Data Structures and Algorithms for Game Developers

Allen Sherrod

DELMAR
CENGAGE Learning™

Australia • Brazil • Japan • Korea • Mexico • Singapore • Spain • United Kingdom • United States

Data Structures and Algorithms for Game Developers
Allen Sherrod

For product information and technology assistance, contact us at
Cengage Learning Customer & Sales Support, 1-800-354-9706

For permission to use material from this text or product, submit all requests online at **www.cengage.com/permissions**
Further permissions questions can be emailed to
permissionrequest@cengage.com

Library of Congress Control Number: 2007006782

ISBN-13: 978-1-58450-495-5

ISBN-10: 1-58450-495-1

Delmar Cengage Learning
5 Maxwell Drive
Clifton Park, NY 12065-2919
USA

Cengage Learning is a leading provider of customized learning solutions with office locations around the globe, including Singapore, the United Kingdom, Australia, Mexico, Brazil, and Japan. Locate your local office at: **international.cengage.com/region**

Cengage Learning products are represented in Canada by Nelson Education, Ltd.

For your lifelong learning solutions, visit **delmar.cengage.com**

Visit our corporate website at **www.cengage.com**

NOTICE TO THE READER
Publisher does not warrant or guarantee any of the products described herein or perform any independent analysis in connection with any of the product information contained herein. Publisher does not assume, and expressly disclaims, any obligation to obtain and include information other than that provided to it by the manufacturer. The reader is expressly warned to consider and adopt all safety precautions that might be indicated by the activities herein and to avoid all potential hazards. By following the instructions contained herein, the reader willingly assumes all risks in connection with such instructions. The publisher makes no representation or warranties of any kind, including but not limited to, the warranties of fitness for particular purpose or merchantability, nor are any such representations implied with respect to the material set forth herein, and the publisher takes no responsibility with respect to such material. The publisher shall not be liable for any special, consequential, or exemplary damages resulting, in whole or part, from the readers' use of, or reliance upon, this material.

Printed in the United States of America
10 11 12 7 6 5 4 3 2

DATA STRUCTURES
AND ALGORITHMS FOR
GAME DEVELOPERS

Contents

Acknowledgments

With every book I write I learn a lot about myself as a writer and as a person. Along my journey I've received a lot of help and support that went a long way to making each of my book projects possible. I would like to thank my friends, family, and the men and women at Charles River Media and Thomson Learning who believed in me from the beginning. I would also like to thank the readers of each of my books and the loyal visitors of www. UltimateGameProgramming.com.

I would like to give a special thanks to Jenifer Niles of Charles River Media for believing in me and giving me this chance.

Introduction

- What to Expect in the First Edition
- Who this Book is For
- What You Need to Know Before Reading this Book
- The Software Needed for this Book
- How this Book Is Organized

WHAT TO EXPECT IN THE FIRST EDITION

The creation of a video game is no easy task for anyone to undertake. When it comes to programming, a lot of knowledge needs to be obtained to create an efficient and solid product. The game industry is a very competitive business, where games are defined heavily by the products that came before them. These products have raised the bar in terms of what is considered cutting-edge and standard in the industry. The more advanced games become, the more data is required to realize a game, especially from a graphics point of view. As games continue to push the envelope of what can be done and as they continue to increase gamers' expectations, it becomes harder to create top-of-the-line quality products.

This book is the first edition of Data Structures for Game Developers. In this book you can expect to walk away with detailed knowledge about various data structures and the algorithms that can be performed on them. This combination is the key to creating real-time simulations that push the envelope on what is considered cutting-edge. Along with game- and simulation-related data structures, this book will cover common data structures and algorithms that are heavily used in general computer programming.

THE PURPOSE OF THIS BOOK

The purpose of this book, Data Structures for Game Developers, is to cover, in general, the huge topic of data structures that are used in game development and is targeted to beginner, student, and hobbyist C++ game and simulation programmers. The information in this book can be used by any programmer outside the field of game development, a few chapters cover information that applies more to individuals creating graphical simulations that need to run at interactive rates, which fits in with game development. These chapters cover scene management techniques used to help process a 3D scene in real time for rendering as well as physics and collisions, to name a few.

This project is my third book, with the first being Ultimate Game Programming with DirectX and the second being Ultimate 3D Game Engine Design and Architecture. Data structures and algorithms drive object-oriented software and are key subjects to tackle for serious developers. Data structures and algorithms are the topics programmers learn after learning a programming language and are used in almost every kind of application, even simple ones that rely on arrays. Video games have a lot of data that need to be managed and processed efficiently, so this book is ideal for those getting into the topics for the first time or for those looking for a reference.

WHO THIS BOOK IS FOR

This book is for C++ programmers who are looking for a reference and for those learning the topics for the first time. The target experience level is beginners, but anyone at any level can find some value in this book. It can be used in data structure and algorithm courses in either general computer programming or in game development courses. The material in this book is easy to understand and is straightforward, which also makes it appropriate as a supplemental text. Many readers of different levels can benefit from having this book in their development library.

WHAT YOU NEED TO KNOW BEFORE READING THIS BOOK

The focus of this book is the C++ programming language, but the topics and information presented here are not exclusive to any one language. The key throughout this book is to make use of object-oriented programming languages and features to create a meaningful result. The information in this book can be generally applied to Java, C#, or any other object-oriented programming language. Because C++ is a highly successful and popular programming language in the game industry, it is used in this book to illustrate the various topics and information. For the graphics sections, the OpenGL® graphics API will be used for the following reasons:

- OpenGL is not specific to any one operating system, allowing this book to be used by Windows®, Macintosh®, Linux®, and any other operating system and hardware that supports it.
- This book will be using the OpenGL utility toolkit and will focus on only graphics topics that are needed to illustrate the points in question, allowing you to focus on the information at hand.
- Performing general rendering on OpenGL is easy and does not distract from the main concepts and topics.

THE SOFTWARE NEEDED FOR THIS BOOK

For this book you will need a C++ compiler to compile any source code into an executable and, for some of the later chapters, an OpenGL-compatible graphics card. All chapter code for this book was compiled and tested on Windows XP, Mac OS X, and the latest Ubuntu® distribution of Linux. Any operating system and hardware that supports OpenGL 1.4 should be compatible with everything that will be done in this book. To run the executable files that come packaged on the CD-ROM, you'll need Windows 98 or higher, Mac OS X or higher, or Linux. Users with other operating systems can compile the chapter code using their compiler of choice for their platform.

HOW THIS BOOK IS ORGANIZED

This book is made up of 15 chapters. Each chapter goes over the manual creation of a set of data structures and, where applicable, the C++ Standard Template Library (STL) counterpart. The first 12 chapters deal with data structures and algorithms that are used in general computer programming. Chapters 13 and 14 discuss data structures that can be found in game and simulation applications, and Chapter 15 provides a summery. The breakdown of the chapters of the book is as follows:

- Chapter 1, Introduction to Data Structures, introduces the topic of data structures and algorithms in general. This chapter also gives readers some insight into what they can expect from the remainder of the book.
- Chapter 2, Arrays, covers arrays, which are the most basic data structure that exists in programming languages that support them. In this chapter we discuss single- and multidimensional arrays, various algorithms that can be applied to arrays (e.g., insertion, removal, and so forth), bit arrays, ordered arrays, and the STL implementation of dynamic arrays, the `vector` template class.

- Chapter 3, Recursion, deals with the topic of recursive methods in programming using self-referencing functions and algorithms.

- Chapter 4, Introduction to Sorting, discusses sorting algorithms that can be performed in data structures. This chapter is an introduction to sorting and covers topics such as the merge sort, the bubble sort, the selection sort, and the insertion sort.

- Chapter 5, Link Lists, looks at the link list data structure by discussing three variations known as the singly linked list, the doubly linked list, and the double-ended linked list. Also discussed in this chapter are iterators, which can be used to move through the elements of a data structure, and the C++'s implementation for linked lists in a template class called `list`.

- Chapter 6, Stacks and Queues, discusses three types of data structures known as stacks, queues, and priority queues. This chapter also discusses the C++ STL implementation for each of these data structures.

- Chapter 7, Hash Tables, focuses on creating hash table data structures and the algorithms that operate on them. In this chapter we'll also look at different types of hash tables and algorithms such as quadric probing, separate chaining, and linear probing.

- Chapter 8, Advanced Sorting, builds off of Chapter 4, Introduction to Sorting, by discussing more advanced sorting algorithms. These algorithms include the radix sort, the quick sort, the shell sort, and partitioning.

- Chapter 9, Trees, discusses the general and binary tree data structures and the algorithms that are commonly performed on them. An understanding of binary trees can go a long way toward understanding binary space partition trees, which are discussed later in the book.

- Chapter 10, Heaps, is a straightforward discussion about heap data structures and the common algorithms that can be performed on them.

- Chapter 11, Graphs, deals with the graph data structure, which is shaped by an abstract problem. Weighted graphs and their use in artificial intelligence are also discussed.

- Chapter 12, Additional STL Algorithms, overviews the remaining C++ STL. Because the STL is so useful to C++ programmers, the chapter covers as much information as possible.

- Chapter 13, Scene Management, discusses bounding volume hierarchies such as quad trees and octrees and talks about creating and rendering a special type of binary tree called the BSP tree, variations of which are used in many games such as Half-Life® 2 and Doom® 3. Other topics are also discussed such as portal rendering, potential visibility sets, and level of detail.

- Chapter 14, Data Compression, deals with algorithms that can compress and encrypt data. This chapter also discusses various texture compression techniques that are very useful to game developers.

- Chapter 15, Conclusions, is the final chapter in the book and concludes the discussion of data structures and algorithms.
- Appendix A, Additional Resources, is a list of resources that can be beneficial for those wanting to learn more about general computer programming and game development.
- Appendix B, Chapter Review Question Answers, provides the answers to all chapter questions in the book.
- Appendix C, OpenGL, gives a brief review of the OpenGL graphical API and the OpenGL utility toolkit (GLUT). These tools are used for the graphics-related chapters of the book, and this appendix gives brief information for those who need a refresher or for those using it for the first time.
- Appendix D, Nonstandard Containers and Algorithms, is a more detailed look at a few resources that provide STL implementations, nonstandard code, and documentation for STL-related code.

BEYOND THIS BOOK

The topic of data structures and algorithms is huge. There is a lot to learn, especially when game development is involved. To further complicate matters, optimizations and efficiency is also a crucial area when dealing with this subject. Appendix A has a list of helpful book and Web resources that might be of great value to you. Also, www.UltimateGameProgramming.com is a community of hobbyist game programmers looking to learn as much as they can from one another.

About the Author

Allen Sherrod (Smyrna, GA) is the host of the game programming website www.UltimateGameProgramming.com for beginner, student, and hobbyist game programmers, where he writes regular columns and develops code for this popular site. He has been programming in many different languages such as C, C++, C#, Java, QBasic, Visual Basic, and Assembly for the past seven years. He graduated from DeVry University with a bachelor's degree in computer information systems. Allen Sherrod is also the author of the books Ultimate Game Programming with DirectX, Game Graphics Programming, and Ultimate 3D Game Engine Design and Architecture as well as a contributor to Game Programming Gems 6, Game Developers Magazine, and Gamastura.

1 Introduction to Data Structures

In This Chapter

- Data Structures and Algorithms
- Data Structures in Games and Simulations
- C++ versus Java and C#
- The C++ STL
- Template Classes and Functions
- Big-O Notation

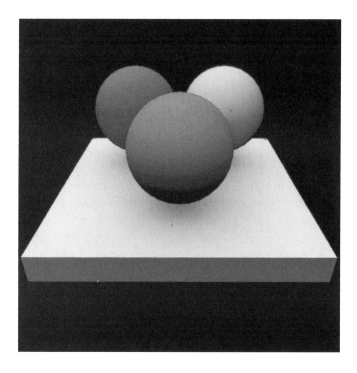

The purpose of this chapter is to define data structures and algorithms in terms of what they are, why they exist, and how they are used in computer programming. This chapter will also introduce topics such as how data structures fit into game development, template classes and their benefits, C++'s Standard Template Library, and the big-O notation and how it can be used to measure the performance of algorithms. This chapter is an introduction on which the following chapters will build.

This book assumes that you have some experience with the C++ programming language and object-oriented programming (either with C++ or another high-level object-oriented programming language such as Java or C#). Although you do not need an expert level of knowledge, you do need at least some understanding of classes in C++. Experience with data structures and various algorithms is not assumed beyond the basic data structure known as arrays.

DATA STRUCTURES AND ALGORITHMS

Data structures are the building blocks of software engineering. Every application has to manage and manipulate data in some meaningful way to perform a task. In modern video games this data is used to create a complex interactive experience in which gamers can have many different experiences. By themselves data structures are not very useful, but when they are combined with algorithms, some meaningful output takes place. In this book we will look at many different data structures and algorithms that are common in general computer programming as well as games and simulations development.

DEFINITION OF DATA STRUCTURES

A data structure defines how data is arranged in memory and can be operated on by using various algorithms. One of the most basic data structures used in general computer programming is the array. An array is a data structure because it defines how data is arranged in memory, in this case a heap of variables or objects of a specific type (or types in typeless languages), which can be operated on by various algorithms (e.g., insertion into the array, deletion, searching, sorting, and so forth). The data structures that will be examined in this book include the following:

- Arrays
- Link lists
- Queues

- Stacks
- Heaps
- Graphs
- Scene graphs
- Octrees
- Quad-trees
- Binary trees
- Minimax trees
- *kd* trees
- Sphere trees
- Bounding volume hierarchies
- Hash tables
- Portals and sectors

Another way to look at a data structure is as a structure that is often user-defined and represents some kind of physical object. Data structures are also objects that contain objects.

DEFINITION OF ALGORITHMS

An algorithm is code that manipulates data in data structures. Most algorithms examined in this book apply to general data structures that include inserting items into a data structure, deleting items, sorting, and iterating. Some of the algorithms that will be looked at throughout this book include the following:

- Recursion
- Insertions
- Deletions
- Merging
- Various sorting algorithms
- Various searching algorithms
- Transversal
- Various algorithms for balancing trees
- Data compression
- Texture compression
- Data encryption
- Texture filters

DATA STRUCTURES IN GAMES AND SIMULATIONS

Data structures form the foundation of many techniques performed in modern video games and are essential to creating the kinds of experiences gamers expect. Alone, a data structure is an arrangement of data in memory, but when combined with special-purpose algorithms those data can be processed and used efficiently and effectively. Because of the nature of a data structure, by definition, the subject alone is a general topic. Data structures and algorithms in game development are often used to speed up the processing of a game's data. In the following sections we'll take a brief look at some of their uses and why they are important to a game application. Later in the book we will take a more detailed look at the data structures used in video games.

This book focuses on how we can manage data objects in a gaming application. These data describe entities that need to be processed in a manner that benefits the overall application's performance, performs some calculations needed to create an effect (e.g., artificial intelligence, physics, etc.), or takes data in one form and transforms them into another. The main questions that will be addressed in this book are:

- How to store data efficiently in the computer's memory
- How to process data efficiently
- What algorithms work best under what situations and why
- How various popular algorithms compare to one another in specific situations
- What data structures can help the processing of game data in certain situations

Some data structures that we'll look at model real-world situations and objects. For example, a queue data structure, which we'll look at in Chapter 6, can be used to store a queue of networking messages for an online game. Another example of this can be seen in a graph where the nodes of the graph represent cities across the United States, which we'll look at in Chapter 13.

DATA STRUCTURES FOR SCENE MANAGEMENT

Complex virtual environments in modern video games are often more complex than the hardware can handle all at once. In games thousands of polygons are rendered and processed, special effects are updated and drawn, and physics need to be processed that can quickly overwhelm any system's hardware. Since the beginning of 3D games, data structures and algorithms have been used to speed up the rendering of complex scenes that otherwise would bring an application's performance down to noninteractive (unplayable) rates.

Using data structures for managing scenes often comes down to situations such as needing a fast means of determining what geometry is visible to avoid sending geometry down the pipeline that can't be seen by the viewer, avoiding or minimizing bottlenecks and state changes in the system, and efficiently managing the static and dynamic objects that exist in the game world. Scene and resource management are two of the topics that are essential to all modern 3D games and their frameworks, also known as the game engine.

As an example of state management, consider a situation where a game has 20 high-resolution textures that are shared among 500 surfaces. If the rendering code sets up the texture and other effect parameters, renders the surface, and then moves onto the next object and does the same thing for all objects, the application could be wasting a lot of processing time with unnecessary rendering state changes. Grouping surfaces together that use the same states (textures, shaders, and so forth) reduces the number of state changes, which increases performance. Not only does this mean rendering all surfaces that use texture A together before moving to all that use texture B, but it also means not wasting processing time moving the same data down the system if it is already there (e.g., sending the same shader uniform values that are already there or re-applying the current shader). State changes such as textures and shaders are very expensive, and spending time reducing them is far more beneficial than allowing them to take place in a complex gaming environment. This kind of optimization occurs in many areas of game development, especially rendering, and can be used to push the envelope of what a system can do in real time.

DATA STRUCTURES FOR ARTIFICIAL INTELLIGENCE

Artificial intelligence (AI) drives many gaming experiences. It can be simple or complex. Even in simple AI systems various data structures and algorithms are used to control the behavior of dynamic game elements. As the AI gets more complex, speed becomes more of an issue because the more complex the algorithms, the more processing time is needed to complete its operations. Combine that with multiple objects, each needing to execute AI algorithms, and you can find yourself trying to balance realism with performance, much like rendering and physics. For this reason, game AI is often not as complex and extensive as AI used in robotics and other such technologies, but game AI is a very complex and growing field. As gamers' demands increase, so will this and other areas of game development.

DATA STRUCTURES FOR PHYSICS DYNAMICS AND COLLISIONS

Physics is becoming a standard feature in modern 3D games. Physics in games deals with the realistic representation of a game object as well as how it interacts with its environment. This includes forces that act on the objects (e.g., gravity, wind, and so forth) as well as the resulting forces that result from objects interacting with each other, mainly through collisions.

Physics and collisions have their own set of data structures and algorithms (e.g., point masses, rigid bodies, algorithms to apply external forces, resolve interactions, and so forth) that are performed to allow objects to interact in real time with each other and their environment. Because physics and collisions are so expensive, other data structures and algorithms that are used for scene management are also used in physics to help eliminate unnecessary calculations, such as trying to find collisions between two objects that have no way of being able to touch one another in order to improve performance.

Data structures can be seen in many areas of application design. Being able to efficiently define data structures and the algorithms that operate on them is the key to creating a solid and effective product.

C++ versus Java and C#

Many differences distinguish C++, Java, and C# from each other. Java and C# have very similar syntax, and anyone familiar with one will have an easier time learning the other. One of the biggest differences that set Java and C# apart from C++ is memory management. With Java and C# automatic memory management takes place within the runtime environment. This frees the programmer from a great deal of memory management responsibilities. It also means that Java and C# programmers do not have to worry about dangling pointers, accidental memory leaks, and, to a degree, memory fragmentation. With C++ the management of memory is the responsibility of the programmer working on a project. This further complicates the development of an application. In C++ an error with the memory (e.g., dangling pointers, buffer overflow, and so forth) can crash an application or the system, as well as other potentially disastrous scenarios that for the most part are unpredictable. Memory management is also tied with performance, which is always crucial in game development.

NOTE

C++ has pointers, whereas Java and C# do not. All three languages support references.

Memory management is very important for C++ game developers, and learning about it is highly recommended.

The differences in the syntax of the languages are somewhat minor. In C++ all memory that is allocated must be unallocated by the programmer, or else a memory leak can occur. Java and C#, on the other hand, automatically handle the reuse and deletion of memory (memory recycling), so the programmer does not have to. A simple example of the need to manually delete memory in C++ can be seen in Listing 1.1, Listing 1.2, and Listing 1.3, where the bubble sort algorithm (which will be examined later in this book) is being performed on an array in C++, Java, and C#, respectively.

LISTING 1.1   An Example of the Bubble Sort in C++

```
void BubbleSort(int *array, int size)
{
   if(!array || !size)
      return;

   for(int k = size - 1; k > 0; k-)
   {
      // Loop through every number.
      for(int i = 0; i < k; i++)
      {
         if(array[i] > array[i + 1])
         {
            // Swap values.
            int temp = array[i];
            array[i] = array[i + 1];
            array[i + 1] = temp;
         }
      }
   }
}


int main(int args, char *arg[])
{
   // Create array of unordered numbers.
   int array[] = new int[5];

   array[0] = 80;
   array[1] = 64;
   array[2] = 99;
   array[3] = 76;
   array[4] = 5;

   cout << "Bubble Sort Algorithm" << endl << endl;
```

```
cout << "Unordered Array: ";

// Display unordered numbers.
for(int i = 0; i < 5; i++)
   cout << array[i] << " ";

cout << endl;

// Sort array using bubble sort algorithm.
BubbleSort(array, 5);


cout << "Ordered Array: ";

// Display ordered numbers.
for(int i = 0; i < 5; i++)
   cout << array[i] << " ";


delete[] array;
array = NULL;


cout << endl << endl;

return 1;
}
```

LISTING 1.2   An Example of the Bubble Sort in Java

```
public class BubbleSort
{
  public static void main(String args[])
  {
    int array[] = new int[5];

    array[0] = 80;
    array[1] = 64;
    array[2] = 99;
    array[3] = 76;
    array[4] = 5;

    System.out.print("\nBubble Sort Algorithm\n\n");
```

```java
        System.out.print("Unordered Array: ");

        // Display unordered numbers.
        for(int i = 0; i < 5; i++)
           System.out.print(array[i] + " ");

        System.out.print("\n");

        // Sort array using bubble sort algorithm.
        BubbleSort(array);


        System.out.print("Ordered Array: ");

        // Display ordered numbers.
        for(int i = 0; i < 5; i++)
           System.out.print(array[i] + " ");

        System.out.print("\n\n");


        System.exit(0);
    }

    public static void BubbleSort(int[] array)
    {
        for(int k = array.length - 1; k > 0; k-)
        {
           // Loop through every number.
           for(int i = 0; i < k; i++)
           {
              if(array[i] > array[i + 1])
              {
                 // Swap values.
                 int temp = array[i];
                 array[i] = array[i + 1];
                 array[i + 1] = temp;
              }
           }
        }
    }
}
```

LISTING 1.3   An Example of the Bubble Sort in C#

```csharp
public class BubbleSort
{
   public static void Main()
   {
      Console.Write("Bubble Sort Algorithm\n\n");

      int[] array = { 80, 64, 99, 76, 5 };


      Console.Write("Unordered Array: ");

      // Display unordered numbers.
      for(int i = 0; i < 5; i++)
         Console.Write(array[i] + " ");

      Console.Write("\n");

      // Sort array using bubble sort algorithm.
      BubbleSortArray(array);


      Console.Write("Ordered Array: ");

      // Display ordered numbers.
      for(int i = 0; i < 5; i++)
         Console.Write(array[i] + " ");

      Console.Write("\n\n");
   }

   public static void BubbleSortArray(int[] array)
   {
      for(int k = array.GetLength(0) - 1; k > 0; k--)
      {
         // Loop through every number.
         for(int i = 0; i < k; i++)
         {
            if(array[i] > array[i + 1])
            {
               // Swap values.
               int temp = array[i];
               array[i] = array[i + 1];
```

```
                array[i + 1] = temp;
            }
        }
    }
  }
}
```

THE C++ STL

The C++ programming language has a standard set of template classes known as the Standard Template Library (STL). This library is used for both code reuse and maintainability and is composed of many efficiently designed components and algorithms that are seen often in general computer programming. The STL is composed of containers, iterators, and algorithms. Containers are the template classes that represent a data structure, while an iterator is used to transverse through a data structure. One of the major goals of the STL is to be abstract while maintaining efficiency. This allows the STL to be used in a variety of different applications.

Using the STL can save programmers a lot of time and effort when it comes to generic data structures. Each STL container is implemented with speed performance efficiency in mind and uses allocators and deallcators rather than the `new` and `delete` operators. STL containers are designed to provide similar functionality to one another so that each container uses the same name for a function or object that another container uses for the same thing. Some functions that are conveniently common to STL containers are the overloaded operators:

- `<`
- `>`
- `<=`
- `>=`
- `==`
- `!=`

The STL containers will be examined throughout this book. Along with how to use the containers, there will also be tips and techniques that can be useful when working with STL containers and algorithms in commercial applications. The STL containers we will look at are as follows:

- `vector`
- `queue`
- `priority_queue`
- `list`

- deque
- stack
- map
- multimap
- set
- multiset
- hash_set
- hash_multiset
- hash_map
- hash_multimap

Additional containers we will also be looking at that are part of the C++ standard include the following:

- bitset
- string
- valarray

Avoid wasting time creating your own data structures instead of using the STL. In this book we look at both for educational purposes, but for the most part the STL will be sufficient in all types of applications. In some unique circumstances the STL might not be the best option, depending on specific application needs versus the STL implementation.

We will revisit the STL throughout this book, starting with `vectors` and `bitset` in Chapter 2, Arrays. Because the STL is efficient and widely used, it is important for all C++ programmers to be familiar with it on some level. Although it is possible to write and use our own data structures and algorithms in a commercial product, it might be beneficial to use the STL for the following reasons:

- The STL is standard.
- The STL is widely used.
- The STL is optimized and efficient.
- Using the STL saves time and effort.
- The STL comes with C++.

TEMPLATE CLASSES AND FUNCTIONS

C++ has a feature that allows template classes and functions to be created and used in code. A template is a way to create code that is evaluated during compile time rather than runtime. Templates allow for the same code to be used with different data and user-defined types, which minimizes the need to write duplicate code for every type that is to be supported. As long as the evaluation passes and the code written is valid, templates can be created and used in C++.

C++ has two types of templates: one for functions and one for classes. Function templates allow programmers to specify function parameters to the template. In C++ overloaded functions are used to perform similar operations in different functions based on the parameter data types. When a template function is used, the general operations only need to be written once, and the compiler will create the necessary overloaded function code objects at compile time. If the code cannot pass the evaluation, the compiler produces an error message describing the problem. One of the benefits to using templates is that they are type safe, unlike macros.

Classes can be made into templates by specifying one or more template names to be used within the class. All function and class templates begin with the keyword `template`, which is followed by a list of type parameters that are enclosed in angle brackets (`<` and `>`). For every function and class body that is to accept template parameters, template parameters must define this keyword before every body of code. Within the angle brackets each type must be specified using the `class` or `typename` keyword or can define a constant. The `class` and `typename` keywords mean that the type is user defined or is a built-in data type. The purpose of specifying a class to be a template is to allow some member variables or the parameters of class functions to use the template type(s). Listing 1.4 shows an example using both template functions and classes. On the CD-ROM in the Chapter 1/Templates folder is a C++ demo application, called Templates, for the code in Listing 1.4.

ON THE CD

LISTING 1.4   An Example Using Template Classes and Functions

```
#include<iostream>


template<typename T>
T min(T lVal, T rVal)
{
    if(lVal > rVal)
        return rVal;

    return lVal;
}


template<typename T>
T max(T lVal, T rVal)
```

```
{
   if(lVal < rVal)
      return rVal;

   return lVal;
}


template<typename P>
class TemplateClass
{
   public:
      TemplateClass(P val)
      {
         m_val = val;
      }


      bool operator<(TemplateClass &rVal)
      {
         return m_val < rVal.GetVal();
      }


      bool operator>(TemplateClass &rVal)
      {
         return m_val > rVal.GetVal();
      }


      P GetVal()
      {
         return m_val;
      }


   private:
      P m_val;
};



int main(int args, char **argc)
{
```

```
std::cout << "C++ Templates" << std::endl;
std::cout << "Chapter 1: Templates" << std::endl;
std::cout << std::endl;


std::cout << "Min = " << min(32, 54) << std::endl;
std::cout << "Max = " << max(49.3, 38.98) << std::endl;
std::cout << "Max (objects) = " << max(TemplateClass<int>(7),
           TemplateClass<int>(4)).GetVal() << std::endl;


TemplateClass<int> obj(10);

std::cout << "obj = " << obj.GetVal() << std::endl;


std::cout << std::endl << std::endl;

return 1;
}
```

Templates are used heavily in this book and are a major part of the STL classes. When working with data structures and algorithms, it is often useful to declare them using templates so that near-duplicate code does not need to be written to support every built-in or user-defined data type that might occur in a programming project. This can be very useful when expanding functions to work with other data types.

BIG-O NOTATION

Big-O notation is used to describe the theoretical performance of an algorithm. This measurement is usually made to measure the time or memory consumption used by an algorithm. The purpose of big-O notation is to be able to create a representation of the performance of an algorithm to compare it to others. This gives coders a general way to compare algorithms based on a set of inputs.

The problem with the performance of algorithms is that it can fluctuate depending on the number of items that were inserted and are present in a data structure. For example, if algorithm A runs faster than algorithm B with 1,000 items but runs slower with 100,000 items, it can be hard to get an accurate picture when comparing the two. Big-O notation gives an idea of an algorithm's performance based on the number of items in the structure (its growth).

Big-O notation is used in software engineering as a way to measure a function's growth and was introduced in 1894 by Paul Bachmann. Big-O notation has some properties that are helpful when estimating the general efficiency of various algorithms and can be used to compare algorithms.

Discussions of algorithms later in this book mention the algorithms' performance in big-O notation. For example, when inserting an item into an unordered array, the operation is not dependent on the number of items in the list. This means that the insertion is constant. When writing big-O notation, we don't need to worry about any constants, which are the particulars of a CPU chip and a compiler, but instead we can use the uppercase letter "O" and a label that represents what the algorithm depends on for its operation. The insertion of an item into an unordered array does not depend on anything other than placing the new item at the end of the list. This gives the insertion into an unordered array of:

O(1)

The performance of a linear search on an unordered array depends on the number of items in the list. In general a linear search is a search through half of the list. Because the linear search algorithm depends on the number of items, its big-O notation would look like the following (where N is the number of items):

O(N)

The big-O notation of O(N²) is considered to result in a worse performance than O(N), O(1), or O(log N).

In a binary search the base 2 logarithm can be used by the constant to represent the performance of the algorithm with an ordered array. This would look like the following in big-O notation:

O(log N)

Looking at big-O notation with the operations we've discussed so far for arrays shows that the insertion of an item in an array takes a fast O(1) operation, while a linear search takes a slow O(N) operation. On the other hand, an insertion into an ordered array takes a slow O(N) operation because the insertion is based on the number of items in the list, while the binary search through an ordered array takes a somewhat fast O(log N) operation. Deletion by both arrays can take a O(N) operation because the deletion is the same in both cases and the deletion would work by creating a new array, copying over the data up to the point to be deleted and then copying the data after the point that was to be deleted one index lower than the original array. In other words, the performance of the deletion is dependent on the number of items in the array.

Big-O notation is used to give a meaningful idea of the performance of an algorithm. We will look at big-O notation in upcoming chapters in more detail.

SUMMARY

In this chapter we talked briefly about data structures and algorithms, object-oriented programming languages, template classes, the C++ STL, and big-O notation. This chapter introduced material to come and reviewed information that every C++ programmer should be familiar with before moving on to the next chapter.

In the next chapter we will look at traditional arrays, ordered arrays, bit arrays, basic searching algorithms (linear and binary), insertion and deletion algorithms, and the STL's vector class. Chapter 2, Arrays, will allow beginners to start getting deeply involved in the world of data structures and algorithms.

CHAPTER REVIEW QUESTIONS

Answers to the following chapter review questions can be found in Appendix B.

1. A data structures define an arrangement of data in
   a. Source code
   b. A template class
   c. Memory
   d. None of the above
2. What are algorithms?
3. A type of data structure is a
   a. Template class
   b. Array
   c. Binary tree
   d. Compression
   e. b and c
   f. None of the above

4. STL is an acronym for
   a. Structured Template Language
   b. Standard Template Library
   c. Structured Template Library
   d. None of the above
5. Three STL data structures include
   a. Array, vector, list
   b. Hash table, bubble sort, list
   c. List, vector, queue
   d. None of the above
   e. All of the above
6. Java and C# use automatic memory management.
   a. True
   b. False
7. C++ places memory management on the responsibility of the programmer.
   a. True
   b. False
8. Template classes are used to allow inheritance in object-oriented programming.
   a. True
   b. False
9. Big-O notation can be used to measure performance.
   a. True
   b. False
10. O(log N) is generally worst than O(N²).
    a. True
    b. False

2 Arrays

In This Chapter

- The Data Structures Known as Arrays
- Algorithms: Insertion and Deletion
- Ordered Arrays
- Algorithms: Basic Searches
- STL Arrays
- Bit Arrays

Binary Search for 95

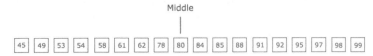

Middle

45 49 53 54 58 61 62 78 80 84 85 88 91 92 95 97 98 99

Not Found
Cut range in half and search upper bounds
since 95 is larger than 80

Middle

84 85 88 91 92 95 97 98 99

Not Found so check upper (95 > 92)

Middle

92 95 97 98 99

Not Found so check lower (95 < 97)

Found After 4 Checks

92 95 97

The most common form of data structure is the array because it is built into many different programming languages and is easy to learn and work with in any type of application. Every C and C++ programmer of any level should be familiar with arrays, so they are a good place to start. In this chapter we will explore arrays in detail beyond the language-specific implementation. Later in the chapter we will look at the STL implementation of arrays by using a template STL class known as the vector. Arrays are very important in application programming, and a solid understanding of them beyond the syntax can be very beneficial to all types of applications. Also in this chapter, we'll look at ordered arrays, the C++ valarray, and various bit arrays.

Chapters 3 and 4, Recursion and Introduction to Sorting, will use the code developed in this chapter to help illustrate their topics and algorithms. This chapter will use C++ templates, which were discussed in Chapter 1, and classes. By creating an array class, you can get an intimate look inside the data structure outside of the STL vector as well as have the ability to add methods and operations to your own custom data structure. Although the manual data structures and algorithms covered in this chapter are not as complex as the STL vector, they are a good starting point for those new to the subject.

Arrays have great use in all kinds of applications, especially games and simulations. Arrays can be used in any game where a list of objects with the same data type is needed. This list can be an array of character models, an array of textures, an array of sounds, and so forth. Arrays are simple data structures, and sometimes the simple path is the best option.

THE DATA STRUCTURES KNOWN AS ARRAYS

The most common data storage structure is the array. Arrays are very convenient to use because most programmers, even novices, are familiar with them because they are built into many programming languages. Listing 2.1 shows a simple example of arrays. The code for this example, called Arrays, can be found on the CD-ROM in the Chapter 2/Arrays folder along with its executable. Later in the chapter we will look at creating a template class that will be used as a container for a list of objects. In Listing 2.1 the example program code creates two arrays, one static and one dynamic, fills them with data, and displays that information to the screen. Because of the nature of arrays, it is assumed that you have some prior experience with them in the C++ programming language.

ON THE CD

LISTING 2.1   A Simple Example of the Use of Arrays

```cpp
#include<iostream>


int main(int args, char **argc)
{
   std::cout << "1D Array Example" << std::endl;
   std::cout << "Chapter 2: Arrays01" << std::endl;
   std::cout << std::endl;


   const int size = 5;
   int array[size] = { 10, 32, 53, 91, 21 };

   std::cout << " Static array contents (" << size << "): ";

   for(int i = 0; i < size; i++)
   {
      std::cout << array[i] << " ";
   }

   std::cout << std::endl;


   int *array2 = new int[size];

   array2[0] = 99;
   array2[1] = 67;
   array2[2] = 23;
   array2[3] = 49;
   array2[4] = 12;

   std::cout << "Dynamic array contents (" << size << "): ";

   for(int i = 0; i < size; i++)
   {
      std::cout << array2[i] << " ";
   }

   delete[] array2;
```

```
        std::cout << std::endl << std::endl;

        return 1;
    }
```

Keep in mind that you can also use using namespace std; *to avoid having to specify the namespace before any of the standard library objects such as* cout *and* endl, *as shown in Listing 2.1.*

C++ arrays can be single or multidimensional as well as static or dynamic. Dynamic arrays require at least basic manual memory management to avoid unwanted side effects from errors that cause undefined behavior and so forth. This means that to use a dynamic array we must manually create and destroy the array within code as well as keeping track of the allocated memory through pointers. Failing to destroy an array once a program is done with it can lead to memory leaks, which occur when memory goes outside an application's reach by pointers (i.e., no pointers are pointing to that allocated memory). When enough memory leaks occur, they can cause future allocations to fail, and will effect the overall application and system performance.

When memory is allocated, it must be carefully tracked. Trying to access memory that has been deleted through an invalid pointer can cause a host of undesirable and often unpredictable side effects, which happens when a behavior is undefined, as in the case of trying to use or delete an invalid pointer. One example of such a side effect is that the application can abruptly crash when the pointer is accessed or some time afterwards. Errors caused by dangling pointers, as well as other types of errors, can be unpredictable, and the side effects can be either obvious or silent (such as corrupting memory).

Automatic memory management as well as advanced manual memory management techniques are used in computer science. Although they are very useful in game development and general application development, the topic of advanced memory management is outside the scope of this book.

Memory management is handled automatically in some languages such as C# and Java. Users learning C++ after learning one of these languages will have to adjust to manually managing their memory consumption.

Memory must be tracked by pointers, and those pointers must be carefully used to avoid dangling pointers, which are pointers to invalid memory in C++. Memory also must be carefully managed to avoid out-of-bound errors, which occur when an attempt is made to access memory outside of the array's range. This kind of error can cause a host of unwanted side effects such as unwanted and unpredictable application behavior, application or system crashing, and so forth. By keeping track of the number of items in an array and by checking to make sure the array does not go out of bounds, we can avoid such errors, althouth such checks add a cost of CPU time in exchange for security. This issue also applies to static memory heaps as well as dynamic memory because C++ does not perform any bounds checks and leaves it up to the programmer. For those new to C++ the information presented in the previous few paragraphs is important to remember when programming.

For those unfamiliar with simple manual memory management, many factors must be taken care of to safely use dynamic, and at times static, arrays in an application. Depending on the application and how it is used, the performance of an array can also be important through controlling memory fragmentation, which is a topic related to memory management. Appendix A lists resources on this subject that can be useful for those wanting to learn more about manual memory management.

CREATING CUSTOM ARRAYS

When working with arrays, it can be beneficial to place the array in a container class. This class can have common operations and algorithms performed on the array such as insertions, deletions, searches, and sorting. Encapsulating an array in a template class can allow us to provide all of our methods in a reusable manner while also using it with many different types. In the following section we will look at doing this for an unordered array and an ordered array. Later in the chapter the same will be done for bit arrays.

This chapter covers the creation, deletion, and management of various arrays as well as a few searching algorithms. In future chapters more algorithms will be added to the arrays built in this class to extend its functionality. The first part of the implementation of the unordered array class includes the ability to create a dynamic array through the constructor, delete the array upon a call to the destructor, store an array that is a template, and determine the size of the array, the size by which we want to expand the array if necessary, and the total number of elements in the array. By allowing the array to expand, we can have a dynamically growing list that can increase its size as needed. Disallowing the growth of an array could be as simple as setting this variable to 0. When inserting new items in the list and when performing certain algorithms, it is important to know how many items are in the list because (a) we only want to process valid items in the array, (b) we need to know where the last item was inserted in the list so we can insert the next item or to remove the last item, and (c) a number of algorithms depend on knowing how big the array is in terms of items inserted (such as the binary searching algorithm). The array itself is a template type, so we can use the code for any built-in and user-defined class without the need to rewrite the data structure for each type it is to support. Listing 2.2 shows the parts of the unordered array class that deal with the ideas discussed in this paragraph.

LISTING 2.2   Partial Look at the Template Array Class

```
template<class T>
class UnorderedArray
{
   public:
      UnorderedArray(int size, int growBy = 1) :
                        m_array(NULL), m_maxSize(0),
                        m_growSize(0), m_ numElements (0)
      {
         if(size)
         {
            m_maxSize = size;
            m_array = new T[m_maxSize];

            m_growSize = ((growBy > 0) ? growBy : 0);
         }
      }


      ~UnorderedArray()
      {
         if(m_array != NULL)
         {
            delete[] m_array;
            m_array = NULL;
         }
      }


   private:
      T *m_array;

      int m_maxSize;
      int m_growSize;
      int m_numElements;
};
```

ALGORITHMS: INSERTION AND DELETION

Inserting items into an array runs in the big-O notation of 0(1) and is not dependant on the number of items in the list. By keeping track of the total number of items in the array, we can immediately know where to insert the next item being placed in the array. This operation's function can have many different names, but in the STL a function used to insert an item into a container is often called push (or a variation such as push_back, or push_front). Removal of items from the end of a container in the STL is often given a function called a pop. For the unordered array class we will be using the function name push for inserting into a container and pop for removing. Inserting into an array is as straightforward as it is outside of the container, which is done by using an assignment operator to make the current array index equal to a value we want stored. The insertion into an unordered array is shown in Listing 2.3. If the maximum size is reached in the array, its size is expanded, which will be discussed later in this chapter.

LISTING 2.3   Inserting (push) into an Unordered Array

```
template<class T>
class UnorderedArray
{
    public:
        virtual void push(T val)
        {
            assert(m_array != NULL);

            if(m_numElements >= m_maxSize)
            {
                Expand();
            }

            m_array[m_numElements] = val;
            m_numElements++;
        }
};
```

Assertions (assert()) are used for debugging purposes that, when failed, will trigger a dialog box to appear. If you are unfamiliar with assertions, look them up in your C/C++ documentation. Assertions are only used in debugging and are excluded from release builds.

Removing an item from an array can be done in a number of different ways. One way can require the array to resize itself and only store the data that was in the original array minus the item to be removed. This might allow applications to conserve memory when many items are removed from an array, but at a huge performance penalty if it is done for large numbers of items and if it is done often. When removing items in this manner, we would be required to create a new array, copy over the data from the original array up to the point of the object being deleted, copy the data after the object being deleted one index down, and delete the old memory. Performing this operation once for every object that is removed is expensive. In games performance is very important so this can be a problem. If new items are inserted into the array after a removal, the array would need to be re-expanded to accommodate the new item (assuming expansion was supported), and a lot of time would be wasted deleting and reexpanding, not to mention copying data to and from different memory locations.

Another option is to simply copy the data that comes after the item to be deleted one element down so that the item to be removed is overridden with the indexes that come after it, leaving an empty spot on the top of the array. We will still need to perform a copy operation on the array, but the memory allocation and deletion will have been avoided. This operation is illustrated in Figure 2.1.

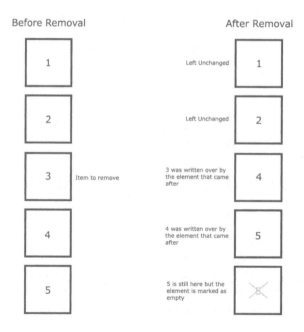

FIGURE 2.1   Removing an item from an array by copying over it.

Later in the book we will see different data structures that are better at deletion of items than the array. One such data structure is called the link list, which will be discussed in Chapter 5, Link Lists. For the array containers in this chapter we will use a function called pop() to remove the last item that was inserted into the container, which will be done by simply decrementing the counter for the total number of items that are in the list. We will use a function called remove() to remove an index from the array by overriding the index to delete. Removing items from an array in the manner described in this and the previous paragraphs is shown in Listing 2.4.

LISTING 2.4   Removing Items from the Unordered Array

```
template<class T>
class UnorderedArray
{
   public:
      void pop()
      {
         if(m_numElements > 0)
            m_numElements--;
      }


      void remove(int index)
      {
         assert(m_array != NULL);

         if(index >= m_maxSize)
         {
            return;
         }

         for(int k = index; k < m_maxSize - 1; k++)
            m_array[k] = m_array[k + 1];

         m_maxSize--;

         if(m_numElements >= m_maxSize)
            m_numElements = m_maxSize - 1;
      }
};
```

What if we wanted to remove all items from the array? Let's say we want to remove all the items so that we can repopulate it with different objects. Although we can remove (remove()) each index one at a time, this would waste CPU time because of the total overhead of the function. We could also keep calling pop() to remove the last item in the list until there were no more, but this too is a waste of CPU time because of the number of pop() calls that would be required for an array with more than one item. A faster method would be to leave the data alone and just reset the counter used to keep track of the total number of items that exist in the container. This will cause all items to be overridden when new items are inserted into the array and only requires one assignment operator. Listing 2.5 shows the process of clearing an array. When working with user-defined classes, it might be necessary to take care of items first, before they can be overridden. This can occur if the array stores pointers to allocated memory or if the items in the array have member variables that require special attention from the programmer.

LISTING 2.5   Quickly Clearing an Array

```
template<class T>
class UnorderedArray
{
   public:
      void clear()
      {
         m_numElements = 0;
      }
};
```

The size of an array is finite. When the array is full, no more items can be inserted into the list without either overriding values in existing indexes or without going out of bounds. The two main options in this situation are to disallow additional items to be inserted or to allocate more memory. The expansion of the array is the option that will be explored for the arrays in this chapter because such an operation can be very useful in an application. Expanding the array gives the container a dynamically growing heap of memory that adjusts as the need arises. To expand the array we need only create a new array that is bigger than the current one, copy the data from the original memory location to the new one, and delete the old memory.

The downside is that the performance hit can add up, depending on the number of items that are inserted into the list and the number of allocates and copies that are needed. One way to minimize such a performance hit is to allocate an array that is more than one element bigger than the original. For example, if the array size is increased by five elements every time it needs to be expanded, that would be faster than increasing the array one element for every expansion. The thing about allocating more space than is needed is that sometimes elements are not used. The number of unused items will depend on how much memory is wasted. This means it is the programmer's responsibility to choose a "grow-by or expansion" value that is generally optimal for the application and use in question. The array containers in this chapter will allow programmers to specify the grow-by size in the constructor. Using a size of 0 will tell the container that it cannot grow larger than its initial size. A function to expand the unordered array container for this chapter is shown in Listing 2.6. The function is private in Listing 2.6 because it is to be used by the container only and not by any application functions outside the class and it works by creating a new memory location, copying the original data to the new location, and deleting the old memory.

LISTING 2.6   Expanding an Array

```
template<class T>
class UnorderedArray
{
   private:
      bool Expand()
      {
         if(m_growSize <= 0)
            return false;

         T *temp = new T[m_maxSize + m_growSize];
         assert(temp != NULL);

         memcpy(temp, m_array, sizeof(T) * m_maxSize);

         delete[] m_array;
         m_array = temp;

         m_maxSize += m_growSize;

         return true;
      }
};
```

One of the most useful operators that C++ arrays support are brackets ([and]). Using brackets allows programmers to directly access specific indexes in the array. C++ has a feature that allows programmers to overload operators with custom code for user-defined objects. Supporting array brackets with custom-made containers will give those classes a feel that is more like traditional arrays.

Accessing elements in an array using brackets brings up the issues of out-of-bound errors, how to not access elements outside of the elements already pushed onto the list, and performance, to name a few. When it comes to performance, the fastest method would be to directly access the array without any safety checks. The problem with this is that some errors might easily occur and be hard to find. Fortunately we can use assertions to announce errors to anyone using the container. Assertions work in the debug builds of applications. Release builds compile assertions down to nothing so that they are not even included and executed. During the debugging process it is common to give a little performance for things like this, which are not included in the release version. Using assertions gives us an indication of where problems are occurring so that they can be fixed before the final version is released. In many containers throughout this book assertions are used to check for potential errors, rather than if statements and other various conditional checks.

Overloading the [] operator to return the reference of an element allows the container to have read and write abilities. This is important when trying to mimic traditional arrays since array elements can have elements read and written to. The operator for [] is shown in Listing 2.7 for the unordered array.

LISTING 2.7 Array Style Access for Elements

```
template<class T>
class UnorderedArray
{
   public:
      virtual T& operator[](int index)
      {
         assert(m_array != NULL && index <= m_numElements);
         return m_array[index];
      }
};
```

Later in this chapter we will revisit unordered arrays and a few algorithms that can be performed with them.

An operation that can operate in constant time has a big-O of $O(1)$ because the performance is unaffected by N. Constant time means that time is unaffected by the number of items in a list.

ORDERED ARRAYS

This section will look at ordered arrays in a C++ template class. An ordered array is an array that has its contents in some kind of order, whether that is larger to smaller or vice versa. With ordered arrays the order is typically determined during the items' insertion. Ordered arrays have benefits for items that must be inserted in a particular order but, as we will see later, there are better options to use in some situations. In this chapter we will create an ordered array that sorts from smaller to larger as an example. A visual look at ordered arrays is shown in Figure 2.2.

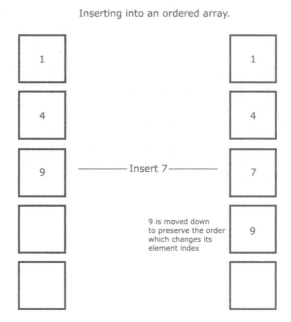

FIGURE 2.2   Ordered arrays.

One way to create an ordered array is to insert the items into the array based on the desired order. This is not always feasible, and logic errors can easily lead to unordered arrays. Another option is to insert the items into the array and allow the insertion code to figure out their order. For example, if there are 10 items in a list and a new item is inserted that needs to be at index 5, the item already at index 5 and every element after it must be moved up the array to allow the new item to take that slot. Doing this every time an item needs to be inserted can be quite expensive in terms of CPU processing time. Inserting into an ordered array has a big-O of $O(N)$ because the insertion is dependant on the number of items in the array. When inserting into the array, conditional checks must be performed until the correct index for the item can be determined. When working with ordered arrays, one must keep in mind that insertion into the array does not mean the item will appear at the end of the array. To determine where inserted items appear in the list, the push() function for the ordered array will return the element's index. This is shown in Listing 2.8.

LISTING 2.8   The Ordered Array Class that Differs from the Unordered Array

```
template <class T>
class OrderedArray
{
  public:
      int push(T val)
  {
          assert(m_array != NULL);

          if(m_numElements >= m_maxSize)
          {
             Expand();
          }

          for(int i = 0; i < m_numElements; i++)
          {
             if(m_array[i] > val)
                break;
          }

          for(int k = m_numElements; k > i; k-)
          {
             m_array[k] = m_array[k - 1];
          }

          m_array[i] = val;
          m_numElements++;

          return i;
      }
};
```

Another option for inserting an item into an ordered array is to use a modified binary search to find the index closest to where the item would need to be inserted and start the stepping from that point. Binary searching will be discussed later in this chapter.

Amortized constant time refers to operations that usually run in constant time but can be affected by N, the number of items in the list.

What do we gain by having an ordered array besides the knowledge that the data is in order? One major advantage, which we'll see in the next section, is that the ordered array is faster to search, using a binary search, than an unordered array, which would use a linear search. One major disadvantage to using an ordered array is that the insertions are much more expensive than with the unordered version. When insertions are rare but searches are frequent, the ordered array would probably be the better choice in most applications. If the opposite is true, the unordered array might be the better choice. In the following section we will look at two searching algorithms that can be performed on unordered or ordered template arrays.

ALGORITHMS: BASIC SEARCHES

This chapter discusses two searching algorithms: the linear search and the binary search. Being able to find a value in an array might prove useful in a container. Because these algorithms are relatively simple, they are a great introduction to the world of algorithms. An algorithm is a set of operations that are performed on a data structure, with the data structure in this case being the array. Linear searches are used on unordered arrays, while binary searches are better to use on ordered arrays. Each will be discussed in more detail in the following sections.

LINEAR SEARCHES

When we are looking for a value in an unordered array, our main option is the linear search. The linear search is a brute-force-style search. The algorithm works by stepping through each element of the array, starting with the first element, and checking to see if the value of that element matches the value of what is being searched for. If it is found, then the algorithm can report that the item exists in some meaningful fashion, and it can also report where in the array the item is positioned.

During a linear search the algorithm can find the first occurrence or all occurrences of a value. If duplicates are allowed in the array, then more than one value can exist. In this chapter we'll discuss finding the first occurrence. If there are times when you know you need to know how many occurrences there are, or even how many and where they are, then the searching function of the unordered array class can be expanded to accommodate those needs. Searching beyond the first occurrence can be a waste of CPU time if there is no need to look for duplicates. Figure 2.3 illustrates the linear search. The search() function used to perform a linear search in the unordered array class is shown in Listing 2.9, where the function returns the index of the value if it is found, or else it returns -1 to indicate that the value was not found.

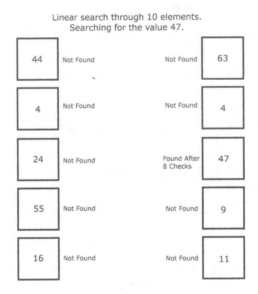

FIGURE 2.3   A linear search.

LISTING 2.9   The Linear Search of an Unordered Array

```
template<class T>
class UnorderedArray
{
    public:
        virtual int search(T val)
        {
            assert(m_array != NULL);
```

```
for(int i = 0; i < m_numElements; i++)
{
    if(m_array[i] == val)
        return i;
}

return -1;
    }
};
```

A linear search can become slow for arrays with large numbers of items. On average, the algorithm requires half the total number of items to find a value. If there were 100 items in a list, then the average would be 50. Because the linear search's performance is based on the number of items in the array, it has a big-O of `O(N)`. The linear search is the most basic, yet slowest, search because it must check potentially every item (half on average) before finding a value, assuming the value even exists in the array. If the value does not exist, the search would have checked every element in the array and come up with nothing.

Binary Searches

A binary search can be performed on an ordered array. It works by taking a value that is being searched for and testing it by the element in the middle of the array. If the value being searched for is lower than the item in the middle of the ordered array, it can be determined that if the value exists, it is in the first half of the array. If the value is larger than the element in the middle, the value might exist in the upper half. Once the direction is known, half of that new section is tested to further narrow down where the value can be. This is repeated until the value is found or until there are no more elements left. The binary search gets its name from the fact that the remaining elements are always split in half (binary equals 2). An illustration of a binary search is shown in Figure 2.4. Because a binary search requires the elements to be in order, this algorithm cannot work for an unordered array since the unordered array can be unpredictable in terms of item positions.

The binary search can eliminate large sections of an array in an effort to narrow down the list to find the value, assuming it exits. When compared to the linear search, this can result in a huge difference in performance as *N* grows larger. For example, an array being searched with a linear algorithm that is made up of 1 million elements will take on average 500,000 steps for items that exist, which can mean that some checks can go up to the whole million depending on the item. Using a binary search on an ordered array with that same number of elements will take 20 comparisons. To go from an average of 500,000 comparisons to just 20 is a huge difference. To go from 1 million comparisons to 20 with items that are not found

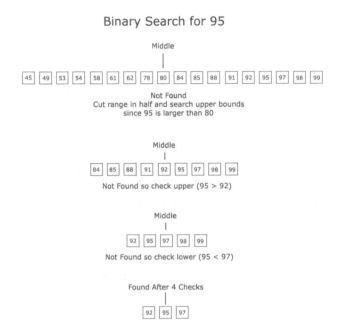

FIGURE 2.4   A binary search.

in the array is tremendous. Such a difference can have a huge impact on a container's performance in any situation. The function for the binary search in shown in Listing 2.10, where a while loop is used to split through the array until the element is found or is proven to not exist in the container. The binary search has a big-O of O(log N).

LISTING 2.10   Binary Search for an Ordered Array

```
template <class T>
class OrderedArray
{
   public:
      int search(T searchKey)
      {
         assert(m_array != NULL);

         int lowerBound = 0;
         int upperBound = m_numElements - 1;
         int current = 0;
```

```
while(1)
{
    current = (lowerBound + upperBound) >> 1;

    if(m_array[current] == searchKey)
    {
        return current;
    }
    else if(lowerBound > upperBound)
    {
        return -1;
    }
    else
    {
        if(m_array[current] < searchKey)
            lowerBound = current + 1;
        else
            upperBound = current - 1;
    }
}

return -1;
    }
};
```

The binary search in Listing 2.10 starts off by defining the bounds that make up the search range, which is initially set to the entire array. Once the range is set, the middle of the range is determined and the element at the position is tested. If the item is found, the index is returned; if the lower bound's value becomes higher than the upper bound's value (which will happen when the search has stepped through the entire array), then the value is not found. If neither of these two cases are true, the lower bound, which is the minimum search range position, is adjusted if the item is greater than the item in the middle, or else the upper bound is adjusted. Adjusting the range values will quickly shrink the search range until the value is found or until there are no more elements to check. As shown in Figure 2.4, this operation is pretty fast as N grows larger.

Operations that run in logarithmic time need more time to operate as N grows larger. The time that is required by the operation is proportional to the logarithm of N.

In general, the time required to run an operation in constant time is faster than one in logarithm time, and an operation in logarithm time is faster than one that is linear. Sometimes, however, if N is small enough, some operations that have slower theoretical performance can outperform ones that one would think are faster.

In upcoming chapters we'll look at adding algorithms to the array classes discussed in this chapter. Both arrays have the ability to insert items, remove items, expand when necessary, perform searching, and allow for element access through overloading the [ ] operator. Accessing elements with the unordered array class allows reading and writing, but the ordered array does not allow this without risking unintentionally unordering the array with logic errors. The entire unordered and ordered arrays discussed in this chapter appear in Listing 2.11.

LISTING 2.11   The Entire Ordered and Unordered Array Classes

```
template<class T>
class UnorderedArray
{
   public:
      UnorderedArray(int size, int growBy = 1) :
                     m_array(NULL), m_maxSize(0),
                     m_growSize(0), m_numElements(0)
      {
         if(size)
         {
            m_maxSize = size;
            m_array = new T[m_maxSize];
            memset(m_array, 0, sizeof(T) * m_maxSize);

            m_growSize = ((growBy > 0) ? growBy : 0);
         }
      }


      virtual ~UnorderedArray()
      {
         if(m_array != NULL)
         {
            delete[] m_array;
            m_array = NULL;
         }
      }
```

```
virtual void push(T val)
{
    assert(m_array != NULL);

    if(m_numElements >= m_maxSize)
    {
        Expand();
    }

    m_array[m_numElements] = val;
    m_numElements++;
}


void pop()
{
    if(m_numElements > 0)
        m_numElements-;
}


void remove(int index)
{
    assert(m_array != NULL);

    if(index >= m_maxSize)
    {
        return;
    }

    for(int k = index; k < m_maxSize - 1; k++)
        m_array[k] = m_array[k + 1];

    m_maxSize-;

    if(m_numElements >= m_maxSize)
        m_numElements = m_maxSize - 1;
}


virtual T& operator[](int index)
{
    assert(m_array != NULL && index <= m_numElements);
    return m_array[index];
}
```

```
virtual int search(T val)
{
   assert(m_array != NULL);

   for(int i = 0; i < m_numElements; i++)
   {
      if(m_array[i] == val)
         return i;
   }

   return -1;
}


void clear()       { m_numElements = 0; }
int GetSize()      { return m_numElements; }
int GetMaxSize()   { return m_maxSize; }
int GetGrowSize()  { return m_growSize; }

void SetGrowSize(int val)
{
   assert(val >= 0);
   m_growSize = val;
}


private:
   bool Expand()
   {
      if(m_growSize <= 0)
         return false;

      T *temp = new T[m_maxSize + m_growSize];
      assert(temp != NULL);

      memcpy(temp, m_array, sizeof(T) * m_maxSize);

      delete[] m_array;
      m_array = temp;

      m_maxSize += m_growSize;

      return true;
   }
```

```cpp
   private:
      T *m_array;

      int m_maxSize;
      int m_growSize;
      int m_numElements;
};


template <class T>
class OrderedArray
{
   public:
      OrderedArray(int size, int growBy = 1) :
                  m_array(NULL), m_maxSize(0),
                  m_growSize(0), m_numElements(0)
      {
         if(size)
         {
            m_maxSize = size;
            m_array = new T[m_maxSize];
            memset(m_array, 0, sizeof(T) * m_maxSize);

            m_growSize = ((growBy > 0) ? growBy : 0);
         }
      }


      virtual ~OrderedArray()
      {
         if(m_array != NULL)
         {
            delete[] m_array;
            m_array = NULL;
         }
      }


      void push(T val)
      {
         assert(m_array != NULL);

         if(m_numElements >= m_maxSize)
         {
```

```
        Expand();
    }

    for(int i = 0; i < m_numElements; i++)
    {
        if(m_array[i] > val)
            break;
    }

    for(int k = m_numElements; k > i; k-)
    {
        m_array[k] = m_array[k - 1];
    }

    m_array[i] = val;
    m_numElements++;
}


void pop()
{
    if(m_numElements > 0)
        m_numElements-;
}


void remove(int index)
{
    assert(m_array != NULL);

    if(index >= m_maxSize)
    {
        return;
    }

    for(int k = index; k < m_maxSize - 1; k++)
        m_array[k] = m_array[k + 1];

    m_maxSize-;

    if(m_numElements >= m_maxSize)
        m_numElements = m_maxSize - 1;
}
```

```
// Making this const allows for reading but not writing.
virtual const T& operator[](int index)
{
   assert(m_array != NULL && index <= m_numElements);
   return m_array[index];
}


int search(T searchKey)
{
   if(!m_array)
      return -1;

   int lowerBound = 0;
   int upperBound = m_numElements - 1;
   int current = 0;

   while(1)
   {
      current = (lowerBound + upperBound) >> 1;

      if(m_array[current] == searchKey)
      {
         return current;
      }
      else if(lowerBound > upperBound)
      {
         return -1;
      }
      else
      {
         if(m_array[current] < searchKey)
            lowerBound = current + 1;
         else
            upperBound = current - 1;
      }
   }

   return -1;
}


void clear()     { m_numElements = 0; }
int GetSize()    { return m_numElements; }
```

```
int GetMaxSize()  { return m_maxSize; }
int GetGrowSize() { return m_growSize; }

void SetGrowSize(int val)
{
   assert(val >= 0);
   m_growSize = val;
}


private:
   bool Expand()
   {
      if(m_growSize <= 0)
         return false;

      T *temp = new T[m_maxSize + m_growSize];
      assert(temp != NULL);

      memcpy(temp, m_array, sizeof(T) * m_maxSize);

      delete[] m_array;
      m_array = temp;

      m_maxSize += m_growSize;

      return true;
   }


private:
   T *m_array;

   int m_maxSize;
   int m_growSize;
   int m_numElements;
};
```

ON THE CD

On the CD-ROM in the Chapter 2 folder is a demo application called Array Template that demonstrates the use of both the unordered and ordered arrays. Each function and operator is tested in a C++ console application, whose main source file is shown in Listing 2.12.

LISTING 2.12   The Main Source File

```cpp
void UnorderedArrayTest()
{
    UnorderedArray<int> array(3);

    array.push(3);
    array.push(53);
    array.push(83);
    array.push(23);
    array.push(82);

    array[2] = 112;

    array.pop();
    array.remove(2);

    cout << "Unordered array contents: ";

    for(int i = 0; i < array.GetSize(); i++)
    {
        cout << array[i] << " ";
    }

    cout << endl;

    cout << "Search for 53 was found at index: ";
    cout << array.search(53);

    cout << endl << endl;
}


void OrderedArrayTest()
{
    OrderedArray<int> array(3);

    array.push(43);
    array.push(8);
    array.push(23);
    array.push(94);
    array.push(17);
```

```
        array.pop();
        array.remove(2);

        cout << "Ordered array contents: ";

        for(int i = 0; i < array.GetSize(); i++)
        {
            cout << array[i] << " ";
        }

        cout << endl;

        cout << "Search for 12 was found at index: ";
        cout << array.search(12);

        cout << endl << endl;
    }


int main(int args, char **argc)
{
    UnorderedArrayTest();
    OrderedArrayTest();

    return 1;
}
```

*To use user-defined classes in an ordered array, the array must specify the neces-
sary operators such as the less-than sign (<).*

NOTE

DEALING WITH DUPLICATES

By default, C++ arrays cannot check for duplicate data. When working with arrays
that require unique data elements, one option is to search the list before inserting
new items into it. If an item exists, the insertion can be avoided; otherwise the
operation adds the item to the list and returns. Using the code developed so far, one
could prevent duplicates by running the search() function before push(). For both
arrays this can be expensive because linear searching is costly with unordered arrays
with a large *N* and so is the insertion into ordered arrays. One way to deal with
keeping out duplicates with an ordered array is to slightly alter the push() function

to check for the value as it searches for the spot in which it will be placed. If the item is found, the insertion can stop immediately. This can be controlled by using a flag that can be passed to the constructor to inform the container it if is allowed to have duplicates or not. For unordered arrays a linear search would have to be performed each time. An example of using the code developed so far in this chapter to keep duplicates out of an array is shown in Listing 2.13. The type of array used will depend on the application and how the application interacts with the structure. If insertions are not frequent throughout the course of the application but searchers are (and the need for unique data is a must), then the ordered array may be the better option. There is never a clear general winner, and the one to use is determined by the programmer. Other options include using other data structures exclusively or in conjunction with arrays, for example, using a hash table to store hash values of items already inserted so that a quick test can be performed to see if an item already exists.

LISTING 2.13   Checking for Duplicates

```
UnorderedArray<int> array(3);


if(array.Search(3) != -1)
    array.push(3);

if(array.Search(53) != -1)
    array.push(53);

if(array.Search(83) != -1)
    array.push(83);

if(array.Search(23) != -1)
    array.push(23);

if(array.Search(82) != -1)
    array.push(82);
```

STL ARRAYS

The STL is a set of classes that are intended to be generic, tested, portable, and convenient. One STL data structure that will be discussed in this chapter is the vector container. Other classes that will be looked at are the valarray and the bitset, which is not a container but is useful and available to C++ programming in the standard library. Applications of all sorts can benefit from having arrays that need to expand and contract, and by using the STL `vector`, programmers can get just that in an efficient and powerful template class.

The STL sequence containers include `vector`, `string`, `deque`, *and* `list`. *The STL associative containers include* `set`, `multiset`, `map`, *and* `multimap`. *The STL nonstandard associative containers include* `hash_set`, `hash_multiset`, `hash_map`, *and* `hash_multimap`. *The STL nonstandard sequence containers include* `slist` *and* `rope`.

THE STL Vector

The `vector` container (with container being synonymous with list and collection) permits the construction of a generic type of data structure and is one of the STL sequence container types that also include `deque`, `list`, `set`, `map`, `multiset`, and `multimap`, each of which will be encountered throughout this book. This section will present the `vector` class and a few of the algorithms that can be performed on it as well as other STL data structures. Throughout the book more algorithms will be discussed in detail, but this chapter will focus on the algorithms mentioned so far, which include the searching algorithms.

Items are copied into containers with vectors. If the object being copied is expensive to copy, this can cause a serious bottleneck in an application. The expense can have many causes, the major one being lots of memory allocated in the object's construction.

The `vector` class is made up of various methods and operations that allow for the manipulation of the container, with many of these methods and operations being common among STL data structures. Whenever possible, it is recommended that you use container functions and algorithm functions when working with containers, as those functions are highly efficient and in most situations can outperform any custom code that you provide. Table 2.1 summarizes the various STL `vector` class methods and operator functions.

The `vector` *class, along with other STL data structures, uses allocators to allocate memory used by the data structure. Earlier in this chapter we used* `new` *and* `delete` *to handle the allocation and de-allocation of memory.*

TABLE 2.1   Summary of the `vector` Class's Methods and Operators

Method and Operator Names	Descriptions
`vector<type>()`	Constructor that creates an empty vector container
`vector<type>(n)`	Constructor that creates a vector of size *n*
`vector<type>(source)`	Copy constructor that creates a vector that is a copy of the `source` object
`vector<type>(n, val)`	Constructor that creates a vector of size *n* that has its elements initialized to `val`
`vector<type>` `(src.begin, src.end)`	Constructor that creates a vector out of the elements in the `src` vector defined by its beginning and ending iterators
`~vector<type>()`	Destructor that destroys the vector
`assign(n, val)`	Assigns to the vector *n* elements of the value `val`
`at(index)`	Returns a reference to the element specified by `index`
`back()`	Returns a reference to the last element
`begin()`	Returns a random-access iterator to the beginning of the vector
`capacity()`	Returns the number of elements the vector could contain without needing to allocate more memory
`clear()`	Erases the elements of a vector
`empty()`	Returns true if the vector is empty, or else false
`end()`	Returns a random-access iterator to the end of the vector
`erase(index)` `erase(begin, end)`	Erases the element specified by `index` or a range of elements specified by the iterators `begin` and `end`
`front()`	Returns a reference to the beginning of the first element in the vector
`get_allocator()`	Returns the allocator used by the vector container
`insert(index, val)` `insert(index, n, val)`	

→

Method and Operator Names	Descriptions
insert(index, begin, end)	Inserts a value specified by val or a range of values specified by the begin and end iterators into the position index. N is the total number of times to insert into the container.
max_size()	Returns the maximum size of the container
push_back(val)	Adds a value val to the end of the container
pop_back()	Removes the value at the end of the container
rbegin()	Returns an iterator to the first element in a reverse vector container
rend()	Returns an iterator to the last element in a reverse vector container
resize(n)	Specifies a new size n for the container
reserve(n)	Reserves the minimum size n for the container
size()	Returns the number of elements in the container
swap(source)	Swaps two vectors with one another
operator[index]	Returns a reference to an element at index
operator==	Boolean operator that returns true if two vectors are equal, or else it returns false
operator!=	Boolean operator that returns true if two vectors are not equal, or else it returns false
operator<	Boolean operator that returns true if the first vector is less than the second
operator>	Boolean operator that returns true if the first vector is greater than the second
operator<=	Boolean operator that returns true if the first vector is less than or equal to the second
operator>=	Boolean operator that returns true if the first vector is greater than or equal to the second

In addition to the methods and operators in Table 2.1 there is a list of STL algorithms that can also be performed on STL containers. In this chapter we will look at the binary search, search, copy, and accumulate algorithms in the code examples that follow. Commonly used STL algorithms include but are not limited to those described in Table 2.2.

To use STL algorithms you will need to include the header file <algorithm>.

TABLE 2.2   Commonly Used STL Algorithms

`accumulate(begin, end, val)`	Returns the sum of all of the elements in the range of the `begin` and `end` iterators (and adds `val` to each element)
`copy(src.begin, src.end, dst.begin)`	Copies the elements in `src` to `dst` in the range of the `src`'s `begin` and `end` iterators
`copy_backward(src.begin, src.end, dst.begin)`	Same as `copy()` but with the elements in reverse
`count(begin, end, val)`	Counts the number of elements that match `val` in the range specified by the `begin` and `end` iterators
`fill(begin, end, val)`	Fills a container in the range specified by `begin` and `end` with the value `val`
`find(begin, end, val)`	Returns an input iterator to the first occurrence of `val` in the range specified by `begin` and `end`
`min_element(begin, end)`	Returns the minimum element in the range specified by `begin` and `end`
`max_element(begin, end)`	Returns the maximum element in the range specified by `begin` and `end`
`random_shuffle(begin, end)`	Randomly shuffles elements in a range
`remove(begin, end, val)`	Removes a value `val` from the container in a range without changing the order of the remaining elements
`replace(begin, end, oldVal, newVal)`	Replaces the elements that match `oldVal` with `newVal` in a range
`reverse(begin, end)`	Changes the order of the elements in the specified range
`search (begin1, end1, begin2, end2)`	Searches for the first occurrence of a set of values specified in `begin2` and `end2` with those in `begin1` and `end1`
`sort (begin, end)`	Sorts the elements in the range into ascending order
`swap(vec1, vec2)`	Swaps the elements between two vectors
`unique(begin, end)`	Removes duplicate elements within the range

This book will cover more STL algorithms in the following chapters.

Slicing can occur when objects of a derived type are copied into a container that is set up to store objects of the base type. Slicing occurs when objects are copied using the base class instead of the derived class (derived-ness of the objects is removed). One way to avoid this is to use a container of base class pointers, but this can have its own problems, as we will see later on.

In this section we will look at a few C++ console demo applications that use the STL `vector` template class. The first demo application is called stlvector and can be found on the CD-ROM in the Chapter 2 folder. The demo is made up of one source file called main.cpp. In the demo the code will demonstrate passing vectors by reference to functions, calling the `size()` and `capacity()` functions of the container class, inserting items with `push_back()`, removing items with `pop()`, accessing elements with the `[]` operator, reserving space with the `reserve()` function, declaring an integer vector container `clear()` for clearing the container, and calling the `empty()` function to see if the container is empty. The entire main.cpp source file from the stlvector demo application is shown in Listing 2.14.

LISTING 2.14   The Main Source File of the stlvector Demo Application

```cpp
#include<iostream>
#include<vector>

using namespace std;


void PrintVector(vector<int> &array)
{
   cout << "Contents (" << "Size: " << (int)array.size() <<
          " Max: " << (int)array.capacity() << ") - ";

   for(int i = 0; i < (int)array.size(); i++)
   {
      cout << array[i] << " ";
   }

   cout << endl;
}
```

```
int main(int args, char **argc)
{
   cout << "STL Vector Example" << endl;
   cout << "Data Structures for Game Developers" << endl;
   cout << "Allen Sherrod" << endl << endl;


   vector<int> array;
   array.reserve(5);

   array.push_back(10);
   array.push_back(20);
   array.push_back(30);
   array.push_back(40);

   cout << "  Inserted into vector.  ";
   PrintVector(array);


   array.pop_back();
   array.pop_back();

   cout << "Popped two from vector.  ";
   PrintVector(array);


   array.clear();

   cout << "        Cleared vector.  ";
   PrintVector(array);

   cout << endl;

   if(array.empty() == true)
      cout << "Vector is empty.";
   else
      cout << "Vector is NOT empty.";

   cout << endl << endl;

   return 1;
}
```

In Listing 2.14 the demo application creates an integer array and populates it with data using the push_back() method (see Table 2.1 for more information). The container is empty until items are pushed onto it. Once on the list, the array [] operators can be used to access the element by reading or writing to it. In the example code in Listing 2.14 four items are pushed onto the list before popping (removal) of the last two and displaying the contents of the container.

The container is cleared, displayed again, and tested to see if it is empty. Inside the function used to print a container, the code uses size() to determine how many valid elements are currently pushed onto the container while capacity() is used to determine how much space the container can hold without being resized. To access the elements, we use the array operators [] for convenience.

ITERATORS

Iterators are similar to pointers in that they point to elements in a container. Iterators are commonly used in C++ and are very important when using the STL. In Tables 2.1 and 2.2 a number of functions dealt with iterators, and in the following section we will take a closer look at them and how they relate to the vector template class.

Iterators can be created to point to an element in a container. In the case of a vector class, an iterator can point to one of the elements in the array. The iterator supports operators such as (*), which is used for dereferencing iterators so you can use them almost as variables that hold the value for that element (just as with pointers), and (++) and (–) for moving to the next and previous elements in the container. Iterators work on sequence containers, which include our vector class.

Iterators include container iterators (forward, bidirectional, and random access), input iterators, and output iterators, and we'll see each type throughout this book. As a demonstration of using iterators with a vector class, there is a demo application called stlvector 2 on the CD-ROM in the Chapter 2 folder. The main source file of the demo application is shown in Listing 2.15.

ON THE CD

LISTING 2.15   The Main Source File for the stlvector 2 Demo Application

```
#include<iostream>
#include<vector>
#include<algorithm>
#include<numeric>

using namespace std;


void PrintVector(vector<int> &array)
{
```

```
         cout << "Contents (" << "Size: " << (int)array.size() <<
               " Max: " << (int)array.capacity() << ") - ";

      ostream_iterator<int> output(cout, " ");
      copy(array.begin(), array.end(), output);

      cout << endl;
}


int main(int args, char **argc)
{
      cout << "STL Vector Example 2: Iterators" << endl;
      cout << "Data Structures for Game Developers" << endl;
      cout << "Allen Sherrod" << endl << endl;


      vector<int> array;
      array.reserve(5);

      // Add items then print.
      array.push_back(10);
      array.push_back(20);
      array.push_back(30);
      array.push_back(40);
      array.push_back(50);


      // Calling the copy algorithm.
      vector<int> array2;
      for(int i = 0; i < 5; i++)
         array2.push_back(0);

      copy(array.begin(), array.end(), array2.begin());


      cout << "  Inserted into vector:   ";
      PrintVector(array);


      // Run the accumulate algorithm.
      cout << "             Accumulate:   "
           << accumulate(array.begin(), array.end(), 0)
           << endl;
```

```
// Pop off the container.
array.pop_back();
array.pop_back();

cout << "Popped two from vector:  ";
PrintVector(array);


// Clear the container.
array.clear();

cout << "        Cleared vector:  ";
PrintVector(array);

cout << endl;

// Test if the container is empty.
if(array.empty() == true)
    cout << "Vector is empty.";
else
    cout << "Vector is NOT empty.";


cout << endl << endl;

return 1;
}
```

The demo application stlvector 2 in Listing 2.15 starts in the same manner as the demo application stlvector in Listing 2.14 by creating an integer container and filling it with elements. Once the container is filled, the STL copy algorithm is used to copy the first container into another. Before the copying, a loop is used to create the element space in the second container because to copy the first container into the second, the second must have at least the number of elements required by the range, which is specified by the iterators begin (first element or [0]) and end (last element or [4] in this case).

After the copy algorithm is performed and the container is displayed, the accumulate STL algorithm is performed to demonstrate that to get the sum of all the elements, a few pop() calls are performed, the container is cleared, and it is tested for emptiness. Inside the function used to print the container is new code that replaces the for loop in the first vector demo application stlvector. In this function an output iterator is created and the STL copy algorithm is called. The call states that the range of elements from the first parameter (the beginning of the container in this case) to the second parameter (the end of the container in this case) should be copied to the output iterator. The output iterator for this demo application is set up to point to the C++ STD `cout` object. This is an example of how to use algorithms and iterators together to perform fast tasks in C++ code. Using a `for` loop is one option, which was seen in the first stlvector demo, but it is slower than using STL algorithms. Whenever possible use STL algorithms for traditional arrays and containers because the performance is efficient. The output iterator that is set up in Listing 2.15 points to the `cout` object and appends a " " character to every element that is passed to it. This is what gives the output a space between each element that is printed.

To use `accumulate()` *we also must include the header file* `<numeric>`.

NOTE

STL vector Tips and Tricks

In this section we will look at some tips to keep in mind when using `vector` classes. Throughout this book, especially in the next few chapter, we will discuss more tips and how they relate to the topics at hand.

Tip 1

Unless there is a reason not to, you should always use `vector` classes with user-defined classes or even class pointers. This is suggested because with traditional arrays, if you were to do the following,

```
SomeClass someArray[100];
```

100 constructors, one for each object, would be executed. If those constructors have special needs, such as large and expensive memory allocation, this can be not only a performance bottleneck but also a waste of time if not all elements are to be used. The same can be said for dynamic arrays. Use the following instead:

```
vector<SomeClass> someVec;
someVec.reserve(100);
```

No constructors are executed and, assuming you know you need at least 100 elements, the container will be ready to store at least 100 objects.

Tip 2

Use `reserve()` to avoid unnecessary reallocations whenever possible. If you know the minimum or even maximum number of elements your container will use, using `reserve()` can avoid or minimize the number of reallocations the container will need to perform. Depending on the application, the savings can add up and prove to be beneficial.

Tip 3

Avoid using `vector<bool>`. Because of the nature of Booleans used with the `vector` container, they cannot be used to create true containers. The container will attempt to use bit fields instead of bools to save space, and it uses proxy classes instead of references with the `[]` operator. A container of bools can't be created because the following won't compile (it does not follow the Standard for C++ as specified in Section 23.1):

```
vector<bool> array;
bool *ptr = &array[0];
```

The above won't compile because what is returned is a proxy class and not a reference to a Boolean. An alternative to using `vector<bool>` is to use an STL `bitset`, which we'll discuss later in this chapter.

For some compilers, if you do not specify a copy constructor and a copy assignment operator for containers that need them, the compiler will attempt to create them for you. This code creation can happen without your knowledge at compile time for your user-defined classes whenever the compiler can step in and do so.

Tip 4

Manually delete pointers of new-ed memory that was stored in a container, because the container will not delete that memory for you. When a container is destroyed, so are the elements in the container. Unfortunately, although the elements are destroyed, their destructors are not called when working with pointers because they did not use the `delete` keyword. Deleting memory is the responsibility of the programmer, not the containers. Because of this, if you don't delete dynamically allocated objects that were placed in a container, you will have a memory leak. This happens because what was pushed onto the container is a copy of the pointer. There is no way for the container to know that it has pointers to dynamically allocate memory, and even if it knew that, it would have no way of knowing if it was free to delete that memory, because other pointers can still be using it.

 To demonstrate how to delete memory that was inserted in a container, a demo application called stlvector 3 is in the Chapter 2 folder on the CD-ROM. The main source file for the demo application is shown in Listing 2.16.

LISTING 2.16   The Main Source File for the stlvector 3 Demo Application

```cpp
#include<iostream>
#include<vector>
#include<algorithm>

using namespace std;


class ExampleClass
{
   public:
      ExampleClass()
      {
         cout << "Item created!" << endl;
      }

      ~ExampleClass()
      {
         cout << "Item deleted!" << endl;
      }
};


struct DeleteMemObj
{
   template<typename T>
   void operator()(const T* ptr) const
   {
      delete ptr;
      ptr = NULL;
   }
};


int main(int args, char **argc)
{
   cout << "STL Vector Example 3: Deleting New Pointers" << endl;
   cout << "Data Structures for Game Developers" << endl;
   cout << "Allen Sherrod" << endl << endl;


   vector<ExampleClass*> array;
   array.reserve(5);
```

```
        array.push_back(new ExampleClass);
        array.push_back(new ExampleClass);
        array.push_back(new ExampleClass);
        array.push_back(new ExampleClass);
        array.push_back(new ExampleClass);


        cout << endl;


        for_each(array.begin(), array.end(),
                DeleteMemObj());

        cout << endl;

        cout << "Array items deleted!";

        cout << endl << endl;

        return 1;
    }
```

The demo application stlvector 3 in Listing 2.16 works by calling the for_each() algorithm on the container class. When it is time to delete the memory, the algorithm goes through each element, as specified by the begin() and end() iterators, and applies the structure DeleteMemObj to it. The structure has an over-loaded () operator and is a template type that allows us to sneak in a delete key-word. Technically you could have written a loop to go through and delete each pointer by performing:

```
    for(vector<ExampleClass*>::iterator it = array.begin();
        it != array.end(); it++)
    {
        if((*it) != NULL)
        {
            delete (*it);
            (*it) = NULL;
        }
    }
```

Using the code above on an iterator that was de-referenced using pointer no-tation would work, but because the for_each() STL algorithm is faster than our hand-coded loops, it was used in the demo application in Listing 2.16.

Tip 5

Hold off from creating a container until the last possible moment. Containers such as `vector` allocate memory upon construction. Because of this, there can be a wasted construction in many cases where the container was not used. For example,

```
void SomeFunc(SomeClass *ptr)
{
    vector<AnotherClass> exampleVec;

    if(ptr == NULL)
        return;

    // ... INSERT CODE HERE ...
}
```

Because the code in the previous example has a condition that could cause the container to never be used, it is a waste to declare the container in such situations. A better solution would be the following:

```
void SomeFunc(SomeClass *ptr)
{
    if(ptr == NULL)
        return;

    vector<AnotherClass> exampleVec;

    // ... INSERT CODE HERE ...
}
```

C++ gives programmers the freedom to declare objects and variables anywhere they want as long as it is in scope and is declared before it is used. Therefore, C++ programmers should take advantage of this feature, unlike C programmers.

Trick 1

The following can be used to clear a `vector` by swapping the contents in an empty `vector` (by calling the constructor) with one you want to clear:

```
vector<int> vec;
vector<int>().swap(vec);
```

The same trick can be used to trim a vector with excess space by doing the following:

```
vector<int> vec;
vector<int>(vec.begin(), vec.end()).swap(vec);
```

THE valarray

The next class that will be discussed is the valarray, which is a template class used to hold a sequence of elements for fast mathematical operations. When fast math operations are a must, the valarray might be a great choice over a vector. The types used with a valarray must be able to have mathematical operations performed on them or the benefit is lost. The class is made up of a one-dimensional "smart" array that checks the subscript references (by [ ]) at runtime to ensure that they are in bounds. When compared to a vector, the valarray is a near-container, in that it does not fully support the features of a sequence container. One noticeable difference is that there are no iterators with a valarray as there are with vector classes.

ON THE CD

An example of using a valarray, called Valarray, can be found on the CD-ROM in the Chapter 2 folder. The demo application creates and fills a valarray, applies a multiplication to all of its elements, and has the ability to print the array. Since the valarray has no iterators, we can not use the for_each() algorithm as we did in the stlvector 2 demo application. The main source file for the Valarray demo application is shown in Listing 2.17. Note how value_type objects are used to apply mathematical operations on the valarray.

LISTING 2.17   An Example of Using a valarray

```
#include<iostream>
#include<valarray>

using namespace std;


void PrintValArray(const valarray<int> &valArray)
{
   cout << "Contents of valArray: ";

   for(int i = 0; i < 10; i++)
   {
      cout << valArray[i] << " ";
   }

   cout << endl << endl;
}
```

```
int main(int args, char **argc)
{
    cout << "STL Val Array Example" << endl;
    cout << "Data Structures for Game Developers" << endl;
    cout << "Allen Sherrod" << endl << endl;


    valarray<int> valArray(10);

    // Placing numbers 1 through 10 on for demonstration.
    for(int i = 0; i < 10; i++)
    {
        valArray[i] = i;
    }

    PrintValArray(valArray);


    valarray<int>::value_type rVal = 5;

    cout << "The value of rVal before multiplication: "
        << rVal << endl << endl;

    valArray *= rVal;

    PrintValArray(valArray);

    return 1;
}
```

BIT ARRAYS

The next class that will be discussed is the manual bit array class. A bit is one-eighth of a byte. Since there are no data types smaller than a char (byte) in C++, we have to use bit-wise operators to access and manipulate individual bits of a byte. There are many benefits to using arrays of bits. The first benefit is storage. For every one char, we have eight bits. In situations in which boolean values are needed, this 8:1 compaction can be very beneficial for a large number of bits. Also, bit-wise operators are very fast, and working with them is efficient. Later we will use arrays of bits for various algorithms, with one example being compression.

In this chapter we will create a simple bit array class. This class will be able to allocate an array of bits with one byte for every eight bits, clear all bits to false, set all bits to true, set an entire byte, and set and clear an individual bit. The class also supports the [ ] operator, which takes the bit that is to be accessed (read-only), returns a true or false value if it is set or not, and uses an STL vector data structure. The reasoning behind the setting of a byte is that in future chapters we will write code that will create bytes from a file that stores useful bit information. Since a single byte suffers from no endian complications, this bit array code will work on all platforms. The bit array class is shown in Listing 2.18.

LISTING 2.18 A Class for Bit Arrays

```
#define BYTE_BITS          8
#define BIT_TO_CHAR(bit)   ((bit) / BYTE_BITS)
#define BIT_IN_CHAR(bit)   (1 << (BYTE_BITS - 1 -
                            ((bit) % BYTE_BITS)))
#define MIN_CHARS(bits)    ((((bits) - 1) / CHAR_BIT) + 1)
#define MAX_UCHAR          0xff


class BitArray
{
   public:
      BitArray(unsigned int size)
      {
         assert(size > 0);

         m_totalBits = size;
         m_totalBytes = MIN_CHARS(m_totalBits);

         m_bits.reserve(m_totalBytes);

         for(unsigned int i = 0; i < m_totalBytes; i++)
            m_bits.push_back(0);
      }


      ~BitArray()
      {

      }


      void ClearAllBits()
      {
```

```cpp
      m_bits.assign(m_bits.size(), 0);
}


void SetAllBits()
{
   m_bits.assign(m_bits.size(), MAX_UCHAR);

   int bits = m_totalBits % BYTE_BITS;

   if(bits != 0)
   {
      unsigned char mask = MAX_UCHAR << (BYTE_BITS - bits);
      m_bits[BIT_TO_CHAR(m_totalBits - 1)] = mask;
   }
}


void SetByte(unsigned int byte, unsigned char val)
{
   assert(m_totalBits > byte);

   m_bits[byte] = val;
}


void SetBit(unsigned int bit)
{
   assert(m_totalBits > bit);

   m_bits[BIT_TO_CHAR(bit)] |= BIT_IN_CHAR(bit);
}


void ClearBit(unsigned int bit)
{
   assert(m_totalBits > bit);

   unsigned char mask =  BIT_IN_CHAR(bit);
   mask = ~mask;

   m_bits[BIT_TO_CHAR(bit)] &= mask;
}
```

```
bool operator[](unsigned int bit) const
{
    assert(m_totalBits > bit);

    return((m_bits[BIT_TO_CHAR(bit)] &
            BIT_IN_CHAR(bit)) != 0);
}


private:
    vector<unsigned char> m_bits;
    unsigned int m_totalBits, m_totalBytes;
};
```

The bit array class in Listing 2.18 starts off with a constructor and a destructor. The destructor isn't needed because the vector class can clean up after itself. The constructor, on the other hand, reserves enough space for the bits (in bytes) and pushes enough elements onto the container. The functions ClearAllBits() and SetAllBits() are used to set all bits in the array to false for the clear and true for the set. During the SetAllBits() function all bits are set to true and then any excess bits are set to false. Excess bits are bits that are left over from having to use whole bytes instead of bits. For example, if we had 36 bits, that would be 5 bytes since the first 4 bytes make 32 bits and the remaining 4 bits must be carried over to the fifth byte. Although this is not necessary since the excess bits aren't accessible, it was done as a demonstration.

The function following SetAllBits(), SetByte(), performs an unsigned char copy (byte copy). The next two functions clear and set individual bits using the |= bit-wise operator and the &~ operator. The final function is the overloaded operator for the []. Using the brackets allows the class to access true or false values for individual bits by using the bit, not the byte, as an array index. This makes reading bits as easy as:

```
bool result = bitArray[16];
```

ON THE CD
On the CD-ROM in the Chapter 2 folder is a demo application called Bitarray that uses the code in Listing 2.18. The demo application tests each of the class functions and operators. The main source file for the demo application, main.cpp, is shown in Listing 2.19.

LISTING 2.19 The Main Source File for the Bitarray Demo Application

```
int main(int args, char **argc)
{
```

```
        BitArray bitArray(16);

        cout << "Bit Array Example" << endl;
        cout << "Data Structures for Game Developers" << endl;
        cout << "Allen Sherrod" << endl << endl;


        cout << "Initial bit values for 2, 3 and 14." << endl << endl;

        cout << "Bit  2 = " << bitArray[ 2] << "." << endl;
        cout << "Bit  3 = " << bitArray[ 3] << "." << endl;
        cout << "Bit 14 = " << bitArray[14] << "." << endl << endl;


        cout << "Set bits 2 and 14." << endl << endl;

        bitArray.SetBit(2);
        bitArray.SetBit(14);

        cout << "Bit  2 = " << bitArray[ 2] << "." << endl;
        cout << "Bit  3 = " << bitArray[ 3] << "." << endl;
        cout << "Bit 14 = " << bitArray[14] << "." << endl << endl;


        cout << "Set all bits" << endl << endl;

        bitArray.SetAllBits();

        cout << "Bit  2 = " << bitArray[ 2] << "." << endl;
        cout << "Bit  3 = " << bitArray[ 3] << "." << endl;
        cout << "Bit 14 = " << bitArray[14] << "." << endl << endl;


        cout << "Clear all bits" << endl << endl;

        bitArray.ClearAllBits();

        cout << "Bit  2 = " << bitArray[ 2] << "." << endl;
        cout << "Bit  3 = " << bitArray[ 3] << "." << endl;
        cout << "Bit 14 = " << bitArray[14] << "." << endl << endl;

        return 1;
}
```

THE bitset CLASS

The last class we will look at is the C++ standard `bitset` class. The `bitset` class is used to store a sequence of bits much like the bit array class discussed in the previous section. The application for the Bitset demo, which can be found on the CD-ROM in the Chapter 2 folder, is the same as the Bitarray demo, with the exception of creating a `bitset<16>` instead of a `BitArray(16)`. Along with bit-wise operators, the `bitarray` uses the methods seen in Table 2.3. The main.cpp source file from the Bitset demo application is shown in Listing 2.20.

TABLE 2.3   The `bitset` Methods

Method Name	Description
any()	Tests if any bit in the set is set to 1
count()	Returns the number of bits there are in a sequence
flip()	
flip(size_t pos)	Flips all bits or a specific bit. Bits that are true become false and bits that are false become true.
none()	Tests if no bits have been set to 1
reset()	
reset(size_t pos)	Resets all bits in the set to 0 or resets an individual bit in pos
set()	
set(size_t pos, bool val)	Set all bits to true or sets an individual bit at pos to a specified value val
size()	Returns the number of bits in a `bitset` object
test(size_t pos)	Tests whether a bit at pos is set to 1
to_string()	Converts a `bitset` to a string
to_ulong()	Converts a `bitset` to an unsigned long

LISTING 2.20   The Bitset Demo Application's main.cpp File

```
#include<iostream>
#include<bitset>
```

```cpp
using namespace std;


int main(int args, char **argc)
{
   bitset<16> bitArray;

   cout << "STL Bit Set Example" << endl;
   cout << "Data Structures for Game Developers" << endl;
   cout << "Allen Sherrod" << endl << endl;


   cout << "Number of bits: " << bitArray.size() << endl;
   cout << "Bits not set (T or F): " << bitArray.none() << endl;

   cout << endl;


   cout << "Initial bit values for 2, 3 and 14." << endl << endl;

   cout << "Bit  2 = " << bitArray[ 2] << "." << endl;
   cout << "Bit  3 = " << bitArray[ 3] << "." << endl;
   cout << "Bit 14 = " << bitArray.test(14) << "." << endl << endl;


   cout << "Set bits 2 and 14." << endl << endl;

   bitArray[ 2] = true;
   bitArray[14] = true;

   cout << "Bit  2 = " << bitArray[ 2] << "." << endl;
   cout << "Bit  3 = " << bitArray[ 3] << "." << endl;
   cout << "Bit 14 = " << bitArray.test(14) << "." << endl << endl;


   cout << "Set all bits" << endl << endl;

   bitArray.set();

   cout << "Bit  2 = " << bitArray[ 2] << "." << endl;
   cout << "Bit  3 = " << bitArray[ 3] << "." << endl;
   cout << "Bit 14 = " << bitArray.test(14) << "." << endl << endl;
```

```
        cout << "Clear all bits" << endl << endl;

        bitArray.reset();

        cout << "Bit  2 = " << bitArray[ 2] << "." << endl;
        cout << "Bit  3 = " << bitArray[ 3] << "." << endl;
        cout << "Bit 14 = " << bitArray.test(14) << "." << endl << endl;

        return 1;
    }
```

SUMMARY

This chapter covered the array data structures the STL `vector`, `bitset`, `valarray` and three custom-created classes, one for unordered arrays, one for ordered arrays, and one for bits. The algorithms covered in this chapter included the linear and binary searches as well as various STL algorithms such as accumulate, copy, and for-each. Arrays are very useful in applications, and the information covered in this chapter can go a long way toward using arrays efficiently.

The next two chapters will focus on adding algorithms to the array classes built in this chapter as well as covering their STL counterparts. As we've seen so far, algorithms and their data structures are very useful tools to have in any library. The STL makes using these tools easier than ever before.

CHAPTER REVIEW QUESTIONS

Answers to the following chapter review questions can be found in Appendix B.

1. What kind of container is the STL vector?
   a. A standard STL associative container
   b. A nonstandard STL associative container
   c. A standard STL sequence container
   d. A nonstandard STL sequence container
2. A memory leak occurs when:
   a. An index attempts to access an element outside of the array's bounds
   b. An application tries to access a deleted pointer
   c. No pointers are pointing to a memory location and can't release the resource.

3. An ordered array's insertion runs in the big-O:
   a. O(N)
   b. O(1)
   c. O(log N)
   d. O(N²)
4. A binary search is the big-O of:
   a. O(N)
   b. O(1)
   c. O(log N)
   d. O(N²)
   e. None of the above
5. What is the purpose of the vector::reserve() function?
6. What are iterators? What kind of iterators were discussed in this chapter?
7. vector<bool> should not be used because it does not implement actual bools.
   a. True
   b. False
8. vector classes should be used for mathematical operations over valarray.
   a. True
   b. False
9. Bit arrays contain elements where each element is an individual bit.
   a. True
   b. False
10. The bitset is a typedef for vector<unsigned char>.
    a. True
    b. False

PROGRAMMING PROJECTS

Exercise 1: Modify the ordered array to use a binary search as a means to find the position at which an item is to be inserted. The new search function should find the best index position of where the item will be placed rather than an actual value.

Exercise 2: Create a function that takes as parameters a bit array and a string that holds the file name to a text file of bytes. Allow this function to load all of the bytes from the file into the bit array. Create an alternate function that allows bit arrays to be saved out to a file.

Exercise 3: Add overloaded operators for each of the C++ bit-wise operators. Also add two functions, with one used to flip all bits in the bit array and the other used to flip a specific bit in the array.

3 Recursion

In This Chapter

- Recursion Defined
- Triangular Numbers
- Factorials

Triangular Numbers: 8th Term

| 36 | 28 | 21 | 15 | 10 | 6 | 3 | 1 |

In computer programming there are definitions that have the ability to call themselves within code. Left unchecked, such an event can lead to an infinite cycle that can have negative, or even catastrophic, effects on the executing code. Normally such an event is a logic error, such as a function calling itself, due to a typo or some other human error. Once an infinite cycle, or loop, has occurred, there is little or nothing that can be done to stop it outside of forcing the application to quit. This can be trouble, especially in a gaming application.

Not all definitions that can call themselves are bad in the world of programming. Assuming there is some uniqueness inside the code being executed, the definition itself can choose when to stop the cycle. An example of this can be seen with loops where a condition is chosen to indicate when the loop should end. Uniqueness in this case is often a variable used as some form of counter such as in the following for-loop example:

```
for(int i = 0; i < 10; i++)
{
    // Code executed within the loop.
}
```

Uniqueness means that there is some difference, even if minor, in the executing code during the iterations of its execution. Without such a difference, it would be hard to tell when an algorithm should stop. Sometimes this is not bad, especially if some user-required interaction is desired. An example of this can be seen in many game loops where the loops are infinite but some user-controlled action can cause a break in their executions at specific times. The bad kind of infinite cycles are the ones that are not intentional and have no way out of their execution. When learning about loops, one has to tackle the topic of avoiding infinite loops.

Using such a cycle that can be interrupted is known as recursion. Recursion has many useful applications in programming and can be beneficial to the design of code. In this chapter we will look at what recursion is, how to perform it, and some uses it has in programming and game development. Later in the book we will look at data structures that can rely on recursion to build various trees. One popular tree used in game development that we will be looking at is the BSP (binary space partitioning) tree. When it comes to performing repetitive tasks on data structures, recursion can be very useful and the code can be easy to read.

NOTE

Recursion will be used heavily in some of the later chapters in this book. For those not familiar with recursion, it is important to study the concept before moving on.

In this chapter we will explore a few areas in which recursion can be used to great effect. These areas include factorials, triangular numbers, and binary searching. The binary search will be used in the ordered array since the algorithm requires data to be in order.

RECURSION DEFINED

Recursion occurs when a method calls itself within the body of its definition. It is a technique used in programming to help solve various problems. Recursive functions execute their contents under some condition that, when met, causes the recursion to cease. The purpose of a recursive function is to find the solution to a small piece of a bigger problem, and each time the body of a recursive function is called, another piece of that puzzle is solved. The condition with recursive functions revolves around the completion of the original problem.

Recursion is used to simplify a problem conceptually. This simplification does not mean that the code will always be more efficient.

THE PROS AND CONS OF RECURSION

Recursion can be very useful in computer programming, and, as we will see later, in game development, but there are a few pros and cons that all programmers should keep in mind when learning about recursion. These pros include the following things to remember:

- It is conceptually easier to code.
- It is easier to maintain and modify in some situations.

The cons are:

- There is overhead with the calling of functions that can quickly add up with recursion.
- When enough functions and their arguments are pushed onto the stack, it can cause a stack overflow when the recursive function gets to a point where it exceeds the system's capacity.
- Using recursion can be less effective in performance than using loops.

In cases where the efficiency loss is great, you should avoid using recursion if it becomes a serious source of a bottleneck in the application.

TAIL RECURSION AND NONTAIL RECURSION

A recursive method can be defined by making the method either tail recursive or nontail recursive, where the differences are small but have large implications. Tail recursion is a type of recursive definition that calls itself at the end of the function, where no statements follow it and no recursive statements come before it. An example of tail recursion can be seen in the following:

```
int recursion(int param)
{
   if(param < 1)
      return 0;


   // Perform some task


   return recursion(param - 1);
}
```

Nontail recursion is a method that defines statements after the recursive call and/or if there is more than one recursive call in the same body. An example of nontail recursion can be seen in the following:

```
int recursion(int param)
{
   if(param < 1)
      return 0;


   recursion(param - 1);


   // Perform some task


   recursion(param - 1);
}
```

In both tail and nontail recursion, a condition is specified somewhere in the function that keeps the calls from becoming infinite. By altering the parameter each time the recursive function is called, the code can allow for some uniqueness in each of the iterations of its execution, which allows the condition to exist to monitor the depth of the method.

AN EXAMPLE OF RECURSION

As an example of recursion, we will consider an application that will display a series of positive numbers in reverse order. This will work by supplying the recursive function with an integer value and displaying that number along with all numbers before it until it reaches 0. Using the whole number 10 as an example, the output would look like the following:

10   9   8   7   6   5   4   3   2   1

ON THE CD

On the CD-ROM in the Chapter 3 folder is a demo application called Recursion. The Recursion demo application will perform the task described above by printing a series of numbers from a number *N* to 0. Look at Listing 3.1 for the main source file from the Recursion demo application. A screenshot of the running Recursion demo application is shown in Figure 3.1.

LISTING 3.1   An Example of Recursion

```cpp
#include<iostream>
#include<cassert>

using namespace std;


void PrintNumReverse(int x)
{
   if(x <= 0)
      return;

   cout << " " << x;

   PrintNumReverse(x - 1);
}


int main(int args, char **argc)
{
   cout << "Recursion Example" << endl;
   cout << "Chapter 3: Recursion" << endl << endl;

   cout << "Example of a recursive call:";
```

```
        PrintNumReverse(10);

        cout << "." << endl << endl;

        return 1;
    }
```

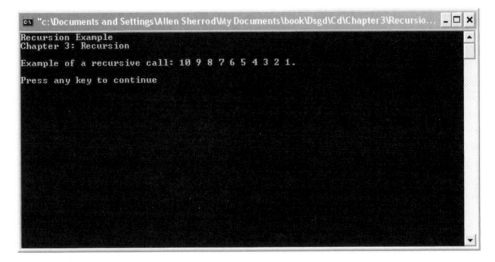

FIGURE 3.1 A screenshot of the Recursion demo.

In Listing 3.1 the demo application defines a recursive function called `PrintNumReverse()`. This function is a tail recursive function that works by printing out the parameter passed into it before calling itself with the parameter minus 1. The condition that needs to be met before this function can return without calling itself again recursively is that the parameter passed in be less than 1. Until that condition is met, the series of numbers from the parameter, `param`, until 0 is displayed one after the other in order.

RECURSIVE BINARY SEARCH

As another example of recursion, we will look at modifying the binary search of the ordered array created in Chapter 2 to use recursion instead of a loop. The recursive binary search looks exactly the same as the loop version, with the exception of the loop itself and that the return value is based on either –1 (for not found), the index for found, or the recursive call for cases where we must keep searching. Listing 3.2 shows the new binary search, where the `search()` function has been modified to call a new private function called find(). The find() method takes as parameters the value we are searching for and the upper and lower bounds of the search. The bounds, which are the minimum and maximum array elements to search, are used as the condition for which we can determine if the recursion should stop if the value is not found. Because we don't want the bounds to be the responsibility of anyone using the class, we can code it so search() is used by the outside code but binarySearch() performs the actual work.

LISTING 3.2   The Modified search() and the New find() of the Ordered Array

```
template <typename T>
class OrderedArray
{
   public:

      int search(T searchKey)
      {
         return binarySearch(searchKey, 0, m_numElements - 1);
      }


   private:

      int binarySearch(T searchKey, int lowerBound, int upperBound)
      {
         assert(m_array != NULL);
         assert(lowerBound >= 0);
         assert(upperBound < m_numElements);

         int current = (lowerBound + upperBound) >> 1;

         if(m_array[current] == searchKey)
         {
            return current;
         }
         else if(lowerBound > upperBound)
         {
            return -1;
         }
         else
         {
```

```
                    if(m_array[current] < searchKey)
                        return binarySearch(searchKey, current+1,
                                                    upperBound);
                    else
                        return binarySearch(searchKey, lowerBound,
                                                    current - 1);
                }

                return -1;
            }
        };
```

A demo application called Recursive Binary Search on the accompanying CD-ROM in the Chapter 3 folder demonstrates that this new code works. The new code was added to the ordered array because, as discussed in Chapter 2, the unordered array does not use a binary search but instead uses a linear search that would have no benefit to recursion. The code for the Recursive Binary Search demo application is shown in Listing 3.3. Figure 3.2 shows a screenshot of the application running.

LISTING 3.3 The Main Source File of the Recursive Binary Search Demo

```
#include<iostream>
#include"Arrays.h"

using namespace std;


int main(int args, char **argc)
{
    cout << "Recursive Binary Search Example" << endl;
    cout << "Chapter 3: Recursion" << endl << endl;


    OrderedArray<int> array(3);

    array.push(43);
    array.push(8);
    array.push(23);
    array.push(94);
    array.push(17);
    array.push(83);
    array.push(44);
    array.push(28);
```

```
cout << "Ordered array contents:";

for(int i = 0; i < array.GetSize(); i++)
{
   cout << " " << array[i];
}

cout << "." << endl;


cout << "Search for 43 was found at index: ";
cout << array.search(43) << ".";


cout << endl << endl;

return 1;
}
```

FIGURE 3.2   A screenshot of the Binary Search demo.

TRIANGULAR NUMBERS

As an exercise in using recursion, we will next discuss triangular numbers that deal
with the Pythagorian theorem, in which a series of numbers are created using the

*n*th term. For example, given the numbers, 1, 3, 6, 10, 15, 21, 28, 36, 45, 55, the 11th term would be 66 because adding 11 to 55 gives us 66. The *n*th term is added to the value that came before it. For 3, which is the second term, we add 2 to the previous value, 1, and get 3. For the 6, we added 3 to the previous term, which was 3; for 10 we added 4 to the previous term of 6, and so forth. The 12th term would be added to 66 to get 78, after which 13 would be used to get 91, and so on.

The triangular numbers get their name from the fact that, when using rows and columns, they form a triangle, as shown in Figure 3.3.

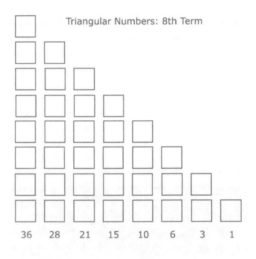

FIGURE 3.3 An example of triangular numbers.

To find the value of any term in Figure 3.3, we must add each column starting with the column for the term we want and all columns to the right of that. For example, when looking for the sixth term, we could use simple addition as shown in Figure 3.4.

Looking at the problem and solving it this way is one thing, but code is another. In the following sections we will discuss how to find the value of any term using both a loop and recursion. Afterwards we will look at another potential use of recursion by finding the factorial of a term.

FINDING THE TERM IN A LOOP

To find the term inside a loop in a function—let's call it `TriangularNumber()`—we can simply take a variable—let's call it `value`—and make it equal to itself plus the term for each iteration of the loop. At the end of each loop iteration that is exe-

Triangular Numbers: 8th Term

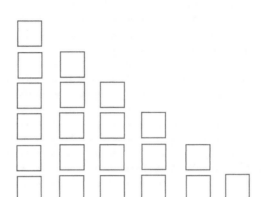

21 (15 + 6) 15 (10 + 5) 10 (6 + 4) (3 + 3) 3 (2 + 0) 1 (1+0)

FIGURE 3.4 Finding the sixth term's value.

cuted, the term can be decremented by one so that the condition for the loop can be to test that the term is greater than 0. By the time the loop is done executing, the value for whatever term was being looked for would be known and could be returned to the caller. An example of such a function is shown in Listing 3.4.

LISTING 3.4 Finding a Term in a Loop

```
int TriangularNumber(int term)
{
   int value = 0;

   for(; term > 0; term--)
   {
      value += term;
   }

   return value;
}
```

Using the code in Listing 3.4 as an example, we can find the fifth term by stepping through each iteration of the loop. In the first iteration we add the total of 0 to the term, which is the number 5. In the next iteration we add the total of 5 to the decremented term of 4, giving a total of 9. After that iteration we add 3 to the total of 9 to get a new total of 12, add 2 to get 14, and then add 1 to get the final value of 15. As we know from Figure 3.4 the sixth term has a value of 15, which confirms that our code worked as intended.

FINDING THE TERM WITH RECURSION

Using recursion to find the term requires a slightly different way of thinking. One way to find the value of a term, as shown in Figure 3.4, is to add up the columns starting from the left, which is the column of the term, to the right. In code this can be done by using recursion to simulate moving from the term's column all the way down to the first column. Once there, the function can start returning values for each term. The first term would return 1, the second term would return its parameter term with what was returned from the last call (1), and so on until the original column's function ends and the final value is passed to the caller. An example of this can be seen in the modified `TriangularNumber()` function in Listing 3.5.

LISTING 3.5 Finding a Term Using Recursion

```
int TriangularNumber(int term)
{
   assert(term >= 1);

   if(term == 1)
      return 1;

   return (TriangularNumber(term - 1) + term);
}
```

If you step through the code using 4 as the term, you will find that the recursion keeps happening until the condition of the term being greater than 1 is broken. When that happens, the last `TriangularNumber()` function returns 1, the next function returns 2 plus what was returned (1), the function after that returns 3 plus what was returned (3), and the last function returns 4 plus what was returned (6), which gives us a total of 10. Without the condition to check that the term has reached its minimum of 1, the function will keep calling itself until, most likely, the application crashes.

ON THE CD

On the accompanying CD-ROM a demo application called Triangular Numbers in the Chapter 3 folder demonstrates using a loop and using recursion to find the value of the nth term. The functions used in the demo's main.cpp source file are the same as the code in Listing 3.4 and Listing 3.5. The entire main.cpp source file is shown in Listing 3.6. This is a simple test of the information discussed in this section. Figure 3.5 shows a screenshot of the demo.

LISTING 3.6   Triangular Number Demo's main.cpp Source File

```cpp
#include<iostream>
#include<cassert>

using namespace std;


int TriNumLoop(int term)
{
   int value = 0;


   for(; term > 0; term-)
   {
        value += term;
   }

   return value;
}


int TriNumRecursion(int term)
{
   assert(term >= 1);


   if(term == 1)
      return 1;

   return(TriNumRecursion(term - 1) + term);
}


int main(int args, char **argc)
{
   cout << "Triangular Numbers Example" << endl;
   cout << "Chapter 3: Recursion" << endl << endl;


   cout << "The value of the 18th term using a loop: ";
   cout << TriNumLoop(18);
   cout << "." << endl;
```

```
        cout << "The value of the 25th term using recursion: ";
        cout << TriNumRecursion(25);
        cout << "." << endl;


        cout << endl;

        return 1;
    }
```

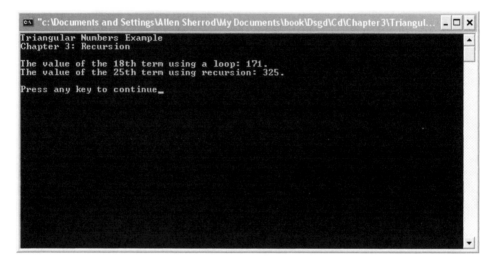

FIGURE 3.5 Screenshot from the Triangular Numbers demo.

FACTORIALS

Next we will look at another example of using recursion to calculate factorials and double factorials. A factorial is similar in concept to a triangular number in that to find the value of the *n*th term we take the multiplication of the term and the term −1 recursively instead of the term plus the term −1 recursively. Calculating the factorial of the fourth term would look like the following, where we have 1 * 1, which equals 1; that result * 2 equals 2; 2 * 3 is 6; and 6 * 4 (the original term) equals 24:

$$((((1 * 1) = 1 * 2) = 2 * 3) = 6 * 4) = 24$$

Finding the term of 0 when looking at factorials, by definition, returns a value of 1. This is also true for 1 itself.

Calculating a double factorial is the same as calculating a factorial, with the exception that we are subtracting 2 from the term with each call instead of 1. The code for factorials in general looks exactly like the triangular numbers counterpart, with the exception that we are looking for 0, which returns 1 by definition of factorials, and we are using multiplication during each step instead of addition. Listing 3.7 shows a pair of example functions used to calculate the factorial and double factorial of a number.

LISTING 3.7   Calculating Factorials

```
int factorial(int x)
{
   assert(x >= 0);

   if(x == 0)
      return 1;

   return(factorial(x - 1) * x);
}


int doubleFactorial(int x)
{
   assert(x >= 0);

   if(x == 0)
      return 1;

   return (doubleFactorial(x - 2) * x);
}
```

On the accompanying CD-ROM a demo application called Factorials in the Chapter 3 folder shows how to use the functions in Listing 3.7. The main source file for the Factorials demo application is in Listing 3.8, and a screenshot of the running executable is shown in Figure 3.6.

LISTING 3.8   Factorial and Powers Demo's main.cpp

```
#include<iostream>
#include<cassert>
```

```
using namespace std;


int factorial(int x)
{
assert(x >= 0);

   if(x == 0)
      return 1;

   return(factorial(x - 1) * x);
}


int doubleFactorial(int x)
{
assert(x >= 0);

   if(x == 0)
      return 1;

   return (doubleFactorial(x - 2) * x);
}


int main(int args, char **argc)
{
   cout << "Factorials" << endl;
   cout << "Chapter 3: Recursion" << endl << endl;


   cout << "The factorial of 3: ";
   cout << factorial(3);
   cout << "." << endl;


   cout << "The double factorial of 4: ";
   cout << doubleFactorial(4);
   cout << "." << endl;


   cout << endl;

   return 1;
}
```

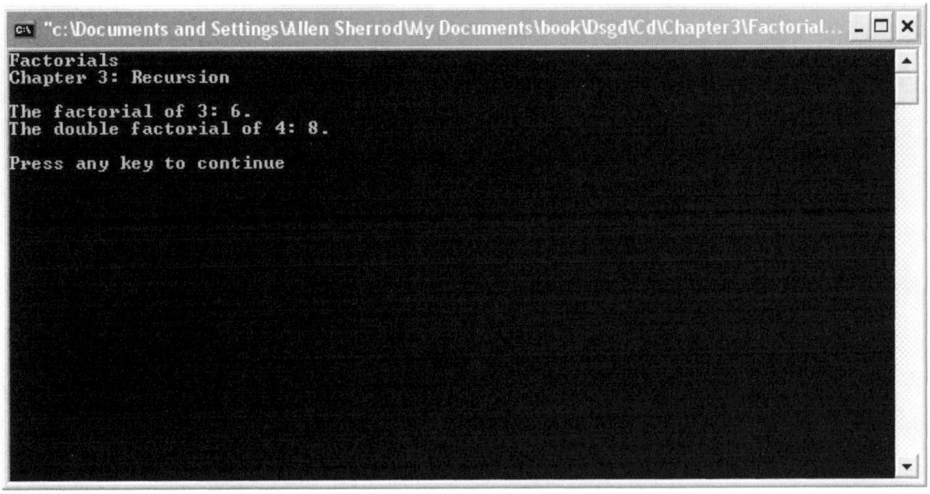

FIGURE 3.6 Screenshot from the Factorials demo.

SUMMARY

Recursion is a very useful operation that will be explored more throughout this book and, as we will see later, is great for building trees. In this chapter we explored recursion by looking at examples dealing with factorials, binary searching, triangular numbers, and more. An understanding of recursion is important, as it will help with the examples to come later on. Care must be taken to keep recursive methods from becoming potential problems that can bring down an entire application.

In the next chapter we will discuss various sorting algorithms, using arrays as an example. Often in application programming the data stored in a data structure need to be ordered. This order can be based on value, size, priority, or some other means.

CHAPTER REVIEW QUESTIONS

Answers to the following chapter review questions can be found in Appendix B.

1. What is recursion?
2. What is the difference between tail and nontail recursion.
3. What are triangular numbers? Why are they called triangular numbers?

4. What is the value of the seventh term in triangular numbers?
   a. 45
   b. 17
   c. 28
   d. 33
   e. None of the above
5. What is the main difference between factorials and triangular numbers?
6. What is the value of the seventh term in factorials?
   a. 5040
   b. 64
   c. 28
   d. 1278
   e. None of the above
7. Recursion is always more efficient than loops.
   a. True
   b. False
8. Recursion can make the conceptual design of an algorithm's implementation easier.
   a. True
   b. False
9. Recursion gone wrong can lead to overflow stack errors.
   a. True
   b. False
10. Recursion incurs no function overhead since it is calling a function that is already on the stack.
    a. True
    b. False

PROGRAMMING PROJECTS

Exercise 1: Suppose you needed to raise a number to a power but didn't have any standard math library functions to use. Write a recursive function that will perform this task in a function called RecursivePow().

4 | Introduction to Sorting

In This Chapter

- Introduction to Sorting
- The Bubble Sort
- The Selection Sort
- The Insertion Sort
- STL Sorting
- The Merge Sort

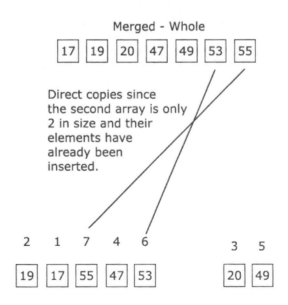

Often in application development data need to be sorted in some particular order or, in the case of the binary search, it is necessary for certain algorithms to perform their task correctly and/or efficiently. Data can be sorted by name, by age, by size, by serial number, by priority, by value, by type, and so forth, as well as being in ascending or descending order. Sorting has been an area of study that has resulted in many different algorithms, each with their own strengths and weaknesses in various situations.

The purpose of this chapter is to look at some algorithms that can be used for sorting. Although most of these algorithms are simple to read and not as fast as other algorithms that we'll consider later on, they are still useful in many situations and they can be great for learning to sort. In this chapter we will use the unordered array class created in Chapter 2 to demonstrate each of these algorithms.

The ability to sort objects in an application can be very important in many situations. In a video game we may want to sort players at a status screen based on how many points they have from greatest to least or we may want to sort items in the player's inventory based on their importance. Whatever the application, arrays can be simple and effective solutions. Of course not all situations will benefit from an array, and the need to look for other data structures will arise, which we'll discuss throughout this book.

INTRODUCTION TO SORTING

Sorting in computer programming is conceptually different from what we human beings do naturally. Computers can only compare two objects at a time, while humans can look at the problem as a whole and compare items in a less strict and mechanical way. When working with data structures, it is sometimes useful to be able to organize data based on a relationship. To sort data that exist in memory we have to perform an algorithm in said data structures while taking into account the efficiency of the algorithm with a certain number of items.

Visually sorting is easy. We can quickly pick out which object is smaller than the rest, which object is the biggest, and which objects are in between. Visually sorted objects are shown in Figure 4.1.

In programming sorting is not as straightforward. Not only does an algorithm have to move through the list and order each object based on how it compares to the others, but, in many situations, the algorithm also has to be efficient in terms of speed and memory consumption. In some applications where performance is not an issue, it would be possible to get away with using inferior algorithms, but in games, where performance is critical, this is something that needs to be addressed. The same can be said for other speed-critical applications such as databases.

FIGURE 4.1   A visual representation of sorting.

In this chapter we will look at the bubble sort, the selection sort, the insertion sort, the stable sort, and the merge sort. In Chapter 8, Advanced Sorting, we will examine more-advanced sorting algorithms. Whenever possible we will also look at C++ STL implementations as well, using `vector` data structures.

The bubble sort, selection sort, and insertion sort are also known as elementary sorting algorithms.

THE BUBBLE SORT

The bubble sort algorithm is simple to implement and understand but is very slow. It works by comparing two values in the data structure. If the object on the left is bigger, or satisfies some condition that makes it "larger," than the object on the right, then the two are swapped. If this is done on the first two objects, the next two objects (the second and third) will be compared and swapped if necessary. This continues until the entire array has been processed, which, at the time, would have moved the largest object to the end of the list. A single pass using the bubble sort is shown in Figure 4.2.

The bubble sort works in multiple passes. The first pass moves the largest object from its position in the array to the far right. The second pass moves the second-largest object to one element before the largest and so on until all items are in their sorted positions. This means that in an array the bubble sort needs to loop through the array once for each object (total elements minus 1) in the list. For example, if there are 20 items in the list, we must perform 19 passes over the list, and during each pass we must loop through the entire list and perform a variable number of

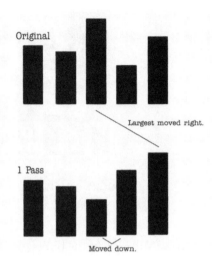

FIGURE 4.2   One pass over an array using the bubble sort.

comparisons and copies. By the final pass we would have gone from having the order in Figure 4.2 to the one seen in Figure 4.3.

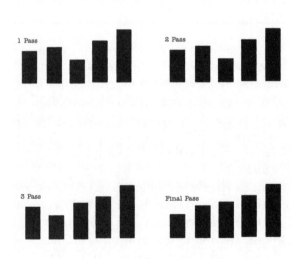

FIGURE 4.3   The array from Figure 4.2 after all bubble sort passes.

The bubble sort gets its name from the fact that the large items bubble up at the top of the list until all items are in order. Because of the number of passes, comparisons, and copies and the brute-force style of the algorithm, it is slow. When working with user-defined objects, this can be worse because the comparison and copying of objects can be quite expensive, especially when objects have other objects inside of them that are or use dynamic memory allocation.

The bubble sorting algorithm runs in $O(N^2)$.

BUBBLE SORT EXAMPLE WITH ARRAYS

To implement the bubble sort algorithm, we can use a pair of nested loops where the inner loop performs the comparisons and necessary copyings throughout the entire list and the other loop ensures that this is done once for each item in the list. By the last iteration of the loop, the entire list will be sorted. In this chapter we will be sorting objects from smaller to larger. Listing 4.1 shows code used to perform the bubble sort algorithm in a function called `BubbleSort()` that was added to the unordered array class from Chapter 2.

LISTING 4.1   The Bubble Sorting Method Added to the Unordered Array Class

```
template<typename T>
class UnorderedArray
{
    public:

        void BubbleSort()
        {
            assert(m_array != NULL);


            T temp;


            for(int k = m_numElements - 1; k > 0; k--)
            {
                for(int i = 0; i < k; i++)
                {
                    if(m_array[i] > m_array[i + 1])
                    {
                        temp = m_array[i];
                        m_array[i] = m_array[i + 1];
```

```
                        m_array[i + 1] = temp;
                    }
                }
            }
        }

    };
```

On the accompanying CD-ROM a demo application called Bubble Sort is in the Chapter 4 folder. Inside this folder is an updated Array.h header file with the bubble sorting algorithm added to the unordered array class, which was shown in Listing 4.1, and a main.cpp source file for demonstrating the code in a console window. The main.cpp source file creates a list of integers, displays them unsorted, sorts them, and then displays the sorted data to the console window. The main.cpp source file for the Bubble Sort demo application is shown in Listing 4.2. Figure 4.4 shows a screenshot of the Bubble Sort demo application.

LISTING 4.2 The Bubble Sort Demo Application's Main Source File

```
#include<iostream>
#include"Arrays.h"

using namespace std;


int main(int args, char *arg[])
{
    cout << "Bubble Sort Algorithm" << endl;
    cout << "Chapter 4: Recursion" << endl << endl;


    UnorderedArray<int> array(5);
    array.push(80);
    array.push(64);
    array.push(99);
    array.push(76);
    array.push(5);


    cout << "Before sort:";
```

```
for(int i = 0; i < 5; i++)
{
   cout << " " << array[i];
}

cout << endl;


array.BubbleSort();


cout << "After sort:";

for(int i = 0; i < 5; i++)
{
   cout << " " << array[i];
}


cout << endl << endl;

return 1;
}
```

FIGURE 4.4   A screenshot of the Bubble Sort demo application.

THE SELECTION SORT

The selection sort gives some improved performance over the bubble sort algorithm. With the selection sort there are not as many swaps, on average, but there are still many comparisons and passes over the data structure. Whereas the bubble sort runs in $O(N^2)$, the selection sort has a swap that operates in $O(N)$ but has comparisons in $O(N^2)$. Because of the larger number of swaps in the bubble sort, the selection sort is slightly faster. This speed difference in performance can add up as N grows larger.

The selection sort works by looping through the list and keeping a record of which item is considered the smallest in the group. Once a pass over the list is complete, the smallest item in the list is swapped with the first item (at index position 0). From this you can see that there is only one swap per pass, but the number of comparisons is the same, whereas the bubble sort constantly swaps large items until they get to the end of the list. The number of passes depends on the number of elements, just like with the bubble sort, and as items are sorted in the beginning of the list, they can be ignored since they're already in their final positions. A visual representation of the selection sort is shown in Figure 4.5.

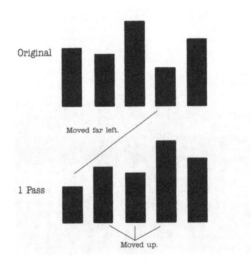

FIGURE 4.5 The selection sort.

The selection sort will sort items from the left to the right, while the bubble sort will sort items from the right to the left.

Selection Sort Example with Arrays

Implementing the selection sort is as straightforward as implementing the bubble sort. The differences include keeping track of which object is the smallest and only performing the swap once a complete iteration over the list has occurred. As with the bubble sort, the selection sorting algorithm was added in its own function, `SelectionSort()`, to the unordered array class. Listing 4.3 shows this algorithm's code.

LISTING 4.3   The Selection Sort Algorithm Added to the Unordered Array

```cpp
template<typename T>
class UnorderedArray
{
   public:

      void SelectionSort()
      {
         assert(m_array != NULL);


         T temp;
         int min = 0;


         for(int k = 0; k < m_numElements - 1; k++)
         {
            min = k;


            for(int i = k + 1; i < m_numElements; i++)
            {
               if(m_array[i] < m_array[min])
                  min = i;
            }


            if(m_array[k] > m_array[min])
            {
               temp = m_array[k];
               m_array[k] = m_array[min];
               m_array[min] = temp;
            }
```

```
            }
        }
    };
```

On the accompanying CD-ROM is a demo application called Selection Sort in the Chapter 4 folder that demonstrates the selection sort algorithm in Listing 4.3. The main.cpp source file from this demo is the same as the one for the Bubble Sort demo, with the exception that the values being inserted into the list are different and that the demo calls the SelectionSort() function instead of the BubbleSort() function. The main.cpp source file from the Selection Sort demo application is shown in Listing 4.4. Figure 4.6 shows a screenshot of the application.

LISTING 4.4   The Main Source File of the Selection Sort Demo

```cpp
#include<iostream>
#include"Arrays.h"

using namespace std;


int main(int args, char *arg[])
{
    cout << "Selection Sort Algorithm" << endl;
    cout << "Chapter 4: Recursion" << endl << endl;


    UnorderedArray<int> array(5);
    array.push(136);
    array.push(489);
    array.push(28);
    array.push(1);
    array.push(393);


    cout << "Before selection sort:";

    for(int i = 0; i < 5; i++)
    {
        cout << " " << array[i];
    }

    cout << endl;
```

```
array.SelectionSort();


cout << " After selection sort:";

for(int i = 0; i < 5; i++)
{
    cout << " " << array[i];
}


cout << endl << endl;

return 1;
}
```

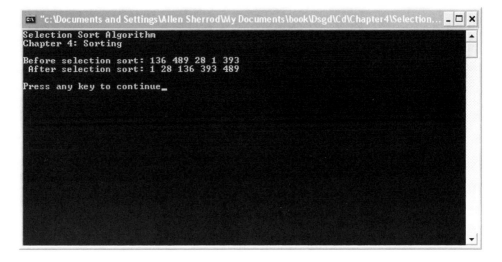

FIGURE 4.6   A screenshot of the Selection Sort demo application.

THE INSERTION SORT

The insertion sort works by comparing two elements, let's say element[0] and element[1], and swapping them if necessary. After those two objects are processed, the algorithm looks at the next object and inserts it into its proper place if it is smaller than either of the two elements that came before it. By inserting an object into its place, we are moving all objects up the array at the point of insertion, and then we are moving the object in question to the newly empty slot. During the insertion sort a number of shifts are done on the array, whereas the other two algorithms we looked at focus only on swapping individual items. When the insertion sort is being performed, it is only executing on a small portion of the list with each cycle, and this portion grows larger as more cycles are executed. When the algorithm reaches its last pass over the list, the entire list is looked at as a whole. The algorithm has the ability to quit early with lists that are already sorted. Figure 4.7 shows a visual representation of the insertion sort.

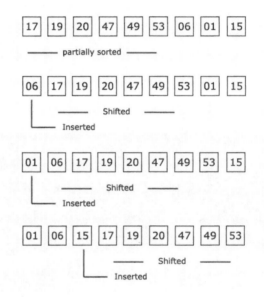

FIGURE 4.7 The insertion sort.

The insertion sort algorithm runs in $O(N^2)$ but is slightly faster than the selection sort algorithm in most cases and is faster than the bubble sort algorithm. In the worst case the insertion sort is as fast as the bubble sort, which can happened if the items in the list are in the reverse order from their sorted state (e.g., in descending order when the sorting will place them in ascending order). If the items are in reverse order, then the maximum comparisons, shifts, and swaps must be done, which makes it as slow as the bubble sort.

INSERTION SORT EXAMPLE WITH ARRAYS

As with the previously discussed sorting algorithms, a function was added to the unordered array class to perform the insertion sort. In this function two loops are nested together. The outer loop performs a pass on the inner loop once for every object in the list. In the inner loop the comparisons are made to the first item, which is defined by the outer loop, and all items before it. This means the sort is partial, because with each cycle of the outer loop, the range of the inner loop grows. With lists that are almost in order, close to being in order, or are in order, this algorithm is very fast. The only case to look out for is a list in reverse or near-reverse order, as that will cause various "worst-case" operations to be performed. The insertion sorting algorithm is shown in a function that was added to the unordered array class, called InsertionSort()(Listing 4.5).

LISTING 4.5 The Insertion Sorting Algorithm Added to the Unordered Array

```
template<typename T>
class UnorderedArray
{
   public:

      void InsertionSort()
      {
         assert(m_array != NULL);


         T temp;
         int i = 0;


         for(int k = 1; k < m_numElements; k++)
         {
            temp = m_array[k];
            i = k;


            while(i > 0 && m_array[i - 1] >= temp)
            {
               m_array[i] = m_array[i - 1];
               i--;
            }


            m_array[i] = temp;
         }
      }
};
```

On the accompanying CD-ROM is a demo application called Insertion Sort in the Chapter 4 folder. In this demo the main function is similar to the Bubble Sort and Selection Sort demos, with the exception of the values inserted into the list and the call to `InsertionSort()` instead of `BubbleSort()` or `SelectionSort()`. The main.cpp source file for the Insertion Sort demo application is in Listing 4.6. A screenshot of the demo application running is shown in Figure 4.8.

LISTING 4.6   The main.cpp Source File of the Insertion Sort Demo

```cpp
#include<iostream>
#include"Arrays.h"

using namespace std;


int main(int args, char *arg[])
{
   cout << "Insertion Sort Algorithm" << endl;
   cout << "Chapter 4: Recursion" << endl << endl;


   UnorderedArray<int> array(5);
   array.push(348);
   array.push(112);
   array.push(847);
   array.push(999);
   array.push(264);


   cout << "Before insertion sort:";

   for(int i = 0; i < 5; i++)
   {
      cout << " " << array[i];
   }

   cout << endl;


   array.InsertionSort();


   cout << " After insertion sort:";
```

```
for(int i = 0; i < 5; i++)
{
   cout << " " << array[i];
}


cout << endl << endl;

return 1;
}
```

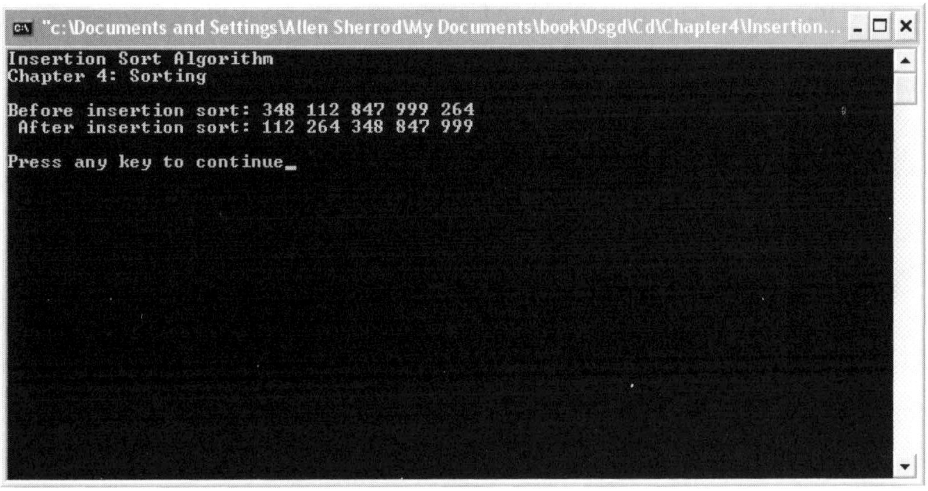

FIGURE 4.8 A screenshot of the Insertion Sort demo application.

STL SORTING

In this section we will look at a few algorithm functions defined in the header file <algorithms> that can be used to perform sorting using the STL in C++. The functions we will look at in this section include the STL sort(), stable_sort(), and partial_sort(). At the end of this section we will see each of these algorithms in action in one demo application called STL Sorting.

> *There is also* sort_heap(), *which we'll look at later in this book when we talk about heaps.*

NOTE

The function sort() is used to sort objects into ascending or descending order based on a binary predicate. This function takes as parameters a random access iterator to the first element in the data structure to be sorted, a random access iterator to the last element in the data structure to be sorted, and the optional binary predicate. The sort() algorithm is not stable, which means that items in the data structure can be equivalent but not equal, so neither element is less than the other element. Earlier versions of the sort() STL function used the quick sort algorithm, which will be examined later in the book, while more current implementations use the intro sort algorithm.

The function stable_sort() is the same as the sort() function, with the exception that the stable_sort() function is stable. The stable_sort() function uses the merge sort algorithm, discussed later in this chapter, and takes the same parameters as the sort() function. One use of stable sorting algorithms is if you have objects that have multiple fields, where some fields are equal but others are not. This can occur if you are trying to order a list of names in which the last names of some people might be equal but the first names are not (or vice versa).

The partial_sort() function allows a data structure to be partially sorted based on a binary predicate. In other words, the sorting algorithm can occur on the entire data structure or only on a few of its internal elements. The partial_sort() function takes as parameters a random access iterator to the first element in the range to be sorted, a random access iterator to the last element in the range to be sorted, a random access iterator to the end of the list (which might not be the end of the sorting range), and optionally a binary predicate such as greater<>, less<>, greater_equal<>, less_equal<>, and so forth.

To use less<>, greater<>, *or other binary predicates you will need to include the header file* <functional>. *To use the sorting algorithms you will need to include the header file* <algorithms>.

A demo application called STL Sorting can be found on the accompanying CD-ROM in the Chapter 4 folder. This demo application is a simple one that demonstrates how to use the sort(), stable_sort(), partial_sort(), and binary predicates. In the demo application two arrays and a vector container are sorted. Before and after each sort the data structures are displayed to show that the algorithms indeed performed their jobs. The main.cpp source file for the STL Sorting demo application is shown in Listing 4.7. Figure 4.9 shows a screenshot of the STL Sorting demo application.

LISTING 4.7   The STL `sort()`, `partial_sort()`, and `stable_sort()` Functions

```
#include<iostream>
#include<vector>
#include<algorithm>
#include<functional>

using namespace std;


inline bool CompareNoCase(char lVal, char rVal)
{
   return tolower(lVal) < tolower(rVal);
}


int main(int args, char *arg[])
{
   cout << "STL Sorting Algorithm" << endl;
   cout << "Chapter 4: Sorting" << endl << endl;


   char str1[] = "lekiamhjdqn";
   char str2[] = "peuyxknasdb";
   vector<int> int1;

   int1.push_back(58);
   int1.push_back(23);
   int1.push_back(1);
   int1.push_back(53);
   int1.push_back(33);
   int1.push_back(84);
   int1.push_back(12);


   cout << "Original str1 data: " << str1 << "." << endl;
   sort(str1, str1 + (sizeof(str1) - 1), CompareNoCase);
   cout << "  Sorted str1 data: " << str1 << "." << endl;

   cout << endl;
```

```
    cout << "Original str2 data: " << str2 << "." << endl;
    stable_sort(str2, str2 + (sizeof(str2) - 1), CompareNoCase);
    cout << "  Sorted str2 data: " << str2 << "." << endl;

    cout << endl;


    ostream_iterator<int> output(cout, " ");

    cout << "Original int1 data: ";
    copy(int1.begin(), int1.end(), output);
    cout << endl;

    partial_sort(int1.begin(), int1.begin() + int1.size(),
                 int1.end(), less<int>());

    cout << "  Sorted int1 data: ";
    copy(int1.begin(), int1.end(), output);
    cout << endl << endl;

    return 1;
}
```

The partial_sort() *function is a stable sorting algorithm.*

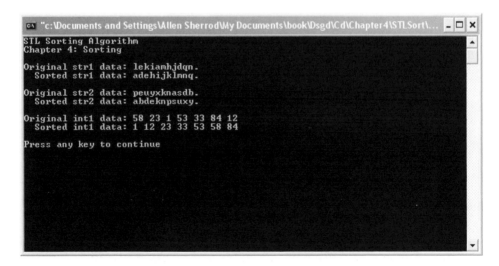

FIGURE 4.9 A screenshot of the STL Sorting demo application.

THE MERGE SORT

The merge sort is the most efficient sorting algorithm discussed in this chapter. The merge sort has a big-O of `O(N * log N)`, which is better than the `O(N²)` the first three sorting algorithms work in (although selection had a swap set of operations of `O(N)`). This means that with a list of 25,000 elements, `O(N²)` would have an *N* of 625,000,000, while `O(N * log N)` would have an *N* of only 109,949 (109,948.5 rounded up). The merge sort should outperform any of the other sorting algorithms we've discussed so far in most cases that arise, especially with large *N*. In Chapter 8 we'll look at some other advanced algorithms for sorting as well.

The merge sort algorithm can work recursively. The algorithm recursively splits the list into two halves. This recursion continues until only one element remains on each side of the original half, as shown in Figure 4.10. In other words, the algorithm starts by splitting the list in half, then splits each half into half (a quarter of the original size), and so on until no more splits can be done.

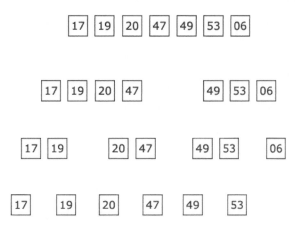

FIGURE 4.10   Splitting through the list.

Once one element remains on both sides they are merged together and sorted. Merging means that the elements from both sides are combined into one list. Once those two elements are merged, the recursive function returns. On the higher level of the recursive heap the results from the previous merge from both sides of the list are merged together. This keeps happening until we are at the top of the list. Once there, the entire list has been sorted and merged into one array. This is shown in Figure 4.11. The second-to-last level will leave us with two halves of the array that are both sorted individually.

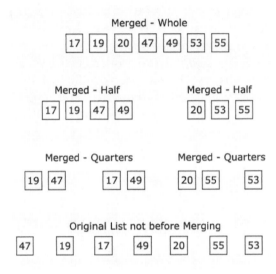

FIGURE 4.11   Merging until we have a sorted list.

During the merge the items are sorted, so if we have four items, we sort them before returning from the recursive function to the higher-level call. Recursion is used to first single out two elements on each side of the list half. The sorting occurs as we are moving back up to the top of the recursive stack. The merge sort has the disadvantage of needing another array that is equal in size to the array that is being sorted. In situations where memory is not a problem, creating this extra array is no big deal. If it is a big deal, we might have to look elsewhere for another sorting algorithm. This is especially true for lists that have large numbers of objects and/or are made up of memory-expensive objects.

MERGE SORT EXAMPLE WITH ARRAYS

Like the previously discussed sorting algorithms, the merge sort will be added to the unordered array class in a function called `MergeSort()`. As we will discuss soon, it is beneficial to use multiple functions for this process. The `MergeSort()` function can be used to create the temporary array used throughout the algorithm, delete that array once the sorting is complete, and call the recursive function used to perform the actual work. This recursive function can be a private overloaded `MergeSort()` function for convenience.

The private `MergeSort()` function would be used to recursively split the elements in half until each side is left with one element. Once there is only one element on each side, the function will start to return without calling itself further. For each return another function is called and used to merge the data into the temporary array. The merging function (let's call it `Merge()`) will copy data into the temporary array in ascending order while both arrays still have elements. When one array is out of elements, which can happen when the merging arrays have different numbers of elements, the other array's data is simply copied to fill in the remaining slots of the temporary array, as shown in Figure 4.12. Once complete, the data in the temp array can be moved back to the original list. By doing this each time we will eventually have a sorted array and we'll be able to delete the temporary array.

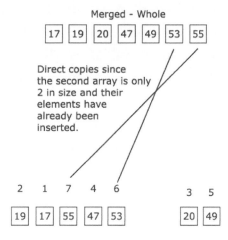

FIGURE 4.12   Merging arrays of different sizes.

To recap, the algorithm first splits the list into halves, which are further split in half recursively until no more splits can be done (one element left on each side). Once at the bottom of the recursive heap, we can start returning from the recursive calls. For each return we merge the elements at that level into a temporary array, which is sorted and copied back into the original array. By the time we make it to the top of the recursive heap, the entire list has been sorted. The code for the two `MergeSort()` functions and the `Merge()` function are shown in Listing 4.8. The first `MergeSort()` function is the function called outside of the class, while the second one sets up parameters that shouldn't be left up to the programmers (i.e., it shouldn't be left up to the programmers to create the temporary array of the correct type and supply it to the sorting function along with the desired range). The second `MergeSort()` is recursive, while `Merge()` will merge and sort together two ranges of data.

LISTING 4.8 The Merge Sort Algorithm Added to the Unordered Array

```
template<typename T>
class UnorderedArray
{
   public:

      void MergeSort()
      {
         assert(m_array != NULL);


         T *tempArray = new T[m_numElements];
         assert(tempArray != NULL);


         MergeSort(tempArray, 0, m_numElements - 1);
         delete[] tempArray;
      }

   private:

      void MergeSort(T *tempArray, int lowerBound, int upperBound)
      {
         if(lowerBound == upperBound)
            return;


         int mid = (lowerBound + upperBound) >> 1;


         MergeSort(tempArray, lowerBound, mid);
         MergeSort(tempArray, mid + 1, upperBound);
```

```
            Merge(tempArray, lowerBound, mid + 1, upperBound);
        }

        void Merge(T *tempArray, int low, int mid, int upper)
        {
            int tempLow = low, tempMid = mid - 1;
            int index = 0;


            while(low <= tempMid && mid <= upper)
            {
                if(m_array[low] < m_array[mid])
                {
                    tempArray[index++] = m_array[low++];
                }
                else
                {
                    tempArray[index++] = m_array[mid++];
                }
            }


            while(low <= tempMid)
            {
                tempArray[index++] = m_array[low++];
            }


            while(mid <= upper)
            {
                tempArray[index++] = m_array[mid++];
            }


            for(int i = 0; i < upper - tempLow + 1; i++)
            {
                m_array[tempLow + i] = tempArray[i];
            }
        }
    };
```

ON THE CD

On the accompanying CD-ROM in the Chapter 4 folder is a demo application called Merge Sort that demonstrates the merge sorting algorithm discussed in this chapter. The demo's main.cpp source file is similar to the other demo applications discussed in this chapter, with the exception that the MergeSort() function is being called and the values differ slightly. For convenience the entire main.cpp source file for the Merge Sort demo application is shown in Listing 4.9. Figure 4.13 shows a screenshot of the Merge Sort demo application.

LISTING 4.9   The main.cpp Source Code for the Merge Sort Demo

```cpp
#include<iostream>
#include"Arrays.h"

using namespace std;


int main(int args, char *arg[])
{
   cout << "Merge Sort Algorithm" << endl;
   cout << "Chapter 4: Sorting" << endl << endl;

   UnorderedArray<int> array(5);
   array.push(645);
   array.push(294);
   array.push(777);
   array.push(789);
   array.push(119);
   array.push(100);
   array.push(823);


   cout << "Before merge sort:";

   for(int i = 0; i < 5; i++)
   {
      cout << " " << array[i];
   }

   cout << endl;


   array.MergeSort();


   cout << " After merge sort:";
```

```
    for(int i = 0; i < 5; i++)
    {
        cout << " " << array[i];
    }

    cout << endl << endl;

    return 1;
}
```

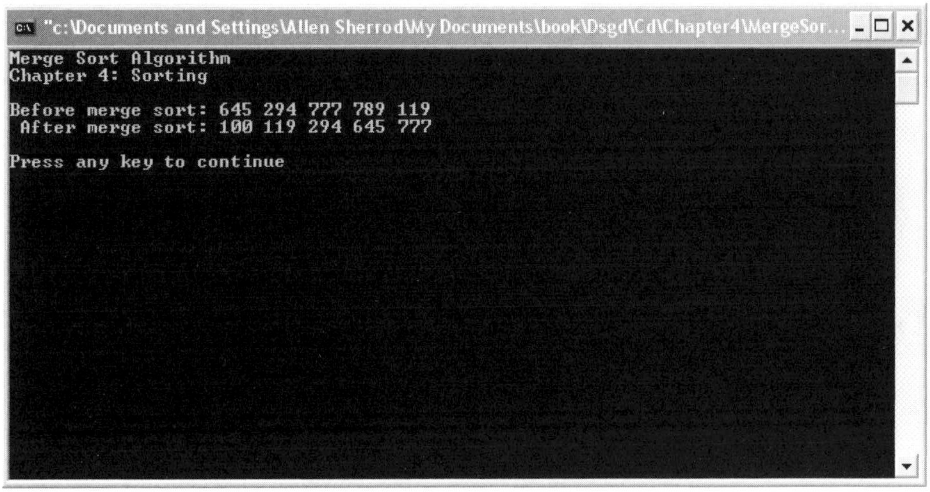

FIGURE 4.13   A screenshot of the Merge Sort demo application.

SUMMARY

In this chapter we took an introductory look at sorting algorithms that can be performed on data structures. Sorting can be very useful in applications that require data to be in a specific order. As seen with the binary searching algorithm in Chapters 2 and 3, some algorithms require data to be in a specific order to accomplish its task. In this chapter we looked at the following algorithms:

- Bubble sort
- Selection sort
- Insertion sort
- Merge sort
- STL functions `sort()`, `stable_sort()`, `partial_sort()`, and binary predicates

Later in the book we will look at more advanced, complex sorting algorithms. Many of the algorithms discussed in this chapter are called elementary sorting algorithms, which include the bubble sort, the selection sort, and the insertion sort. In later chapters we will be discussing the following algorithms:

- Quick sort
- Partitioning
- Radix sort
- Shell sort
- Intro sort
- Heap sort

In the next chapter we will discuss a different kind of data structure known as the link list. Link lists have advantages that solve some of the disadvantages of arrays, but they have a few disadvantages that are advantages for arrays. Link lists are a very popular type of data structure, and we will learn more about them after Chapter 5, Link Lists.

CHAPTER REVIEW QUESTIONS

Answers to the following chapter review questions can be found in Appendix B.

1. The bubble sort runs in:
   a. `O(1)`
   b. `O(N)`
   c. `O(N²)`
   d. `O(N * log N)`
   e. None of the above

2. The selection sort comparison runs in:
   a. `O(1)`
   b. `O(N²)`
   c. `O(log N)`
   d. `O(N * log N)`
   e. None of the above

3. The selection sort swapping runs in:
   a. `O(N)`
   b. `O(N²)`
   c. `O(log N)`
   d. `O(N * log N)`
   e. None of the above

4. The insertion sort comparison runs in:
   a. O(N²)
   b. O(N)
   c. O(log N)
   d. O (N * log N)
   e. None of the above
5. The merge sort comparison runs in:
   a. O(1)
   b. O(N²)
   c. O(log N)
   d. O(N * log N)
   e. None of the above
6. The earlier STL sort() function uses what algorithm internally?
   a. Bubble sort
   b. Quick sort
   c. Radix sort
   d. Intro sort
   e. None of the above
7. The more recent STL sort() function uses what algorithm internally?
   a. Bubble sort
   b. Quick sort
   c. Radix sort
   d. Intro sort
   e. None of the above
8. The STL stable_sort() function uses what algorithm internally?
   a. Bubble sort
   b. Quick sort
   c. Radix sort
   d. Intro sort
   e. Merge sort
   f. None of the above
9. A binary predicate is used for what purpose?
10. Which is faster: the bubble sort or the selection sort? Why?
11. The bubble sort got its name because the sorted objects bubble on the top of the list throughout the algorithm.
    a. True
    b. False
12. The selection sort bubbles sorted objects at the beginning of the list.
    a. True
    b. False

13. Even in the worst-case scenario, the selection sort is still slightly faster than the bubble sort.
    a. True
    b. False
14. The merge sort will merge the items into a new list before sorting them.
    a. True
    b. False
15. The STL `partial_sort()` is stable.
    a. True
    b. False

PROGRAMMING PROJECTS

Exercise 1: Create an application that allows you to store a list of employee information in an array. Allow that array to sort the information by employee ID. The employee information to store is the employee ID, first name, last name, email, address, and phone number. Create a class called `EmployeeList` that stores the data structure, which can be an STL `vector`, and has member functions for sorting by ID and for printing out the information to the console window. For the sorting create a function that uses the bubble sort.

Exercise 2: Modify the application you created in Exercise 1 and allow the information to be read in from a file. Also modify the application to allow the programmer using your employee list to sort the data by ID, first name, or last name and create functions that use the selection and insertion sorting algorithms.

Exercise 3: Modify the application you created in Exercise 2 and add support for the merge sort. Also modify the application so that it can save the current list of employees to the file on command, can remove employees from the list, and can insert new employee records.

5 Link Lists

In This Chapter

- Introduction to Link Lists
- Singly and Double-Ended Linked Lists
- Doubly Linked Lists
- STL Link Lists
- Tips and Things to Remember When Using Link Lists

Doubly Linked List

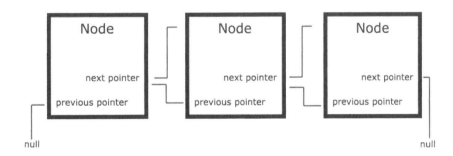

S o far we've looked at only one general type of data structure known as the array. The array is a common data structure and is easy to work with, but it is not without its disadvantages; for example, deletion is slow, searching in unordered arrays is slow, insertion into ordered arrays is slow, and growing and shrinking arrays is slow. Not all situations that arise in computer programming are suited to arrays, and some other data structures can do the job. One thing to keep in mind is that not all data structures are suited for all needs. When one data structure does not work in application development, a different, more efficient, data structure must be chosen. Being able to recognize the need to switch and choose a data structure for a specific task is important.

In this chapter we will look at another data structure known as the link list. Link lists have a number of advantages that solve the array's disadvantages such as the ability to quickly grow and shrink as well as fast removal (deletion). However, link lists still have some disadvantages that can determine whether or not the data structure is used in an application. In this chapter we'll look at a few types of linked lists including singly linked lists, doubly linked lists, double-ended linked lists, and various STL implementations for the linked list data structure.

INTRODUCTION TO LINK LISTS

Link lists are a type of data structure that allows elements of the list to be linked to one another to form a dynamic chain. In a link list each item in the list is referred to as a node (also called a link). With a link list you start off with a root node and add elements to that node to form the chain. Each node has a pointer to the next item in the chain and, in some cases, pointers to the item that comes before it and even pointers to the start and end of the list. An example of this is shown in Figure 5.1, where the link list starts off with a single node and more elements are added to the list by "chaining" them together using pointers. Link lists have many applications in general programming and in game development. They have very fast insertions and expansion, which makes them ideal in real-time applications such as video games when random access is not needed and the list can expand and shrink at a variable rate.

One of the keys to link lists is the use of pointers. A pointer pointing to the next node in a chain is often called the "next pointer." The initial root node is created to start the chain. When a new item is added to the chain, the root node's next pointer is created and used for that object. When a third node is added to the link, it does so by allocating the second node's next pointer and so forth. This was seen in Figure 5.1, where a root node exists and additional nodes are attached by linking them together using next pointers. A way of thinking about this process is to imagine children holding hands in a line, where the left hand is the hand that attaches to the

Visual Example of a Link List

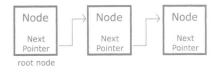

root node

Nodes are connected by pointers.

FIGURE 5.1   A link list.

next person in the chain ("next pointer") while the right hand is the hand that attaches to the previous person in the chain ("previous pointer"). Since a root node is the top node, it has no previous link. In code this is done by making such a node NULL. The same goes for the last node since it would have no next node in the list.

If the last node's next pointer points to the root and the root's previous node points to the last node, that is known as a circular link list. The link forms a chain that is completely circular.

At this point it should be clear that the elements of a link list are connected by pointers that can be allocated at any time. This means the data do not have to exist side by side in the computer's memory. This also means random access is not possible because you can't use array indexes to access any elements you want. Instead you have to start at the root and traverse through the list. In arrays random access is an advantage, while in link lists the loss of random access is a disadvantage. As previously mentioned, not all data structures are perfect for all situations. When random access is important, the link list does not work as well.

A link list is normally made up of three parts: the node, an iterator, and the link list itself. Later we'll look at iterators and the link list, which is itself a node. The node's definition can be a structure or a class that has some kind of data member and a self-referencing pointer, which is a pointer to an object of the same data type as itself. Such a structure for a singly linked list, which consists of nodes that go in one direction and is specified by the next pointer, can look like the following in pseudo-code:

```
class Node
{
    T data;
    Node *next;
}
```

The data member of the example node class can be any type. In C++ it is often useful to make this member a template data type so that different types can be used with the code, which has been seen throughout this book. The next pointer is only allocated when a new link is to be added in the chain. If this wasn't a pointer, the constructor of the member will be called, which will recursively call constructors on its member objects and cause trouble. In C++ this is not allowed.

In the Java and C# programming languages objects are declared using references and are not created until the new keyword is used. In C++ when a nonpointer object is declared, it is instantiated.

The elements of a link list have a relationship to one another instead of just a position as with an array. In later chapters the topic of relationships and the role they play with nodes of a data structure will be very important. With arrays each element has a position from the start of the list, which is accessed using an index. In an array writing code to access an element can look like the following:

```
someVar = array[4];
```

This would be the same as writing the following:

```
someVar = *(array + 4);
```

It is possible to simulate random access with linked lists using overloaded operators, but the simulation would be just that, a simulation, and would not be actual random access. Luckily not all situations in computer programming require random access, so this might at times be a disadvantage that can be ignored.

Later in this chapter we will look at the implementation of singly linked lists. These are nodes that can go in one direction by means of a next pointer, double-ended link list, which is a link list in which nodes can be inserted in the front of or back of the list, and a doubly linked list, which has nodes that have a previous pointer that allows backward movement through the link list. We'll also be looking at various STL link lists in C++.

ITERATORS

Chapter 2 disucssed STL vector iterators and how they are used to access elements in the data structure. Iterators are very useful in linked lists as well, and we will implement a structure that can be used for the custom data structures developed throughout this chapter. By creating an iterator, we will have a way to access the elements of the link list since using array indexes, which was done in the previously

described data structure (array), would not work. Even if we overloaded the operators so that the class can use indexes to access elements, we still need a way to traverse
through the container.

An iterator points to an element within the list. Once an iterator has been created,
it can be used to access the data of the element, which is often done by using various
dereferencing operators, and it can be used to traverse through the remaining elements of the list. An iterator in a link list would be simple when looked at from
a general point of view. An iterator could work by internally storing a pointer to a
node. Whenever an operation is applied to the iterator, it can be transferred to the
node pointer. For example, to move to the next element using an iterator, we could
set the iterator's node pointer to its next pointer. An illustration of iterators is shown
in Figure 5.2.

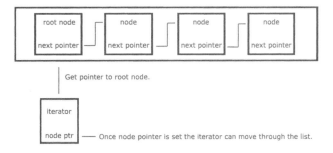

FIGURE 5.2   A visual representation of iterators.

One great thing about C++ is that overloaded operators can be specified for almost every type of operator the language supports. This means that using operators
on an iterator class can be very useful. For example, using the ++ operator on the iterator can cause the iterator to move one forward through the list while the operator — could move backward. Pointer dereferencing, which is also used in STL
iterators, can also be used to access the actual data. A data structure iterator using
overloaded operators might look like the following:

```
Iterator it = dataStructure.GetBeginIterator();

for(; it != dataStructure.GetEndIterator(); it++)
{
    Display("Element: " + (*it));
}
```

In the following section we will look at creating an iterator class for the link list data structure. Those familiar with STL are probably already aware of the usefulness of iterator structures.

SINGLY AND DOUBLE-ENDED LINKED LISTS

This section will focus on singly and double-ended link lists. Singly linked lists are list with nodes that go in one direction, while double-ended linked lists allow for insertions in the front or in the back of the list. Each type of link list will build off of the previous one. First we'll examine the singly linked list before moving onto the double-ended and doubly linked lists.

EXAMPLE OF A SINGLY LINKED LIST

The singly linked list is the most straightforward to implement. The items that will need to be represented are the iterator, the node, and the link list itself. The node is never directly used and only exists in the link list, the iterator is the structure that will be used to access and traverse through the link list data structure, and the link list is the container class for everything. The node class in this chapter will generally only need two members: the next pointer and the data that the link will store. The data member will be a template type so that this class can be reused for different applications and types. The link list's node class, LinkNode, is shown in Listing 5.1. Since the LinkNode is never used outside of the link list, its data members are private and specify friends to the necessary classes that will use it.

LISTING 5.1   The Link List's Node Class

```
template<typename T> class LinkIterator;
template<typename T> class LinkList;


template<typename T>
class LinkNode
{
   friend class LinkIterator<T>;
   friend class LinkList<T>;

   private:
      T m_data;
      LinkNode *m_next;
};
```

The class for the iterator is mainly made up of overloaded operators, a constructor, and a destructor. These operators can make using the custom made iterator class a bit more like using STL iterators while making them convenient for the programmers using the class. The operators specified in this chapter (more can be added if desired) are the = operator, the * dereferencing operator, the ++ post- and pre-increment operators, and a few boolean comparison operators. Later we'll see each of these operators in action, but for now the code is shown in Listing 5.2.

LISTING 5.2   Link List Iterator Class

```
template<typename T>
class LinkIterator
{
   public:
      LinkIterator()
      {
         m_node = NULL;
      }


      ~LinkIterator()
      {

      }


      void operator=(LinkNode<T> *node)
      {
         m_node = node;
      }


      T &operator*()
      {
         assert(m_node != NULL);

         return m_node->m_data;
      }


      void operator++()
      {
         assert(m_node != NULL);
```

```
            m_node = m_node->m_next;
        }


        void operator++(int)
        {
            assert(m_node != NULL);

            m_node = m_node->m_next;
        }


        bool operator!=(LinkNode<T> *node)
        {
            return (m_node != node);
        }


        bool operator==(LinkNode<T> *node)
        {
            return (m_node == node);
        }


    private:
        LinkNode<T> *m_node;
};
```

The link list class is very straightforward. The one thing the link list will need is a member pointer for the root of the chain. In the link list class that will be shown in this section, there is also a member variable for the container's size that is incremented every time a new item is inserted into the list and decremented every time one is removed.

For member functions our implementation in this section will have a constructor for initializing member variables, a destructor that will make sure all the elements have been deleted from the container, a function used to insert items into the list, a function used to remove the last item in the list, and a function used to get the root node and one for the end. The ability to get the root node allows the iterator to gain access to the chain. The end of the list is used to give the class an appearance that is somewhat closer to the STL iterator that we will see later on for link lists. The code for the link list is shown in Listing 5.3.

LISTING 5.3   The Link List Class

```cpp
template<typename T>
class LinkList
{
   public:
      LinkList() : m_size(0), m_root(0), m_lastNode(0)
      {

      }


      ~LinkList()
      {
         while(m_root != NULL)
         {
            Pop();
         }
      }


      LinkNode<T> *Begin()
      {
         assert(m_root != NULL);

         return m_root;
      }


      LinkNode<T> *End()
      {
         return NULL;
      }


      void Push(T newData)
      {
         LinkNode<T> *node = new LinkNode<T>;

         assert(node != NULL);
         node->m_data = newData;
         node->m_next = NULL;
```

```
    if(m_lastNode != NULL)
    {
       m_lastNode->m_next = node;
       m_lastNode = node;
    }
    else
    {
       m_root = node;
       m_lastNode = node;
    }

    m_size++;
}


void Pop()
{
    assert(m_root != NULL);

    if(m_root->m_next == NULL)
    {
       delete m_root;
       m_root = NULL;
    }
    else
    {
       LinkNode<T> *prevNode = m_root;

       while(prevNode->m_next != NULL &&
             prevNode->m_next != m_lastNode)
       {
          prevNode = prevNode->m_next;
       }

       delete m_lastNode;
       prevNode->m_next = NULL;
       m_lastNode = prevNode;
    }

    m_size = (m_size == 0 ? m_size : m_size - 1);
}
```

```
int GetSize()
{
    return m_size;
}


private:
    int m_size;
    LinkNode<T> *m_root;
    LinkNode<T> *m_lastNode;
};
```

In Listing 5.3 we look for the previous node because there is no way to move from the last node backward in a singly linked list. In upcoming link list examples this problem will be solved.

The link list class seen in Listing 5.3 starts with a constructor that clears the class's member variables and destructor that empties the container. The Begin() function is used to return the root node, and the End() function returns a value to mark when a list has ended, which here is set to NULL to make things easy. Both the Begin() and End() functions are used by the class for the iterator.

The function for inserting items into the link list, push(), works by creating a link node, setting its data members, and attaching the newly created node to the end of the list. The pop() function, which is used to remove the last item inserted into the list, works by deleting the last node that was inserted into the list. Both operations are made possible by keeping track of which node is the last node. Without this marker we would have to traverse through the list until one of the elements was found to have a NULL next pointer, which would tell us we are at the last node. For the removal function we have to search for the previous node anyway, because in a singly linked list there is no way to go backward.

The application that demonstrates the use of the node, link list, and iterator code is called Link List and can be found on the companion CD-ROM in the Chapter 5 folder. The demo application creates a link list, pushes five values onto it to create the chain of nodes, and uses the iterator to traverse the data structure container and display its values. The main.cpp source file for the Link List demo application is shown in Listing 5.4. The code for the link list itself is in the header file LinkList.h on the CD-ROM.

LISTING 5.4   The main.cpp Source File for the Link List Demo

```
#include<iostream>
#include"LinkList.h"
```

```
using namespace std;


int main(int args, char **argc)
{
    cout << "Link List Example" << endl;
    cout << "Chapter 5: Link Lists" << endl;
    cout << endl;


    LinkList<int> lList;

    lList.Push(101);
    lList.Push(201);
    lList.Push(301);
    lList.Push(401);
    lList.Push(501);

    lList.Pop();

    lList.Push(601);


    LinkIterator<int> it;

    cout << "Contents of the link list:";

    for(it = lList.Begin(); it != lList.End(); it++)
    {
        cout << " " << *it;
    }


    cout << "." << endl << endl;

    return 1;
}
```

In Listing 5.4 the iterator is used much like it is used with the STL version seen with the vector class in Chapter 2. Because of the operators that were specified, the iterator can be used directly in the for loop. By using the dereferencing operator, we can gain direct access to the node's data, which is definitely a feature worth having. A screenshot of the Link List demo application is shown in Figure 5.3.

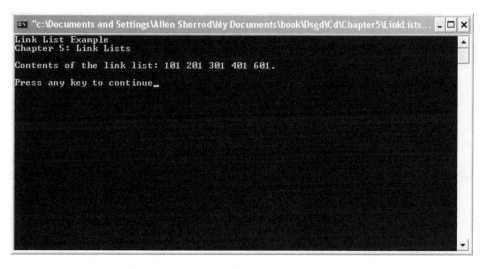

FIGURE 5.3 A screenshot of the Link List demo.

EXAMPLE OF A DOUBLE-ENDED LINK LIST

The next type of link list that will be discussed is the double-ended link list. A double-ended link list is one that allows for insertions and removals from either end of the container. Up until this point we've only inserted and removed items at the end of the link list, but now we will look at inserting and removing items at the start. A visual example of a double-ended link list in shown in Figure 5.4. Adding this feature is straightforward, as we will soon see.

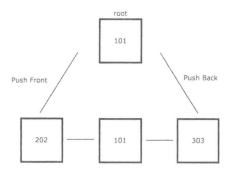

FIGURE 5.4 A double-ended link list.

A useful feature, which can be added if desired, is the ability to insert and re-move elements from particular locations within the link list container. Another useful feature would be to allow for the removal of a range of elements from the link list. This can be done using iterators and overloaded push() and pop() functions and will be done as an exercise at the end of this chapter.

To add support for double-ended link lists, we will need to add two new functions for inserting and removing elements from the front of the container. The link list in this chapter will call these functions Push_Front() and Pop_Front(). The Push_Front() function basically replaces the root node with a new node and takes the old root node and attaches it to the newly created node. The Pop_Front() function deletes the current root node and makes the object that comes next in the list the new root. Because both functions manipulate the root node, the last node pointer is never altered, aside from when Push_Front() is used to insert the first item into the container (i.e., when the root is NULL). The updated link list class that allows for double-ended insertions and removals is shown in Listing 5.5.

LISTING 5.5 The Push_Front() and Pop_Front() Class Methods

```
template<typename T>
class LinkList
{
   public:
      void Push_Front(T newData)
      {
         LinkNode<T> *node = new LinkNode<T>;

         assert(node != NULL);

         node->m_data = newData;
         node->m_next = NULL;

         if(m_root != NULL)
         {
            node->m_next = m_root;
            m_root = node;
         }
         else
         {
            m_root = node;
            m_lastNode = node;
         }
```

```
            m_size++;
        }


        void Pop_Front()
        {
            assert(m_root != NULL);

            LinkNode<T> *temp = m_root;

            m_root = m_root->m_next;
            delete temp;

            m_size = (m_size == 0 ? m_size : m_size - 1);
        }
    };
```

On the CD-ROM there is a demo application called Double-Ended in the Chapter 5 folder that demonstrates the features of a double-ended link list. The main.cpp source file for this demo application combines calling Push(), Push_Front(), Pop(), and Pop_Front()to test the calls. The main.cpp source file for the Double-Ended demo application is shown in Listing 5.6. Figure 5.5 shows a screen-shot of the Double-Ended executable.

LISTING 5.6   The main.cpp File of the Double-Ended Demo

```
#include<iostream>
#include"LinkList.h"

using namespace std;


int main(int args, char **argc)
{
    cout << "Double- Ended Link List Example" << endl;
    cout << "Chapter 5: Link Lists" << endl;
    cout << endl;


    LinkList<int> lList;

    lList.Push(101);
    lList.Push_Front(201);
```

```
lList.Push(301);
lList.Push_Front(401);
lList.Push(501);

lList.Pop();
lList.Push(601);
lList.Pop_Front();


LinkIterator<int> it;

cout << "Contents of the link list:";

for(it = lList.Begin(); it != lList.End(); it++)
{
    cout << " " << *it;
}


cout << "." << endl << endl;

return 1;
}
```

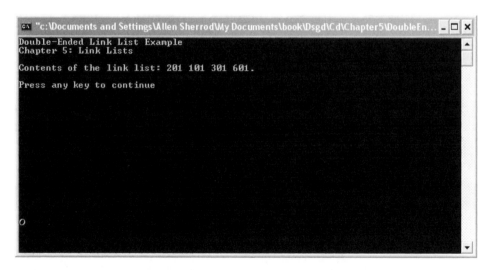

FIGURE 5.5   A screenshot of the Double-Ended Link List demo.

DOUBLY LINKED LISTS

A doubly linked list is similar to a singly linked list, but the doubly linked list can move forward by use of a next pointer and backward by use of a previous pointer. Up until this point our link list, or more specifically the iterator for the link list, was only able to move in one direction. With this section we'll add the ability for the iterator to move in both directions. An example of a doubly linked list is shown in Figure 5.6.

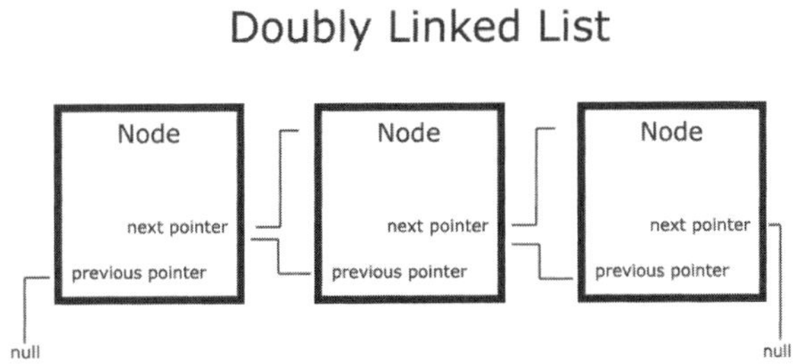

Doubly Linked List

FIGURE 5.6 Visual representation of a doubly linked list.

The doubly linked list works by specifying a pointer in the node class called the previous pointer. Whenever new items are inserted or removed from the container, the next and previous pointers must be able to reflect the current state of the list. All nodes have a previous node in the chain, with the exception of the root node because the root node is the root, which means no other node comes before it. The same can be said for the last node, in that the node with a next pointer that is equal to NULL must be the last node in the container.

Adding support for a doubly linked list to the link list code developed throughout this chapter requires us to make minor changes to the insertion and removal functions, add a few new overloaded operators to the iterator class, and add a new node pointer type to the link list's node class. In the following section we'll look at doing just that to the code developed so far.

EXAMPLE OF A DOUBLY LINKED LIST

The first class to examine is the node class LinkNode. This class has the least amount of new code and it adds a new pointer type and initializes it to NULL in the constructor. Because the node class is the basis for everything in the system, this is an important place to start. The newly updated LinkNode class is shown listed in Listing 5.7.

LISTING 5.7 The Updated Node Class for Adding Doubly Linked List Support

```
template<typename T>
class LinkNode
{
    friend class LinkIterator<T>;
    friend class LinkList<T>;

    private:
        LinkNode() : m_next(0), m_previous(0)
        {

        }


        T m_data;
        LinkNode *m_next;
        LinkNode *m_previous;
};
```

The next class to look at is the iterator class. Since our node class now has the ability to track the next element in the container as well as the previous one, the iterator class can be updated with a few new overloaded operators to make use of this newly added code. The two new operators are the – prefix and postfix operators, which are used to decrement, or move backward, through the container. These new operators are the opposite of the ++ operators and are shown in Listing 5.8.

The difference between specifying the pre- or the postfix increment or decrement operator is the existence of an unused (int) parameter. Specifying this parameter tells the compiler that it is a postfix operator; otherwise, it is a prefix operator.

LISTING 5.8 The Overloaded Operators Added to the Iterator Class

```
template<typename T>
class LinkIterator
{
    public:
        void operator-()
        {
            assert(m_node != NULL);
```

```
                    m_node = m_node->m_previous;
                }


                void operator-(int)
                {
                    assert(m_node != NULL);

                    m_node = m_node->m_previous;
                }
        };
```

The last class to look at is the link list itself. Because of the addition of a previous pointer, the link list container must be sure to link all pointers to elements added to the list. This is important because in order to traverse in both directions, the pointers must be valid. The methods affected by this change include Push_ Front(), Push(), Pop_Front(), and Pop().

In the Push_Front() function the old root's previous pointer is attached to the new root node when root is not already a node (i.e., the container is not empty). The Push() function sets the new node's previous pointer to the last node in the list and then sets the last node's next pointer to the new node.

The Pop_Front() function only has to set the previous pointer of the node next to the root to NULL before deleting the root node and promoting the node that came after it to the root position. The Pop() function previously used a loop to find the node that came before the last node. This was done because we already had a way to keep track of the last node but no way to backtrack to find the node that came before it. Since we now have a fast way to traverse backward with the previous pointer, we do not need this loop, and we already have access to all we need to perform a clean pop. The updated link list class is shown in Listing 5.9.

LISTING 5.9   The Updated Link List Class

```
        template<typename T>
        class LinkList
        {
            public:
                void Push_Front(T newData)
                {
                    LinkNode<T> *node = new LinkNode<T>;

                    assert(node != NULL);
```

```
      node->m_data = newData;
      node->m_next = NULL;
      node->m_previous = NULL;

      if(m_root != NULL)
      {
         node->m_next = m_root;
         m_root->m_previous = node;
         m_root = node;
      }
      else
      {
         m_root = node;
         m_lastNode = node;
      }

      m_size++;
   }


   void Pop_Front()
   {
      assert(m_root != NULL);

      LinkNode<T> *temp = m_root;

      m_root = m_root->m_next;

      if(m_root != NULL)
         m_root->m_previous = NULL;

      delete temp;

      m_size = (m_size == 0 ? m_size : m_size - 1);
   }


   void Push(T newData)
   {
      LinkNode<T> *node = new LinkNode<T>;

      assert(node != NULL);
```

```cpp
      node->m_data = newData;
      node->m_next = NULL;
      node->m_previous = NULL;

      if(m_lastNode != NULL)
      {
         m_lastNode->m_next = node;
         node->m_previous = m_lastNode;
      }
      else
      {
         m_root = node;
      }

      m_lastNode = node;

      m_size++;
   }


   void Pop()
   {
      assert(m_root != NULL);

      if(m_root->m_next == NULL)
      {
         delete m_root;
         m_root = NULL;
      }
      else
      {
         LinkNode<T> *prevNode = m_lastNode->m_previous;

         prevNode->m_next = NULL;
         delete m_lastNode;
         m_lastNode = prevNode;
      }

      m_size = (m_size == 0 ? m_size : m_size - 1);
   }
};
```

On the accompanying CD-ROM in the Chapter 5 folder is a demo application called Doubly Linked List that demonstrates the use of a doubly linked list in C++.

The main.cpp source file for this demo application uses the newly added operators in the iterator class to traverse in both directions of the container. The demo application displays the elements of the container in both forward and backward order to show that the code works as expected. The main.cpp source file is shown in Listing 5.10. The code for the link list can be found in the header file LinkList.h on the CD-ROM in the Chapter 5/Doubly Linked List folder. A screenshot of the Doubly Linked List demo application is shown in Figure 5.7.

ON THE CD

LISTING 5.10 The main.cpp Source File for the Doubly Linked List Demo

```
#include<iostream>
#include"LinkList.h"

using namespace std;


int main(int args, char **argc)
{
    cout << "Doubly Link List Example" << endl;
    cout << "Chapter 5: Link Lists" << endl;
    cout << endl;


    LinkList<int> lList;

    lList.Push(101);
    lList.Push_Front(201);
    lList.Push(301);
    lList.Push_Front(401);
    lList.Push(501);

    lList.Pop();
    lList.Push(601);
    lList.Pop_Front();


    LinkIterator<int> it;

    cout << "Contents of the link list (forward):";

    for(it = lList.Begin(); it != lList.End(); it++)
    {
        cout << " " << *it;
    }
```

```
        cout << "." << endl;


        cout << "Contents of the link list (reverse):";

        for(it = lList.Last(); it != NULL; it-)
        {
           cout << " " << *it;
        }


        cout << "." << endl << endl;

        return 1;
}
```

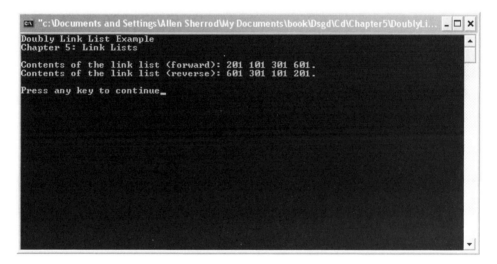

FIGURE 5.7   A screenshot of the Doubly Linked List demo.

STL LINK LISTS

The STL has a link list called the list container. The STL's link list is implemented as a doubly linked list that can push and pop elements from the front and the back of the container (double-ended). The STL's implementation of the link list is similar to its array in terms of the function names, algorithms that can be performed on them, and the operators. The underlying STL algorithms internally treat the two data structures as needed.

The STL link list can be accessed by including the <list> *header file.*

The STL's link list has many of the same functions as the array in Chapter 2. These functions include various push and pop methods, empty(), clear(), overloaded operators, and much more. The list of methods and operators that are part of the list container is shown in Table 5.1.

TABLE 5.1   Methods and Operators for the list STL Class

Method and Operator Names	Descriptions
list<type>()	Constructor that creates an empty container.
list<type>(n, val)	Constructor that creates a list of number of copies n that has its elements initialized to val.
list<type>(src.begin, src.end)	Constructor that creates a list out of the elements in the src vector defined by its beginning and ending iterators.
~list<type>()	Destructor that destroys the list.
assign(src.begin, src.end)	Assigns a range of values specified by the iterators to the list.
back()	Returns a reference to the last element.
begin()	Returns an iterator to the beginning of the list.
rbegin()	Returns a reverse iterator to the end of the list.
clear()	Erases the elements of a list.
empty()	Returns true if the list is empty, or else false.
end()	Returns an iterator to the end of the vector.
rend()	Returns a reverse iterator from the beginning of the list.
erase(index)	
erase(begin, end)	Erases the element specified by index or a range of elements specified by the iterators begin and end.
front()	Returns an iterator to the beginning of the first element in the list.
get_allocator()	Returns the allocator used by the list container.
insert(index, val)	
insert(index, n, val)	
insert(index, begin, end)	Inserts a value specified by *val* or a range of values specified by the begin and end iterators into the position index. N is the total number of times to insert into the container.

$\longrightarrow$

Method and Operator Names	Descriptions
merge(list2)	Merges the container with that specified by list2; Assumes both lists are sorted.
push_back(val)	Adds a value val to the end of the container.
push_front(val)	Adds a value val to the front of the container.
pop_back()	Removes the value at the end of the container.
pop_front()	Removes the value at the front of the container.
rbegin()	Returns an iterator to the first element in a reverse list container.
rend()	Returns an iterator to the last element in a reverse list container.
resize(n)	Specifies a new size N for the container. Elements outside the new size are deleted.
remove(val)	Removes all elements from the list that have the value of val.
size()	Returns the number of elements in the container.
sort()	Sorts the list in ascending order.
splice(iterator, list2) splice(iterator, list2, list2.begin) splice(iterator, list2, list2.begin, list2.end)	Inserts copies of list2 after the position marked by the iterator iterator. Overloaded functions can specify where to begin the copying in the second list or where to begin and where to end within the second list.
unique()	Removes all duplicate values in the list container. Assumes the list is sorted.
operator==	Boolean operator that returns true if two lists are equal, or else false.
operator!=	Boolean operator that returns true if two lists are not equal, or else false.
operator<	Boolean operator that returns true if the first list is less than the second.
operator>	Boolean operator that returns true if the first list is greater than the second.
operator<=	Boolean operator that returns true if the first list is less than or equal to the second.
operator>=	Boolean operator that returns true if the first list is greater than or equal to the second.

The sort() *function of the list container runs in* O(N * log N).

As shown in Table 5.1, many methods are shared by the list and vector containers. In the following section we will look at an example application that uses the list container, followed by some things to remember and tips for using the containers in applications.

EXAMPLE OF AN STL LINK LIST

ON THE CD On the accompanying CD-ROM is a demo application called STL Link List in the Chapter 5 folder. The application demonstrates the various methods of the list container as well as a few STL algorithms. The main.cpp source file for the demo application is shown in Listing 5.11. Later we'll break down this source file and examine the different parts of it.

LISTING 5.11 The main.cpp Source File for the STL Link List Demo

```cpp
#include<iostream>
#include<list>
#include<algorithm>
#include<numeric>

using namespace std;


void PrintList(list<int> &lList)
{
   cout << "Contents (" << "Size: "
        << (int)lList.size() << ") - ";

   ostream_iterator<int> output(cout, " ");
   copy(lList.begin(), lList.end(), output);

   cout << endl;
}


void PrintListReverse(list<int> &lList)
{
   cout << "Contents (" << "Size: "
        << (int)lList.size() << ") - ";
```

```
    ostream_iterator<int> output(cout, " ");
    copy(lList.rbegin(), lList.rend(), output);

    cout << endl;
}


int main(int args, char **argc)
{
    cout << "STL Link List Example" << endl;
    cout << "Data Structures for Game Developers" << endl;
    cout << "Allen Sherrod" << endl << endl;


    list<int> lList;

    // Add items then print.
    lList.push_back(10);
    lList.push_back(20);
    lList.push_back(30);
    lList.push_back(40);
    lList.push_back(50);


    // Calling the copy algorithm.
    list<int> lList2;

    for(int i = 0; i < 5; i++)
        lList2.push_back(0);

    copy(lList.begin(), lList.end(), lList2.begin());


    // Display list.
    cout << "  Inserted into list:  ";
    PrintList(lList);

    // Display list in reverse.
    cout << "    Reverse contents:  ";
    PrintListReverse(lList);


    // Sort the list.
    lList.sort();
```

```
cout << "    Sorting the list:  ";
PrintList(lList);


// Reverse the list.
lList.reverse();

cout << "    Reverse the list:  ";
PrintList(lList);


// Push and pop from the front.
lList.push_front(60);
lList.push_front(70);
lList.pop_front();
lList.push_front(80);

cout << "       Push/Pop Front:  ";
PrintList(lList);


// Run the accumulate algorithm.
cout << "           Accumulate:  "
    << accumulate(lList.begin(), lList.end(), 0)
    << endl;


// Pop off the container.
lList.pop_back();
lList.pop_back();

cout << "Popped two from list:  ";
PrintList(lList);


// Clear the container.
lList.clear();

cout << "         Cleared list:  ";
PrintList(lList);

cout << endl;
```

```
   // Test if the container is empty.
   if(lList.empty() == true)
      cout << "List is empty.";
   else
      cout << "List is NOT empty.";


   cout << endl << endl;

   return 1;
}
```

The main.cpp source file of the STL Link List demo application has two functions for printing the contents of a list container: one displays the contents in order and the other displays the contents in reverse order and is done using the STL copy() algorithm and the output stream class. To display elements in reverse the rbegin() and rend() iterator functions are used, which were shown in Table 5.1. The first section of the STL Link List demo application's main.cpp source file can be seen by itself in Listing 5.12.

LISTING 5.12   The Global and First Two Functions of the STL Link List Demo

```
#include<iostream>
#include<list>
#include<algorithm>
#include<numeric>

using namespace std;


void PrintList(list<int> &lList)
{
   cout << "Contents (" << "Size: "
         << (int)lList.size() << ") - ";

   ostream_iterator<int> output(cout, " ");
   copy(lList.begin(), lList.end(), output);

   cout << endl;
}
```

```
void PrintListReverse(list<int> &lList)
{
   cout << "Contents (" << "Size: "
        << (int)lList.size() << ") - ";

   ostream_iterator<int> output(cout, " ");
   copy(lList.rbegin(), lList.rend(), output);

   cout << endl;
}
```

The first section of the STL Link List demo's `main()` function starts by creating the STL link list and populates the container with initial data. The function then moves on to testing the STL `copy()` function to copy the elements from one link list to the other, and it displays the contents using both printing functions, which were shown in Listing 5.12. The `sort()` function is then called to sort the elements in order, and then the `reverse()` function is called to reverse the order of the elements. For every operation the contents of the list are displayed to show the state of the containers. This is shown by itself in Listing 5.13.

LISTING 5.13   First Section of the `main()` Function of the STL Link List Demo

```
int main(int args, char **argc)
{
   cout << "STL Link List Example" << endl;
   cout << "Data Structures for Game Developers" << endl;
   cout << "Allen Sherrod" << endl << endl;

   list<int> lList;

   // Add items then print.
   lList.push_back(10);
   lList.push_back(20);
   lList.push_back(30);
   lList.push_back(40);
   lList.push_back(50);


   // Calling the copy algorithm.
   list<int> lList2;

   for(int i = 0; i < 5; i++)
      lList2.push_back(0);
```

```
copy(lList.begin(), lList.end(), lList2.begin());


// Display list.
cout << "  Inserted into list:  ";
PrintList(lList);

// Display list in reverse.
cout << "    Reverse contents:  ";
PrintListReverse(lList);


// Sort the list.
lList.sort();

cout << "    Sorting the list:  ";
PrintList(lList);


// Reverse the list.
lList.reverse();

cout << "    Reverse the list:  ";
PrintList(lList);
```

The next section of the main.cpp source file demonstrates pushing and popping to the front of the container. This is a feature of the double-ended link list discussed earlier in this chapter. The STL algorithm `accumulate()` is also called to test that method with the `list` container. This section of the main.cpp source file is shown by itself in Listing 5.14.

LISTING 5.14   Push/Pop to the Front of the Container and Calling `accumulate()`.

```
// Push and pop from the front.
lList.push_front(60);
lList.push_front(70);
lList.pop_front();
lList.push_front(80);

cout << "      Push/Pop Front:  ";
PrintList(lList);
```

```
// Run the accumulate algorithm.
cout << "           Accumulate:   "
     << accumulate(lList.begin(), lList.end(), 0)
     << endl;
```

The remainder of the main.cpp source file tests the pop_back() method of the link list container, clears the container with the clear() function, and uses the empty() method to test if the container is empty. When using the link list, it is very important to call the empty() function instead of testing if size() returns the value of 0. Although this might sound strange, it isn't when working with link lists. The function empty() is a constant-time operation that is normally implemented as an inline function, that is, very fast. The size() function operates in linear time, which does not make it as fast as calling empty(). When you just need to test if a container is empty, you should use empty() for this reason instead of testing if size() == 0. The remaining section of the STL Link List demo is shown in Listing 5.15. A screenshot of the STL Link List demo is shown in Figure 5.8.

LISTING 5.15   The Remainder of the STL Link List Demo

```
// Pop off the container.
lList.pop_back();
lList.pop_back();

cout << "Popped two from list:   ";
PrintList(lList);


// Clear the container.
lList.clear();

cout << "          Cleared list:   ";
PrintList(lList);

cout << endl;


// Test if the container is empty.
if(lList.empty() == true)
    cout << "List is empty.";
else
    cout << "List is NOT empty.";
```

```
        cout << endl << endl;

        return 1;
    }
```

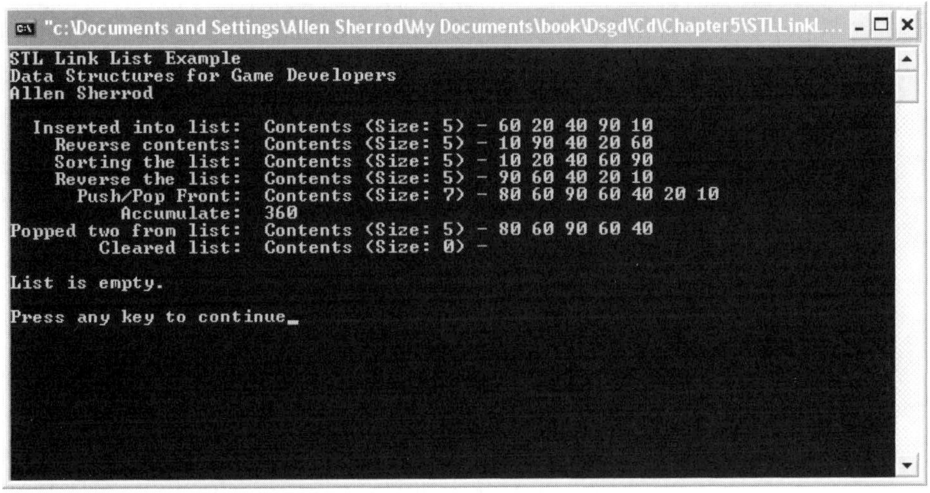

FIGURE 5.8 A screenshot of the STL Link List demo.

TIPS AND THINGS TO REMEMBER WHEN USING LINK LISTS

As mentioned earlier, when using STL link lists it is preferable to call empty() to test if a container is empty instead of testing the return value of size(). Different implementations might handle this differently, but you can't go wrong with calling empty() to test if a container is empty. This is true for all STL containers. The function empty() runs in constant time, while size() might not. Whenever speed is an issue, the empty() function is the way to go without having to worry about what the specific implementation might be doing.

Another tip to keep in mind is to call erase() after calling remove-like algorithm functions to ensure that elements are removed. When calling a remove() function that is not part of the container class (i.e., not a member function but a standalone algorithm function), the function has no way of knowing what container the iterators it takes are pointing to. If it does not know this, because there is no way to go from an iterator back to the container that has created it, then the number of elements can remain, although one would suspect that they wouldn't. This happens because there is no way to call container-specific functions to permanently remove elements. What remove() does internally is move elements around and mark the last "un-removed" element as the last in the container, even though it is technically not the last element in the container. One way to avoid this is to prefer member functions to algorithms with the same name whenever possible. This is also something to keep in mind with other algorithm functions that have container variations as well.

Link lists are very useful data structures to have in a library. Link lists have a number of advantages and disadvantages, which include the following things to remember:

- Link lists have fast insertions and deletions at the end and within the container.
- Link lists can expand and shrink rapidly compared to arrays.
- Link lists can be tighter in terms of memory than arrays, which can often allocate more memory than is needed.
- Doubly linked lists have both forward and reverse iterators for the movement through the list.
- Link lists are slow to search.
- Link lists do not have random access.
- Because the nodes wrap around the data, there is a very small memory gain from using link lists over arrays since arrays are only the data, while link lists are made up of the data plus any pointers, which can result in very large lists.

SUMMARY

In this chapter we looked at singly linked lists, double-ended link lists, doubly linked lists, and the STL link list known as list. Link lists are very good data structures to use when insertions and deletions are frequent but random access is not needed. Although there are many advantages to using link lists, there are also a number of disadvantages. Knowing each of these can make the choice between using a link list and using an array much easier.

In the next chapter we will look at a few new data structures including stacks, queues, double-ended queues (called deque in STL), and priority queues. Each of these data structures have their own uses that can differ from arrays and link lists.

CHAPTER REVIEW QUESTIONS

Answers to the following chapter review questions can be found in Appendix B.

1. List three advantages link lists have over arrays.
2. What are double-ended link lists?

3. What are doubly linked lists?
4. What type of link list is the STL `list` container?
   a. Singly linked list
   b. Doubly linked list
   c. Double-ended-only linked list
   d. None of the above
5. What is the main purpose of an iterator object for link lists?
6. Why should you try to avoid calling algorithm functions when the containers have them implemented as member functions?
7. Link lists have random access through iterators.
   a. True
   b. False
8. Link lists are faster than arrays when it comes to searching but not when it comes to insertions and deletions.
   a. True
   b. False
9. A double-ended link list can traverse in two directions.
   a. True
   b. False
10. It is better to test if `empty()` is true than to test if `size()` == 0 with STL link lists.
    a. True
    b. False

PROGRAMMING PROJECTS

Exercise 1: Add an overloaded `Push()` and `Pop()` set of functions to the link list class developed in this chapter to allow elements to be inserted anywhere within the list's container. The position where the elements are to be inserted or removed should be specified by an iterator.

Exercise 2: Build off of Exercise 1 and add the ability to insert or remove a range of elements from the link list. Allow this to be done using a beginning and ending iterator pair.

Exercise 3: Add a searching algorithm to the link list container class. Allow this function to search for a value and, when it finds it, return an iterator to that element through a pointer parameter. Have the searching function return `true` if the element was found or `false` if not.

6

Stacks and Queues

In This Chapter

- Introduction to Stacks
- STL Stacks
- Introduction to Queues
- STL Queues

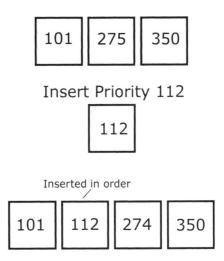

In this chapter we'll be looking at several data structures including the stack, the queue, the double-ended queue, and the priority queue. Along with custom implementations, we'll also be looking at the STL implementations for each of these data structures. Each of the data structures in this chapter are adapters that are built on top of data structures we've previously seen such as arrays and linked lists.

Each data structure discussed in this chapter has its own purpose and usage in general computer programming that differs from the array and link list data structures seen in Chapter 2 and Chapter 5. The benefits of stacks and queues can lend themselves to solving common problems that arise in general computer programming.

The data structures discussed in this chapter are conceptual tools used to aid programmers in completing a task. Normally these data structures are created and used for the sole purpose of processing a task before being discarded, which makes their life span much shorter than the array or the link list. Stacks and queues are restricted-access structures, which we'll discuss later in this chapter, that are built on top of the data structures we've already seen.

Stacks and queues are conceptual aids the programmer can use to process a specific task. An example of this is creating a stack to parse tokens in a script to check that the script is valid. Once the check is done, the container is discarded.

INTRODUCTION TO STACKS

A stack is a last-in, first-out (LIFO) data structure, meaning the last item inserted into the container is the first item removed from the container. This also means that only one item can be inserted or removed at one time. Unlike arrays, where random-access is a normal part of the data structure, stacks restrict the access to only one at a time. To access the elements deep within the container of a stack, items need to be removed from the top. This is true even if the underlying data structure upon which the stack is built is an array. An illustration of a stack data structure is shown in Figure 6.1.

In Figure 6.1 a stack of items forms a list. To help visualize this, imagine that this stack consists of books. Every time a new book is placed on the stack, the stack gets larger. Assuming that it is not possible to remove any books from within the stack other than from the top, the only way to access the books is to remove the topmost book and work downward. You can see that the last book placed on top of the stack is the first book taken off the stack. Restricting access to the elements in this manner is what makes a stack a stack.

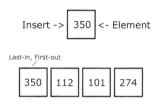

FIGURE 6.1   An example of a stack data structure.

Underneath the stack the elements can be implemented as an array or as a link list. On the higher level the stack container can use either structure with no visible difference to the interface or to the programmers using the code. Because stacks are restricted-access structures, as are queues, there is no access by array indexes, there is no access by searching, and there is no sorting, since that could violate the LIFO order of the container. When working with stacks, the main operations include inserting items onto the stack, removing items from the stack, and taking a peek at the top of the stack. Peeking refers to returning the topmost element without popping it off of the stack and will be discussed in the example programs to come. In a stack it is possible to add a searching algorithm to the container, but access to those elements would violate the LIFO order in some situations and would contradict the purpose of having a stack.

In many cases stacks have great value. Because of the nature of stacks, their uses often differ more than arrays or link lists. For example, an array can be used to store a list of objects that need to exist for a variable amount of time. These items can be accessed and re-accessed many times during the operations of the application. A stack, on the other hand, is a more useful tool to process an algorithm. An example of this can be seen in a scripting system. Let us say there is a list of tokens in an array, with a token being basically a block of text (i.e., a variable name, a colon, a symbol, a function name, etc.), and let us also say that we want to check a script to see if the brackets, parenthesizes, and curly braces match up. To do that we can create a stack and push all open brackes, parentheses, and curly braces onto it as the script is processed. Whenever we come across a closing symbol, we can peek and pop the top off of the stack, which returns the last inserted, and test if that opening symbol matches the closing symbol just encountered. If we reach the end of a file without finding any mismatches, we know the brackets, parentheses, and curly braces are in order. At that point we can discard the stack, but the array of original tokens still exists. In other words, the stack in this example had a much shorter life span than the array used to hold all of the tokens of a script and acted merely as a convenient tool to solve a specific problem. We'll see an example of token matching later on in this chapter. A few uses of a stack data structure include but are not limited to the following:

- They can be useful in any situation where LIFO access is desired.
- They can be useful when implementing a function-call stack for a virtual machine of a game (or general) scripting system.
- They can be useful when writing a compiler for parsing tokens in a game script.
- They are used in artificial intelligence in many different areas, which will be discussed more later in the book.

STACK DATA STRUCTURES

The stack can be implemented on top of an array or a link list. In this chapter we'll look at implementing a stack using both data structures before looking at the STL implementation. A stack needs to support the insertion of items, the removal of items, and a way to access the top of the stack. For consistency we can call the insertion function for a stack container push(), the removal for the container pop(), and the access (but not removal) of the topmost element top(). A stack class built on top of an array data structure is shown in Listing 6.1.

LISTING 6.1   An Array-based Stack

```
#include<cassert>


template<typename T>
class Stack
{
    public:
        Stack(int size, int growBy = 1) : m_size(0),
            m_top(-1), m_array(0), m_growSize(0)
        {
            if(size)
            {
                m_size = size;
                m_array = new T[m_size];

                assert(m_array != NULL);
                memset(m_array, 0, sizeof(T) * m_size);

                m_growSize = ((growBy > 0) ? growBy : 0);
            }
        }


        ~Stack()
        {
```

```
      if(m_array != NULL)
      {
         delete[] m_array;
         m_array = NULL;
      }
   }


   void push(T val)
   {
      assert(m_array != NULL);

      if(isFull())
      {
         Expand();
      }

      m_array[++m_top] = val;
   }


   void pop()
   {
      if(!isEmpty())
      {
         m_top--;
      }
   }


   const T& top()
   {
      assert(m_array != NULL);
      assert(m_top >= 0);

      return m_array[m_top];
   }


   int GetSize()    { return m_top; }
   int GetMaxSize() { return m_size; }
   int isEmpty()    { return (m_top == -1); }
   int isFull()     { return (m_top == m_size - 1); }
```

```
private:
    bool Expand()
    {
        if(m_growSize <= 0)
            return false;

        assert(m_array != NULL);

        T *temp = new T[m_size + m_growSize];
        assert(temp != NULL);

        memcpy(temp, m_array, sizeof(T) * m_size);

        delete[] m_array;
        m_array = temp;

        m_size += m_growSize;

        return true;
    }


private:
    T *m_array;
    int m_top;
    int m_size;
    int m_growSize;
};
```

Instead of growing the list using a constant, it is also possible to grow the list expo-
nentially. For example, instead of growing the size linearly, the size can change
every time the resize *function is called. This can start at a number such as 3, and*
then move to 6, then to 12, and so forth. This will reduce the number of times a list
needs to grow but can waste memory in some cases.

In Listing 6.1 the stack is made up of relatively few functions. The constructor is used to create the initial stack, the destructor deletes this dynamic memory, the push() function inserts a new element onto the array, the pop() function removes an element from the array in a similar manner as the array classes in Chapter 2, the top() function returns the topmost element to the caller, the Expand() function allows us to expand the stack dynamically, and the remaining functions are used to change the size of the container and to test if it is full or empty. The stack class, Stack, in Listing 6.1 is a complete stack based on everything we've discussed so far in this chapter.

ON THE CD

On the accompanying CD-ROM a demo application called Stack can be found in the Chapter 6 folder. This application demonstrates the use of the stack container created in Listing 6.1. In this demo application a stack is created, items are inserted onto the stack, and items are peeked at (by calling `top()`) and removed from the stack. Before the elements are removed from the stack, they are displayed to the console window. The entire main.cpp source file from the Stack demo application is shown in Listing 6.2. A screenshot of the Stack demo application after its execution is shown in Figure 6.2.

LISTING 6.2   The Stack Demo Application's main.cpp Source File

```
#include<iostream>
#include"Stack.h"

using namespace std;


int main(int args, char **argc)
{
   cout << "Stacks Example" << endl;
   cout << "Chapter 6: Stacks and Queues" << endl;
   cout << endl;


   Stack<int> sList(5);

   sList.push(101);
   sList.push(201);
   sList.push(301);
   sList.push(401);
   sList.push(501);

   sList.pop();

   sList.push(601);

   cout << "Contents of the stack:";

   while(sList.isEmpty() == false)
   {
      cout << " " << sList.top();
      sList.pop();
   }
```

```
cout << "." << endl << endl;

    return 1;
}
```

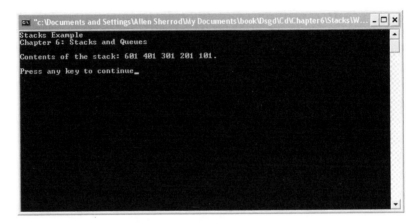

FIGURE 6.2 A screenshot of the Stack demo.

When creating our stack, we could have used the unordered array class developed in Chapter 2 as the underlying array instead of manually recreating the same basic functionality. Listing 6.1 shows the inner workings of a stack as far as an array is concerned, but in the future, since we already have an array class, we can use that to save time on the stack's implementation. Listing 6.3 shows the creation of a stack class using the unordered array class, UnorderedArray, from Chapter 2. Listing 6.4 shows an example of creating a stack by using the linked list class, LinkList, from Chapter 5. The link list is a more natural fit for a stack's underlying data structure and makes the expansion and shrinking of the stack much more efficient. This is especially true since the advantages that arrays hold over link lists do not apply to stacks.

LISTING 6.3 The Stack Implemented with the UnorderedArray Class

```
#include"Arrays.h"


template<typename T>
class Stack
{
    public:
        Stack(int size, int growBy = 1)
```

```
{
   assert(size > 0 && growBy >= 0);

   m_container = new UnorderedArray<T>(size, growBy);
   assert(m_container != NULL);
}


~Stack()
{
   if(m_container != NULL)
   {
      delete m_container;
      m_container = NULL;
   }
}


void push(T val)
{
   assert(m_container != NULL);
   m_container->push(val);
}


void pop()
{
   assert(m_container != NULL);
   m_container->pop();
}


const T& top()
{
   assert(m_container != NULL);
   return (*m_container)[m_container->GetSize() - 1];
}


int GetSize()
{
   assert(m_container != NULL);
   return m_container->GetSize();
}
```

```
                int GetMaxSize()
                {
                    assert(m_container != NULL);
                    return m_container->GetMaxSize();
                }


                bool isEmpty()
                {
                    assert(m_container != NULL);
                    return (m_container->GetSize() == 0);
                }


                bool isFull()
                {
                    assert(m_container != NULL);
                    return (m_top == m_container->GetMaxSize() - 1);
                }


            private:
                UnorderedArray<T> *m_container;
        };
```

LISTING 6.4 The Stack Implemented Using the `LinkList` Class

```
        #include"LinkList.h"


        template<typename T>
        class Stack
        {
            public:
                Stack()  { }
                ~Stack() { }


                void push(T val)
                {
                    m_container.Push(val);
                }
```

```
void pop()
{
   m_container.Pop();
}


const T& top()
{
   LinkIterator<T> it;
   it = m_container.Last();
   return *it;
}


int GetSize()  { return m_container.GetSize(); }
bool isEmpty() { return (m_container.GetSize() == 0); }


private:
   LinkList<T> m_container;
   int m_size;
};
```

CHARACTER MATCHING WITH STACKS

A stack container can be used to match tokens such as brackets, parentheses, and curly braces. This can prove very useful in the implementation of a compiler, such as the ones found in game scripting systems. In this section we will create a simple application that can be used to check that brackets, parentheses, and curly braces match up without error. In C++ programming an opening symbol must be eventually followed by a closing symbol. In a function declaration the opening parenthesis is followed by a parameter list, which is ended by a closing parenthesis. If the closing symbol is anything other than a closing parenthesis, that would be an error. Nesting can occur by encountering more opening symbols, but eventually a closing symbol will need to be encountered.

ON THE CD

On the accompanying CD-ROM is a demo application called Character Matching in the Chapter 6 folder. This is a short application that demonstrates how a stack can be used to match characters that are common in programming. As an example, the characters used are opening and closing brackets, parentheses, and curly braces.

The demo is made up of one source file called main.cpp and uses the linked list version of the stack implementation seen earlier in this chapter. In the main source file are three functions called PrintError(), ParseString(), and main(). The

PrintError() function will display an error message if there is a mismatch found in the string that is being parsed and takes as parameters the character that has caused the error and its index in the string. The second function, ParseString(), takes a string of characters that are to be parsed and checked for errors as well as the size of the string. The ParseString() function creates a stack and pushes the opening symbols we are looking for onto the container. When a closing symbol is encountered, the top of the stack is checked to see if the characters match. If they do not, an error is displayed using the PrintError() function. The PrintError() and ParseString() functions are shown in Listing 6.5.

LISTING 6.5 The First Part of the Character Matching Demo

```
void PrintError(char ch, int index)
{
   cout << "   Error " << ch << " at " << index << "." << endl;
}


void ParseString(char *str, int size)
{
   if(str == NULL || size <= 0)
   {
      cout << "   Error with parameters!" << endl << endl;
      return;
   }


   Stack<char> sList(size);
   char ch = 0;
   int errors = 0;


   for(int i = 0; i < size; i++)
   {
      switch(str[i])
      {
         case '{':
         case '(':
         case '[':
            sList.push(str[i]);
            break;

         case '}':
         case ')':
```

```
                case ']':
                    if(sList.isEmpty() == false)
                    {
                        ch = sList.pop();

                        if((ch != '{' && str[i] == '}') ||
                            (ch != '(' && str[i] == ')') ||
                            (ch != '[' && str[i] == ']'))
                            {
                                PrintError(ch, i + 1);
                                errors++;
                            }
                    }
                    break;
            }
        }

        if(sList.isEmpty() && errors == 0)
        {
            cout << "   No Parsing Errors." << endl << endl;
        }
        else if(sList.isEmpty() == false)
        {
            cout << "   Unclosed Characters: " << sList.GetSize()
                << "." << endl << endl;
        }
    }
```

The `main()` function in the Character Matching demo application is the driver function that calls `ParseString()` to test if the code works. The function `ParseString()` is called twice, the first time for a string of valid characters and the second time for a string of invalid characters. For the invalid character string the second character is purposely wrong to see that the code will catch it. The `main()` function of the Character Matching demo is shown in Listing 6.6. Figure 6.3 shows a screenshot of the Character Matching demo.

LISTING 6.6 The Remainder of the Character Matching Demo

```
int main(int args, char **argc)
{
    cout << "Character Matching with Stacks Example" << endl;
    cout << "Chapter 6: Stacks and Queues" << endl;
    cout << endl;
```

```
char str[] = { '{', '(', 'a', '[', '5', ']', ')', '}' };
int size = strlen(str);

cout << "Parsing str." << endl;
ParseString(str, size);


char str2[] = { '{', ')', 'b', '[', '10', ']', ')', '}' };
size = strlen(str2);

cout << "Parsing str2." << endl;
ParseString(str2, size);

cout << endl;

return 1;
}
```

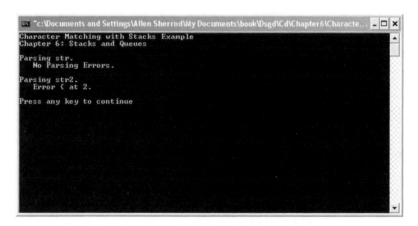

FIGURE 6.3 A screenshot of the Character Matching demo.

STL STACKS

The STL library implements stacks using the template class stack, which is found in the <stack> header file. The STL implementation of a stack is done using a double-ended queue, which in the STL is the template deque class. The STL stack class includes many of the member functions we've already implemented in our custom implementation of the container. These functions are describe in Table 6.1.

TABLE 6.1 The Member Functions of the STL `stack` Class

Function	Description
`stack()` `stack(container)`	Constructors that will create a stack container; an optional second constructor that takes a container from which the stack is to be copied
`empty()`	Returns `true` if the container is empty or `false` if it is not
`pop()`	Removes the last item inserted into the list
`push(T val)`	Inserts the object `val` into the container
`top()`	Returns a reference to the element on the top of the stack
`size()`	Returns the number of elements in the container

NOTE

The STL stack can be implemented using a sequence container. Sequence containers include the STL vector, an STL list, and an STL deque. By default, a stack is implemented with a deque.

When a stack container it created, its functions map to one of the sequence containers that can be used with it. When an object is inserted into the stack, the underlying container's `push_back()` function is called, and when an object is removed from the stack, the underlying container's `pop_back()` function is called. To get the top of the stack, the container calls the underlying container's `back()` function, which returns a reference to the top element. The `empty()` and `size()` functions map directly to the underlying container. Each function is implemented as an inline function for performance by avoiding the overhead of the second function call.

ON THE CD

On the accompanying CD-ROM is a demo application called STL Stack in the Chapter 6 folder. This application demonstrates the STL stack class and each of its member functions (see Table 6.1). The demo creates three different stacks: a `vector` stack, a `list` stack, and a `deque` stack. The demo populates each of these containers with data, displays them by getting a reference to the top element by calling `top()`, and removes the objects in the container by calling `pop()`. The main.cpp source file for the STL Stack demo application is shown in Listing 6.7. Figure 6.4 shows a screenshot of the demo application.

LISTING 6.7 The Main Source File for the STL Stack Demo

```cpp
#include<iostream>
#include<stack>
#include<vector>
#include<list>


using namespace std;


template<typename T>
void DisplayStack(T &stack)
{
   cout << "(Size - " << stack.size() << ") :";

   while(stack.empty() == false)
   {
      cout << " " << stack.top();
      stack.pop();
   }

   cout << "." << endl;
}


int main(int args, char **argc)
{
   cout << "STL Stacks Example" << endl;
   cout << "Chapter 6: Stacks and Queues" << endl;
   cout << endl;


   stack<int> intStack;
   stack<int, vector<int> > vecStack;
   stack<int, list<int> > listStack;

   for(int i = 0; i < 5; i++)
   {
      intStack.push(11 + i);
      vecStack.push(22 + i);
```

```cpp
        listStack.push(33 + i);
    }


    // Display normal (deque) integer stack.
    cout << "        Contents of the int stack ";
    DisplayStack(intStack);


    // Display vector integer stack.
    cout << "Contents of the int vector stack ";
    DisplayStack(vecStack);


    // Display link list integer stack.
    cout << "  Contents of the int list stack ";
    DisplayStack(listStack);

    cout << endl;


    // Calling empty() to test if container is empty.
    if(intStack.empty() == true)
        cout << "The int stack is empty." << endl;
    else
        cout << "The int stack is NOT empty." << endl;

    // Calling empty() to test if container is empty.
    if(vecStack.empty() == true)
        cout << "The vec int stack is empty." << endl;
    else
        cout << "The vec int stack is NOT empty." << endl;

    // Calling empty() to test if container is empty.
    if(listStack.empty() == true)
        cout << "The list int stack is empty." << endl;
    else
        cout << "The list int stack is NOT empty." << endl;

    cout << endl;

    return 1;
}
```

```
c:\Documents and Settings\Allen Sherrod\My Documents\book\Dsgd\Cd\Chapter6\STLStack...
STL Stacks Example
Chapter 6: Stacks and Queues

        Contents of the int stack (Size - 5) : 15 14 13 12 11.
Contents of the int vector stack (Size - 5) : 26 25 24 23 22.
   Contents of the int list stack (Size - 5) : 37 36 35 34 33.

The int stack is empty.
The vec int stack is empty.
The list int stack is empty.

Press any key to continue_
```

FIGURE 6.4 A screenshot of the STL Stack demo.

INTRODUCTION TO QUEUES

In this section we will discuss various types of queue data structures that can be used in general computer programming. A queue data structure has a first-in, first-out order, which is different from the stack data structure discussed earlier in the chapter. A queue has restricted access similar to stacks, where only one element is accessible at a time. There are many similarities between the stack and the queue that we'll see in more detail in this section.

Although stacks and queues seem like the exact same data structure, some differences make them appropriate for different situations. This has a lot to do with the order in which objects are inserted and removed from the container. A visual representation of this is shown in Figure 6.5.

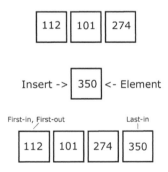

FIGURE 6.5 A visual look at the queue data structure.

Queues have many uses in programming and in game development. One example is a message queue that is used to take incoming messages, place them in a queue, and process them as appropriate. The first message received would need to be processed first, which by definition cannot be done with a stack since it has a LIFO order. A priority queue can go one step further by ordering the elements based on importance so that the critical messages are taken care of before the less important ones. An online game's networking system could work like this within a game's framework, which would allow the most critical game information to be handled as early as possible.

We will look at three types of queues in this chapter. The first type is a traditional queue that allows objects to be inserted into the container and be removed from the back (bottom object) of the container. The second type is a double-ended queue that allows items to be inserted and removed from the front and the back of the container. The third type of queue we'll look at is the priority queue, which can order objects based on priority.

Another type of queue is the circular queue. This type of queue allows for the wrapping of elements. This means that when the data structure is full, the elements inserted to it are wrapped by overriding elements already inside the container.

QUEUE DATA STRUCTURES

The queue data structure is made up of methods that insert objects into the container, remove objects from the container, and peek at the first objects. In this section we will implement a container class called Queue to do just that. The class will also have a function for returning the number of objects in the container and a boolean function for determining if the container is empty. For consistency the insertion function will be called push(), the removal function will be called pop(), and the peeking function will be called front(). In the next section, when we look at double-ended queues, we will also add a back() function so that both ends can be peeked at. Listing 6.8 shows the Queue class as described in this paragraph.

The queue uses a big-O of 0(1) *for its operations.*

LISTING 6.8   The Queue Class

```
template<typename T>
class Queue
{
    public:
```

```cpp
      Queue(int size)
      {
         assert(size > 0);
         m_size = size;
      }


      ~Queue()
      {

      }


      void push(T val)
      {
         if(m_elements.GetSize() < m_size)
            m_elements.Push(val);
      }


      void pop()
      {
         m_elements.Pop_Front();
      }


      const T& front()
      {
         LinkIterator<T> it;
         it = m_elements.Begin();

         return *it;
      }


      int GetSize()    { return m_elements.GetSize(); }
      int GetMaxSize() { return m_size; }
      bool isEmpty()   { return (m_elements.GetSize() == 0); }

      void Resize(int size) { assert(size > 0); m_size = size; }


   private:
      LinkList<T> m_elements;
      int m_size;
};
```

The Queue class in Listing 6.8 uses a doubly linked list (created in Chapter 5) as its underlying data structure. A link list is a better fit for the queue than an array since all we need is fast insertion, removal, and expansion. The insertion function of the Queue class uses push() to insert objects in the back of the link list so that the first object is always in the front. The pop() function of the Queue class uses pop_front() of the underlying data structure to remove the first object from the container (first-in, first-out). The function front() is used to peek at the first object in the container, while the remaining functions are used to determine the size of the container and the maximum size, check if it is empty, and adjust the maximum allowable size. The resizing function adjusts the maximum size so that the container can grow if necessary. For shrinking, the programmers using the class will have to manually call pop()because certain objects that are pushed onto the queue might have special needs that can't be or can't easily be generalized. One example of this is a queue of dynamically allocated objects where the delete or delete[] keywords will need to be used to avoid memory leaks. In this case front() can be used to peek at the front-most pointer for deletion, a keyword can be applied to the element, and pop() can remove the element from the underlying link list.

ON THE CD

On the accompanying CD-ROM, in the Chapter 6 folder, is a demo application called Queue that demonstrates the use of the queue container. The main source file for this demo creates a static integer queue, populates it with elements, and displays its contents. In the demo application all functions of the Queue class are demonstrated within the main() function. The main.cpp source file for the Queue demo application is shown in Listing 6.9. Figure 6.6 shows a screenshot of it.

LISTING 6.9 The Queue Demo's main.cpp Source File

```cpp
#include<iostream>
#include"Queue.h"

using namespace std;


int main(int args, char **argc)
{
   cout << "Queue Data Structures Example" << endl;
   cout << "Chapter 6: Stacks and Queues" << endl;
   cout << endl;


   // Create and populate queue.
   const int size = 5;
   Queue<int> intQueue(size);
```

```
for(int i = 0; i < size; i++)
   intQueue.push(10 + i);


// Display integer queue.
cout << "Queue Contents (Size - "
      << intQueue.GetSize() << ") :";

while(intQueue.isEmpty() == false)
{
   cout << " " << intQueue.front();
   intQueue.pop();
}

cout << "." << endl << endl;


// Calling isEmpty() to test if container is empty.
if(intQueue.isEmpty() == true)
   cout << "The int queue is empty." << endl << endl;
else
   cout << "The int queue is NOT empty." << endl << endl;


   return 1;
}
```

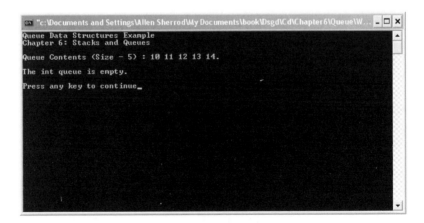

FIGURE 6.6 A screenshot of the Queue demo.

DOUBLE-ENDED QUEUE DATA STRUCTURES

The double-ended queue allows for the insertion, removal, and peeking of objects from both ends of the container. Using the doubly linked list from Chapter 5 makes this process very simple, much like the first queue container created earlier in this chapter.

The double-ended queue uses a big-O of $O(1)$ for its operations, as does the first type of queue seen in this chapter.

NOTE

For the double-ended queue class we can modify the Queue class from the previous section to support this feature. In the new Queue class the insertion functions are called push_front() and push_back(), which maps directly to the underlying data structure. When using the push_front() function, the new objects are inserted into the front of the underlying link list data structure. Because of this, calling pop_front() of the link list in the pop_front() function of the Queue class will remove the item at the front of the list, which is the last item inserted, instead of the first item. When using the Queue class on a high level, this mismatch might be confusing to those who do not understand the inner workings of the containers. To avoid such potential logic errors, and since it makes sense to match functions such as push_front() with pop_front(), the pop_front() function of the Queue class will call the pop() function of the underlying link list. Since the first object inserted in the list will always be at the end, calling pop() on the link list will remove the first item that was inserted, which is what we want. The front() and back() peeking functions work in the same manner, so that at the higher level the front functions can be matched with other front functions and vice versa. The modified Queue class, updated to be a double-ended queue, is shown in Listing 6.10.

LISTING 6.10   The Queue class Updated To Be a Double-Ended Queue

```
template<typename T>
class Queue
{
   public:
      Queue(int size)
      {
         assert(size > 0);
         m_size = size;
      }


      ~Queue()
      {
```

```
    }


    void push_front(T val)
    {
        if(m_elements.GetSize() < m_size)
            m_elements.Push_Front(val);
    }


    void push_back(T val)
    {
        if(m_elements.GetSize() < m_size)
            m_elements.Push(val);
    }


    void pop_front()
    {
        m_elements.Pop();
    }


    void pop_back()
    {
        m_elements.Pop_Front();
    }


    const T& front()
    {
        LinkIterator<T> it;
        it = m_elements.Last();

        return *it;
    }


    const T& back()
    {
        LinkIterator<T> it;
        it = m_elements.Begin();

        return *it;
    }
```

```
    int GetSize()    { return m_elements.GetSize(); }
    int GetMaxSize() { return m_size; }
    bool isEmpty()   { return (m_elements.GetSize() == 0); }

    void Resize(int size) { assert(size > 0); m_size = size; }


private:
    LinkList<T> m_elements;
    int m_size;
};
```

ON THE CD

On the accompanying CD-ROM a demo application called Deque in the Chapter 6 folder demonstrates the newly modified double-ended `Queue` class. In the main source file of this demo the code creates an integer queue, populates it with data, and displays that data to the console window. During the display it displays both sides of the queue before popping from the front, which matches the `push_front()` function of the insertion of the elements. The main source file from the Deque demo application is shown in Listing 6.11. Figure 6.7 shows a screenshot of the Deque demo application.

LISTING 6.11   The Deque Demo's Main Source File

```
#include<iostream>
#include"Queue.h"

using namespace std;


int main(int args, char **argc)
{
    cout << "Deque (Double-Ended Queue) Example" << endl;
    cout << "Chapter 6: Stacks and Queues" << endl;
    cout << endl;


    // Create and populate queue.
    const int size = 5;
    Queue<int> intQueue(size);

    for(int i = 0; i < size; i++)
        intQueue.push_front(20 + i);
```

```
// Display integer queue.
cout << "Queue Contents (Size - "
     << intQueue.GetSize() << ") :" << endl;

while(intQueue.isEmpty() == false)
{
   cout << "   Front: " << intQueue.front();
   cout << "   Back: " << intQueue.back();
   cout << endl;

   intQueue.pop_front();
}

cout << endl << endl;


// Calling isEmpty() to test if container is empty.
if(intQueue.isEmpty() == true)
   cout << "The int queue is empty." << endl << endl;
else
   cout << "The int queue is NOT empty." << endl << endl;


   return 1;
}
```

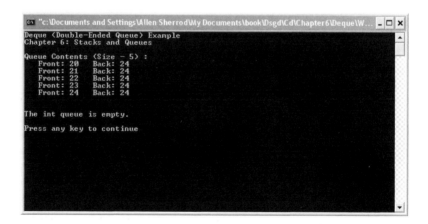

FIGURE 6.7   A screenshot of the Deque demo.

PRIORITY QUEUES

The priority queue differs from the traditional queue in that the objects inserted into the data structure are ordered by importance rather than their insertion order. This has all kinds of uses, including a priority-based online networking system for an online game. Because the objects inserted into the data structure must be ordered, the insertion is slower than the other queues we've seen so far. A visual representation of a priority queue is shown in Figure 6.8.

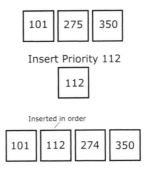

FIGURE 6.8   A priority queue.

Priority queues have an insertion big-O of 0(N) *for the custom implementation because it depends on the number of elements already inserted into the containers. The insertion for the previously discussed types of queues is big-O of* 0(1) *because the insertions do not depend on the number of elements already in the container. All other queue operations have a big-O of* 0(1). *In the STL the big-O for insertions is faster because the STL uses a tree for the internal implementation.*

The priority queue implemented in this chapter will use the link list for speed purposes. Because the priority queue will need to insert elements anywhere within the list, we will need to update the link list class to allow for such insertions. In Chapter 5 this was left as an exercise at the end of the chapter. The solution to that exercise will be given in the upcoming sections.

To be able to insert nodes anywhere within the link list container, the iterator class was first updated to support a new function called isValid(), which is a simple test to see if the iterator's node is not NULL. This can be used to avoid trying to access NULL iterators, which can also prevent bugs and assertions. We'll see why this is needed later on in this section.

Another addition to the link list code can be seen in the link list itself. The link list needs to add functions to allow a new element to be inserted at a particular position. This position can be marked by an iterator to an already existing position within the list. For this two new functions are added called `Insert_Before()` and `Insert_After()`. The `Insert_Before()` function inserts the new element before the node that the iterator points to, while `Insert_After()` inserts it after that node. Both functions take as parameters a link list iterator and an object to insert. Inside each function they both create a new node for the new element and, depending on which function is called, position that new node to either side of the node stored in the iterator. Doing this requires us to manipulate the next and previous pointers of the newly created node, the node in the iterator, and the nodes to either side of the iterator. This must be done to make sure all pointers are correct and the link list is a valid chain. Since we are using the doubly-linked list from Chapter 5, we must be sure to take care of the next and previous pointers of all nodes involved. The updated link list iterator and container code that allow the insertion of elements anywhere inside the containers are shown in Listing 6.12.

LISTING 6.12 Updated Doubly Linked List To Allow Insertions Anywhere Within the Container

```
template<typename T>
class LinkIterator
{
    friend class LinkList<T>;

    public:
        bool isValid()
        {
            return (m_node != NULL);
        }
};


template<typename T>
class LinkList
{
    public:
        void Insert_Before(LinkIterator<T> &it, T newData)
        {
            assert(it.m_node != NULL);


            LinkNode<T> *node = new LinkNode<T>;
            assert(node != NULL);
```

```
            node->m_data = newData;
            node->m_next = it.m_node;
            node->m_previous = it.m_node->m_previous;


            if(node->m_previous != NULL)
                node->m_previous->m_next = node;

            it.m_node->m_previous = node;

            if(it.m_node == m_root)
                m_root = node;


            m_size++;
        }


        void Insert_After(LinkIterator<T> &it, T newData)
        {
            assert(it.m_node != NULL);


            LinkNode<T> *node = new LinkNode<T>;
            assert(node != NULL);

            node->m_data = newData;
            node->m_next = it.m_node->m_next;
            node->m_previous = it.m_node;


            if(node->m_next != NULL)
                node->m_next->m_previous = node;

            it.m_node->m_next = node;

            if(it.m_node == m_lastNode)
                m_lastNode = node;


            m_size++;
        }
};
```

Next is the priority queue container. The priority queue is implemented in its own class called `PriorityQueue`. This class has a `push()` function for inserting elements into the queue, a `pop()` function for removing the element in the front of the queue, functions to peek at both sides of the queue container, and functions to return the size of the container, check if the container is empty, and resize the container. The major difference between the priority queue and the first queue seen in this chapter is that the priority queue class has a more detailed insertion and an additional template parameter. Listing 6.13 shows the `PriorityQueue` class.

LISTING 6.13 The `PriorityQueue` Class

```
template<typename T, typename CMP>
class PriorityQueue
{
   public:
      PriorityQueue(int size)
      {
         assert(size > 0);
         m_size = size;
      }


      ~PriorityQueue()
      {

      }


      void push(T val)
      {
         assert(m_elements.GetSize() < m_size);

         if(m_elements.GetSize() == 0)
         {
            m_elements.Push(val);
         }
         else
         {
            LinkIterator<T> it;
            it = m_elements.Begin();

            CMP cmp;
```

```
      while(it.isValid())
      {
         if(cmp(val, *it))
            break;

         it++;
      }

      if(it.isValid())
         m_elements.Insert_Before(it, val);
      else
         m_elements.Push(val);
   }
}


void pop()
{
   m_elements.Pop_Front();
}


const T& front()
{
   LinkIterator<T> it;
   it = m_elements.Begin();

   return *it;
}


const T& back()
{
   LinkIterator<T> it;
   it = m_elements.Last();

   return *it;
}

int GetSize()    { return m_elements.GetSize(); }
int GetMaxSize() { return m_size; }
bool isEmpty()   { return (m_elements.GetSize() == 0); }

void Resize(int size) { assert(size > 0); m_size = size; }
```

```
    private:
        LinkList<T> m_elements;
        int m_size;
};
```

The first thing to notice about the `PriorityQueue` class is that two items are defined in the template. The first item is the data type that the queue will use, and the second item specifies a comparison operator that the queue will use. For example, if the queue is an integer queue and we want the items to be inserted from greater-than to less-than order, we can create a custom comparison to do so. If we wanted that same queue to sort the elements in the reverse order, we could just change the comparison operator with which the queue is defined. This keeps hardcoded operators out of the class since how the elements are ordered is based on what the programmer wants, which we can't hardcode and predict. Also, and more importantly, user-defined classes can be used with the priority queue as long as the class implements an overloaded operator for the comparison type chosen by the programmer. The purpose of this is to make the class flexible in many different situations by hardcoding as little as possible.

The only difference left to discuss lies within the class's `push()` method, which first checks to see if the container is empty. If it is, the element is simply passed down to the `push()` method of the underlying link list. If the list is not empty, a loop is used to linearly step through the link list and find the position that is right for the new element. To accomplish this, the comparison operator defined by the template parameter is created and used to test the objects. As long as the test fails, it will keep stepping through the link list until the it returns `true` or reaches the end. By using the `++` operator of the link list, it is possible to move past the last node, which would make the iterator's node `NULL`. The purpose of the `isValid()` function that was added to the iterator class is to allow us to determine if the iterator is valid. If it is not valid, we can say that whatever element we are trying to insert must be inserted to the back of the queue since its priority (order) dictates it. If the iterator is valid, we can call `Insert_Before()` since the node that comes before the iterator's location will always be the spot to insert the item because the iterator is always one past where we want to insert.

ON THE CD
On the accompanying CD-ROM in the Chapter 6 folder is a demo application called Priority Queue. The Priority Queue demo application creates a queue of a user-defined class, populates it with elements, and displays each element's member variables to the console windows. Listing 6.14 shows the entire main.cpp source file for the Priority Queue demo application. In the next section we will break up this demo's source code and examine each part for more detailed information.

LISTING 6.14   The Main Source File for the Priority Queue Demo

```cpp
#include<iostream>
#include"PriorityQueue.h"

using namespace std;


template<typename T>
class less_cmp
{
   public:
      inline bool operator()(T lVal, T rVal)
      {
         return (lVal < rVal);
      }
};


template<typename T>
class less_cmp_ptr
{
   public:
      inline bool operator()(T lVal, T rVal)
      {
         return ((*lVal) < (*rVal));
      }
};


template<typename T>
class greater_cmp
{
   public:
      inline bool operator()(T lVal, T rVal)
      {
         return !(lVal < rVal);
      }
};


template<typename T>
class greater_cmp_ptr
{
```

```
        public:
            inline bool operator()(T lVal, T rVal)
            {
                return !((*lVal) < (*rVal));
            }
    };


    class NetworkMessage
    {
        public:
            NetworkMessage() : m_priority(0), m_id(0) { }
            NetworkMessage(int p, int id) : m_priority(p), m_id(id) { }
            ~NetworkMessage() { }


            int GetPriority() { return m_priority; }
            int GetID()       { return m_id; }


            bool operator<(NetworkMessage &m)
            {
                if(m_priority < m.GetPriority())
                    return true;
                else if(m_id < m.GetID())
                    return true;

                return false;
            }

            bool operator>(NetworkMessage &m)
            {
                return !(*this < m);
            }


        private:
            int m_priority, m_id;
    };


    int main(int args, char **argc)
    {
        cout << "Priority Queue Data Structures Example" << endl;
```

```
cout << "Chapter 6: Stacks and Queues" << endl;
cout << endl;


// Create and populate queue.
const int size = 4;
PriorityQueue<NetworkMessage,
              less_cmp<NetworkMessage> > que(size);

que.push(NetworkMessage(3, 100));
que.push(NetworkMessage(2, 286));
que.push(NetworkMessage(1, 362));
que.push(NetworkMessage(3, 435));



// Display integer queue.
cout << "Priority Queue Contents (Size - "
     << que.GetSize() << ") :" << endl;

while(que.isEmpty() == false)
{
   cout << "   Priority: " << que.front().GetPriority();
   cout << " - ID: "       << que.front().GetID();
   cout << endl;

   que.pop();
}

cout << endl;


// Calling isEmpty() to test if container is empty.
if(que.isEmpty() == true)
   cout << "The container is empty." << endl << endl;
else
   cout << "The container is NOT empty." << endl << endl;

return 1;
}
```

The main source file for the Priority Queue demo application starts by defining a few comparison template classes that can be used for the `PriorityQueue` class's template parameter. Although this demo only uses the less-than comparison in the demonstration, others are created as an examples. The first question many readers will have is why there are two versions of each comparison. The answer lies with pointers. If we used the first less-than comparison template class on a pointer, the elements will be ordered based on the pointer's memory address value rather than the priority of the object it points to. This is an easy mistake to make. Since the same template comparison cannot be used on both pointers and nonpointers, different versions are created. To sort based on the object instead of the memory location will require us to deference the pointer with the * operator so that the object's comparison can occur instead of a comparison of the pointer addresses. The example comparison template classes are shown by themselves in Listing 6.15.

LISTING 6.15 The Example Comparison Template Classes of the Priority Queue Demo

```
#include<iostream>
#include"PriorityQueue.h"

using namespace std;


template<typename T>
class less_cmp
{
   public:
      inline bool operator()(T lVal, T rVal)
      {
         return (lVal < rVal);
      }
};


template<typename T>
class less_cmp_ptr
{
   public:
      inline bool operator()(T lVal, T rVal)
      {
         return ((*lVal) < (*rVal));
      }
};


template<typename T>
class greater_cmp
{
   public:
      inline bool operator()(T lVal, T rVal)
```

```
        {
            return !(lVal < rVal);
        }
};


template<typename T>
class greater_cmp_ptr
{
    public:
        inline bool operator()(T lVal, T rVal)
        {
            return !((*lVal) < (*rVal));
        }
};
```

The next section of the Priority Queue demo application's main source file is a user-defined class that will be used with the priority queue. This class is called NetworkMessage and is a simple example of using a user-defined class with the priority queue. The class defines both the greater-than and less-than operators as well as two member variables. The member variables are for the priority of the network message and its id, both of which are used in the comparisons. This is an example of ordering not only by priority but also by other factors. These additional factors can include the size of the object, the time in which the object was created, the object's id, and anything else that is necessary for the application being developed. In the comparisons the priority is tested first. If the priority of one object is the same as the other, the ids are tested. If those match as well, then the objects are equal. In a real networking system the time in which the messages are sent can also play a role in the ordering. The user-defined class NetworkMessage is shown by itself in Listing 6.16.

LISTING 6.16   An Example User-Defined Class Called NetworkMessage

```
class NetworkMessage
{
    public:
        NetworkMessage() : m_priority(0), m_id(0) { }
        NetworkMessage(int p, int id) : m_priority(p), m_id(id) { }
        ~NetworkMessage() { }


        int GetPriority() { return m_priority; }
        int GetID()       { return m_id; }
```

```
        bool operator<(NetworkMessage &m)
        {
            if(m_priority < m.GetPriority())
                return true;
            else if(m_id < m.GetID())
                return true;

            return false;
        }

        bool operator>(NetworkMessage &m)
        {
            return !(*this < m);
        }


    private:
        int m_priority, m_id;
};
```

The remaining code to examine is the main() function of the Priority Queue demo. This function creates a priority queue of NetworkMessage objects, populates it with elements, and loops through the container and displays each object's member variables. The objects are ordered based on priority first and then by id, which was specified in the second template parameter of the priority queue. The remaining code in the Priority Queue demo application's main.cpp source file is shown by itself in Listing 6.17. Figure 6.9 shows a screenshot of the demo application.

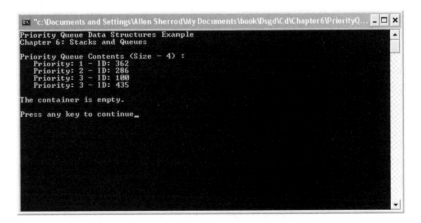

FIGURE 6.9 A screenshot of the Priority Queue demo.

LISTING 6.17   The Remainder of the Priority Queue Demo's Code

```cpp
int main(int args, char **argc)
{
   cout << "Priority Queue Data Structures Example" << endl;
   cout << "Chapter 6: Stacks and Queues" << endl;
   cout << endl;


   // Create and populate queue.
   const int size = 4;
   PriorityQueue<NetworkMessage,
               less_cmp<NetworkMessage> > que(size);

   que.push(NetworkMessage(3, 100));
   que.push(NetworkMessage(2, 286));
   que.push(NetworkMessage(1, 362));
   que.push(NetworkMessage(3, 435));


   // Display integer queue.
   cout << "Priority Queue Contents (Size - "
       << que.GetSize() << ") :" << endl;

   while(que.isEmpty() == false)
   {
      cout << "   Priority: " << que.front().GetPriority();
      cout << " - ID: "       << que.front().GetID();
      cout << endl;

      que.pop();
      }

   cout << endl;


   // Calling isEmpty() to test if container is empty.
   if(que.isEmpty() == true)
      cout << "The container is empty." << endl << endl;
   else
      cout << "The container is NOT empty." << endl << endl;

   return 1;
}
```

STL QUEUES

In this section we will look at three STL queues: the template classes `queue`, `deque`, and `priority_queue`. Each of these types of data structures were already seen in custom implementations earlier in this chapter. In this section we will briefly discuss the STL implementations of each of these classes, which are very similar to the custom implementations for this chapter.

STL `queue` TEMPLATE CLASS

The STL `queue` class enables insertions and removals of elements to occur at the front of the container. By default, the `queue` class is implemented with a `deque`, which will be discussed in the next section, but it can also be implemented using a `list`, which is an STL link list. For performance reasons the operations of the STL `queue` are implemented as inline functions because they map to the underlying data structure. The members of the STL `queue` are shown in Table 6.2.

To get the best performance form a queue it is recommended that the underlying data structure be the default `deque` *instead of the* `list`.

NOTE

TABLE 6.2 The Members of the STL `queue` Template Class

Function	Description
push(val)	Inserts an element to the back of the container
pop()	Removes an element from the front of the container
front()	Returns a reference to the front of the container
back()	Returns a reference to the back of the container
empty()	Boolean check to test if the container is empty
size()	Returns the number of elements in the container

ON THE CD

On the accompanying CD-ROM a demo application called STL Queue is in the Chapter 6 folder. This demo application will create two queues, one using a `deque` and the other using a `list`, populate them with elements, and display those elements to the console window. Because the `queue` does not have random-access iterators, it cannot be used with STL algorithms. The main source file for the STL Queue demo application is shown in Listing 6.18. Figure 6.10 shows a screenshot of the running executable.

LISTING 6.18   The STL Queue Demo Application's Main Source File

```cpp
#include<iostream>
#include<queue>
#include<list>

using namespace std;


template<typename T>
void DisplayQueue(T &que)
{
   cout << "(Size - " << que.size() << ") :";

   while(que.empty() == false)
   {
      cout << " " << que.front();
      que.pop();
   }

   cout << "." << endl;
}


int main(int args, char **argc)
{
   cout << "STL Queue Example" << endl;
   cout << "Chapter 6: Stacks and Queues" << endl;
   cout << endl;


   queue<int> intQueue;
   queue<int, list<int> > listQueue;

   for(int i = 0; i < 5; i++)
   {
      intQueue.push(44 + i);
      listQueue.push(55 + i);
   }


   // Display normal (deque) integer queue.
   cout << "      Contents of the int queue ";
   DisplayQueue(intQueue);
```

```
      // Display link list integer queue.
      cout << "  Contents of the int list queue ";
      DisplayQueue(listQueue);

      cout << endl;


      // Calling empty() to test if container is empty.
      if(intQueue.empty() == true)
         cout << "The int queue is empty." << endl;
      else
         cout << "The int queue is NOT empty." << endl;

      // Calling empty() to test if container is empty.
      if(listQueue.empty() == true)
         cout << "The list int queue is empty." << endl;
      else
   cout << "The list int queue is NOT empty." << endl;

      cout << endl;

      return 1;
}
```

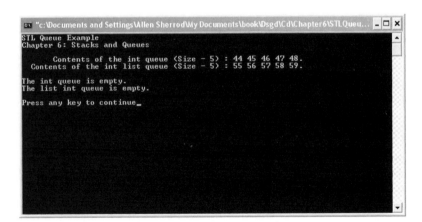

FIGURE 6.10 A screenshot of the STL Queue demo.

STL deque TEMPLATE CLASS

The deque template class is a double-ended queue container. The deque class provides indexed access using subscripting for reading and writing elements and has support of random-access iterators similar to the STL `vector` class. Supporting random-access iterators allows the `deque` class to be used with all STL algorithms. Internally the `deque` manages all of its data by allocating memory in blocks when needed at the end or beginning of the container. These blocks of memory are typically maintained as an array of pointers. The members of the `deque` class can be seen in Table 6.3.

The `deque` does not deallocate blocks of memory until it is destroyed in some implementations. This is done to avoid many allocations and deallocations or reallocations within the container. Although this can provide a performance boost in the container's speed, it comes at the cost of more inefficient memory consumption than that of the vector, for example.

The STL `deque` is a sequence container. The `deque` can be used by including the `<deque>` header.

TABLE 6.3   Members of the `deque` Template Class that Differ from the `vector` Class

Function	Description
push_front(val)	Inserts `val` into the front of the container
pop_front()	Removes an element from the front of the container

On the accompanying CD-ROM is a demo application called STL Deque in the Chapter 6 folder. This application demonstrates creating a `deque`, performing various STL algorithms on it, and displaying its contents. The `deque` supports random access iterators, which makes it possible to use STL algorithms with it. The main source file for the STL Deque demo application is shown listed in Listing 6.19. Figure 6.11 shows a screenshot of the demo application.

LISTING 6.19   The Main Source File for the STL Deque Demo

```
#include<iostream>
#include<deque>
#include<algorithm>
#include<numeric>

using namespace std;
```

```cpp
void PrintDeque(deque<int> &deq)
{
   cout << "Contents (" << "Size: " << (int)deq.size() << ") - ";

   ostream_iterator<int> output(cout, " ");
   copy(deq.begin(), deq.end(), output);

   cout << endl;
}


void PrintDequeReverse(deque<int> &deq)
{
   cout << "Contents (" << "Size: " << (int)deq.size() << ") - ";

   ostream_iterator<int> output(cout, " ");
   copy(deq.rbegin(), deq.rend(), output);

   cout << endl;
}


int main(int args, char **argc)
{
   cout << "STL Deque Example" << endl;
   cout << "Chapter 6: Stacks and Queues" << endl;
   cout << endl;

   deque<int> intDeque;

   for(int i = 0; i < 5; i++)
      intDeque.push_back(66 + i);


   // Display deque.
   cout << "  Inserted into deque: ";
   PrintDeque(intDeque);

   cout << "       Reversed deque: ";
   PrintDequeReverse(intDeque);


   // Display item at the front of deque.
   cout << "        Deque Front(): "
       << intDeque.front() << "." << endl;

   // Display item at the front of deque.
   cout << "         Deque Back(): "
       << intDeque.back() << "." << endl;
```

```
// Pop off the container.
intDeque.pop_back();
intDeque.pop_back();

cout << "Popped two from deque: ";
PrintDeque(intDeque);


// Clear the container.
intDeque.clear();

cout << "          Cleared deque: ";
PrintDeque(intDeque);

cout << endl;


// Test if the container is empty.
if(intDeque.empty() == true)
   cout << "Deque is empty.";
else
   cout << "Deque is NOT empty.";


cout << endl << endl;

return 1;
}
```

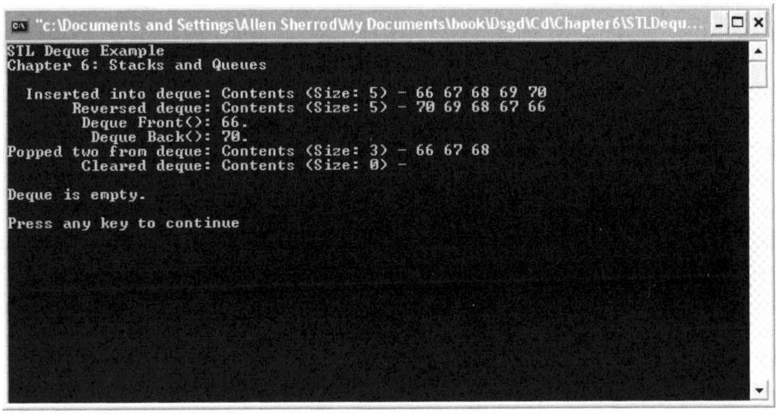

FIGURE 6.11   A screenshot of the STL Deque demo.

STL `priority_queue` TEMPLATE CLASS

The `priority_queue` template class sorts elements, usually using a heap-sort, which we'll talk about later on in the book, and allows for the removal of elements from the front of the container. By default, the `priority_queue` uses a `vector` as its underlying data structure, but it can also use a `deque`. Also by default, the `priority_queue` sorts elements in less-than to greater-than order. This order can be specified by using a comparison template class in the same manner as we did for the custom priority queue implementation earlier in the chapter. The methods of the `priority_queue` class are shown in Table 6.4.

TABLE 6.4   The Methods of the `priority_queue` Class

Method	Description
push(val)	Inserts an element into the front of the container
pop()	Removes an element from the front of the container
top()	Returns a reference to the front of the container
empty()	Returns `true` if the container is empty, or else `false`
size()	Returns the number of elements in the container

ON THE CD

On the accompanying CD-ROM, in the Chapter 6 folder, is a demo application called STL Priority Queue. This application demonstrates using the priority queue with integers that are ordered from less-than to greater-than, which is the default order. Like the STL `queue`, the `priority_queue` does not have random-access iterators. The main source file for the STL Priority Queue demo application is shown in Listing 6.20. Figure 6.12 shows a screenshot from the STL Priority Queue demo.

LISTING 6.20   The STL Priority Queue Demo's Main Source File

```
#include<iostream>
#include<queue>

using namespace std;


int main(int args, char **argc)
{
   cout << "STL Priority Queue Example" << endl;
   cout << "Chapter 6: Stacks and Queues" << endl;
   cout << endl;
```

```
priority_queue<int> priQueue;

for(int i = 0; i < 5; i++)
    priQueue.push(88 + i);


// Display priority queue.
cout << "Priority Queue (int) Contents (" << "Size: "
     << (int)priQueue.size() << ") -";

int size = (int)priQueue.size();

for(int i = 0; i < size; i++)
{
    cout << " " << priQueue.top();
    priQueue.pop();
}

cout << "." << endl;


// Empty test.
if(priQueue.empty() == true)
    cout << "Priority Queue (int) is empty.";
else
    cout << "Priority Queue (int) is NOT empty.";


cout << endl << endl;

    return 1;
}
```

FIGURE 6.12   A screenshot of the STL Priority Queue demo.

The `priority_queue` class can also be used on user-defined classes and can have comparison classes defined for it in the same way that we saw with the custom implementation of the priority queue, `PriorityQueue`, earlier in the chapter. The two are so similar that the same template comparison classes used earlier in the chapter can be used, as is, in the STL `priority_queue`.

On the companion CD-ROM another demo application that uses STL priority queues is STL Priority Queue 2, which can be found in the Chapter 6 folder. This demo application creates two priority queues, one for nonpointer objects and the other for pointer objects. It takes the STL Priority Queue demo created earlier and replaces the custom-created `PriorityQueue` class with the STL `priority_queue`. The demo application also shows how to delete dynamically allocated memory from the STL `priority_queue` as the elements are being popped off of the container. For the nonpointer container the objects are sorted in less-than to greater-than order, while the pointer container specifies the objects in greater-than to less-than order. The entire main source file for the STL Priority Queue 2 demo application is shown in Listing 6.21. Figure 6.13 shows a screenshot of the running demo executable.

LISTING 6.21   The STL Priority Queue 2 Demo's Main Source File

```
#include<iostream>
#include<queue>
#include<vector>

using namespace std;


template<typename T>
class less_cmp
{
   public:
      inline bool operator()(T lVal, T rVal)
      {
         return (lVal < rVal);
      }
};


template<typename T>
class less_cmp_ptr
{
   public:
      inline bool operator()(T lVal, T rVal)
```

```cpp
            {
                return ((*lVal) < (*rVal));
            }
};


template<typename T>
class greater_cmp
{
    public:
        inline bool operator()(T lVal, T rVal)
        {
            return !(lVal < rVal);
        }
};


template<typename T>
class greater_cmp_ptr
{
    public:
        inline bool operator()(T lVal, T rVal)
        {
            return !((*lVal) < (*rVal));
        }
};


class NetworkMessage
{
    public:
        NetworkMessage(int data) : m_data(data) { }
        ~NetworkMessage() { }

        bool operator<(NetworkMessage &obj)
        {
            return (m_data < obj.GetData());
        }


        bool operator>(NetworkMessage &obj)
        {
            return !(m_data < obj.GetData());
        }
```

```
      int GetData()
      {
         return m_data;
      }

   private:
      int m_data;
};


int main(int args, char **argc)
{
   cout << "STL Priority Queue 2 Example" << endl;
   cout << "Chapter 6: Stacks and Queues" << endl;
   cout << endl;


   // Create two test priority queues.
   priority_queue<NetworkMessage, vector<NetworkMessage>,
                  less_cmp<NetworkMessage> > priQueue;

   priority_queue<NetworkMessage*, vector<NetworkMessage*>,
                  greater_cmp_ptr<NetworkMessage*> > priQueuePtr;

   priQueue.push(NetworkMessage(5));
   priQueue.push(NetworkMessage(35));
   priQueue.push(NetworkMessage(2));
   priQueue.push(NetworkMessage(53));

   priQueuePtr.push(new NetworkMessage(14));
   priQueuePtr.push(new NetworkMessage(67));
   priQueuePtr.push(new NetworkMessage(13));
   priQueuePtr.push(new NetworkMessage(12));


   // Display priority queue.
   cout << "Priority Queue Contents:" << endl;

   int size = (int)priQueue.size();

   for(int i = 0; i < size; i++)
   {
      cout << "   " << priQueue.top().GetData() << endl;
      priQueue.pop();
   }
```

```
cout << endl;


// Display priority queue ptr.
cout << "Priority Queue PTR Contents:" << endl;

size = (int)priQueuePtr.size();

for(int i = 0; i < size; i++)
{
   NetworkMessage *ptr = priQueuePtr.top();

   if(ptr != NULL)
   {
      cout << "   " << ptr->GetData();
      delete ptr;
      cout << " (deleted)" << endl;
   }

   priQueuePtr.pop();
}

cout << endl << endl;

return 1;
}
```

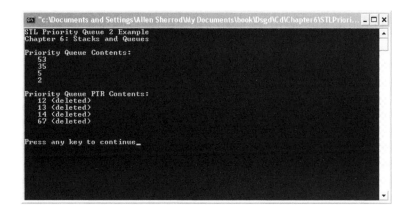

FIGURE 6.13 A screenshot of the STL Priority Queue 2 demo.

SUMMARY

This chapter covered information on stacks and queues in general computer programming. These data structures are restricted-access containers that have a number of useful benefits in application programming. The order in which elements are inserted into these containers can be in first-in, last-out or in first-in, first-out. Often these containers have shorter life spans than other STL containers and are used as tools to aid in some task.

In the next chapter we will look at two more data structures called the hash table and the data port. These data structures are very useful and powerful, and knowledge of them will be a great benefit to general and game programmers. As you can see, data structures and algorithms are very powerful and very important to programmers.

CHAPTER REVIEW QUESTIONS

Answers to the following chapter review questions can be found in Appendix B.

1. Stacks and queues are known as:
   a. Random-access containers
   b. Sequence containers
   c. Restricted-access adapters
   d. None of the above
   e. All of the above
2. Stacks have what access type?
   a. First-in, first-out
   b. First-in, last-out
   c. None of the above
3. Queues have what access type?
   a. First-in, first-out
   b. Last-in, first-out
   c. None of the above
4. With stacks and queues, how many items can be accessed at once?
   a. It is user-defined.
   b. Only one item.
   c. Multiple-items.
   d. Both a and c
5. What is the main purpose of a priority queue?
6. What is the main difference between queues and stacks?

7. What was the main purpose of using a link list instead of an array with the custom implementations of the queue classes in this chapter?
8. The priority queue has an insertion big-O of $O(N^2)$.
    a. True
    b. False
9. A circular queue is also a type of queue container.
    a. True
    b. False
10. STL queues include the `queue`, `circular_queue`, `deque`, and `priority_queue`.
    a. True
    b. False

PROGRAMMING PROJECTS

Exercise 1: Modify the Priority Queue demo application to also be able to sort objects from less-than or equal-to to greater-than range and vice versa. Modify the `NetworkMessage` class to also sort based on the time in milliseconds (time when the message was sent).

Exercise 2: Modify the Queue and Priority Queue demo applications so that the data structures offer a searching function that returns a boolean value based on if the object was found.

Exercise 3: Modify the Priority Queue demo's data structure to use an array instead of a link list as the underlying data structure.

Exercise 4: Implement a circular queue. Circular queues are queues that, when full, wrap by overriding elements already inside of the front of the container.

7 Hash Tables

In This Chapter

- Introduction to Hash Tables
- Hash Functions
- Working with Hash Tables
- Implementing Hash Tables
- Nonstandard Hash Containers

Separate Chaining using an array of Link Lists...

Index	Index	Index	Index	Index
Node	Node		Node	
	Node			

In this chapter we will discuss hash table data structures in detail in terms of what they are, how they are created, and why they exist in general computer programming. A hash table is a fast data structure used to hold a database of information in memory. The speed at which objects can be searched for and retrieved is not only incredibly fast, but is not dependant on the number of objects already inside a container. This means that a hash table with 1,000,000 elements should be as fast, assuming no or minimal internal collisions (more on this later on in the chapter), than a hash table with 1,000 elements.

We will look at implementing different types of hash tables as well as a set of nonstandard C++ template container classes. These classes include the `hash_set`, the `hash_multiset`, the `hash_map`, and the `hash_multimap`. A number of techniques are used for handling hash tables and the data that is inserted into them, which we will examine closely in the following sections of this chapter.

INTRODUCTION TO HASH TABLES

A hash table is a data structure that offers very fast insertions and searching for objects that are inserted into the container. The performance of hash tables is often close to having the big-O `O(1)` in most of its operations, which depends on a number of factors such as the overall collisions, which we'll discuss later in this chapter in more detail. Hash tables are very efficient and useful in all types of applications and a good understanding of them can be very useful. In games a hash table can be used, for example, in a massively multiplayer online role playing game for storing a database of players and their stats, items, weapons and equipment, character information, and so forth. A visual representation of a hash table is shown in Figure 7.1.

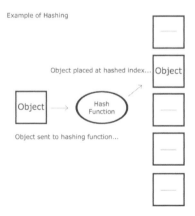

FIGURE 7.1 A hash table.

Hash tables are fast data structures. Even with a large number of items, a search for an object can be almost instant in some situations. This speed comes from the fact that hash tables are based on the array data structure. When the array index of an object is known, the position is nothing more than a table lookup using an array subscript. The trick is calculating an object's array index position, which we'll discuss throughout this chapter, so that it can be placed within the hash table and quickly retrieved at a moment's notice.

Because hash tables are based on arrays, they inherit their weaknesses as well as their strengths. When the size of the hash table can be predicted, some weaknesses might not pose too much of a problem. The following is true about the data structures and the various algorithms that can be performed on hash tables:

- Hash tables are expensive and hard to expand, which is further complicated because the positions of the objects within a hash table depend on the size of the data structure; a change in size invalidates all objects already inside of the container.
- When using open addressing, the performance of hash tables can decrease as the container becomes full.
- Objects cannot be ordered easily within a hash table.
- Looking up objects in a hash table is fast and uses array subscripts.
- Copying hash tables can be expensive and requires that both tables be of the same size to avoid having to rehash all existing elements.
- Insertions into a hash table are fast.

In general, hash tables work by taking an object and hashing it to an integer. This integer is used as the array position for that object in the hash table. Hashing a value refers to executing an algorithm on the object to create an integer that lies within the array bounds of the hash table. Every object that is inserted into the hash table has its own key. This key is an identifier that is hashed into an array index and used for the object. The key can be anything, even the object itself. The code used to hash an object into an array index is called a hash function. A visual representation of hashing is shown in Figure 7.2.

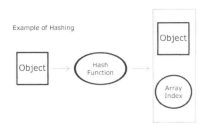

FIGURE 7.2   A visual of hashing.

EXAMPLE OF HASH TABLES

Hash tables have many uses in general computer programming and in game development. When it comes to very large data sets, the speed at which hash tables operate can make them very impressive data structures to use. Some general uses for hash tables include but are not limited to the following:

- Spell checkers
- Database systems
- Dictionaries
- Phone directories
- Implementation of a symbol table for a compiler in a general and game scripting system
- Implementation of a caching system
- Implementation of a transposition table in a chess game
- List of players in a massively multiplayer online role-playing game

Taking a dictionary as an example, the question is how do we create a list of words and definitions that we can quickly search? Using a traditional array wouldn't work because that would require string comparisons to take place on the words we are searching for and, on average, half of the list. In the English language there are tens of thousands of words, and the performance of doing this would be terrible. If we didn't perform string comparisons, the next option would be to look up the words using array indexes, but how do we give a meaningful index to a word? What index would, for example, the word *conscious* have? The answer to these questions would be to perform a fast algorithm on the word to transform it into an array index and use that value to insert and look up the information we want. This is known as hashing, and we'll look at it more later in this chapter. Because hash tables are built from arrays, they can benefit from their look-up speeds as well.

Hash tables are not perfect data structures. There are a few things to keep in mind when deciding to use them:

- Hash tables have poor locality of reference due to objects being accessed in random locations in memory, which can also lead to cache misses in the CPU that can cause delays.
- Writing efficient hash tables and algorithms is error prone and can be difficult with advanced techniques.
- A good hash function is needed, or else the performance and general efficiency of a hash table can degrade in some situations.
- Many factors can affect the performance of a hash table, including the number of collisions as well as how full the container is when open addressing is being considered (more on this later).

EFFICIENCY OF HASHING

The efficiency of the hashing function is very important. Using a poor hash function can lead to collisions in the data structure. A collision occurs when more than one object hashes to the same index. When this happens, there are four things you can do. You can not insert the object, you can replace the old object with the new one, you can find a new position for the object using what is known as open addressing, or you can use separate chaining to allow more than one object to exist at an index. In this chapter we will look closely at open addressing techniques and separate chaining.

The collisions that occur in a hash table can have an adverse affect on overall performance, so the hash function that is used needs to be efficient. No hash function can guarantee that there will be no collisions, but when collisions do occur, they need to be resolved one way or another. The way the collision is resolved can depend on the application itself.

HASH FUNCTIONS

A hash function is an algorithm that takes a value and compresses it into the range of the hash table's array. This value is known as the key, and it can be anything from a string, to a number, and so fourth. The hash value of the key depends on the size of the hash table's array. A change in the array size will invalidate all hashed keys in the table, which will require them to be rehashed and the existing objects repositioned to new elements.

When a hash table is created, its size can be a prime number that is roughly twice the number of elements that will be inserted into the table. As we will see later on, using a prime number is necessary for some algorithms such as double hashing. Using a size that is twice the predicted number of inserted elements will likely decrease the number of collisions in the set.

HASHING VALUES

When hashing a key that is a number, we will use a simple equation to demonstrate how to create a hash function. This hash function will be based on the modulus operator (%) and will be used in conjunction with the array size to return a value that is within the array bounds. An example of this can look like the following line of code:

```
key % m_size;
```

By using this single line, we can hash a number to an index within the table's array, regardless of the number. The larger the size of the hash table's array, the better are the chances that there will not be a collision when a key is being hashed. A visual example of using this hash function on a key is shown in Figure 7.3.

Using a poor hash function can quickly lead to clustering, which means there is a greater probability that a hash function will hash values to the same index (causing collisions) than using a random function.

NOTE

Hashing with a table size of 23...

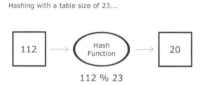

112 % 23

FIGURE 7.3 Hashing a number.

Hashing Strings

Another common type of key that we would like to hash is a string. To hash a string we would use a simple algorithm that loops through each letter of the key and use the modulus operator to build the hash value. When looping through the key, we can use both the current hash value, the total number of letters that can be used, and the value of the letter itself along with the modulus operator to create the hash value. Small strings can be quickly hashed in this manner, and the ability to hash strings is definitely something worth having. A visual example of hashing a string is shown in Figure 7.4. The code to hash a string could look like the following:

```
int HashFunction(string &str)
{
    int hash = 0;

    for(int i = 0; i < (int)str.size(); i++)
    {
        int val = (int)str[i];
        hash = (hash * 256 + val) % m_size;
    }

    return hash;
}
```

A good hash function needs to be computationally fast. Hash tables have the benefit of being fast, so a slow hash function will decrease this advantage.

NOTE

Hashing with a table size of 23...

FIGURE 7.4   Hashing a string.

WORKING WITH HASH TABLES

When working with hash tables, we first must find a position in the hash table that corresponds to an item. If we are inserting into the hash table and if an item is already at the position that we've just hashed another item to, then a collision will occur and a new position must be found for the item we are trying to insert. Even if we are not inserting, but are searching, if the item we are looking for is not the one at the initial hashed index, we must find it elsewhere, assuming it is even in the table. This is known as resolving collision, and we will talk briefly about it in this section.

Resolving collision when working with hash tables includes the major techniques called open addressing and separate chaining. We will discuss a few other types, such as hybrids, in the following section but these are the main two types. With open addressing there are three types: linear probing, quadric probing, and double hashing.

OPEN ADDRESSING: LINEAR PROBING

In linear probing if a collision occurs during an operation within the hash table, a new position must be sought. This is done by sequentially stepping through the hash table and looking for the next empty position. When a position is found, the item is inserted there. During a search we first hash the key to an array index. If the key at that index does not match the key we are searching for, then we must linearly step through the table until we find the value, find an empty slot, or have processed all elements.

Linear probing suffers from clustering, which occurs when a cluster of objects exist next to one another in the table. This slows down searching and will cause objects that actually hash to one of those positions to be inserted elsewhere, which again hurts searching. This is known as primary clustering. Imaging if you hashed item A to index 52. If item B also hashed to 52, it would need to be placed in a different position to resolve the collision. Let's say B is repositioned at 66, so if item C hashed to 66, it would need to be placed elsewhere because B is already there. When searching for B, time is spent looking for it because it is not where it would have normally hashed, and the same can be said for item C. In a large hash table items can be placed quite far from where they would have hashed, causing the linear search to move slowly when trying to find that item. If the item does not exist, a linear search until we have searched all elements or until we find an empty slot can be time consuming. As discussed in Chapter 2, a linear search is very slow. An illustration of linear probing is shown in Figure 7.5.

Linear Probing (searching for 7)...

Check 1	Check 2	Check 3	Check 4	
112	435	37	7	256

Total of 4 checks to find 7 in this small set...

FIGURE 7.5   Linear probing.

The more full a hash table is, the worse the clustering can get.

NOTE

OPEN ADDRESSING: QUADRIC PROBING

When a cluster forms, it continues to grow as items that would hash somewhere within it are pushed to the end of the cluster, which is the next available spot in the array. In linear probing, this cluster can form easily because the stepping through the table is done one at a time. Quadric probing uses the principles of the linear probing, but instead of moving one element at a time, it moves in multiple steps. When the ratio to the number of items to the hash table's size is low, clustering becomes more of a problem. A visual representation of quadric probing is shown in Figure 7.6.

Quadric Probing (searching for 7)...

Check 1			Check 2 (Step += 3)	
112	435	37	7	256

Total of 2 checks to find 7 in this small set...

FIGURE 7.6   Quadric probing.

In quadric probing, when stepping through the array, the operation first checks the first element after the initial hash position. If that position is taken, it tries four steps away from the position. If that position is also taken, it tries nine steps and so fourth until it finds a position or until it determines a position can't be found.

Quadric probing helps eliminate the primary clustering that linear probing suffers from, but it introduces a new problem known as secondary clustering. Although in most situations the secondary clustering might not be as much of a problem as the linear probe's primary clustering, it is still a problem. The secondary clustering occurs because the change in the step sizes is constant. If the changes were random or pseudo-random, the problem would decrease.

OPEN ADDRESSING: DOUBLE HASHING

Double hashing works by using a different hash function to hash the key to a new position when a collision has occurred. Because the new position is based on the key, it will be different for each item. Since the primary reason for clustering is the use of constant steps, double hashing can work quite well to reduce clustering in a hash table. In double hashing the key requirements of the second hash function include that the function can't be the same as the first and can't return an index of 0 to the caller. In this chapter we will use the following equation when looking at double hashing:

```
double hash = constant - (key % constant)
```

where the new step (double hash) is equal to a constant, which is a number that is not 0 and is within the range of the array's size, minus the result of the key % constant. When using this formula, it is important that the array size be prime in order to avoid situations where only a few elements are searched infinitely. An example of this can be seen with an array size of 20 and an initial hash index of 0. If the double hash returns 5, the stepping would go from 0, 5, 10, 15, 20, 5, 10, 15, 20, and so forth. A visual representation of double hashing is shown in Figure 7.7.

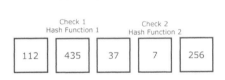

FIGURE 7.7   Double hashing.

MORE ON OPEN ADDRESSING

When looking at opening addressing as a whole compared to separate chaining, which will be discussed in detail in the next section, we find that the following is often true:

- Open addressing does not need to allocate additional memory upon collisions.
- Open addressing with linear and quadric probing suffers from various clustering side effects.
- Open addressing in hash tables is easier to serialize than separate chaining because it is based on arrays.
- Open addressing has a better locality of reference with small tables, which can lead to better performance.
- Open addressing is generally better for smaller tables.
- When using double hashing, it is important to have a prime table size.

The ratio of the total number of items to the hash table's size is known as the load factor.

NOTE

SEPARATE CHAINING

Separate chaining is another technique that can be used to resolve collisions in a hash table. In open addressing the next open position is searched for upon a collision. Instead of looking for another position, separate chaining uses a link list for every element in the hash table's array. This means that if there is a collision, the item is inserted into that index's link list. When searching for an item, we can perform a normal search on the link list at that index. Using a fast searching algorithm can be very useful in the link list when using separate chaining. Separate chaining is illustrated in Figure 7.8. In separate chaining, unlike double hashing and quadric probing, it is not important to have prime table sizes.

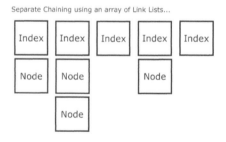

FIGURE 7.8 Separate chaining.

Things to keep in mind when working with separate chaining in hash tables are:

- It is simple to implement with link lists.
- Separate chaining can use less memory than open addressing since the links are only created when necessary.

- Less space is wasted with separate chaining than with large tables using open addressing.
- Using a table with open addressing that stores pointers to external storage can cause them to lose their speed advantage.
- Separate chaining is better for large tables.
- In separate chaining the array size is important to help minimize collisions, but when one occurs, the link list can grow as needed, which is different from resizing the table's array since that would invalidate all hashed keys.

ADDITIONAL TYPES OF HASHING

Additional types of hash tables are used for resolving collisions in the hash table data structure. In this section we will briefly discuss coalesced hashing, robin-hood hashing, perfect hashing, and probabilistic hashing.

Coalesced hashing is a hybrid of open addressing and separate chaining that links together chains of nodes within the table itself. By using coalesced hashing we can achieve the space usage of open addressing while eliminating the clustering effect, which separate chaining is known for solving.

Robin-hood hashing is a variation of double hashing. This is where a key is displaced by an already existing key if the probe count is larger than the key at a position. Robin-hood hashing tries to minimize the performance penalty of searching for items in the data structure when compared to the open addressing techniques that were discussed in this chapter.

In probabilistic hashing when a collision is encountered, it will either drop the new value trying to be inserted or it will simply replace the new value with the one that is already there. This type of hashing system can be used to implement a caching system and to implement a bloom filter with the help of a bit array. When using probabilistic hashing, there are no collisions because values are dropped when collisions might occur. This means there is no need for separate chaining or open addressing since the item is either at the original hash position or it is not.

In perfect hashing a hash table with no collisions can be created if all the keys are known ahead of time and the array size is already known. A slight variation of this is called minimal perfect hashing, in which all elements of the data structure can be occupied by an object, but there are no collisions within the structure.

With perfect hashing there are no collisions; thus there is no need to have collision solvers such as the open addressing methods and separate chaining discussed earlier.

TABLE RESIZING

It is difficult to resize a hash table data structure, because once the table is resized, all keys will need to be rehashed and all items reinserted. For small hash tables and with table resizing being rare, this is not too serious of a problem if resizing the table is the best option at that moment. For larger hash tables the resizing operation can cause a serious delay. Also, when resizing the hash table, incrementing the size by 1 every time a resize needs to happen will result in horrible performance.

If the need to resize a hash table arises, the best option would be to increase the size by a load factor. This factor can be a percentage that tells the data structure how much to increase the size of the array. If the load factor is 1 (100%), the size of the array can double each time a resize is needed. For 10 elements this will create a new size of 20, which if further expanded would create a new size of 40, then 80, and so on. By choosing to not increase the size by 1 you can dramatically reduce the number of resize operations that need to occur, although it would be better to not need to resize at all (if possible) when dealing with very large data sets.

In separate chaining the link list objects would also need to be rehashed. Because the hash table size is different, the objects that collided before will not necessarily collide again. Usually the collisions will change, so there are no short cuts when working with separate chaining.

IMPLEMENTING HASH TABLES

In this section we will implement hash tables using linear probing, double hashing, separate chaining, and various nonstandard C++ template hash table containers. The STL, at this time, does not have hash tables, so we will be using freely available nonstandard hash tables in addition to creating custom implementations. When implementing each type of hash table, we will use prime table sizes because prime numbers can decrease clustering. This is because if many keys share a divisor with the array size, then many keys can end up hashing to the same index. This can happen regardless of the hashing type, so prime numbers will be used for each of the implementations.

HASH KEYS

The keys are the first things that need to be implemented, as this is an important start to creating a hash table. The hash items that will be implemented in this chapter have two member variables: the key and a template object that is to be inserted, along with the key, in the hash table. The key is an integer that is hashed by the hash table, while the object can be anything. The member functions of the class include functions for getting and setting the key, getting and setting the object, making one hash item equal to another, and a boolean comparison function (==) for comparing two hash items. The hash item template class, called HashItem, is shown in Listing 7.1. This class will be used for each of the custom-implemented hash table data structures in this chapter.

LISTING 7.1   The Hash Item Structure that is Inserted into the Table

```
template<typename T>
class HashItem
{
   public:
      HashItem() : m_key(0) {}
      ~HashItem() {}


      int GetKey()        { return m_key; }
      void SetKey(int k) { m_key = k; }


      T GetObject()       { return m_obj; }
      void SetObj(T obj) { m_obj = obj; }


      bool operator==(HashItem &item)
      {
         if(m_key == item.GetKey())
            return true;

         return false;
      }

      void operator=(HashItem item)
      {
         m_key = item.GetKey();
         m_obj = item.GetObject();
      }


   private:
      int m_key;
      T m_obj;
};
```

HASH TABLE WITH LINEAR PROBING

The first hash table that will be implemented is the linear probing hash table. In this hash table, when a collision occurs, the hash table will linearly step through the data structure until it finds a new location for the item. The first functions we will look at are the class's constructor, destructor, and two helper functions for calculating a prime number if one is not supplied. The constructor is responsible for creating the table's array, the destructor will delete the array, and the constructor uses the helper functions for calculating the next prime number after the number that was passed to the constructor, assuming the number is not already prime. This is shown in Listing 7.2.

LISTING 7.2 The First Few Functions of the Hash Table for Linear Probing

```
template<typename T>
class HashTable
{
   public:
      HashTable(int size) : m_size(0), m_totalItems(0)
      {
         if(size > 0)
         {
            m_size = GetNextPrimeNum(size);
            m_table = new HashItem<T>[m_size];
         }
      }


      ~HashTable()
      {
         if(m_table != NULL)
         {
            delete[] m_table;
            m_table = NULL;
         }
      }


   private:
      bool isNumPrime(int val)
      {
         for(int i = 2; (i * i) <= val; i++)
         {
            if((val % i) == 0)
               return false;
         }

         return true;
      }
```

```
int GetNextPrimeNum(int val)
{
   for(int i = val + 1; ; i++)
   {
      if(isNumPrime(i))
         break;
   }

   return i;
}
};
```

The next three functions we'll look at for the linear probing hash table are the insertion function called `Insert()`, the deletion function called `Delete()`, and the searching function called `Find()`. The insertion function takes a key and an object to place in the hash table. As long as there are some empty slots in the hash table, the function can insert the item, or else it returns `false`. The function starts by hashing the key and testing if the index is empty. If it is, the item is directly inserted, or else the code will step through until it finds an empty slot. The modulus operator is used to wrap around the array until that empty slot is found.

The deletion function works in the same manner as the insertion function, with the exception that it nullifies the key of the item to be deleted, which marks it as free in the hash table, instead of adding it. The searching function works using almost the same code as the insertion and deletion functions, with the exception that when the item is found (by comparing the keys), the object is returned to a pointer parameter and either `true` is returned or `false` is returned if the item is not found. In the deletion and searching functions a temporary variable is used to test if the original hash value matches the hash value after being stepped. Since the stepping can wrap around the array, to avoid an infinite loop with full arrays this condition is added to allow the code to know that every item was searched and the item was not found. Each of these three functions are shown in Listing 7.3.

LISTING 7.3   The Insertion, Deletion, and Searching Functions of the Hash Table

```
template<typename T>
class HashTable
{
   public:
      bool Insert(int key, T &obj)
      {
         if(m_totalItems == m_size)
            return false;
```

```
            int hash = HashFunction(key);

            while(m_table[hash].GetKey() != -1)
            {
               hash++;
               hash %= m_size;
            }

            m_table[hash].SetKey(key);
            m_table[hash].SetObj(obj);

            m_totalItems++;

            return true;
         }


         void Delete(int key)
         {
            int hash = HashFunction(key);
            int originalHash = hash;

            while(m_table[hash].GetKey() != -1)
            {
               if(m_table[hash].GetKey() == key)
               {
                  m_table[hash].SetKey(-1);
                  m_totalItems-;

                  return;
               }

               hash++;
               hash %= m_size;

               if(originalHash == hash)
                  return;
            }
         }


         bool Find(int key, T *obj)
         {
            int hash = HashFunction(key);
```

```
        int originalHash = hash;

        while(m_table[hash].GetKey() != -1)
        {
            if(m_table[hash].GetKey() == key)
            {
                if(obj != NULL)
                    *obj = m_table[hash].GetObject();

                return true;
            }

            hash++;
            hash %= m_size;

            if(originalHash == hash)
                return false;
        }

        return false;
    }
```

The remainder of the linear probing hash table includes two hash functions (one for hashing integers and one for strings), a function for returning the total size of the hash table, a function for returning the total number of items in the hash table, and member variables for the table's array, total size, and total number of items already inserted. The hash functions use the same code that was seen earlier in this chapter, while the remainder of the class is straightforward. For strings the class uses the STL class string. We'll cover strings in more detail later on in the book. For now, know that STL strings can be used like an array of characters. The class offers various overloaded operators that make it very similar to working with strings using an array of char variables. The remainder of the linear probing hash table, called HashTable, is shown in Listing 7.4. The entire class is shown in Listing 7.5.

LISTING 7.4   The Remainder of the Linear Probing Hash Table

```
template<typename T>
class HashTable
{
    public:
        int HashFunction(int key)
        {
```

```
                return key % m_size;
        }


        int HashFunction(string &str)
        {
           int hash = 0;

           for(int i = 0; i < (int)str.size(); i++)
           {
              int val = (int)str[i];
              hash = (hash * 256 + val) % m_size;
           }

           return hash;
        }


        int GetSize()
        {
           return m_size;
        }


        int GetTotalItems()
        {
           return m_totalItems;
        }


   private:
        HashItem<T> *m_table;
        int m_size, m_totalItems;
};
```

LISTING 7.5 The Entire `HashTable` Class for Linear Probing

```
template<typename T>
class HashTable
{
   public:
        HashTable(int size) : m_size(0), m_totalItems(0)
        {
           if(size > 0)
```

```
      {
         m_size = GetNextPrimeNum(size);
         m_table = new HashItem<T>[m_size];
      }
   }


   ~HashTable()
   {
      if(m_table != NULL)
      {
         delete[] m_table;
         m_table = NULL;
      }
   }


private:
   bool isNumPrime(int val)
   {
      for(int i = 2; (i * i) <= val; i++)
      {
         if((val % i) == 0)
            return false;
      }

      return true;
   }


   int GetNextPrimeNum(int val)
   {
      for(int i = val + 1; ; i++)
      {
         if(isNumPrime(i))
            break;
      }

      return i;
   }


public:
   bool Insert(int key, T &obj)
```

```
   {
      if(m_totalItems == m_size)
         return false;

      int hash = HashFunction(key);

      while(m_table[hash].GetKey() != -1)
      {
         hash++;
         hash %= m_size;
      }

      m_table[hash].SetKey(key);
      m_table[hash].SetObj(obj);

      m_totalItems++;

      return true;
   }


   void Delete(int key)
   {
      int hash = HashFunction(key);
      int originalHash = hash;

      while(m_table[hash].GetKey() != -1)
      {
         if(m_table[hash].GetKey() == key)
         {
            m_table[hash].SetKey(-1);
            m_totalItems-;

            return;
         }

         hash++;
         hash %= m_size;

         if(originalHash == hash)
            return;
      }
   }
```

```cpp
bool Find(int key, T *obj)
{
    int hash = HashFunction(key);
    int originalHash = hash;

    while(m_table[hash].GetKey() != -1)
    {
        if(m_table[hash].GetKey() == key)
        {
            if(obj != NULL)
                *obj = m_table[hash].GetObject();

            return true;
        }

        hash++;
        hash %= m_size;

        if(originalHash == hash)
            return false;
    }

    return false;
}


int HashFunction(int key)
{
    return key % m_size;
}


int HashFunction(string &str)
{
    int hash = 0;

    for(int i = 0; i < (int)str.size(); i++)
    {
        int val = (int)str[i];
        hash = (hash * 256 + val) % m_size;
    }

    return hash;
}
```

```
        int GetSize()
        {
            return m_size;
        }


    private:
        HashItem<T> *m_table;
        int m_size, m_totalItems;
};
```

On the accompanying CD-ROM a demo application called Linear Probing in the Chapter 7 folder demonstrates the hash table class created in Listing 7.5. In this demo application an integer hash table is created, populated with a few items, and is searched for various keys. When a key is found, a message is displayed with the key and the object it references. When a key is not found, an Item not Found message is displayed. Additionally, the demo application tests that a string is able to be hashed into an index by hashing the word *cats* and displaying its hashed value to the console window. The main.cpp source file of this demo application is shown in Listing 7.6. Figure 7.9 shows a screenshot of the executing application.

LISTING 7.6   The Linear Probing Demo Application

```
#include<iostream>
#include"HashTable.h"

using namespace std;


int main(int args, char **argc)
{
    cout << "Hash Tables - Linear Probing Example" << endl;
    cout << "Chapter 7: Hash Tables" << endl;
    cout << endl;


    // Create table and fill it in.
    HashTable<int> hashTable(20);
    int item = 0;

    item = 348;    hashTable.Insert(112, item);
    item = 841;    hashTable.Insert(87,  item);
    item = 654;    hashTable.Insert(24,  item);
```

```
item = 11;     hashTable.Insert(66,  item);
item = 156;    hashTable.Insert(222, item);


// Search for inserted items.
if(hashTable.Find(87, &item))
   cout << "Item: 87 has a value of " << item << "." << endl;
else
   cout << "Item: 87 not found." << endl;

if(hashTable.Find(112, &item))
   cout << "Item: 112 has a value of " << item << "." << endl;
else
   cout << "Item: 112 not found." << endl;

if(hashTable.Find(66, &item))
   cout << "Item: 66 has a value of " << item << "." << endl;
else
   cout << "Item: 66 not found." << endl;

if(hashTable.Find(100, &item))
   cout << "Item: 100 has a value of " << item << "." << endl;
else
   cout << "Item: 100 not found." << endl;

cout << "\n";


// Test hashing a string.
string str("cats");
int stringHash = hashTable.HashFunction(str);

cout << "The string cats hash to " << stringHash
     << "." << endl << endl;

return 1;
}
```

This demo application can be expanded to perform quadric probing. This can be done by modifying the linear step in the insertion, deletion, and searching functions to use a varying step value instead of doing so by 1, which can be seen in the lines that contain hash++. Since such a modification is trivial, expanding this demo application to perform quadric probing is left as an exercise at the end of the chapter.

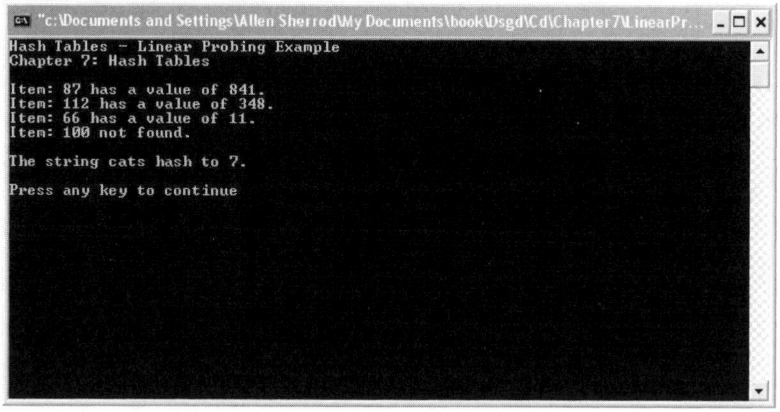

FIGURE 7.9   A screenshot of the Linear Probing demo.

HASH TABLE WITH DOUBLE HASHING

The next type of hashing we will implement in code is the double hashing technique. In this type of hashing a second hash function is used for the hashing of keys that collide with other keys. Double hashing is done in the insertion, deletion, and searching functions of the hash table. Because those are the only functions that differ, we will use the code for the linear probing hash table and modify it for double hashing. The double hashing code, as in what was modified from the linear probing code in Listing 7.5, is shown in listing 7.7.

LISTING 7.7   The Double Hashing Code

```
template<typename T>
class HashTable
{
   public:
      bool Insert(int key, T &obj)
      {
         if(m_totalItems == m_size)
            return false;

         int hash = HashFunction(key);
         int step = HashFunction2(key);

         while(m_table[hash].GetKey() != -1)
         {
            hash += step;
```

```
        hash %= m_size;
    }

    m_table[hash].SetKey(key);
    m_table[hash].SetObj(obj);

    m_totalItems++;

    return true;
}


void Delete(int key)
{
    int hash = HashFunction(key);
    int step = HashFunction2(key);
    int originalHash = hash;

    while(m_table[hash].GetKey() != -1)
    {
        if(m_table[hash].GetKey() == key)
        {
            m_table[hash].SetKey(-1);
            m_totalItems-;

            return;
        }

        hash += step;
        hash %= m_size;

        if(originalHash == hash)
            return;
    }
}


bool Find(int key, T *obj)
{
    int hash = HashFunction(key);
    int step = HashFunction2(key);
    int originalHash = hash;
```

```
        while(m_table[hash].GetKey() != -1)
        {
            if(m_table[hash].GetKey() == key)
            {
                if(obj != NULL)
                    *obj = m_table[hash].GetObject();

                return true;
            }

            hash += step;
            hash %= m_size;

            if(originalHash == hash)
                return false;
        }

        return false;
    }


    int HashFunction(int key)
    {
        return key % m_size;
    }


    int HashFunction2(int key)
    {
        return 3 - key % 3;
    }
};
```

The difference between the code for the double hashing hash table and the linear probe is that the linear probe has a constant step size of 1, while the double hashing step size is determined by the new hash function, HashFunction2(). In Listing 7.7 the second hash function is different from the first. This is a requirement that prevents us from ending up with the same number, which would report a collision (if one existed) and leave us where we started. Also, prime numbers are required with the quadric probing and double hashing to ensure that every element in the hash table's array is visited.

ON THE CD

On the accompanying CD-ROM a demo application in the Chapter 7 folder called Double Hashing demonstrates the double hashing hash table discussed in this section. The main source file for this demo application is the same as the Linear Probing demo, with the exception that different keys and values are used to distinguish between them. The main.cpp source files are, for all intents and purposes, the same because the only real difference occurs inside the data structure and its algorithms. The main.cpp source file for the Double Hashing demo application is shown in Listing 7.8. Figure 7.10 shows a screenshot of the running demo application.

LISTING 7.8   The Double Hashing Demo's main.cpp Source File

```cpp
#include<iostream>
#include"HashTable.h"

using namespace std;


int main(int args, char **argc)
{
   cout << "Hash Tables - Double Hashing Example" << endl;
   cout << "Chapter 7: Hash Tables" << endl;
   cout << endl;


   // Create table and fill it in.
   HashTable<int> hashTable(20);
   int item = 0;

   item = 835;   hashTable.Insert(57, item);
   item = 247;   hashTable.Insert(68, item);
   item = 456;   hashTable.Insert(37, item);
   item = 235;   hashTable.Insert(82, item);
   item = 644;   hashTable.Insert(11, item);


   // Search for inserted items.
   if(hashTable.Find(87, &item))
      cout << "Item: 87 has a value of " << item << "." << endl;
   else
      cout << "Item: 87 not found." << endl;

   if(hashTable.Find(112, &item))
      cout << "Item: 112 has a value of " << item << "." << endl;
   else
      cout << "Item: 112 not found." << endl;
```

```
        if(hashTable.Find(82, &item))
           cout << "Item: 82 has a value of " << item << "." << endl;
        else
           cout << "Item: 82 not found." << endl;

        if(hashTable.Find(37, &item))
           cout << "Item: 37 has a value of " << item << "." << endl;
        else
           cout << "Item: 37 not found." << endl;

        cout << endl;


        return 1;
    }
```

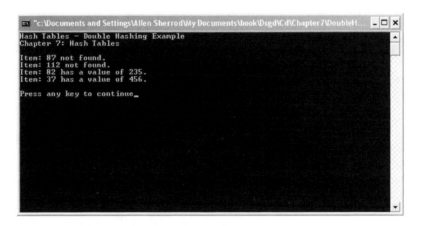

FIGURE 7.10   A screenshot of the Double Hashing demo.

HASH TABLE WITH SEPARATE CHAINING

The last type of custom hash table that will be implemented in this chapter uses separate chaining. For this we will have an array of STL list link list data structures. Since items that collide are added to that index's link list, we do not need to have checks to make sure every element is checked like we did for the first two types of hash tables (which were used to prevent infinite loops). When an element is inserted into the hash table, the key is hashed and that element's push_back() function is called to insert the item into that index's link list. For the deletion and searching functions those work by hashing the key and using STL list iterators to move through that index's link list to find the item we are looking for. Otherwise, the remainder of the separate chaining hash table is the same as the other two types. Since the link list can grow without affecting our hash table at each element, we don't need to keep track of how many items are inserted into the hash table. We had to keep track of that before to avoid trying to insert an item into an array that was full. Since there are no free slots, it would be a waste of CPU time to search the array to come to that conclusion. With arrays that are in the hundreds of thousands or millions, this can add up. In separate chaining we don't have to worry about running out of room, unless we want to limit the number of items.

The hash table code for separate chaining is shown in Listing 7.9. Because we are using STL link lists, the code for some functions is easier to grasp and examine than that for the double hashing and linear probing code.

LISTING 7.9   The Entire Hash Table that Uses Separate Chaining

```
template<typename T>
class HashTable
{
   public:
      HashTable(int size) : m_size(0)
      {
         if(size > 0)
         {
            m_size = GetNextPrimeNum(size);
            m_table = new list<HashItem<T> >[m_size];
         }
      }


      ~HashTable()
      {
         if(m_table != NULL)
         {
            delete[] m_table;
            m_table = NULL;
         }
      }


      bool isNumPrime(int val)
      {
         for(int i = 2; (i * i) <= val; i++)
         {
            if((val % i) == 0)
```

```
               return false;
         }

         return true;
}


int GetNextPrimeNum(int val)
{
    for(int i = val + 1; ; i++)
    {
        if(isNumPrime(i))
            break;
    }

    return i;
}


void Insert(int key, T &obj)
{
    HashItem<T> item;
    item.SetKey(key);
    item.SetObj(obj);

    int hash = HashFunction(key);
    m_table[hash].push_back(item);
}


void Delete(int key)
{
    int hash = HashFunction(key);

    list<HashItem<T> > *ptr = &m_table[hash];
    typename list<HashItem<T> >::iterator it;

    for(it = ptr->begin(); it != ptr->end(); it++)
    {
        if((*it).GetKey() == key)
        {
            ptr->erase(it);
            break;
        }
```

```
        }
    }


bool Find(int key, T *obj)
{
    int hash = HashFunction(key);

    list<HashItem<T> > *ptr = &m_table[hash];
    typename list<HashItem<T> >::iterator it;

    for(it = ptr->begin(); it != ptr->end(); it++)
    {
        if((*it).GetKey() == key)
        {
            if(obj != NULL)
                *obj = (*it).GetObject();

            return true;
        }
    }

    return false;
}


int HashFunction(int key)
{
    return key % m_size;
}


int HashFunction(string &str)
{
    int hash = 0;
    int i = 0;

    for(i = 0; i < (int)str.size(); i++)
    {
        int val = (int)str[i];
        hash = (hash * 256 + val) % m_size;
    }

    return hash;
}
```

```
        int GetSize()
        {
            return m_size;
        }


    private:
        list<HashItem<T> > *m_table;
        int m_size;
};
```

On the accompanying CD-ROM is a demo application called Separate Chaining in the Chapter 7 folder that demonstrates the separate chaining hash table. In the demo application, like the Double Hashing demo, all of the real work occurs inside the data structure, so the main source file is straightforward and is no different than what was already seen (with the exception of different keys and values). The main source file for the Separate Chaining demo application is shown in Listing 7.10. Figure 7.11 shows a screenshot of the running demo application.

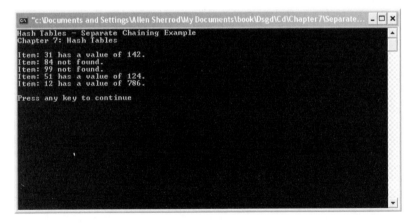

FIGURE 7.11 A screenshot of the Separate Chaining demo.

LISTING 7.10 The Main Source File for the Separate Chaining Demo Application

```
#include<iostream>
#include"HashTable.h"


using namespace std;
```

```cpp
int main(int args, char **argc)
{
   cout << "Hash Tables - Separate Chaining Example" << endl;
   cout << "Chapter 7: Hash Tables" << endl;
   cout << endl;


   HashTable<int> hashTable(21);
   int item = 0;

   item = 142;    hashTable.Insert(31, item);
   item = 756;    hashTable.Insert(42, item);
   item = 432;    hashTable.Insert(24, item);
   item = 124;    hashTable.Insert(51, item);
   item = 786;    hashTable.Insert(12, item);


   // Search for inserted items.
   if(hashTable.Find(31, &item))
      cout << "Item: 31 has a value of " << item << "." << endl;
   else
      cout << "Item: 31 not found." << endl;

   if(hashTable.Find(84, &item))
      cout << "Item: 84 has a value of " << item << "." << endl;
   else
      cout << "Item: 84 not found." << endl;

   if(hashTable.Find(99, &item))
      cout << "Item: 99has a value of " << item << "." << endl;
   else
      cout << "Item: 99 not found." << endl;

   if(hashTable.Find(51, &item))
      cout << "Item: 51 has a value of " << item << "." << endl;
   else
      cout << "Item: 51 not found." << endl;

   if(hashTable.Find(12, &item))
      cout << "Item: 12 has a value of " << item << "." << endl;
   else
      cout << "Item: 12 not found." << endl;

   cout << "\n";


   return 1;
}
```

In some situations it might be better to resize the hash table than to keep allowing link lists to get too large. This depends on many factors, especially the size of the table, but if too many keys are hashing to the same indexes, the issues with collisions might be alleviated by resizing the hash table.

NONSTANDARD HASH CONTAINERS

Hash tables are very useful data structures to have available to programmers. In the STL there are no hash tables to use at this time. This isn't the end of hash tables, as many STL-compatible containers can be used that are created by different sources. In this chapter we will look at the `hash_set`, `hash_multiset`, `hash_map`, and `hash_mutlimap` containers that are part of the STLport. Different sources code their hash implementations differently, so when using other hash containers not from STL-port, which are based on the containers from Silicon Graphics, Inc. (SGI), you'll have to read the documentation. Appendix E provides information for downloading and setting up STLport in an application.

Hashed containers are associate containers. This means, among other things, that we must specify the data type of the objects being stored, a hashing function, a comparison function, and, optionally, the allocator.

hash_set AND hash_multiset CONTAINERS

The `hash_set` container allows an object being inserted into the hash table container to be hashed (i.e., both the key and the object) and inserted. When creating a `hash_set` container, we can specify the object's data type, the hash function, a comparison function, and an allocator (which is always optional). The `hash_set` offers iterators for moving through the hash table data structure.

On the accompanying CD-ROM is a demo application called Hash Set in the Chapter 7 folder. The main source file for the demo application is shown in Listing 7.11 and a screenshot of the demo is shown in Figure 7.12. The demo application is a simple example of how to set up and use the container.

LISTING 7.11   The Hash Set Demo Application

```
#include<iostream>
#include<hash_set>


using namespace _STL;
using namespace std;
```

```
struct cmp
{
   bool operator()(const char *str1, const char *str2) const
   {
      return strcmp(str1, str2) == 0;
   }
};


void Find(const hash_set<const char*, hash<const char*>, cmp> &c,
          const char *str)
{
   hash_set<const char*, hash<const char*>,
           cmp>::const_iterator it = c.find(str);

   if(it == c.end())
      cout << str << " - was not found!" << endl;
   else
      cout << str << " - was found in the hash table!" << endl;
}


int main(int args, char **argc)
{
   cout << "Hash Tables - Hash Set Example" << endl;
   cout << "Chapter 7: Hash Tables" << endl;
   cout << endl;


   hash_set<const char*, hash<const char*>, cmp> hashTable;

   hashTable.insert("Hello");
   hashTable.insert("Goodbye");
   hashTable.insert("So Long");
   hashTable.insert("Take Care");

   Find(hashTable, "Test");
   Find(hashTable, "Example");
   Find(hashTable, "Hello");
   Find(hashTable, "Take Care");
   Find(hashTable, "Good Night");

   cout << endl;


   return 1;
}
```

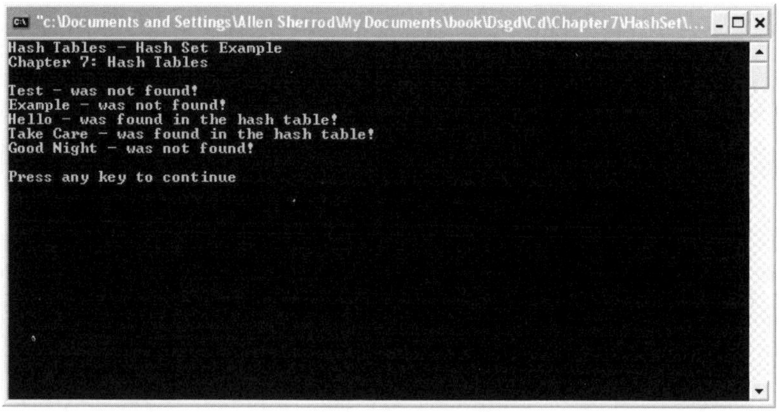

FIGURE 7.12   A screenshot of the Hash Set demo.

hash_multiset containers are useful for objects that need to be searched for quickly. The hash_multiset is very similar to the hash_set. They both specify objects that are also keys, and they both implement the same methods and parameters.

On the CD-ROM another demo application demonstrates using the hash_multiset in code, which is the same as using a hash_set. This application is in the Chapter 7 folder and is called Hash Multiset. The main source file for the Hash Multiset demo application is shown in Listing 7.12 and a screenshot of the demo is shown in Figure 7.13.

LISTING 7.12   The Main Source File for the Hash Multiset Demo

```
#include<iostream>
#include<hash_set>


using namespace _STL;
using namespace std;


struct cmp
{
   bool operator()(const char *str1, const char *str2) const
   {
      return strcmp(str1, str2) == 0;
   }
};
```

```
void Find(const hash_multiset<const char*,
          hash<const char*>, cmp> &c, const char *str)
{
   hash_multiset<const char*, hash<const char*>,
                 cmp>::const_iterator it = c.find(str);

   if(it == c.end())
      cout << str << " - was not found!" << endl;
   else
      cout << str << " - was found in the hash table!" << endl;
}


int main(int args, char **argc)
{
   cout << "Hash Tables - Hash Multi-Set Example" << endl;
   cout << "Chapter 7: Hash Tables" << endl;
   cout << endl;


   hash_multiset<const char*, hash<const char*>, cmp> hashTable;

   if(hashTable.empty() == true)
      cout << "The hash table is now empty." << endl;

   hashTable.insert("Data Structures");
   hashTable.insert("And");
   hashTable.insert("Algorithms");
   hashTable.insert("For Game Developers");


   cout << "The hash table has " << hashTable.size()
        << " items after insertions." << endl << endl;


   Find(hashTable, "Wow");
   Find(hashTable, "And");
   Find(hashTable, "Data Structures");

   cout << endl;


   return 1;
}
```

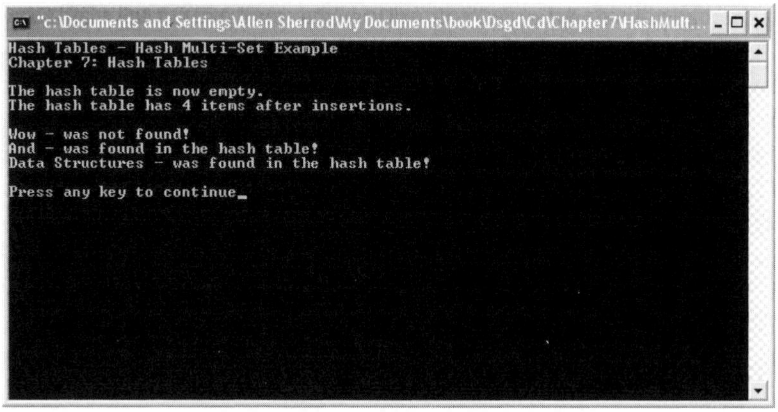

FIGURE 7.13 A screenshot of the Hash Multiset demo.

NOTE

When working with Visual Studio® .NET 2003 and higher be sure to turn off Use Managed Extensions in the properties of the Integrated Development Environment (IDE) when compiling STLport code.

Hash_Map AND Hash_Multimap CONTAINERS

The `hash_map` and the `hash_multimap` are hashed associate containers. With the `hash_map` container you can specify keys by using array subscripts and words instead of having to call functions to insert items as was seen with the `hash_set` and `hash_multiset` containers. For example, inserting a value `val` into the hash table using the key "example" would look like the following:

```
Table["example"] = val
```

The hash table, when using the `hash_map`, will create the hash item that stores `val` and has the key "example" simply by using the overloaded array subscript operators. This can be very useful for many things, such as a dictionary, and can make working with the data structures very easy.

ON THE CD

On the accompanying CD-ROM in the Chapter 7 folder is a demo application called Hash Map. This demo application will create a hash map, of type `hash_map`, and use the overloaded array subscripts to read and write elements to the data structure. All of the hard work is done internally, and on the outside the data structure looks almost like a normal array. The main source file for the Hash Map demo application is shown in Listing 7.13. Figure 7.14 shows a screenshot of it.

LISTING 7.13   The Demo Application for the Hash Map Demo Application.

```cpp
#include<iostream>
#include<hash_map>


using namespace _STL;
using namespace std;


struct cmp
{
   bool operator()(const char *str1, const char *str2) const
   {
      return strcmp(str1, str2) == 0;
   }
};


int main(int args, char **argc)
{
   cout << "Hash Tables - Hash Map Example" << endl;
   cout << "Chapter 7: Hash Tables" << endl;
   cout << endl;


   hash_map<const char*, int, hash<const char*>, cmp> hashTable;

   if(hashTable.empty() == true)
      cout << "The hash table is now empty." << endl;

   hashTable["DVD"] = 30;
   hashTable["Apple"] = 1;
   hashTable["Video Game"] = 59;


   cout << "The hash table has " << hashTable.size()
        << " items after insertions." << endl << endl;


   cout << "DVD - " << hashTable["DVD"] << endl;
   cout << "Apple - " << hashTable["Apple"] << endl;
   cout << "Video Game - " << hashTable["Video Game"] << endl;
   cout << "PS3 - " << hashTable["PS3"] << endl;
```

```
cout << endl;


return 1;
}
```

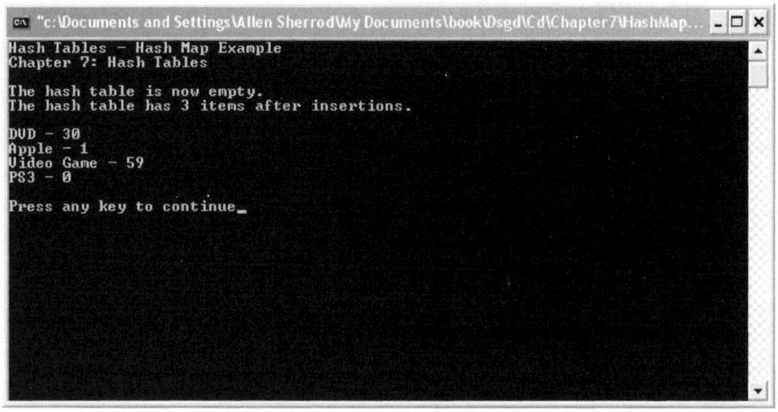

FIGURE 7.14 A screenshot of the Hash Map demo.

The hash_multimap does not use array subscripts like the hash_map container. A hash_multimap is a container that manages an ordered key/value pair, and more than one value can be associated with a key. A hash_multimap is similar to a multimap in its interface. Items are inserted into the container using the value_type of the hash_mutltimap container to pair the key and the object together when calling the insert() function. As with the hash_multiset, the objects in the container can be searched using iterators.

On the CD-ROM is a demo application called Hash Multimap that demonstrates the basics of setting up and using the hash_multimap container. The demo's main source file is shown in Listing 7.14, and a screenshot of the demo is shown in Figure 7.15.

LISTING 7.14 The Hash Multimap Demo's Main Source File.

```
#include<iostream>
#include<hash_map>


using namespace _STL;
using namespace std;
```

```
struct cmp
{
   bool operator()(const char *str1, const char *str2) const
   {
      return strcmp(str1, str2) == 0;
   }
};


typedef hash_multimap<const char*, int, hash<const char*>,
                     cmp> hashType;


void Find(const hashType &hTable, const char *str)
{
   cout << str << " - ";

   pair<hashType::const_iterator,
       hashType::const_iterator> range = hTable.equal_range(str);

   hashType::const_iterator it;

   for(it = range.first; it != range.second; it++)
      cout << (*it).second << " ";

   cout << endl;
}


int main(int args, char **argc)
{
   cout << "Hash Tables - Hash Multi-hTable Example" << endl;
   cout << "Chapter 7: Hash Tables" << endl;
   cout << endl;


   hashType hashTable;

   if(hashTable.empty() == true)
      cout << "The hash table is now empty." << endl;

   hashTable.insert(hashType::value_type("DVD", 30));
   hashTable.insert(hashType::value_type("Apple", 1));
   hashTable.insert(hashType::value_type("Video Game", 59));
```

```
        cout << "The hash table has " << hashTable.size()
            << " items after insertions." << endl << endl;


        Find(hashTable, "DVD");
        Find(hashTable, "Apple");
        Find(hashTable, "Video Game");
        Find(hashTable, "PS3");

        cout << endl;


        return 1;
    }
```

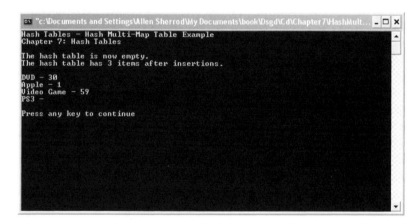

FIGURE 7.15 A screenshot of the Hash Multimap demo.

SUMMARY

In this chapter we've discussed many types of hash tables and collision solvers and implemented hash tables using linear probing, double hashing, and separate chaining. We also discussed and worked with nonstandard hash table containers that are available through the STLport. When working with hash tables the following is important to keep in mind:

■ Hash tables are based on arrays, which makes item lookups fast (although collisions can affect that).

- It is possible to serialize hash tables that use open addressing techniques.
- The load factor is the ratio of the number of items to the size of the array.
- Collisions can have a negative effect on hash table performance.
- Clustering is a problem in open addressing techniques.
- The two types of clustering discussed in this chapter were primary clustering and secondary clustering.
- Cache misses can affect hash table performance.
- A hash function needs to be fast, which fits with the overall benefit of the hash table data structure.

In the next chapter we will revisit sorting by looking at some advanced techniques. The algorithms that will be discussed each have their own strengths and weaknesses that we will discuss in great detail.

CHAPTER REVIEW QUESTIONS

Answers to the following chapter review questions can be found in Appendix B.

1. What is the load factor?
2. What is open addressing? What are the three types that were discussed in this chapter?
3. What is separate chaining?
4. What is linear probing?
5. What is quadric probing?
6. What is double hashing?
7. What is the primary problem that can be encountered with linear probing?
   a. Primary clustering
   b. Secondary clustering
   c. None of the above
8. What is the primary problem that can be encountered with quadric probing?
   a. Primary clustering
   b. Secondary clustering
   c. None of the above
9. Why is it recommended that you use a prime number as the array size when working with double hashing and quadric probing?
10. Describe robin-hood hashing. Describe perfect hashing.
11. Double hashing suffers from primary clustering more than the other open addressing techniques.
    a. True
    b. False

12. The more complex the hashing functions, the better it is.
    a. True
    b. False
13. Double hashing requires using the same hash function to rehash the same key.
    a. True
    b. False
14. Perfect hashing is when the hash keys are known ahead of time and there are no collisions within the table.
    a. True
    b. False
15. Coalesced hashing is a hybrid of open addressing and separate chaining.
    a. True
    b. False

PROGRAMMING PROJECTS

Exercise 1: Modify the Linear Probing demo application to perform quadric probing.

Exercise 2: Implement a caching system using perfect hashing as described in this chapter.

Exercise 3: Implement robin-hood hashing as describe in this chapter. Build off of the Double Hashing demo application to create it.

8

Advanced Sorting

In This Chapter

- Advanced Sorting Topics
- Shellsort
- Partitioning
- Quicksort
- Radix Sort
- Additional Types of Sorting

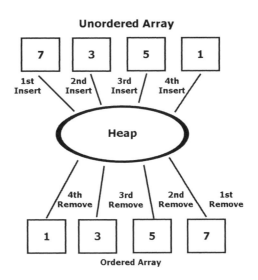

C hapter 4 provided an introduction to sorting by examining a few straightforward and simple techniques. These techniques included the bubble sort, the selection sort, and the insertion sort, as well as the merge sort, which is a much faster sort than the other simple sorts shown in that chapter, but at the cost of twice as much memory.

The problem with the simple sorting algorithms such as the bubble, selection, and insertion sorts is that they are slow, mostly because of the number of comparisons, copies, and loop passes over the container. For small sets of data this might not be that big a problem, but the larger N grows, the worse the performance is. Data sets in the tens of thousands, hundreds of thousands, or millions would require different algorithms with a much more suitable speed for such high numbers.

The purpose of this chapter is to examine a number of very fast sorting algorithms as well as how to implement them in code. These algorithms include the Shellsort, the quicksort, and the radix sort. Additional algorithms discussed in this chapter are partitioning data sets, which are used for the quicksort and will be discussed separately; a brief look at the heap sort, which will be discussed in more detail in Chapter 9, Trees; the bucket sort; and the intro sort.

ADVANCED SORTING TOPICS

Sorting as quickly and efficiently as possible is very important to all types of applications, be they video games or others. For large sets of data the general amount of time the algorithm can be expected to perform is related to the number of items already inside of the container and, at times, how close the container is to being partially sorted or if it is sorted in the inverted direction, which can lead to worst-case performance for many algorithms such as the insertion and selection types.

The algorithms that are implemented in this chapter do not require extra memory like the merge sort does and their performance is much faster than the simple sorts. The Shellsort operates in about the big-O of $O(N * (\log N)^2)$, the quicksort in about $O(N * \log N)$, and the radix sort generally around $O(N * \log N)$. When compared to the simple sorts in Chapter 4, these are much faster, as those simple sorting algorithms operated at around $O(N^2)$.

The first sorting algorithm that will be discussed and implemented is the Shellsort. This will be followed by a discussion of partitioning, followed by the quicksort algorithm and then the radix sort algorithm.

SHELLSORT

The Shellsort algorithm was created by a computer scientist named Donald Shell in the 1950s. The Shellsort algorithm is a great algorithm to use for medium-sized data sets, but for larger sets the quicksort algorithm can outperform it. The algorithm itself is based on the insertion sort but has features and modifications that allow it to outperform the insertion sort algorithm, even though it is based on it.

The size of a data set that is considered small, medium, or large depends a lot on the speed and memory of the machine that is running the code. What is considered large this year might not be considered large a few years from now.

In general you can start out with the Shellsort algorithm, and if the performance is not what you need, you can use the quicksort algorithm.

THE SHELLSORT ALGORITHM

The insertion sort requires many copies and comparisons. During the insertion sort items are shifted (copied) linearly one element as the position for an item is being looked for. During worst-case scenarios where the data set is in the reverse of its sorted order, all items must be copied, moved one element at a time, and compared for a set of N elements. As mentioned in Chapter 4, the insertion sort algorithm works fast for data sets that are partially sorted because the number of copies is kept low, which translates into an increase in performance.

The key idea behind the Shellsort is to minimize the number of copies to increase performance as much as possible. The Shellsort works by performing the insertion sort not on the entire data set but on a few widely spread elements. During each pass the range (gap) is reduced until all elements are in their correct position. Figure 8.1 shows a visual representation of this process with the first three steps of the Shellsort being operated on an array of objects.

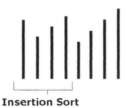

Insertion Sort

FIGURE 8.1   The Shellsort.

In Figure 8.1 the elements 0, 4, and 8 are sorted using the insertion sort. Next the elements 1, 5, and 9 are sorted and so forth. Once an entire pass has been completed on the data set, the range is decreased and another pass is performed. This happens until the step range is 1. The idea behind the Shellsort is to not only reduce the many copies that are performed during the traditional insertion sort but to also get the array close to being partially sorted, which will cause later passes to execute faster. With the insertion sort, if, for example, the smallest element is far to the right and must be on the far left, then the number of copies required just to move that one item is equal to the number of elements in the entire list. If the list has 1,000 elements, then to move that one element would require 1,000 copies. Using the Shellsort that element will be moved over large gaps, which eliminates many of those in-between copies that are common with the insertion sort. In Figure 8.1 notice that the items that were moved are close to where their final position would be in a sorted container. This means that the Shellsort partially sorts the container very quickly and continues until the container is sorted. By performing a variable N-sort using some value, which is 4 in Figure 8.1, we can execute the algorithm over the entire container for one pass and then decrease the range recursively for each additional pass until the range is 1. When the range is 1, the algorithm will translate to a traditional insertion sort that will very quickly sort all elements into their final positions. This process is far faster than using the traditional insertion sort alone because the Shellsort places the elements in a best-case scenario so that during the final pass the insertion sort can quickly process it. When the range of the algorithm reaches 1, the elements in the container are either in their final positions or close to it, in which case the final insertion sort is extremely fast.

You can think of the Shellsort as a multipass insertion sort that works only on a specific range of elements at a time instead of on the entire container.

NOTE

The question now is how we can determine an initial range value for the Shellsort. In Figure 8.1 the value of 4 was used. In an actual application the range would not be constant and would depend on the size of the array. For an array of 500 elements the range might start off at 364 and then be decreased to 121, 40, 13, 4, and finally 1 for each additional pass. This example sequence, called the gap sequence (also known as the interval sequence), is made up of six values, which means six passes over the container in order to sort the elements. In this example sequence the algorithms first look at every 3 elements that are 364 elements apart, then every element that is 121 elements apart, and so forth until it is at 1.

There are a few ways to generate the gap sequence. In this chapter we'll use the Knuth method, which uses the recursive algorithm of the following to find the gap sequence:

```
h = 3 * h + 1
```

where *h* starts out as 1 and keeps going until it is larger than the array. Once *h* is larger than the array, the previous value is the one that starts the gap sequence. For example, when looking at the gap sequence discussed earlier for an array size of 500, the algorithm will start off with 1, then 4, 13, 40, 121, 364, and 1,093. Since the array has 500 elements, it can't use 1,093, so 364 is the first choice. Once the initial gap sequence value is known, the previous ones can be calculated on the fly, so they do not need to be stored, which can also save memory by using the inverse algorithms of:

```
h = (h - 1) / 3
```

When it come to picking an algorithm for generating the gap sequence, the algorithm either must be able to end with 1 or, when the sequence gets small enough, it must be able to jump to 1 for the final step. The gap sequence is very important because it will contribute to the overall performance of the Shellsort algorithm. If the initial gap sizes are too small, more copies and comparisons might be performed than are necessary. As the gap size approaches 1, the final pass might require more work than it should. Using prime numbers will also improve performance, as it will keep items sorted in a step within a pass from being sorted in another step in the same pass (loop iteration). In general the Shellsort is faster than the simple sorts (i.e., bubble, selection, and insertion) but is not generally faster than the quicksort for very large numbers of elements. It is slightly faster than the quicksort for small sets of data.

IMPLEMENTING THE SHELLSORT

The Shellsort algorithm in this chapter will be implemented using the unordered array class from Chapter 2. The implementation will use loops to create the gap sequence as well as to execute the algorithm. The code will be implemented in a function called `Shellsort()` (shown in Listing 8.1) that is added to the `UnorderedArray` class created in Chapter 2.

LISTING 8.1   The `Shellsort()` Function of the Modified Unordered Array

```
void Shellsort()
{
   assert(m_array != NULL);

   T temp;
   int i = 0, k = 0;

   // Sequence...
   int seq = 1;
```

```
        while(seq <= m_numElements / 3)
           seq = seq * 3 + 1;


    while(seq > 0)
    {
       for(k = seq; k < m_numElements; k++)
       {
          temp = m_array[k];
          i = k;

          while(i > seq - 1 && m_array[i - seq] >= temp)
          {
             m_array[i] = m_array[i - seq];
             i -= seq;
          }

          m_array[i] = temp;
       }

       seq = (seq - 1) / 3;
    }
}
```

The assert() *used in Listing 8.1 is for debugging purposes.*

The Shellsort() function in Listing 8.1 starts off by finding the largest value in the gap sequence that will be used as a step size in the first pass of the Shellsort algorithm. The function moves onto the first loop, which is used to keep execution going as long as the sequence step size is valid. Within the first loop is a nested for and while loop pair used to partially sort a range of elements that are separated by the step size. The while loop in this pair is used to sort the elements throughout the step range, and the for loop is used to perform the while loop partial sorting for all elements in the container. Once these loops finish executing, the step size is adjusted and the entire process repeats itself until it is done.

On the CD-ROM is a demo application called Shellsort in the Chapter 8 folder. This demo application will test that the algorithm works by creating an array of 10 random integer values. In the main source file of this demo the code sets up the array, displays its unordered contents, sorts the array, and then displays its ordered contents to the console window. The source code to the Shellsort demo application is straightforward and is shown in Listing 8.2. Figure 8.2 shows a screenshot of the demo application.

LISTING 8.2   The `main()` Function for the Shellsort Demo

```cpp
#include<iostream>
#include"Arrays.h"

using namespace std;


int main(int args, char *arg[])
{
   cout << "Shellsort Algorithm" << endl;
   cout << "Chapter 8: Advance Sorting" << endl << endl;

   const int size = 10;
   int i = 0;

   UnorderedArray<int> array(size);

   for(i = 0; i < size; i++)
      array.push(rand() % 100);


   cout << "Before shellsort sort:";

   for(i = 0; i < size; i++)
      cout << " " << array[i];

   cout << endl;


   array.Shellsort();


   cout << " After shellsort sort:";

   for(i = 0; i < size; i++)
      cout << " " << array[i];

   cout << endl << endl;

   return 1;
}
```

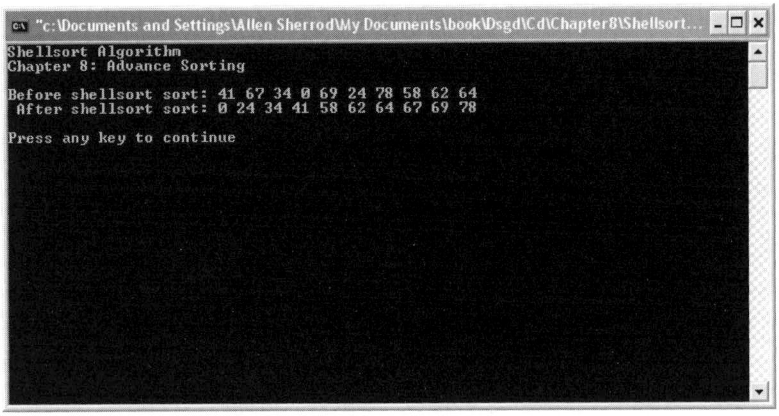

FIGURE 8.2 A screenshot of the Shellsort demo application.

PARTITIONING

Partitioning is the process of splitting something into two sections. In one group will be all items that are related based on a specific condition, and on the other side are the remaining items. The partitioning algorithm is used as the basis for the quicksort algorithm, and understanding the partitioning algorithm will make learning the quicksort algorithm much easier. The sole purpose of a partition is to split data into two sections. When a hard drive is partitioned, the memory is normally split into two sections, where one section is the new partition, which is a size within the original memory's size, and the second section is the modified old partition whose new size is the original size minus the size of the new partition.

Outside of the quicksort algorithm there might be other times when it is useful to partition data into two sections. Maybe a game application needs to partition players in a game into two sections, where all players above a specific ranking level are on one side and all players under a specific level are on the other. Or maybe there is a game application where a partition can be used to separate online players from offline players on a friend list so that the online players are displayed above the offline players, which can be further partitioned to have players that are playing the same game as the user of the application from those that are not. There are endless uses for partitioning, so the discussion of the algorithm here is useful for more than just learning the quicksort algorithm.

THE PARTITIONING ALGORITHM

The partitioning algorithm starts by taking a data set that needs to be partitioned and a condition by which it is to be split. In an array of integers, for example, the data can be partitioned into two sections, where one section is lower than the number 100 and the other section is greater than or equal to it. This number is called the pivot value and is the condition that is used to partition the data. In the partition algorithm the elements on both ends of the container are checked, starting with the left end before moving to the right end. If the element on the left side is under 100, it stays where it is. The left side loop keeps moving until it finds a value that does not meet the condition. Once it finds it, the algorithm moves to the right end and keeps checking values until it finds one that doesn't meet the requirement of the value being greater than or equal to 100. Once it finds a value on the left and one on the right that do not meet the conditions, those two values are swapped. The algorithm continues where it left off by moving from the left end and searching elements until it finds another value that does not belong, and then it does the same for the right end. Once a pair on the left and right is found, they are swapped.

This continues until the left-end index and right-end index pass one another. At that point it can be determined that the algorithm is complete and that the point of crossing, the point where left index equals right index, is what is known as the pivot index. A pivot index is an index that marks the position in the array that specifies where one section ends and the other begins. When a partition occurs, the two sections are not necessarily equal in size. A visual example of partitioning is shown in Figure 8.3.

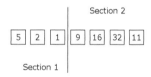

FIGURE 8.3   A visual example of partitioning.

Partitioning is not a sorting algorithm. It simply loops through both ends of a container and swaps when necessary until all elements have been processed. The partition is not stable, which means that the order of each group is not necessarily the original order of the elements before the partition. Although the partitioned data is not sorted, it is one step closer to being sorted, which we'll look at in the quicksort algorithm later in this chapter.

The pivot value is the value used as a condition in the partition, while the pivot index marks the position in the container where the first section ends and the second section begins. Remember the difference between the two.

The partition algorithm runs in big-O O(N) on average.

IMPLEMENTING PARTITIONING

Implementing the partitioning algorithm requires creating a function that can loop through both ends of a container and swap elements when necessary. The swapping of elements can be placed in its own function, which we'll call SwapElements(), and will only switch two valid elements specified by two indexes. During partitioning the first step is to move from the left end to the right until an element is found that needs to be swapped. Once such an element is found, a loop from the right end does the same thing with the right side moving toward the left. When an element is found on the right side that needs to be swapped, the two elements are swapped. This action continues until both indexes point to the same element, which would mean that the algorithm has processed the entire container. The element that both the left and right are equal to is the pivot index, and this value can be returned when the function is finished for applications that need to know where the index is. The code added to the UnorderedArray class that allows for the container to be partitioned is shown in Listing 8.3.

LISTING 8.3 The SwapElements() and Partition() Functions of the UnorderedArray Class

```
template<typename T>
class UnorderedArray
{
   public:
      void SwapElements(int index1, int index2)
      {
         assert(index1 >= 0 && index1 < m_numElements);
         assert(index2 >= 0 && index2 < m_numElements);
         assert(m_array != NULL);


         T temp = m_array[index1];
         m_array[index1] = m_array[index2];
         m_array[index2] = temp;
      }


      int Partition(T pivot)
      {
         return Partition(0, m_numElements - 1, pivot);
      }
```

```
int Partition(int lIndex, int rIndex, T pivot)
{
    int currentLeft = lIndex;
    int currentRight = rIndex;


    while(1)
    {
        while(currentLeft < rIndex &&
              m_array[currentLeft] < pivot)
        {
            // Searching left for val bigger than pivot.
            // This will break when it finds it or moves
            // to the end.

            currentLeft++;
        }


        while(currentRight > lIndex &&
              m_array[currentRight] > pivot)
        {
            // Same as left side.

            currentRight++;
        }


        if(currentLeft >= currentRight)
        {
            // Done with partition (no more to search).
            break;
        }


        // Swap elements if we get here.
        SwapElements(currentLeft, currentRight);
    }


    // Returns position of the pivot.
    return currentLeft;
}
};
```

On the accompanying CD-ROM a demo application called Partitioning is in the Chapter 8 folder. The purpose of this demo application is to test the code in Listing 8.3 by creating an array of 10 random integers and partitioning them based on the pivot value of 60. In the demo application the contents of the array are displayed twice: before the partition and after the algorithm's execution. The main source file for the Partitioning demo application is shown in Listing 8.4. Figure 8.4 shows a screenshot of the running demo application.

LISTING 8.4 The Partitioning Demo's Main Source File

```
#include<iostream>
#include"Arrays.h"

using namespace std;


int main(int args, char *arg[])
{
   cout << "Partitioning Algorithm" << endl;
   cout << "Chapter 8: Advance Sorting" << endl << endl;

   const int size = 10;
   int i = 0;
   int pivotValue = 60;

   UnorderedArray<int> array(size);


   // Insert elements and print basic stats.
   for(i = 0; i < size; i++)
      array.push(rand() % 100);

   cout << "Array size - " << size << " pivot value - "
        << pivotValue << "." << endl << endl;


   // Display elements.
   cout << "Before partitioning:";

   for(i = 0; i < size; i++)
      cout << " " << array[i];

   cout << endl << endl;
```

```
      // Partition then display results.
      int pivot = array.Partition(0, size - 1, pivotValue);

      cout << "After partitioning (pivot index - " << pivot << "):";

      for(i = 0; i < size; i++)
         cout << " " << array[i];

      cout << endl << endl;

      return 1;
   }
```

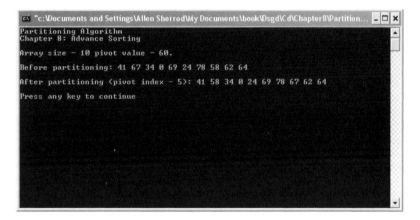

FIGURE 8.4   A screenshot from the Partitioning demo.

QUICKSORT

The quicksort algorithm is very popular for large data sets. It is based on the partitioning algorithm and has a big-O of O(N * log N). The quicksort was developed in 1962 by C.A.R. Hoare and is among the algorithms of choice to use for very large sets of data. In this section we will look at a straightforward implementation of the quicksort algorithm and an implementation that uses what is called the median-of-three.

THE QUICKSORT ALGORITHM

The quicksort algorithm works by using recursion and the partitioning algorithm to partition data sections until the lowest level is reached. At that point the entire data set is sorted. Recall that after a partition the data is not sorted but is partially sorted. Continuing to partition each half, then each quarter, and so on until there is only one element left (which means the algorithm is done) will sort the entire data set. A visual example of the quicksort is shown in Figure 8.5.

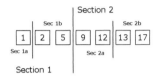

FIGURE 8.5 The quicksort.

The quicksort algorithm can be described in a few steps. First, pick a pivot value and partition the array into two sections. The pivot value can simply be the center element in this example. The next step is to recursively partition the two sections further and further until there is only one element left, which means the algorithm is complete. As shown in Figure 8.5, this will eventually lead to a sorted container. The key to the quicksort algorithm is choosing a good pivot value. Simply choosing the center value, as shown in the example in Figure 8.5, will not always lead to the most balanced partitions. In the next section we will discuss the implementations of the quicksort algorithm in two demo applications.

IMPLEMENTING THE QUICKSORT

To implement the quicksort algorithm we will use recursion and the partition function. The quicksort recursive function will be simple in that it will always use the right-most element (the last element) as the pivot value in the partition. Once the pivot index from this partition is returned, the quicksort recursive function is called twice, once to partition the left section and once for the right. Since the right-most element is always being used, we must add a function to swap indexes in the partitioning function. For an example, take a look at Figure 8.6. After a partition, since the right-most element is used as the pivot value, it will always need to be swapped with the element at the pivot index to ensure that the partition has created two valid sections. The quicksort algorithm code is shown in Listing 8.5, in which the source code is added to the UnorderedArray class from Chapter 2.

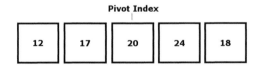

FIGURE 8.6 The need to swap the end element with the element at the pivot index after a partition.

LISTING 8.5   The Quicksort Algorithm Added to the `UnorderedArray` class

```cpp
template<typename T>
class UnorderedArray
{
    public:
        void SwapElements(int index1, int index2)
        {
            assert(index1 >= 0 && index1 < m_numElements);
            assert(index2 >= 0 && index2 < m_numElements);
            assert(m_array != NULL);

            T temp = m_array[index1];
            m_array[index1] = m_array[index2];
            m_array[index2] = temp;
        }


        void Quicksort()
        {
            QuickSort(0, m_numElements - 1);
        }


    private:
        void QuickSort(int lVal, int rVal)
        {
            if((rVal - lVal) <= 0)
                return;

            int pivotIndex = Partition(lVal, rVal,
                                       m_array[rVal]);

            QuickSort(lVal, pivotIndex - 1);
            QuickSort(pivotIndex + 1, rVal);
        }


        int Partition(int lIndex, int rIndex, T pivot)
        {
            int currentLeft = lIndex;
            int currentRight = rIndex - 1;
```

```
                while(1)
                {
                   while(m_array[currentLeft] < pivot)
                   {
                      // Searching left for val bigger than pivot.
                      // This will end when it finds it.

                      currentLeft++;
                   }

                   while(currentRight > 0 &&
                         m_array[currentRight] > pivot)
                   {
                      // Same as left side.

                      currentRight-;
                   }

                   if(currentLeft >= currentRight)
                   {
                      // Done with partition (no more to search).
                      break;
                   }

                   // Swap elements if we get here.
                   SwapElements(currentLeft, currentRight);
                }


                SwapElements(currentLeft, rIndex);

                // Returns position of the pivot.
                return currentLeft;
             }
      };
```

In Listing 8.5 there is a function used to swap elements, a public Quicksort() function to sort an entire array, a recursive private Quicksort() function that does the work, and a partitioning function. The partitioning function is private since it is only used by the recursive Quicksort() function. It has been modified to have an extra swap for the right-most element and the one at the pivot index to ensure two value sections. Understanding the quicksort algorithm requires an understanding of the partitioning algorithm. The quicksort is basically a recursive set of partitioning algorithms that are performed until the entire container is sorted.

Recursion is one option for implementing these functions, but you could also use an iterative approach using loops. Loops are harder to implement and are often much less intuitive.

On the accompanying CD-ROM is an example demo application called Quicksort that will demonstrate the use of the code in Listing 8.5. The demo application will create an integer array, populate it with random integers, display the contents of the container before the sort, sort the container using the quicksort algorithm, and display the contents of the container after the sorting algorithm has been processed. The main source file for the Quicksort demo application is shown in Listing 8.6. Figure 8.7 shows a screenshot of the demo application.

LISTING 8.6   The Main Source File for the Quicksort Demo

```cpp
#include<iostream>
#include"Arrays.h"

using namespace std;


int main(int args, char *arg[])
{
   cout << "Quicksort Algorithm" << endl;
   cout << "Chapter 8: Advance Sorting" << endl << endl;


   const int size = 10;
   int i = 0;
   UnorderedArray<int> array(size);


   // Insert elements and print basic stats.
   for(i = 0; i < size; i++)
      array.push(10 + rand() % 90);


   // Display elements.
   cout << "Before Quicksort:";

   for(i = 0; i < size; i++)
      cout << " " << array[i];

   cout << endl << endl;
```

```
        // Sort then display results.
        array.Quicksort();

        cout << " After Quicksort:";

        for(i = 0; i < size; i++)
           cout << " " << array[i];

        cout << endl << endl;

        return 1;
    }
```

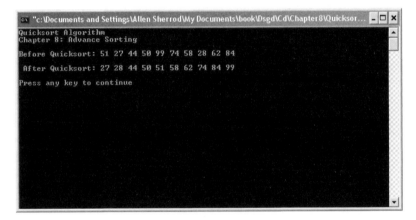

FIGURE 8.7 A screenshot from the Quicksort demo.

QUICKSORT: MEDIAN-OF-THREE

It is important to pick a good pivot value for the partitioning algorithm. In the Quicksort demo the right-most element was chosen as the pivot value each time. This was good in the sense that it was a fast and simple process of picking a pivot value, but since the data in the element is random, this can lead to some bad pivot value choices. The key to coming up with a pivot value is to make the process as quick as possible to allow the overall performance of the quicksort algorithm to be as fast as possible. Examining all of the elements in a container just to choose the best pivot value is not practical and could not only hurt performance but could even take longer than the quicksort algorithm itself.

In this section we will look at what is known as the median-of-three. This method is used to pick pivot values that have the chance of being better than always going with the right-most element. In the median-of-three the first, middle, and last elements in the container are examined and the median of the three (the value that is in the middle) is used as the pivot value. As an example, Figure 8.8 shows a visual representation of picking the median-of-three numbers. Using this method will not guarantee that the best or even a good pivot value is chosen, but it can be a better option than always using the element at the end of the container regardless of its value. When checking for the median-of-three values, those elements can also be sorted among themselves. This will ensure that the left-most and right-most elements are already on their proper sides.

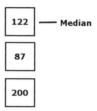

FIGURE 8.8   Median-of-three.

The problem with the median-of-three is that you can't use it on sections with less than three items, and the quicksort algorithm wouldn't be efficient enough to use it on small sections, whose number depends on the computer's CPU power, memory, and so on. In such a case another sort can be used as a fallback to the quicksort, such as the selection or insertion sort. For the implementation we are about to look at, we will fall back to the insertion sort for data sections that are too small to further partition using the median-of-three.

Implementing the median-of-three in the quicksort algorithm will require us to update the Quicksort() recursive function. This function will calculate the median as well as swap the elements as necessary to at least partially sort those three elements. The partitioning function and the functions for the insertion sort are the same as those we've seen before. In the recursive Quicksort() function if the elements that are trying to be sorted are smaller than the macro QUICKSORT_CUTOFF, it will fall back to the insertion sort. The cutoff value is 4 in the upcoming demo (Listing 8.7) because the array is only 10 elements in size. In practice a value of 9 would probably be good to use. The median-of-three modified code for the quicksort algorithm is shown in Listing 8.7.

LISTING 8.7   Implementing the Quicksort Using the Median-of-Three

```
#define QUICKSORT_CUTOFF   4
```

```cpp
template<typename T>
class UnorderedArray
{
    public:
        void InsertionSort()
        {
            InsertionSort(0, m_numElements - 1);
        }


        void SwapElements(int index1, int index2)
        {
            assert(index1 >= 0 && index1 < m_numElements);
            assert(index2 >= 0 && index2 < m_numElements);
            assert(m_array != NULL);


            T temp = m_array[index1];
            m_array[index1] = m_array[index2];
            m_array[index2] = temp;
        }


        void Quicksort()
        {
            QuickSort(0, m_numElements - 1);
        }


    private:
        void QuickSort(int lVal, int rVal)
        {
            if((rVal - lVal + 1) < QUICKSORT_CUTOFF)
            {
                InsertionSort(lVal, rVal);
                return;
            }

            int center = (lVal + rVal) / 2;

            if(m_array[lVal] > m_array[center])
                SwapElements(lVal, center);
```

```
   if(m_array[lVal] > m_array[rVal])
      SwapElements(lVal, rVal);

   if(m_array[center] > m_array[rVal])
      SwapElements(center, rVal);


   int pivotIndex = Partition(lVal, rVal, center);


   QuickSort(lVal, pivotIndex - 1);
   QuickSort(pivotIndex, rVal);
}


int Partition(int lIndex, int rIndex, int pivot)
{
   while(1)
   {
      while(m_array[++lIndex] < m_array[pivot]);
      while(m_array[-rIndex] > m_array[pivot]);


      if(lIndex >= rIndex)
         break;


      SwapElements(lIndex, rIndex);
   }


   // Returns position of the pivot.
   return lIndex;
}


void InsertionSort(int lVal, int rVal)
{
   assert(m_array != NULL);

   T temp;
   int i = 0;
```

```
        for(int k = lVal + 1; k <= rVal; k++)
        {
            temp = m_array[k];
            i = k;

            while(i > lVal && m_array[i - 1] >= temp)
            {
                m_array[i] = m_array[i - 1];
                i-;
            }

            m_array[i] = temp;
        }
    }
};
```

On the accompanying CD-ROM is a demo application called Quicksort 2 that demonstrates the median-of-three code created in Listing 8.7. The main source file for the demo application is shown in Listing 8.8, and a screenshot of the demo is shown in Figure 8.9.

LISTING 8.8 The Main Source File for the Quicksort 2 Demo

```
#include<iostream>
#include"Arrays.h"

using namespace std;


int main(int args, char *arg[])
{
    cout << "Median-Of-Three Quicksort Algorithm" << endl;
    cout << "Chapter 8: Advance Sorting" << endl << endl;


    const int size = 10;
    int i = 0;
    UnorderedArray<int> array(size);


    // Insert elements and print basic stats.
    for(i = 0; i < size; i++)
        array.push(10 + rand() % 90);
```

```
// Display elements.
cout << "Before Quicksort:";

for(i = 0; i < size; i++)
   cout << " " << array[i];

cout << endl << endl;


// Sort then display results.
array.Quicksort();

cout << " After Quicksort:";

for(i = 0; i < size; i++)
   cout << " " << array[i];

cout << endl << endl;

return 1;
}
```

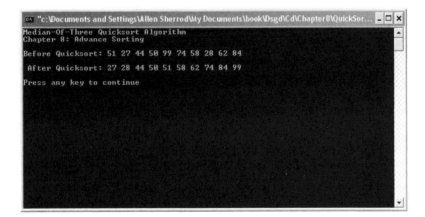

FIGURE 8.9   A screenshot from the Quicksort 2 demo.

RADIX SORT

The sorting algorithms we've seen in this book up to this point work by comparing elements in the sorting process. Along with comparisons, the algorithms discussed up to this point also have a number of copying operations that take place throughout the algorithm. When it comes to sorting, not all algorithms need to do comparisons. In this section we will look at a sorting algorithm that can quickly sort the elements in a container without performing comparisons of internal elements.

THE RADIX SORT ALGORITHM

The radix sort creates a number of internal containers that it uses to perform its job. Let's start with an example. Say we want to sort numbers that use the decimal system. In the decimal system we have the ones position, the tens position, the hundreds position, and so forth. Each of these positions can have a value that is a 0, 9, or some number in between. If we have 10 containers, with the first container being 0, the second being 1, and so on, we can use those 10 containers for the sorting process.

The algorithm in this example would first take the ones position of every element and use that value as an array index into the list of containers we have standing by for the algorithm. Once all elements have been inserted into one of the containers, we have effectively ordered the ones position of all elements in the container. The containers in question can be something like a link list, queue, and so on (see Figure 8.10). So far there are no comparisons. A modulus operator can allow us to extract the ones position from a number that is used directly as an array index (index into an array of secondary containers).

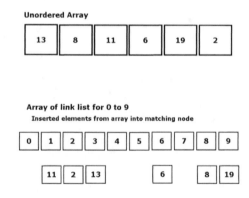

FIGURE 8.10 Sorting the ones position.

Once the elements have been placed in the ones position container they belong to, we can remove all elements from each of the containers, starting with the container for 0 and moving toward the container for 9, and place those values back into the original array, which will give us an array with all elements sorted by the ones position. The next pass would do the same thing for the tens position, then the hundreds position, and so on until all necessary decimal positions have been processed. If the biggest number in the array is 100, the most times we'll have to do this is three since the algorithm would have to be performed for the ones, tens, and hundreds positions. This is shown in Figure 8.11.

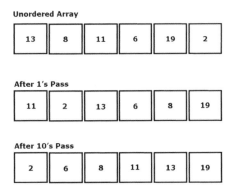

FIGURE 8.11   Sorting using the radix sort for six elements.

When all positions have been processed, we will end up with a completely sorted array of numbers. There are no comparisons, and the only copying that occurs is when the values from the secondary containers are being transferred back to the original array. In practice this can lead to a very fast sort.

The radix sort can be used for other things such as numbers in the binary system, hexadecimal system, letters in the alphabet, and so forth. Although there is copying going on, it is pretty minimal when compared to some of the sorts we saw earlier in the book. Also, the algorithm requires temporary, secondary containers to be created to hold the values for each pass. Using a link list allows the elements to grow and shrink as needed, but additional memory is needed, as well as various memory allocations and de-allocations.

IMPLEMENTING THE RADIX SORT

ON THE CD

On the accompanying CD-ROM in the Chapter 8 folder a demo application called Radix Sort implements the radix sort. The demo application is a simple one to help make it easier to understand what is going on. First we will look at the function used to perform the radix sort algorithm, called RadixSort().

The RadixSort() function creates the secondary containers that it will need. For the demo application we will be sorting numbers in the decimal system, so 10 containers will be needed for numbers 0 through 9. The next part of the function loops through each decimal position and performs two internal loops that do the hard work of the algorithm. The first inner loop adds each element to a container based on the value of the current decimal position. The second loop removes each of the elements of each container and places the values back onto the original array. That's it. Once this function has executed, the array is completely sorted. The RadixSort() function is show in Listing 8.9. The macro MAX_POSITIONS is the number of decimal positions the demo uses, is this case two, because the numbers being sorted range from 10 to 99, which means we will only be looking at the ones position and the tens position.

LISTING 8.9 A Function to Perform the Radix Sort on Integers

```
#define BASE              10
#define MAX_POSITIONS     2


void RadixSort(int *array, int size)
{
   // Base index, radix index, counter.
   int b = 0, r = 0, i = 0;

   // Container conter, base factor.
   int index = 0, factor = 0;

   // List of containers for the sort.
   deque<int> qList[BASE];


   // Place in containers then take them off for every base.
   for(b = 1, factor = 1; b <= MAX_POSITIONS; factor *= BASE, b++)
   {
      for(r = 0; r < size; r++)
      {
         index = (array[r] / factor) % BASE;
         qList[index].push_back(array[r]);
      }


      for(r = 0, i = 0; r < BASE; r++)
      {
         while(qList[r].empty() != true)
         {
            array[i++] = qList[r].front();
            qList[r].pop_front();
         }
      }
   }
}
```

The main source file for the Radix Sort demo application creates an array of integers, fills it in with random data that range between 10 and 99, displays the array's contents before the sort, sorts the array, and then displays the contents of the array after the sort. The main source file for the Radix Sort is straightforward and uses the code in Listing 8.9. The `main()` function of the Radix Sort demo application is shown in Listing 8.10. Figure 8.12 shows a screenshot of the demo application.

LISTING 8.10   The Main Source File for the Radix Sort Demo

```cpp
int main(int args, char **argc)
{
   cout << "Radix Sort Example" << endl;
   cout << "Chapter 8: Advanced Sorting" << endl;
   cout << endl;

   const int size = 10;
   int array[size];
   int i = 0;


   // Populate array.
   for(i = 0; i < size; i++)
      array[i] = 10 + rand() % 89;


   // Display array contents.
   cout << "Array contents before sort: ";

   for(i = 0; i < size; i++)
      cout << " " << array[i];

   cout << endl;


   // Radix sorting.
   RadixSort(array, size);


   // Display array contents.
   cout << " Array contents after sort: ";

   for(i = 0; i < size; i++)
      cout << " " << array[i];

   cout << endl << endl;

   return 1;
}
```

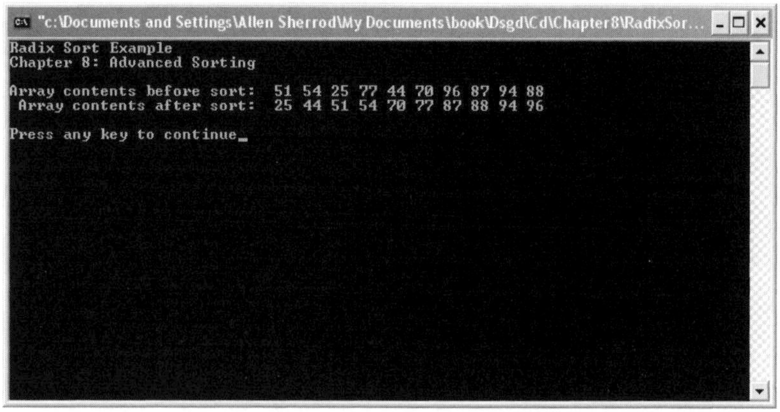

FIGURE 8.12   A screenshot from the Radix Sort demo.

THE BIT RADIX SORT

The bit radix sort can be used to sort bits in an array instead of a series of bytes as was done with the integers in the Radix Sort demo application. The bit radix sort only requires two containers since binary values are either a 0 or a 1. When extracting the values, instead of using the modulus operator, we use the bit-wise operator &.

The main thing to consider is the number of elements that would be created in the secondary containers. A 32-bit value such as an integer is made up of 32 bits. Even with a small array of 100 elements, that would be 32 * 100 elements for each container, which is 3,200. For link lists that expand and shrink a lot, this can lead to many memory allocations and de-allocations. Using memory heaps and manual memory management can improve this, but the topic of memory management is a complex subject. If larger bits are used, such as 64, the amount of overhead can increase considerably and can degrade performance, especially with large arrays in the thousands, hundreds of thousands, and so forth.

ADDITIONAL TYPES OF SORTING

Many more types of sorting algorithms exist in the world of computer programming. Each algorithm has strengths and weaknesses that depend highly on the situations in which they are used. In this section we will talk a little about the heap sort algorithm, the introspective sort algorithm, and the bucket sort algorithm. Other sorting algorithms are the bead sort, the bidirectional bubble sort, the comb sort, and a host of others.

HEAP SORT

The heap sort algorithm is a general-purpose sorting algorithm that uses a heap data structure to sort elements in a container. The heap is a data structure that we will look at in the next chapter. When items are inserted into the heap data structure, the minimum values (or maximum values, depending on the implementation) can be quickly retrieved. If the values can be extracted from the heap in order, then a sort can occur quickly. For example, if we take the elements in an array and add them to a heap, we can extract the values from the heap and place them back into the array sorted. An illustration of the heap sort is shown in Figure 8.13. Using a heap data structure requires additional memory for the algorithm, but it is fast and can compete with the quicksort seen earlier in this chapter with a big-O of `O(N log N)`. The heap sort and the heap data structure will be examined in more detail in Chapter 9, Trees.

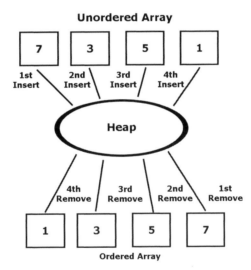

FIGURE 8.13   The heap sort.

INTROSPECTIVE SORT

The introspective sort (intro sort for short) is another general-purpose sorting algorithm. The intro sort starts with a quicksort algorithm and then it switches to a heap sort once the recursion depth reaches a certain value. The worst case for the intro sort is big-O `O(N log N)`. The combination of the quicksort and the heap sort can allow for a very fast combination much like how the Shellsort modified the traditional insertion sort and improved its speed drastically.

BUCKET SORT

The bucket sort, also known as the bin sort, is a sorting algorithm that is based on partitioning, much like the quicksort. The bucket sort works by partitioning an array into a finite number of sections (buckets). Elements of the container are added to the buckets they belong to, and each bucket is sorted separately. For example, a container with 100 elements can have 10 buckets, with the first bucket being for numbers 0 through 9, the second bucket being for numbers 10 through 19, and so forth. By sorting each of these smaller buckets separately, an entire container can be sorted. Buckets used in this manner are similar to the containers we used for the radix sort.

SUMMARY

This chapter covered a few advanced sorting algorithms that can be very useful in general applications and game development. The algorithms discussed included the Shellsort, the quicksort, the radix sort, the heap sort, the intro sort, and partitioning.

In the next chapter we'll look at the heap sort in more detail. Also in the next chapter we'll be looking at trees in general, and specifically binary trees, before moving onto more tree data structures and algorithms. Trees are used a lot in application development and in various techniques in game development, which makes them very important topics to cover in this book.

CHAPTER REVIEW QUESTIONS

Answers to the following chapter review questions can be found in Appendix B.

1. Who invented the Shellsort?
2. What sorting algorithm is the Shellsort based upon?
   a. Bubble sort
   b. Selection sort
   c. Insertion sort
   d. Quicksort
   e. None of the above
3. What is the range of values used as step sizes called?
   a. Step sequence
   b. Gap sequence
   c. Size sequence
   d. None of the above

4. Why is the Shellsort faster than the insertion sort?
5. The Shellsort has a big-O of:
   a. `O(N)`
   b. `O(N²)`
   c. `O(log N)`
   d. `O(N * log N)`
   e. `O(N * (log N)²)`
   f. None of the above
6. Using an array size of 1,000, what would be the first step size in the gap sequence using the Shellsort (using the Knuth method)?
   a. 364
   b. 512
   c. 121
   d. 789
   e. None of the above
7. What is the partition algorithm?
8. What is the big-O for partitioning?
   a. `O(1)`
   b. `O(N)`
   c. `O(N²)`
   d. `O(log N)`
   e. `O(N * log N)`
   f. None of the above
9. What is the pivot value?
10. What is the pivot index?
11. Partitioning is an algorithm that what other algorithm is based on?
    a. Shellsort
    b. Heap sort
    c. Intro sort
    d. Quicksort
    e. Radix sort
    f. None of the above
12. The quicksort has a big-O of:
    a. `O(N)`
    b. `O(N²)`
    c. `O(N * log N)`
    d. `O(N * (log N)²)`
    e. None of the above
13. What is the median-of-three when talking about the quicksort?

14. The quicksort should be used for medium-sized data sets, while the Shell-sort should be used for large data sets.
    a. True
    b. False
15. The quicksort is based on the insertion sort.
    a. True
    b. False
16. What is the radix sort?
17. The radix sort has a big-O of:
    a. $O(N)$
    b. $O(N^2)$
    c. $O(N * \log N)$
    d. $O(N * (\log N)^2)$
    e. None of the above
18. How many containers does a bit radix sort use?
19. The radix sort is based on the quicksort.
    a. True
    b. False
20. The radix sort performs on average half the number of swaps (copying two elements) as there are elements in the container.
    a. True
    b. False

PROGRAMMING PROJECTS

Exercise 1: Create an application that takes an array of players and sorts them based on whether they are online or offline. Create a gamer (player) class that stores the player's gamer name and a boolean flag for whether or not they are online.

Exercise 2: Implement the bit radix sort algorithm based on the information discussed in this chapter.

Exercise 3: Implement the intro sort algorithm based on the information discussed in this chapter.

Exercise 4: Implement the bucket sort using the information learned from the partitioning algorithm and from the radix sort.

9 Trees

In This Chapter

- Introduction to Trees
- Tree Example
- Binary Trees
- *k*-dimensional Trees
- Additional Types of Trees

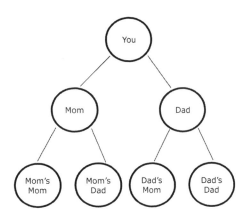

Throughout this book we've looked at data structures that create lists of elements using an array or using a chain of pointers. Each of these data structures has their strengths and weaknesses depending on how they are used. Data structures based on arrays often allow for random-access, fast searching with ordered data and fast insertions in unordered containers but it is expensive to increase and decrease the container's size, insert data in order, and so forth. Data structures based on link chains such as the link list allow for fast insertions, deletions, and expansion and shrinkage of the container but do not offer random access to the elements and are also slow to search.

In this chapter we will talk about data structures that are trees. Trees can be used for maintaining a hierarchy of data, and some types of trees also offer fast searches, fast insertions, fast deletions, and fast resizing and can store ordered data easily. In this chapter we'll be looking at the following types of tree:

- General trees
- Binary trees
- *kd*-trees

We'll also discuss other tree data structures in this and the next chapter, including:

- B-trees
- 2-3 trees
- 2-3-4 trees
- AVL trees
- Red-black trees
- Heaps

In the following chapters we'll discuss heaps (Chapter 10, Heaps), graphs and weighted graphs (Chapter 11, Graphs). We'll also use trees in various ways in Chapter 13, Scene Management, and Chapter 14, Data Compression, so an understanding of them is very important. Trees are used throughout game and general application development in many different ways, a few of which will be discussed throughout the remainder of this book.

The STL does not have general-purpose trees.

NOTE

INTRODUCTION TO TREES

A tree in computer science is a data structure that forms some kind of meaningful hierarchy. Trees start off with what is called the root. The root can be thought of as the first node in a link list in the sense that it is the starting point of the data structure's container. A tree is made up of a hierarchy of nodes that are connected by what are called edges. The edges, as far as C++ is concerned, are abstract and are represented by pointers that connect to other nodes, similar to a link list data structure. A visual example of a tree data structure is shown in Figure 9.1.

Instead of using pointers to connect nodes, indexes can be used. This is done in trees that are implemented using arrays instead of using connecting pointers in C++.

NOTE

The nodes of a singly linked list are connected by a one-directional edge that is represented by the next pointer.

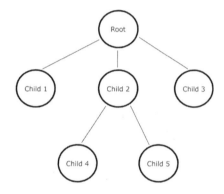

FIGURE 9.1 A visual representation of a tree.

A tree is a type of graph, and we'll discuss graphs in more detail in Chapter 11, Graphs. In link lists nodes are associated with one another using the next and previous pointers. These pointers have no special meaning other than acting as links that keep the chain intact. In trees the relationships between nodes often take on more meaning. We'll discuss more on the different parts of a tree in the following section.

PARTS OF TREES

Which type of tree we are talking about depends on its parts. In general a tree is made up of nodes and edges. The edges in a tree can be any means of connecting one node to another. Connecting nodes can be indexes or pointers. The nodes are subcontainers that hold the data and edges. The relationship between nodes is a parent-child relationship. An easy way to think of a tree data structure is to imagine a family tree in which the nodes are the members of the family, the edges are the branches that connect family members, and the tree is organized by parents, children, and siblings. See Figure 9.2 for an example.

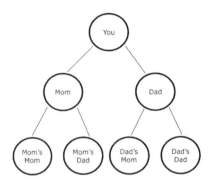

FIGURE 9.2 A family tree.

In the family tree in Figure 9.2 each generation is a different level. For example, the root of the tree is the first level, which we'll call person A. The nodes that make up the root's children are level 1, with the mother on the left and the father on the right. The nodes that make up the root's level 2 nodes can be the grandparents on both sides of the family, and so forth. The only major difference between general trees and a family tree is that a node's subnodes are the children, while in the example in Figure 9.2 they are the parents.

Other terms used to describe the parts of a tree include the following:

- Leaf nodes
- Keys
- Traversing
- Parent nodes

A leaf node is a type of node that has no children nodes attached to it, while a leafless node is a node with one or more children attached.

A key is used to determine how nodes are to be inserted into a tree. Not all trees use keys, but some do, which we'll see first with binary trees. A key can be a separate object or it can be the object itself. For example, in the STL set the key was used as the object.

Traversing is the process of moving through the nodes of the tree, which is normally done to perform some set of algorithms on the tree. The order of traversal is either in-order, pre-order, or post-order.

A parent node is like the previous node pointer in a link list in the sense that it is the node that the current node is attached to. The only node that does not have a parent is the root node. Keeping track of a parent node is not necessary but could be helpful for some algorithms.

Sibling nodes are nodes that share the same parent node.

NOTE

Types of Trees

The topic of trees is a broad one in computer science. There are many different kinds of tree, each of which serves a different general purpose. Among the trees that will be discussed and implemented throughout the remainder of this book are the following:

- General hierarchical trees
- Binary trees
- *kd*-trees
- Heaps
- Scene graphs (graphs used to store scene information in a game)
- Binary space partitioning (BSP) trees
- Quad trees
- Octrees (three-dimensional versions of the quad tree)

We'll also discuss the following types of tree data structures later in this chapter and throughout the remainder of this book:

- Red-black trees
- AVL trees
- 2-3 trees
- 2-3-4 trees
- B-trees
- Potential visibility sets
- Portals and sectors

Tree Example

In this section we are going to implement a simple tree data structure using the information discussed so far. This data structure will allow for any number of children per node. To accomplish this we can create a node class that has both a child pointer and a sibling pointer. The child pointer is used to point to the first child node, while any additional children of a node can be accessed through the sibling pointer of the first child and so on, thus creating a link list. A visual representation of this is shown in Figure 9.3.

In this example we will use a node for the entire tree and we will link nodes of subtrees to it. We could have also created a tree class along with a node class, but that would complicate things, as you'll see soon. The first section of the node class is shown in Listing 9.1, where there is a constructor and a destructor. The constructor

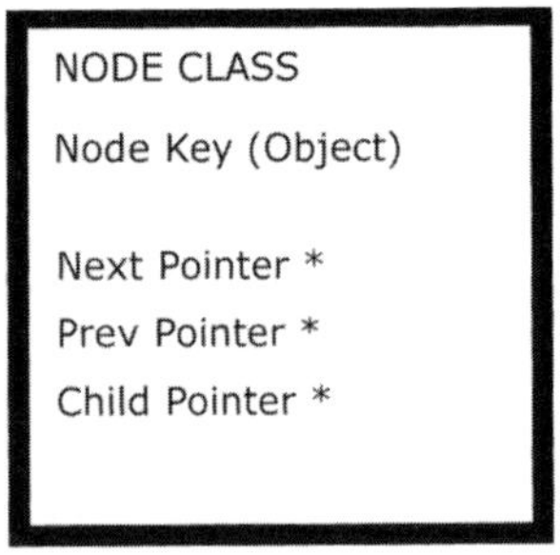

```
NODE CLASS

Node Key (Object)


Next Pointer *
Prev Pointer *
Child Pointer *
```

FIGURE 9.3 The node class we will create for the first tree example.

sets the default values for each of the members, while the destructor deletes any allocated memory. In this example we will assume the nodes store a single object, which will be an integer as a way to have something to print out during the example's demo application later on.

The integer object in the node class for the example tree data structure will serve as a simple key that has no other use other than being displayed to the console window and to be used during the searching algorithm we will look at. This is just a simple example.

LISTING 9.1 The Constructor and Destructor of the Node Class

```cpp
class Node
{
   public:
      Node(int obj) : m_object(obj), m_next(NULL),
                         m_prev(NULL), m_child(NULL)
      {
         cout << "Node created!" << endl;
      }


      ~Node()
      {
         m_prev = NULL;

         if(m_child != NULL)
            delete m_child;
```

```
        if(m_next != NULL)
            delete m_next;

        m_child = NULL;
        m_next = NULL;

        cout << "Node deleted!" << endl;
    }


private:
    int m_object;
    Node *m_next, *m_prev, *m_child;
};
```

A node needs to be able to add a child and a sibling. When adding a child node, there are two cases that can exist using the setup we have so far. There is either no children, in which case we would allocate the child pointer to the node that is being attached, or there is a child already, in which case we will call a function to add a sibling to that already-existing child node. Adding a sibling is similar in that there are either no siblings, which would mean we would allocate the sibling pointer to the node that is being added, or there is already a sibling, so we would call the function to add a sibling to that node, which will keep being called until we reach the end of the sibling list. This process for adding a sibling is the same as adding a node to the end of a link list. The functions we'll create for both of these operations are called AddChild() and AddSibling(), both of which are shown in Listing 9.2.

LISTING 9.2   The AddChild() and AddSibling() Functions

```
class Node
{
    public:
        void AddChild(Node *node)
        {
            if(m_child == NULL)
                m_child = node;
            else
                m_child->AddSibling(node);
        }


        void AddSibling(Node *node)
        {
            Node *ptr = m_next;
```

```
            if(m_next == NULL)
            {
               m_next = node;
               node->m_prev = this;
            }
            else
            {
               while(ptr->m_next != NULL)
                  ptr = ptr->m_next;

               ptr->m_next = node;
               node->m_prev = ptr;
            }
         }
      };
```

The last two functions we'll add to the example node class for the example general tree data structure are a function to display from the current node downward and a function to search for a value. The displaying function, called DisplayTree(), is for output purposes only for the upcoming demo application. The function will work by displaying the value of the integer member using std::cout and then calling the DisplayTree() function on all siblings and children that are attached to the node. This will keep occurring until all attached nodes have been displayed.

The searching function is a simple function used to search from the current node downward by checking all children and across the node by checking all siblings until the entire tree has been searched, which would mean the object was not found, or until it finds what it is looking for. The searching function works like the DisplayTree() function, with the exception that we start off by testing if the key we are searching for matches the key of the current node. If it does, the function will return true, or else it will check all children and siblings until it either reaches the end of the tree or finds the value. The DisplayTree() and Search() functions are shown in Listing 9.3.

LISTING 9.3 The DisplayTree() and Search() Functions

```
class Node
{
   public:
      void DisplayTree()
      {
         cout << m_object;
```

```
        if(m_next != NULL)
        {
            cout << " ";
            m_next->DisplayTree();
        }

        if(m_child != NULL)
        {
            cout << endl;
            m_child->DisplayTree();
        }
    }


    bool Search(int value)
    {
        if(m_object == value)
            return true;

        if(m_child != NULL)
        {
            if(m_child->Search(value) == true)
                return true;
        }

        if(m_next != NULL)
        {
            if(m_next->Search(value) == true)
                return true;
        }

        return false;
    }
};
```

One thing to note about the searching function from Listing 9.3 is that the search is slow. This example of a general tree is not a search tree built for speed. For a fast searching algorithm we could use other types of trees such as the kd-tree or the binary tree, which we'll look at in the upcoming sections of this chapter. Because there is no way to organize the data to the point where a searching algorithm can quickly traverse through the data structure, we are left with a linear approach. As mentioned earlier, not all trees are search trees. In Chapter 13 we'll look at data structures such as the scene graph, which is not a search tree and can be built using the approach that is implemented by this general example tree.

A scene graph is a graph that describes the hierarchy relationship of a virtual scene.

On the accompanying CD-ROM a demo application called Simple Tree in the Chapter 9 folder demonstrates the creation of a simple tree data structure using the code discussed so far. The demo application will create a subtree, create a root node that will act as the starting point for the main tree, add the subtree as a child to the root node, and add a few additional children to the root node. The node creation will look like the illustration in Figure 9.4.

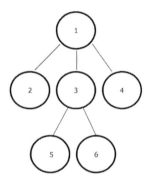

FIGURE 9.4 The nodes of the Simple Tree demo application.

In Figure 9.4 the subtree holds what will be the grandchildren to the root node, and the subtree itself is a child node. The root node also has additional children, which makes the root's children nodes 2, 3, and 4 (with 1 being the root node). Nodes 5 and 6 are the root node's grandchildren, the children of node 3. Because of the nature of the tree that is being created, we create subtrees and bind them together to create the one larger tree. The entire Node class for the Simple Tree demo application is shown in Listing 9.4.

LISTING 9.4 The Node Class for the Simple Tree Demo Application

```
class Node
{
   public:
      Node(int obj) : m_object(obj), m_next(NULL),
                      m_prev(NULL), m_child(NULL)
      {
         cout << "Node created!" << endl;
      }
```

```cpp
~Node()
{
   m_prev = NULL;

   if(m_child != NULL)
      delete m_child;

   if(m_next != NULL)
      delete m_next;

   m_child = NULL;
   m_next = NULL;

   cout << "Node deleted!" << endl;
}


void AddChild(Node *node)
{
   if(m_child == NULL)
      m_child = node;
   else
      m_child->AddSibling(node);
}


void AddSibling(Node *node)
{
   Node *ptr = m_next;

   if(m_next == NULL)
   {
      m_next = node;
      node->m_prev = this;
   }
   else
   {
      while(ptr->m_next != NULL)
         ptr = ptr->m_next;

      ptr->m_next = node;
      node->m_prev = ptr;
   }
}
```

```
void DisplayTree()
{
    cout << m_object;

    if(m_next != NULL)
    {
        cout << " ";
        m_next->DisplayTree();
    }

    if(m_child != NULL)
    {
        cout << endl;
        m_child->DisplayTree();
    }

}


bool Search(int value)
{
    if(m_object == value)
        return true;

    if(m_child != NULL)
    {
        if(m_child->Search(value) == true)
            return true;
    }

    if(m_next != NULL)
    {
        if(m_next->Search(value) == true)
            return true;
    }

    return false;
}


private:
    int m_object;
    Node *m_next, *m_prev, *m_child;
};
```

In the `main()` function of the Simple Tree demo application, once the nodes have been created and combined into one tree, the demo application displays all levels of the tree starting with the root node by calling `DisplayTree()`. This function will list, line by line, each generation of the tree. The first generation is the root node; the second generation is nodes 2, 3, and 4; and the third generation is nodes 5 and 6. Once complete, the demo application tests the `Search()` function to see if it can find a node with the key 5 and one with the key 9. The main source file for the Simple Tree demo application is shown in Listing 9.5, and a screenshot of the running demo application is shown in Figure 9.5.

LISTING 9.5 The `main()` Function of the Simple Tree Demo

```
int main(int args, char *arg[])
{
    cout << "Simple Tree Data Structure" << endl;
    cout << "Chapter 9: Trees" << endl << endl;


    // Manually create the tree...
    Node *root = new Node(1);
    Node *subTree1 = new Node(3);

    root->AddChild(new Node(2));

    subTree1->AddChild(new Node(5));
    subTree1->AddChild(new Node(6));

    root->AddChild(subTree1);
    root->AddChild(new Node(4));

    cout << endl;


    // Display the tree...
    cout << "Tree contents by level:" << endl;

    root->DisplayTree();

    cout << endl << endl;


    // Test seaching...
    cout << "Searching for node 5: ";
```

```
        if(root->Search(5) == true)
           cout << "Node Found!" << endl;
        else
           cout << "Node NOT Found!" << endl;

        cout << "Searching for node 9: ";

        if(root->Search(9) == true)
           cout << "Node Found!" << endl;
        else
           cout << "Node NOT Found!" << endl;

        cout << endl;


        // Will delete entire tree...
        delete root;

        cout << endl << endl;

        return 1;
     }
```

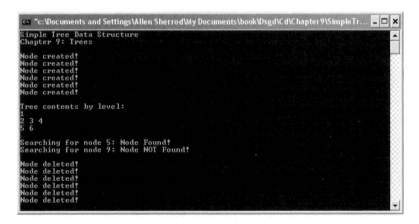

FIGURE 9.5   A screenshot from the Simple Tree demo.

BINARY TREES

A binary tree has a maximum of two child nodes per node. This differs from the tree created in the Simple Tree demo, where each node can have any number of children it wants. These two nodes of a binary tree are often referred to as the left and right child nodes. In this section we'll look at a binary search tree, which is a binary tree used for fast searches. In Chapter 13 we will look at a binary space partitioning tree, which is used in game development and related areas to speed up the processing of algorithms being performed on a virtual scene.

The left and right child nodes of a binary search tree are called left and right because when most people draw binary trees, one node is always to the lower left of its parent and the other is to the lower right. This is shown in Figure 9.6.

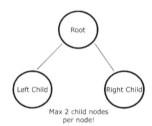

FIGURE 9.6   A binary tree.

The binary tree offers very fast insertions, deletions, and searching compared to the general tree discussed earlier in this chapter because the keys in a binary tree play an important role, as we will discuss in the following sections.

INSERTING INTO THE TREE

When a node is being inserted into a binary tree, its placement depends on its key. If the key is lower than the root node, the new node is allocated at the left node; otherwise, it is allocated at the right. If child nodes already exist, the child node is evaluated and the new node would either be allocated to the left or right node of the child. An example of this is shown in Figure 9.7.

As Figure 9.7 shows, the placement of a node depends on its key value instead of where it is manually placed by the programmer as seen in the Simple Tree demo earlier in this chapter. Also, as you can see from Figure 9.7, it does not take many checks to correctly place a node in a binary tree data structure. The larger the tree is, the more efficient it can be for processing various algorithms. For example, when inserting a new node in an ordered array of 1,000,000 elements, it will take on average 500,000 comparisons before it finds the position where the item is to be inserted (which is followed by copying operations, if necessary, to place the object there). In a binary tree of 1,000,000 elements it would take at most 20 comparisons to find the position of the node, and the node would be directly placed (allocated)

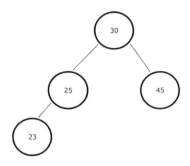

Inserting the node 23...

FIGURE 9.7   Inserting a node into a binary tree.

there. There is a huge difference in comparisons when working with arrays versus working with a binary tree. To calculate how many maximum comparisons would be needed for a binary tree you would use this equation:

$$C = \log_2(N - 1).$$

The value you come up with for the maximum number of comparisons depends on if the tree is balanced or not. A balanced tree means that on average there are as many left nodes as there are right nodes. An unbalanced tree is a tree with uneven sides. Unbalanced trees take longer to process. The worst-case scenario for unbalanced trees is when nodes are inserted in ascending or descending order, which would put all nodes on one side of the tree. An unbalanced tree can be created based on the order in which nodes are created. An example of this is shown in Figure 9.8.

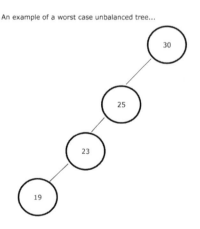

An example of a worst case unbalanced tree...

FIGURE 9.8   Balance versus unbalanced trees.

Balancing a tree can be difficult. Later in this chapter we will discuss a few balanced trees. A binary search tree is not automatically going to be balanced, unless the nodes are inserted in a way that ensures that it is. As shown in Figure 9.8, the order in which nodes are created has an impact on whether or not the tree is balanced and how unbalanced it gets. Later we'll discuss different types of balanced binary trees such as the red-black tree.

SEARCHING THROUGH THE TREE

Searching through a binary tree is much faster than it is for the example tree we saw earlier in this chapter. As trees grow, the difference in searching efficiency becomes extremely large. To search for a node in a tree with 1 million elements will take up to 20 comparisons using a binary tree, and that is the worst-case scenario. Like an ordered array, the binary tree uses what is known as the binary search, but in the binary tree the direction of the traversal depends on the value of the current node and the value of the key that is being searched. If the key is lower than the key of the current node, then the object, if it exists in the tree, would be on the left branch or on the right. Recursively moving, or using a loop, through a tree using that premise will quickly allow the algorithm to find an object or at least know that it is not in the tree once it reaches the bottom. The algorithm used to search a tree is similar to inserting a node in the tree, with the exception that when the algorithm has moved to the end of the tree without finding the key it was looking for, it will exit knowing the item was not found instead of allocating a spot for it.

Moving through a tree, called traversal, can be done in three different orders. It can be done in-order, pre-order, and post-order. Each of these types will be seen later in this chapter.

FINDING THE MINIMUM OR MAXIMUM KEY

Finding the node with the minimum or maximum key is easy in a binary tree. To find the minimum key you start at the root node and continue moving through left pointers until you reach a node with no left node. Once there, you know that you have arrived at the minimum key value in the tree. The same goes for the maximum key value, but instead you are moving to the right of the root node until you get to a node that has no right child. An illustration of this is shown in Figure 9.9.

REMOVAL FROM THE TREE

The most involved and slightly difficult part of implementing a binary search tree deals with deleting nodes. When you are deleting nodes from a tree, three general cases will come up in the implementation. The first case deals with deleting a node

The min value is the left- most value of 23.
The max value is the right-most value of 57.

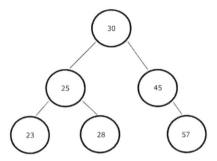

FIGURE 9.9 Finding the minimum and maximum keys.

that has no children. In this case the node can be deleted because there is nothing attached to it and no special treatments need to take place. If the node has only one child, that child node will replace the node that will be deleted. Both of these cases are shown in Figure 9.10.

Deleting a node without children (57)

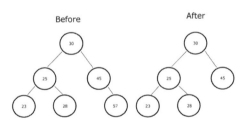

FIGURE 9.10 Deleting a node without children and one with children.

When there are two children, the work that must be done is a bit more involved. It is not possible to simply delete the node because the tree will become invalid. An example of this is shown in Figure 9.11.

Instead we have to find the smallest key under the node we will be deleting. This is called the in-order successor. This node will replace the one to be deleted. This allows us to delete the node while maintaining a valid tree and is shown in Figure 9.12.

Deleting a node with children (25)

Replace with 28 then what happens to 23?
What happens with to 10 and its children if 23
replaces 25?

The best option is to use 27, the in-order successor.

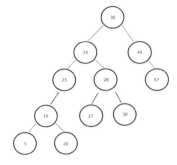

FIGURE 9.11   Simply deleting a node will lead to an invalid tree.

Using the in-order successor, 20, keeps the tree valid.

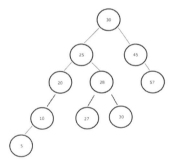

FIGURE 9.12   Replacing the node with its in-order successor leaves the tree valid.

An additional case is if the in-order successor has a right child node (it wouldn't have a left child because the left child would be the successor or the smallest key). In that case the right child node replaces the in-order successor, and the in-order successor replaces the node that is to be deleted, as shown in Figure 9.12.

If deleting nodes is not a feature that is desired in the tree, it can be avoided altogether. In this chapter we will implement a binary search tree with the ability to delete nodes.

IMPLEMENTING A BINARY TREE

ON THE CD

On the accompanying CD-ROM a demo application called Binary Tree is in the Chapter 9 folder. This demo application will create a binary search tree that allows for insertions, deletions, and searching throughout the tree structure. For the implementation a class will be created to represent a node. Inside this node is a template object for the key and left and right child nodes. The class's constructor, destructor, and member objects are shown in Listing 9.6. For this tree's implementation we will use both a node class and a tree class. For many trees the details of how they are implemented is more a matter of preference than anything else. For example, in the first tree implementation of the Simple Tree demo we used a node. Either way is fine, but the direction taken will determine how the code is implemented. Using a tree class allows more general information about the entire tree to be stored. Although this can be done using just the node class, it would require static member variables and would not look as straightforward since the nodes would have members that do not particularly pertain to it.

LISTING 9.6   The Node Class's Constructor, Destructor, and Members

```
template<typename T>
class BinaryTree;


template<typename T>
class Node
{
   friend BinaryTree<T>;

public:
   Node(T key) : m_key(key), m_left(NULL), m_right(NULL)
   {

   }


   ~Node()
   {
      if(m_left != NULL)
      {
         delete m_left;
         m_left = NULL;
      }
```

```
        if(m_right != NULL)
        {
            delete m_right;
            m_right = NULL;
        }
    }


    T GetKey()
    {
        return m_key;
    }


private:
    T m_key;

    Node *m_left, *m_right;
};
```

The binary tree itself only has one member object, which is a root node pointer. The tree's constructor marks the root node as NULL, and the destructor deletes the root node's memory if necessary. This will cause the entire tree to be deleted because the destructor of the node deletes the two child nodes.

Nodes are added to the binary tree using a function called push() (to be consistent with previous data structures). The push() function will need to handle two different cases. The first case is if there is no root node, so the node that is being added to the tree will become the root. The second case is if there is already a root node, then the left node would be used if the key is smaller than the root node, or the right node if it is not. If the appropriate child node already exists, the child node and both its children are examined until a free spot is found. The tree's constructor, destructor, and push() functions are shown in Listing 9.7.

LISTING 9.7   The BinaryTree Class's Constructor, Destructor, and push() Functions

```
template<typename T>
class BinaryTree
{
    public:
        BinaryTree() : m_root(NULL)
        {

        }
```

```
~BinaryTree()
{
   if(m_root != NULL)
   {
      delete m_root;
      m_root = NULL;
   }
}


bool push(T key)
{
   Node<T> *newNode = new Node<T>(key);

   if(m_root == NULL)
   {
      m_root = newNode;
   }
   else
   {
      Node<T> *parentNode = NULL;
      Node<T> *currentNode = m_root;

      while(1)
      {
         parentNode = currentNode;

         if(key == currentNode->m_key)
         {
            delete newNode;
            return false;
         }

         if(key < currentNode->m_key)
         {
            currentNode = currentNode->m_left;

            if(currentNode == NULL)
            {
               parentNode->m_left = newNode;
               return true;
            }
         }
         else
```

```
            {
                currentNode = currentNode->m_right;

                if(currentNode == NULL)
                {
                    parentNode->m_right = newNode;
                    return true;
                }
            }
        }
    }

    return true;
    }
};
```

Handling duplicates can be quite tricky and is not needed in most cases. The first thing the push() function does is to check to make sure the key does not match the current node. If a match is found, the function returns false. If a match is not found, the keys are examined and traversal through the tree continues until an empty spot is found.

The next function is used to perform a binary searching algorithm on the tree data structure. This function is straightforward. It examines the current node's key with the key that is being searched. If there is a match, then true is returned; otherwise, the appropriate child node is examined, which would be the left node if the key is smaller than the current node, or the right node is examined. This continues until there are no more nodes to check or until a match is found. The searching algorithm is shown in Listing 9.8 in a function called search() that, for this demo, simply tests if a key is found in the tree.

LISTING 9.8   The search() Function for the BinaryTree

```
template<typename T>
class BinaryTree
{
    public:
        bool search(T key)
        {
            if(m_root == NULL)
                return false;

            Node<T> *currentNode = m_root;
```

```
            while(currentNode->m_key != key)
            {
               if(key < currentNode->m_key)
                  currentNode = currentNode->m_left;
               else
                  currentNode = currentNode->m_right;

               if(currentNode == NULL)
                  return false;
            }

            return true;
         }
   };
```

The next set of functions is the `DisplayPreOrder()`, `DisplayPostOrder()`, and `DisplayInOrder()` member functions of the `BinaryTree` class. These functions display the keys of each node in the tree. For the pre-order traversal a node is operated on before moving to its left child and then to its right. This operation is recursive and will visit all nodes in the entire tree if starting at the root node. The post-order traversal visits the left child and then visits the right child before operating on the node itself. The in-order traversal visits the left child node first, operates on the current node, and then visits the right child node. Each of these traversal-displaying functions are shown in Listing 9.9.

LISTING 9.9   Traversal Displaying Functions

```
         template<typename T>
         class BinaryTree
         {
            public:
               void DisplayPreOrder()
               {
                  DisplayPreOrder(m_root);
               }


               void DisplayPostOrder()
               {
                  DisplayPostOrder(m_root);
               }
```

```cpp
        void DisplayInOrder()
        {
           DisplayInOrder(m_root);
        }


    private:
        void DisplayPreOrder(Node<T> *node)
        {
           if(node != NULL)
           {
              cout << node->m_key << " ";

              DisplayPreOrder(node->m_left);
              DisplayPreOrder(node->m_right);
           }
        }


        void DisplayPostOrder(Node<T> *node)
        {
           if(node != NULL)
           {
              DisplayPostOrder(node->m_left);
              DisplayPostOrder(node->m_right);

              cout << node->m_key << " ";
           }
        }


        void DisplayInOrder(Node<T> *node)
        {
           if(node != NULL)
           {
              DisplayInOrder(node->m_left);

              cout << node->m_key << " ";

              DisplayInOrder(node->m_right);
           }
        }
};
```

The last function in the `BinaryTree` class is the `remove()` function and it takes as a parameter the key of the node to delete. This function starts off by looking for the node that is to be deleted. If it does not find it, the function returns because the key does not exist in the tree. If it does find it, it must handle one of three main cases. If the node has no children, it is simply deleted from the tree. Since there is a pointer pointing to the node to be deleted, the code will first test if the root node is the one being deleted. If so, it sets the root to NULL or else it sets the corresponding node of the parent to NULL. This ensures that these nodes have nullified pointers. If the code tries to access a pointer to memory that has been deleted, the application can crash. Making them NULL now will ensure we have a way to test if a pointer has already been deleted. After that we can delete the temporary pointer that was pointing to the node that was to be deleted so that memory can be freed.

The second case is if the node to be deleted has one child. When this happens, the parent of the node that will be deleted replaces the deleted node with the node's child. Once that is done, the temporary pointer that was pointing to the node to be deleted is freed from memory.

The third case is if the node to be deleted has two children. In this case the in-order successor to the node that is going to be deleted is found by finding the left-most node of the right child of the node that will be deleted. This in-order successor is used to replace the deleted node. If the in-order successor has a right child, then the parent node of the node that will be deleted replaces the soon-to-be-deleted node with that child. Once done, the temporary pointer pointing to the node to be deleted can be freed, and the removal from the tree is complete. The `remove()` function of the `BinaryTree` class is shown in Listing 9.10.

LISTING 9.10 The `remove()` function of the `BinaryTree`

```
template<typename T>
class BinaryTree
{
   public:
      void remove(T key)
      {
         if(m_root == NULL)
            return;

         Node<T> *parent = m_root;
         Node<T> *node = m_root;
         bool isLeftNode = false;

         while(node->m_key != key)
         {
            parent = node;
```

```
   if(key < node->m_key)
   {
      node = node->m_left;
      isLeftNode = true;
   }
   else
   {
      node = node->m_right;
      isLeftNode = false;
   }

   if(node == NULL)
      return;
}

if(node->m_left == NULL && node->m_right == NULL)
{
   if(node == m_root)
      m_root = NULL;
   else if(isLeftNode == true)
      parent->m_left = NULL;
   else
      parent->m_right = NULL;
}
else if(node->m_left == NULL)
{
   if(node == m_root)
      m_root = node->m_right;
   else if(isLeftNode == true)
      parent->m_left = node->m_right;
   else
      parent->m_right = node->m_right;
}
else if(node->m_right == NULL)
{
   if(node == m_root)
      m_root = node->m_left;
   else if(isLeftNode == true)
      parent->m_left = node->m_left;
   else
      parent->m_right = node->m_left;
}
else
{
```

```
            Node<T> *tempNode = node->m_right;
            Node<T> *successor = node;
            Node<T> *successorParent = node;

            while(tempNode != NULL)
            {
                successorParent = successor;
                successor = tempNode;
                tempNode = tempNode->m_left;
            }

            if(successor != node->m_right)
            {
                successorParent->m_left = successor->m_right;
                successor->m_right = node->m_right;
            }

            if(node == m_root)
            {
                m_root = successor;
            }
            else if(isLeftNode)
            {
                node = parent->m_left;
                parent->m_left = successor;
            }
            else
            {
                node = parent->m_right;
                parent->m_right = successor;
            }

            successor->m_left = node->m_left;
        }

        // Nullify so the destructor does not delete any nodes
        // they might point to.
        node->m_left = NULL;
        node->m_right = NULL;
        delete node;
    }
};
```

The last code to discuss is the main source file for the Binary Tree demo application. In this demo application an integer binary tree is created and is populated with eight nodes. The node with the key 27 is then removed from the tree to test the remove() function. Once this is completed, the search() function is called to test if it can find a key of 20, 14, and 27. Since 27 was deleted, it should not be able to find that node. The main() function wraps up by calling DisplayInOrder(), DisplayPreOrder(), and DisplayPostOrder() to display the keys of each of the tree's nodes using the various types of traversals. The main source file for the Binary Tree demo application is shown in Listing 9.11. A screenshot of the demo application executing is shown in Figure 9.13.

LISTING 9.11   The Main Source File for the Binary Tree Demo

```cpp
#include<iostream>
#include"BinaryTree.h"

using namespace std;


int main(int args, char **argc)
{
    cout << "Binary Trees" << endl;
    cout << "Chapter 9: Trees" << endl;
    cout << endl;


    BinaryTree<int> binaryTree;

    binaryTree.push(20);
    binaryTree.push(10);
    binaryTree.push(12);
    binaryTree.push(27);
    binaryTree.push(9);
    binaryTree.push(50);
    binaryTree.push(33);
    binaryTree.push(6);

    binaryTree.remove(27);


    if(binaryTree.search(20) == true)
        cout << "The key 20 found!" << endl;
    else
        cout << "The key 20 NOT found!" << endl;
```

```
   if(binaryTree.search(14) == true)
      cout << "The key 14 found!" << endl;
   else
      cout << "The key 14 NOT found!" << endl;


   if(binaryTree.search(27) == true)
      cout << "The key 27 found!" << endl;
   else
      cout << "The key 27 NOT found!" << endl;

   cout << endl;


   cout << " Pre-order: ";
   binaryTree.DisplayPreOrder();
   cout << endl;

   cout << "Post-order: ";
   binaryTree.DisplayPostOrder();
   cout << endl;

   cout << "  In-order: ";
   binaryTree.DisplayInOrder();
   cout << endl << endl;

   return 1;
}
```

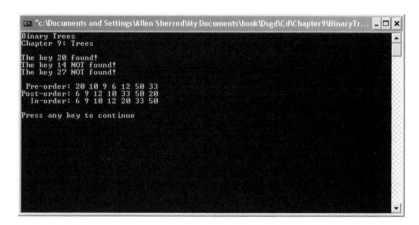

FIGURE 9.13 A screenshot from the Binary Tree demo.

K-DIMENSIONAL TREES

The data structure known as a *k*-dimensional tree, *kd*-tree for short, is a type of binary tree that uses keys that have multiple dimensions. This multidimensional key can vary—hence the k in *kd*-tree. In this section we will look at *kd*-trees more closely and we will create a straightforward implementation.

NOTE *kd-trees are spelled with a lowercase italicized k and lowercase d. Some people use different variations such as KD-tree or Kd-tree, but this is the most common spelling.*

A *kd*-tree can be used for range searches, nearest neighbor searches, space partitioning, and so forth. By sending in a range of key values, a *kd*-tree can find all nodes that fall within that range or that match it. In this chapter we will create a demo application that will allow us to create a three-dimensional *kd*-tree and perform a range search algorithm on it.

When inserting nodes into a *kd*-tree, the current depth of the tree is used to determine which dimension of the key is used when determining the direction of traversal. For example, the root node is level 1 and would use the first dimension of the key. The next level is level 2 and would use the second dimension of the key and so on. If there are three dimensions to the key, which can be represented as an array that is the size of 3, then the following level will start back at the first dimension. An example of this is shown in Figure 9.14. A *kd*-tree with one dimension is no different than a traditional binary tree.

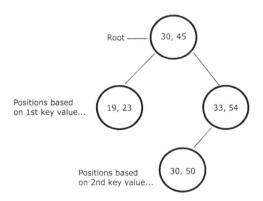

FIGURE 9.14 Nodes of a *kd*-tree.

A *kd*-tree can also be used for space partitioning like a BSP tree. This is done by finding the median point of all the vertices for a node and defining a plane based on the current depth of the tree. For example, a three-dimensional *kd*-tree can be used where level 1 would create a plane along the *x*-axis, level 2 the *y*-axis, and level 3 the *z*-axis. We'll discuss this more in Chapter 13, Scene Management.

IMPLEMENTING A *KD*-TREE

The implementation of a *kd*-tree starts with the node. The node is similar to the node of a binary tree, with the exception that the key is not one-dimensional but can vary. For this implementation we will use a `std::vector` array as well as having a left and right child node. There is no limit to the number of dimensions the tree can have, but it has to be more than one. The constructor, destructor, and member variables for the *kd*-tree's node class are shown in Listing 9.12.

LISTING 9.12 The Node of a *kd*-Tree

```
template<class TYPE>
class KdTree;


template<class TYPE>
struct KdNode
{
   friend KdTree<TYPE>;

   public:
      KdNode(vector<TYPE> &key) : m_key(key), m_left(NULL),
                                  m_right(NULL)
      {

      }


      ~KdNode()
      {
         if(m_left != NULL)
         {
            delete m_left;
            m_left = NULL;
         }

         if(m_right != NULL)
         {
```

```
            delete m_right;
            m_right = NULL;
         }
      }

   private:
      vector<TYPE> m_key;

      KdNode *m_left;
      KdNode *m_right;
};
```

The class for the *k*d-tree has a root node and a dimensional depth as member variables. The depth is used to keep track of how many dimensions this *k*d-tree is. When a node is being inserted into the tree, a loop is used to traverse through the container until the spot for the node is found. Every time the code goes to a deeper level by moving to one of the child nodes, that will determine which key dimension is used. In the upcoming demo application that will use this code we will specify three dimensions for the key. This means the root uses the first index of the key, the child of the root uses the second index, the child of the root's children use the last index of the key, the children a level deeper than that use the first index of the key, and so on. The tree class is called KdTree, and its member objects, constructor, destructor, and insertion (push()) functions are shown in Listing 9.13.

LISTING 9.13 The KdTree Class

```
template<typename TYPE>
class KdTree
{
   public:
      KdTree(int depth) : m_root(0), m_depth(depth)
      {
         assert(depth > 0);
      }


      ~KdTree()
      {
         if(m_root != NULL)
         {
            delete m_root;
            m_root = NULL;
```

```
        }
    }


    void push(vector<TYPE> &key)
    {
        KdNode<TYPE> *newNode = new KdNode<TYPE>(key);

        if(m_root == NULL)
        {
            m_root = newNode;
            return;
        }

        KdNode<TYPE> *currentNode = m_root;
        KdNode<TYPE> *parentNode = m_root;
        int level = 0;

        while(1)
        {
            parentNode = currentNode;

            if(key[level] < currentNode->m_key[level])
            {
                currentNode = currentNode->m_left;

                if(currentNode == NULL)
                {
                    parentNode->m_left = newNode;
                    return;
                }
            }
            else
            {
                currentNode = currentNode->m_right;

                if(currentNode == NULL)
                {
                    parentNode->m_right = newNode;
                    return;
                }
            }

            level++;
```

```
            if(level >= m_depth)
                level = 0;
        }
    }


    private:
        KdNode<TYPE> *m_root;
        int m_depth;
};
```

The last functions in the class are the functions used to display all keys that match a range of values. This function tests to see if all the dimensions of a key fall within a range that is passed in as parameters. If so, the key is displayed to the console window. The traversal continues through all nodes until the entire tree has been processed. The functions (shown in Listing 9.14) are called `displayRange()`.

LISTING 9.14   The `displayRange()` Functions

```
template<typename TYPE>
class KdTree
{
    public:
        void displayRange(const vector<TYPE> &low,
                          const vector<TYPE> &high)
        {
            displayRange(0, low, high, m_root);
        }


    private:
        void displayRange(int level, const vector<TYPE> &low,
                          const vector<TYPE> &high,
                          KdNode<TYPE> *node)
        {
            if(node != NULL)
            {
                for(int i = 0; i < m_depth; i++)
                {
                    if(low[i] > node->m_key[i] ||
                        high[i] < node->m_key[i])
                        break;
                }
```

```
              if(i == m_depth)
              {
                 cout << "(";

                 for(int j = 0; j < m_depth; j++)
                 {
                    cout << node->m_key[j];

                    if(j != m_depth - 1)
                       cout << ", ";
                 }

                 cout << ")" << endl;
              }

              level++;

              if(level >= m_depth)
                 level = 0;

              if(low[level] <= node->m_key[level])
                 displayRange(level, low, high, node->m_left);

              if(high[level] >= node->m_key[level])
                 displayRange(level, low, high, node->m_right);
           }
        }
     };
```

ON THE CD

On the accompanying CD-ROM is a demo application called KD Tree in the Chapter 9 folder. This demo application will create a *kd*-tree and populate it with random three-dimensional keys. Once created, the displayRange() function is called to test that the code can find a range of values within a high and low range and display them. The display is for output purposes only. The code for the main() function for the KD Tree demo is shown in Listing 9.15. Figure 9.15 shows a screen-shot from the application.

LISTING 9.15   The Main Source File for the KD Tree Demo

```
     #include<iostream>
     #include"KDTree.h"

     using namespace std;
```

```
int main(int args, char **argc)
{
   cout << "KD Trees" << endl;
   cout << "Chapter 9: Trees" << endl;
   cout << endl;


   // Create KD tree and populate it.
   KdTree<int> kdTree(3);

   for(int i = 0; i < 100; i++)
   {
      vector<int> key(3);

      key[0] =  rand() % 100;
      key[1] =  rand() % 100;
      key[2] =  rand() % 100;

      kdTree.push(key);
   }


   // Display range of values that falls within the range.
   vector<int> low(3), high(3);

   low[0] = 20;
   low[1] = 30;
   low[2] = 25;

   high[0] = 90;
   high[1] = 70;
   high[2] = 80;

   cout << "Range (20, 30, 25) (90, 70, 80) Match:" << endl;

   kdTree.displayRange(low, high);


   cout << endl << endl;

   return 1;
}
```

NOTE

Another popular algorithm to use for kd-trees is the n-nearest neighbor search, which can get a number of elements that is closest to a key.

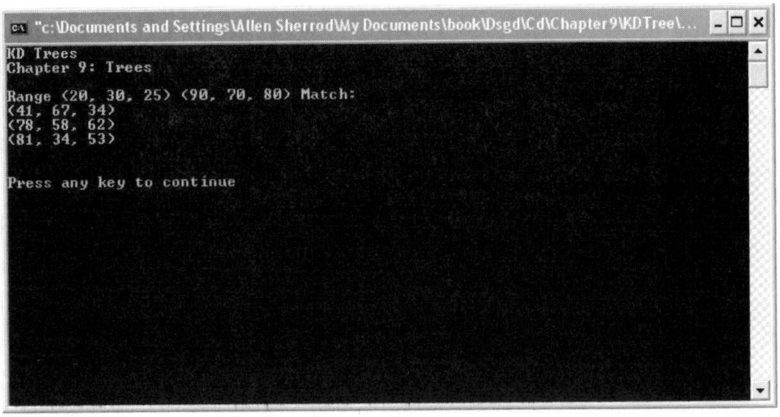

FIGURE 9.15 A screenshot from the KD-Tree demo.

ADDITIONAL TYPES OF TREES

There are many different types of tree data structures in computer science. In this chapter we will briefly discuss general b-trees, AVL trees, red-black trees, heaps, 2-3 trees, and 2-3-4 trees.

B-TREES

A b-tree is a balanced tree data structure with multiple child nodes that can be attached to one node. B-trees keep the number of child nodes within a certain range, which can be predefined, so when a node violates this range, the tree is altered so that it follows the rules of a b-tree. This is done by joining nodes together or splitting them. The range of nodes determines what type of b-tree it is. Types of b-trees are 2-3 trees and 2-3-4 trees, which we'll discuss later in this section.

B-trees can waste more space with nodes that are not full than other balanced trees but often don't need to be rebalanced as much. B-trees are kept balanced by keeping all leaf nodes on the same depth. They are more complicated to implement than other trees, but they can be powerful data structures. They can also be used in applications such as database systems.

AVL TREES

An AVL tree is a self-balancing binary search tree, which means there are two child nodes for every node. The heights of the child nodes in an AVL tree differ at most by one, which makes them height-balanced trees. When items are inserted or deleted from the tree, they alter the structure of the tree as needed to keep it balanced. This is done with tree rotations, which red-black trees use to balance nodes as well.

NOTE

A height value, also known as the balance factor, is the value you get from adding up all child node keys on both sides (left and right). In an AVL tree the difference between these totals should be 1, 0, or −1, or else the tree is not balanced.

In an AVL tree there is something known as the balance factor. The balance factor of a node is the height of the right child minus the height of the left child of any given node. As long as the balance factor is in the range of −1 to 1, the node is balanced. If a node has any other value for its balance factor, an algorithm must be performed to rebalance the tree.

Red-Black Trees

Red-black trees are balanced binary trees. In a red-black tree the algorithms for searching are the same but the algorithms for insertions and deletions are very different. When nodes are inserted into a red-black tree, they alter the structure of the tree as needed to keep it balanced. Insertions can be either top-down or bottom-up, where top-down insertions insert nodes that descend down the tree while bottom-up insertions work from the bottom to the top of the tree when looking for a place to insert a node. The insertions and deletions of a red-black tree are not as fast as a traditional binary tree, but it is worth the cost in most applications and algorithms to have a fast, balanced tree. The red-black tree is more complicated to implement than a binary tree but is considered easier than most b-trees.

2-3 and 2-3-4 Trees

2-3 trees are b-trees of order 3, which means they can have up to three child nodes for each node. This tree is another self-balancing tree like the other balanced trees. In a 2-3 tree a node with a data item cam have two children, and a node with two data items can have three children. The elements in 2-3 trees, as well as other b-trees, are ordered.

NOTE

2-3 trees are also called multiway trees of the order of 2, while 2-3-4 trees have an order of 4.

2-3-4 trees are similar to 2-3 trees, but 2-3-4 trees can have up to four child nodes. They are another type of multiway tree. 2-3-4 trees are harder to implement than red-black trees, but they are considered equivalent. A 2-3-4 tree can be converted easily into a red-black tree and vise versa. 2-3-4 trees are isomorphic to red-black trees.

Heaps

A heap is a weakly ordered binary tree that keeps the node with the largest key (root node) on the top of the tree. All nodes within the heap are not necessarily in order, unlike in a binary tree. The only thing that is certain in a heap is that the child nodes of any given node have a key that is less than their parent.

NOTE *The STL priority queue uses a heap as its underlying data structure.*

Heaps will be discussed in more detail in Chapter 10, Heaps. The heap data structure is very useful, but because it is weakly ordered, it cannot be used for searching using the binary algorithm. The phrase *weakly ordered* in this case means that the child nodes of any given node are smaller than their parents but are not in any particular order other than that. Because of this, it would be hard to determine which child nodes to visit to get to the node that is being searched for the fastest.

Heaps are often implemented as arrays. Although arrays do not offer fast insertions, this can be handled by making sure the expansion size is not linear. The STL vector array increases its size by nonlinear means and is recommended when speed is critical but the possibility for wasted memory is not a huge disadvantage.

Summary

There is a lot of information on tree data structures in computer science. Trees have may uses that can aid in the processing of a set of data. In game development trees are used in great numbers for all kinds of applications such as speeding up rendering time, speeding up real-time physics and collision detection and response, representing scene information, speeding up advance lighting contributions, and so forth.

Trees will be discussed throughout the remainder of this book. In the next chapter, Heaps, we'll look at the heap data structure, which uses a weakly ordered binary tree. In Chapter 11, Graphs, we'll look at graphs. A tree is an instance of a graph, which can be used for numerous applications such as artificial intelligence. In Chapter 13 we'll take another look at trees and how they fit in with game and simulation development.

Chapter Review Questions

Answers to the following chapter review questions can be found in Appendix B.

1. What is a tree in computer science?
2. What is a root node?

3. A node with no children is known as a:
   a. Child node
   b. Successor node
   c. Leaf node
   d. None of the above
4. What is the name for a node that shares a parent with another node?
   a. Sibling node
   b. Left and right children
   c. In-order successor
   d. None of the above
5. What is an edge?
6. How many nodes can a binary tree have attached to a node?
   a. 1
   b. 2
   c. 3
   d. None of the above
7. How many siblings can a binary tree node have?
   a. 1
   b. 2
   c. 3
   d. None of the above
8. On average, what is the maximum number of comparisons needed to find a key in a balanced binary tree with 1 million nodes?
   a. 10
   b. 15
   c. 20
   d. 30
   e. None of the above
9. What are the types of traversals talked about in this chapter?
   a. In-order, pre-order, post-order
   b. Front-to-back, back-to-front
   c. In-order, pre-order, post-order, successor
   d. None of the above
10. To delete a node in a binary tree that has two children requires the algorithm to find what node?
   a. The node with the maximum key underneath the deleted node's subtree
   b. The parent node
   c. The smallest sibling node
   d. The in-order successor
   e. None of the above

11. How do *kd*-trees differ from binary trees?
12. A *kd*-tree inserts nodes based on:
    a. Key value
    b. Depth level, key dimension, and key value
    c. The best way to make the tree balanced
    d. None of the above
13. What are b-trees?
14. How many edges does a 2-3 tree's node have? How many edges does a 2-3-4 tree's node have?
15. What are AVL trees?
16. All binary trees are balanced.
    a. True
    b. False
17. A heap is a data structure based on link lists.
    a. True
    b. False
18. A *kd*-tree is a type of binary tree.
    a. True
    b. False
19. An edge is a connection from one node to another.
    a. True
    b. False
20. A red-black tree has three edges for each node.
    a. True
    b. False

PROGRAMMING PROJECTS

Exercise 1: Based on the information in this chapter, implement a binary tree using an array instead of pointers to nodes.

Exercise 2: Build off Exercise 1 and allow the array-based binary tree to be saved and loaded from a file.

Exercise 3: Implement a binary tree that allows you to change the key of a node. When a key is changed, it will need to be removed from the tree and reinserted.

10 Heaps

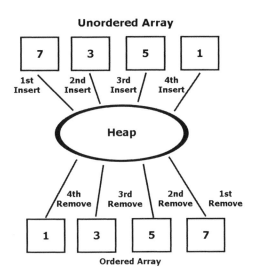

A bstract data types are data structures that can be implemented using a variety of underlying data structures. One such abstract data type seen in this book is the priority queue in Chapter 5. A priority queue is an abstract data type because it can be implemented using an array, link list, or another data structure such as a tree. An array is an example of a basic data structure, and those types of data structures are normally used internally by other, more abstract data structure containers.

In this chapter we will look at the heap abstract data type (ADT) data structure. We'll also look at the heap sort algorithm, which uses heaps to perform a fast sorting operation, and we'll look at how heaps are a natural fit to create a priority queue by implementing a new container that uses the heap. Most standard STL implementations of the `priority_queue` data structure use a heap for its underlying implementation.

INTRODUCTION TO HEAPS

A heap container is a binary tree data structure that is not used for searching, unlike the binary search tree in Chapter 9, which is used specifically for searching for specified key values. In a heap data structure the node keys are always larger than their children nodes, but their children nodes are not in any particular order. This differs from the binary tree, in which the left child is always the smaller node, while the right node is always the larger value when compared to their parents. In a heap this is not the case because both children are smaller than the parent. A visual representation of this is shown in Figure 10.1.

The binary search tree specifies its condition that the left child be smaller than its parent while the right child be greater than or equal to its parent. This data structure condition is not one for a traditional binary tree that is not used for searching.

An example of a heap as a tree...

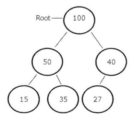

FIGURE 10.1 A heap.

Three major characteristics make a heap data structure what it is: (a) A heap is a binary tree. (b) A heap is a complete data structure, meaning the rows of nodes are completely filled in from left to right without any gaps, as shown in the left-hand illustration in Figure 10.1. (c) Every node in a heap is larger than or equal to its child nodes. The root node of every heap is either the largest or smallest value in the container, depending on the sorting condition, unlike in a binary tree where the largest value in the container is the right-most node from the root and the smallest value is the left-most node from the root.

A CLOSER LOOK AT HEAPS

A heap is a weakly ordered binary tree. This means that the child nodes of any given node are smaller than their parent but are not necessarily in any particular order in relation to one another. This was seen in Figure 10.1, where some nodes are not in any order except for being smaller than or equal to their parents. In a binary search tree the order is strict, which allows for the possibility of performing a binary search. When traversing a heap, the direction of traversal cannot be assumed. If a search was to be performed on a heap, every node would potentially need to be visited. When searching, you can exit from some paths early if the keys of the current nodes become less than the search key, but other than that the traversal is much slower than that of a binary search tree. The big-O of a searching algorithm performed on a heap would run at `O(N)`.

HEAP INSERTIONS

Although a heap is weakly ordered, the purpose of the data structure is to allow for fast removal from the top of the heap. When an item is inserted into the data structure, it is initially placed on the bottom of the list. The element cannot stay at this position because its value might violate the heap condition that states that every child must be smaller than its parent. Thus, when an element is inserted into the container, it is moved up through the list until it finds an index where the element is smaller than its parent but larger than its children. This is shown in Figure 10.2.

HEAP REMOVAL

Removing is done from the top of the heap. When a heap is implemented as an array, this means removing element 0 since the element at index 0 is always the root node. Once the root has been removed, the heap is no longer complete because of the newly made hole, and it must be replaced with the next elements in line. One method is simply to move all elements in the array down one. Another method, which will be used in this chapter, is to take the last element in the array, place it at index 0, and move that element down until it is below an element that is larger than

An example of a heap as a tree...

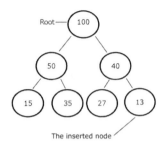

FIGURE 10.2 Inserting into a heap.

it but is above an element that is smaller. Using a simple algorithm, which we'll discuss in the implementation, can allow us to quickly perform this operation without having to move $N - 1$ elements by using the first method. A visual representation of the removal process is shown in Figure 10.3.

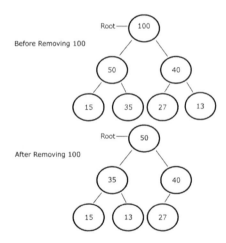

FIGURE 10.3 Removing from a heap.

Moving elements up or down a container is called bubbling up or down (also known as percolating and trickling). During the bubbling process a value is checked to see whether it is in a position that satisfies the data structure's conditions. If so, it can be left where it is; otherwise, the process continues until the correct position is found. This process not only satisfies the heap condition but also keeps the heap complete when elements are removed, each of which is illustrated in Figure 10.3.

When elements are bubbled up or down, they traverse parent to parent.

HEAP RESIZING

In this chapter the heap will be implemented using an array. As you'll see later in this chapter, using an array is easy and straightforward when compared to other basic data structures such as the link list. A binary tree that uses pointers and references could also be used, but the insertion and removal algorithms can perform slower and can be harder to implement than when using only an array. This will be demonstrated in the next section during the implementation of a heap. Although arrays are not as easy to expand as basic data structures that use pointers, expanding the array using nonlinear means can be very beneficial and it does not affect the elements already inside the container.

STL vector arrays expand nonlinearly.

Using a tree implementation for the heap would make it very difficult to access the last item inserted into the data structure. With an array this element would be $N - 1$, but in a tree how would one know where the last element was inserted? Also, by initially inserting a new item onto the list, you'll have to locate that end position for the element, which can take quite a while with a large tree. Since a heap is not a search tree, this can be very difficult using an algorithm. Regardless of the tree size, the initial insertion for an array is constant $0(1)$. Whether using a tree or an array, the last item would have to be bubbled up through the container, so a tree implementation does not offer any benefit.

IMPLEMENTING HEAPS

The heap implementation will use an array. Because the STL is such a useful tool for programmers, the implementation for the heap data structure will use the `std::vector`. The heap in this section will be implemented as a template class. This class has only one member object, which is the vector array, and several functions. The first constructor of the heap implementation will be a default empty function, and the second constructor will allow a minimal size to be specified. This can be useful to prevent the `vector` array from having to resize if the minimal size or the total size of the heap is already known.

The heap data structure has two functions called `push()` and `pop()`. The `push()` function will insert a new element into the end of the array. Once the element is there, the function will move the element up until it finds the best position for it. The parent of any element is found using the following equation:

```
pIndex = (index - 1) / 2
```

where pIndex is the parent index and index is the current node's index. A loop inside the push() function executes until it finds the best position for the element or until it reaches the top, at which point it can be determined that the element belongs at the top of the heap.

The pop() function works by first taking the last element of the std::vector array and putting it in the top position at index 0. The array size is decremented, and the code enters a loop. Inside this loop the code finds the right position to insert the element that has been moved to the top. Once it finds this, the code will set that index to the element and exit.

The last two functions are used to peek at the top of the container and to return the size. The size of the container is the size of the vector array. The peeking function is used to look at the topmost element so that our code has a way of accessing that data. The Heap class is shown in Listing 10.1.

LISTING 10.1 The Heap Class

```
#include<vector>

using namespace std;


template<typename KEY>
class Heap
{
   public:
      Heap()
      {

      }


      Heap(int minSize)
      {
         m_heap.reserve(minSize);
      }


      void push(KEY key)
      {
         m_heap.push_back(key);

         int index = (int)m_heap.size() - 1;
         KEY temp = m_heap[index];
         int parentIndex = (index - 1) / 2;
```

```
    while(index > 0 && temp >= m_heap[parentIndex])
    {
       m_heap[index] = m_heap[parentIndex];
       index = parentIndex;
       parentIndex = (parentIndex - 1) / 2;
    }


    m_heap[index] = temp;
}


void pop()
{
    int index = 0;

    m_heap[index] = m_heap[(int)m_heap.size() - 1];
    m_heap.pop_back();

    KEY temp = m_heap[index];

    int currentIndex = 0, leftIndex = 0, rightIndex = 0;


    while(index < (int)m_heap.size() / 2)
    {
       leftIndex = 2 * index + 1;
       rightIndex = leftIndex + 1;


       if(rightIndex < (int)m_heap.size() &&
          m_heap[leftIndex] < m_heap[rightIndex])
       {
          currentIndex = rightIndex;
       }
       else
       {
          currentIndex = leftIndex;
       }


       if(temp >= m_heap[currentIndex])
          break;
```

```
                m_heap[index] = m_heap[currentIndex];
                index = currentIndex;
            }


            m_heap[index] = temp;
        }


        KEY peek()
        {
            return m_heap[0];
        }


        int size()
        {
            return (int)m_heap.size();
        }


    private:
        vector<KEY> m_heap;
};
```

ON THE CD

On the accompanying CD-ROM a demo application called Heap can be found in the Chapter 10 folder. The Heap demo application creates a heap using the Heap class from Listing 10.1 and populates it with 10 elements. The contents of the heap are displayed to the console window, which by default will display the contents from greatest to smallest. The main source file for the Heap demo application is shown in Listing 10.2. Figure 10.4 shows a screenshot of the application.

LISTING 10.2 The Heap Demo's Main Source File

```
#include<iostream>
#include"Heap.h"

using namespace std;


int main(int args, char **argc)
{
    cout << "Heap" << endl;
    cout << "Chapter 10: Heaps" << endl;
    cout << endl;
```

```
Heap<int> heap(10);

heap.push(30);
heap.push(33);
heap.push(43);
heap.push(23);
heap.push(20);
heap.push(10);
heap.push(22);
heap.push(90);
heap.push(95);
heap.push(86);


cout << "Heap Contents:";

while(heap.size() != 0)
{
   cout << " " << heap.peek();
   heap.remove();
}


cout << "." << endl << endl;

return 1;
}
```

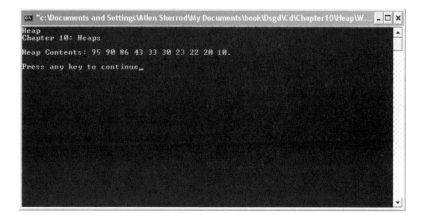

FIGURE 10.4   A screenshot of the Heap demo.

HEAP SORT

A heap data structure can be used to perform what is called a heap sort, an algorithm that uses a heap to sort the elements of another data structure. This is done by inserting all the elements of an unordered data structure into a heap and then moving the elements from the heap one by one back into the original data structure. Because a heap stores the largest or smallest value on the top of the container, simply removing elements from it will remove the elements in order. This was shown in the Heap demo application when the contents of the container were displayed to the console window in descending order. The insertion and removal operations by themselves for the heap data structure run in O(logN), and the heap sort runs in O(N * log N) because to complete the sort a heap sort must eventually call each of these functions for every element in the unordered data structure. An illustration of the heap sort algorithm is shown in Figure 10.5.

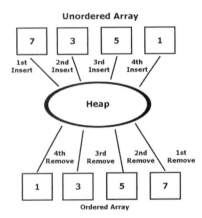

FIGURE 10.5 The heap sort.

IMPLEMENTING THE HEAP SORT

Implementing the heap sort is straightforward. In this demo application the heap code will be the code used in Listing 10.1 and will keep the largest element on the top of the tree. To perform the heap sort a loop is used to place all elements from one container into a heap, and then another loop is used to move the elements from the heap back into the original container.

On the CD-ROM a demo application called Heap Sort in the Chapter 10 folder demonstrates the heap sort algorithm. The Heap Sort demo application sorts an array in ascending and descending order. The main() function of the Heap Sort demo application creates an array, displays the unordered contents to the console window, sorts the array in ascending order, displays the contents again, and then it does the same in descending order. The main source file for the Heap Sort demo application is shown in Listing 10.3. Figure 10.6 shows a screenshot.

Performing the heap sort on the unordered container instead of copying to a second container (heap) can reduce the memory footprint of the algorithm.

LISTING 10.3   The Heap Sort Algorithm

```cpp
#include<iostream>
#include<vector>
#include"Heap.h"

using namespace std;


void HeapSortAscending(vector<int> &array)
{
   Heap<int> heap;
   int i;


   for(i = 0; i < (int)array.size(); i++)
      heap.push(array[i]);

   for(i = (int)array.size() - 1; i >= 0; i-)
   {
      array[i] = heap.peek();
      heap.pop();
   }
}


void HeapSortDescending(vector<int> &array)
{
   Heap<int> heap;
   int i;


   for(i = 0; i < (int)array.size(); i++)
      heap.push(array[i]);
```

```
   for(i = 0; i < (int)array.size(); i++)
   {
      array[i] = heap.peek();
      heap.pop();
   }
}


void DisplayVector(vector<int> &array)
{
   for(int i = 0; i < (int)array.size(); i++)
   {
      cout << " " << array[i];
   }


   cout << ".";
}


int main(int args, char **argc)
{
   cout << "Heap Sort" << endl;
   cout << "Chapter 10: Heaps" << endl;
   cout << endl;


   // Create container and populate it.
   vector<int> array;

   array.push_back(33);
   array.push_back(43);
   array.push_back(23);
   array.push_back(20);
   array.push_back(10);
   array.push_back(22);
   array.push_back(90);
   array.push_back(95);
   array.push_back(86);


   // Display before sort.
   cout << "Array contents before sort:";
   DisplayVector(array);
   cout << endl;
```

```
        // Display after sort (ascending).
        HeapSortAscending(array);

        cout << "Array contents after sort (ascending ):";
        DisplayVector(array);
        cout << endl;


        // Display after sort (descending).
        HeapSortDescending(array);

        cout << "Array contents after sort (descending):";
        DisplayVector(array);
        cout << endl << endl;


        return 1;
}
```

FIGURE 10.6   A screenshot of the Heap Sort demo.

PRIORITY QUEUES USING HEAPS

A priority queue is an ADT data structure that internally sorts its elements based on their priority level. When elements are removed from the container, the largest or smallest (depending on the specified sorting condition) element is removed. In a priority queue only one element is accessible at a time, like a queue and a stack, and when elements are pushed onto the container, an element will only be available when it has the highest priority.

A heap is a natural fit for a priority queue. In a priority queue only the highest-priority element is removed or accessible. This can also be seen with the heap data structure in that only one element is accessible at a time. Using a heap data structure that allows for the sorting condition to be specified will allow us to create a priority queue by using the heap as an underlying data structure. The heap is a fast data structure, so this speed is beneficial to the priority queue, especially with large sets of data.

IMPLEMENTING PRIORITY QUEUE USING HEAPS

The implementation for the priority queue in this chapter starts by modifying the Heap class so that the order of the elements can be determined by the programmer. Earlier the heap kept the highest value on the top of the container, but now it will be altered to allow for either the highest or the lowest. The changes made to this class involve specifying another template parameter, which will be used for the comparison operator. Altering the push() and pop() functions to make use of the comparison operator instead of assuming that the largest value element will be on top. The modified Heap data structure class is shown in Listing 10.4.

LISTING 10.4 The Altered Heap Class

```
#include<vector>

using namespace std;


template<typename KEY, typename CMP>
class Heap
{
    public:
        Heap()
        {

        }


        Heap(int minSize)
        {
            m_heap.reserve(minSize);
        }
```

```
void push(KEY key)
{
   m_heap.push_back(key);

   int index = (int)m_heap.size() - 1;
   KEY temp = m_heap[index];
   int parentIndex = (index - 1) / 2;

   CMP cmp;


   while(index > 0 && (cmp(temp, m_heap[parentIndex]) ||
         temp == m_heap[parentIndex]))
   {
      m_heap[index] = m_heap[parentIndex];
      index = parentIndex;
      parentIndex = (parentIndex - 1) / 2;
   }

   m_heap[index] = temp;
}


void pop()
{
   int index = 0;

   m_heap[index] = m_heap[(int)m_heap.size() - 1];
   m_heap.pop_back();

   KEY temp = m_heap[index];

   int currentIndex = 0, leftIndex = 0, rightIndex = 0;

   while(index < (int)m_heap.size() / 2)
   {
      leftIndex = 2 * index + 1;
      rightIndex = leftIndex + 1;

      CMP cmp;

      if(rightIndex < (int)m_heap.size() &&
         (cmp(m_heap[rightIndex], m_heap[leftIndex]) ||
          m_heap[rightIndex] == m_heap[leftIndex]))
```

```
        {
            currentIndex = rightIndex;
        }
        else
        {
            currentIndex = leftIndex;
        }

        if(cmp(temp, m_heap[currentIndex]) ||
            temp == m_heap[currentIndex])
            break;

        m_heap[index] = m_heap[currentIndex];
        index = currentIndex;
    }

    m_heap[index] = temp;
}


KEY peek()
{
    return m_heap[0];
}


int size()
{
    return (int)m_heap.size();
}


private:
    vector<KEY> m_heap;
};
```

The priority queue data structure will implement a function to insert items, peek at the top of the container, remove items from the container, test if the container is empty, and return the number of elements. Each of these operations can wrap around the heap data structure. The function used to test if the container is empty, called empty(), can be a boolean test to see if the size is equal to 0. Because the priority queue of this chapter uses a heap, the code is much shorter than it was in Chapter 5. The priority queue class, PriorityQueue, is shown in Listing 10.5.

LISTING 10.5   The Priority Queue

```
#include"Heap.h"


template<typename T, typename CMP>
class PriorityQueue
{
   public:
      PriorityQueue()
      {

      }


      void push(T val)
      {
         m_elements.push(val);
      }


      void pop()
      {
         m_elements.remove();
      }


      T peek()
      {
         return m_elements.peek();
      }


      int size()
      {
         return m_elements.size();
      }


      bool empty()
      {
         return (m_elements.size() == 0);
      }
```

```
private:
    Heap<T, CMP> m_elements;
};
```

The main source file for the priority queue creates a priority queue using the code in Listing 10.5 and populates it with elements. Once filled, it displays the contents of the container to the console window. The code for the Priority Queue demo application of this chapter (located on the accompanying CD-ROM) is similar to the Priority Queue demo application of Chapter 5. In this demo the comparison operators can be specified in the same way as in Chapter 5. The main source file for the Priority Queue demo application is shown in Listing 10.6. Figure 10.7 shows a screenshot of the running application.

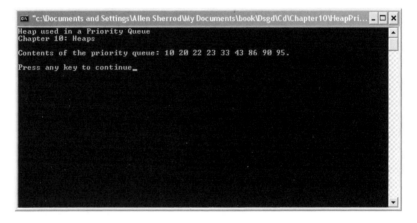

FIGURE 10.7 A screenshot of the Heap Priority Queue demo.

LISTING 10.6 The Priority Queue Demo's Main Source File

```
#include<iostream>
#include"PriorityQueue.h"

using namespace std;


template<typename T>
class less_cmp
{
    public:
```

```
        inline bool operator()(T lVal, T rVal)
        {
            return (lVal < rVal);
        }
};


template<typename T>
class greater_cmp
{
    public:
        inline bool operator()(T lVal, T rVal)
        {
            return !(lVal < rVal);
        }
};


int main(int args, char **argc)
{
    cout << "Heap used in a Priority Queue" << endl;
    cout << "Chapter 10: Heaps" << endl;
    cout << endl;


    // Create the container and populate it.
    PriorityQueue<int, less_cmp<int> > pq;

    pq.push(33);
    pq.push(43);
    pq.push(23);
    pq.push(20);
    pq.push(10);
    pq.push(22);
    pq.push(90);
    pq.push(95);
    pq.push(86);


    // Display queue.
    cout << "Contents of the priority queue:";

    while(pq.empty() != true)
    {
```

```
        cout << " " << pq.peek();
        pq.pop();
    }

    cout << "." << endl << endl;

    return 1;
}
```

STL HEAP FUNCTIONS

Although there is no heap data structure in the STL, a few heap-related functions are part of the STL. Using these functions on a data structure, for example, a `vector` array, can create a heap out of the elements, which places the largest value at the front of the container. Using the STL heap functions to push, pop, and create the elements can create a heap without a heap container. These heap functions include the following:

- `make_heap()`
- `push_heap()`
- `pop_heap()`
- `sort_heap()`

The `make_heap()` function is used to take a range of elements and create a heap out of them. The first element after the function is called is the largest element. Optionally the function allows for a binary predicate to be specified for the element comparisons. The function prototypes for the `make_heap()` function are:

```
template<class RandomAccessIterator>
void make_heap(RandomAccessIterator _First,
            RandomAccessIterator _Last);


template<class RandomAccessIterator, class BinaryPredicate>
void make_heap(RandomAccessIterator _First,
            RandomAccessIterator _Last,
            BinaryPredicate _Comp);
```

The `push_heap()` function adds a range of elements to a heap, which could have been created by calling `make_heap()`. The function takes a range of elements as well as an optional binary predicate if you choose to specify that. The function prototypes for the `push_heap()` functions are:

```
template<class RandomAccessIterator>
void push_heap(RandomAccessIterator _First,
               RandomAccessIterator _Last);



template<class RandomAccessIterator, class BinaryPredicate>
void push_heap(RandomAccessIterator _First,
               RandomAccessIterator _Last,
               BinaryPredicate _Comp);
```

The pop_heap() function removes the largest element from the container. This function is the inverse of the push_heap() function and takes as parameters a range that specifies the elements of the heap, which is the first element to the next-to-last element, and an optional binary predicate. The function prototypes of the pop_heap() function are:

```
template<class RandomAccessIterator>
void pop_heap(RandomAccessIterator _First,
              RandomAccessIterator _Last);



template<class RandomAccessIterator, class BinaryPredicate>
void pop_heap(RandomAccessIterator _First,
              RandomAccessIterator _Last,
              BinaryPredicate _Comp);
```

The last function is the sort_heap(). This function takes as parameters the range of elements that make up the heap and an optional binary predicate. Calling this function on a heap will sort the elements in the range. After this function is called, the heap is no longer a heap. For example, if a heap was created out of a vector array and this function was called, the heap would have been changed into an ordered array. The function prototypes for the sort_heap() are:

```
template<class RandomAccessIterator>
void sort_heap(RandomAccessIterator _First,
               RandomAccessIterator _Last);



template<class RandomAccessIterator, class BinaryPredicate>
void sort_heap(RandomAccessIterator _First,
               RandomAccessIterator _Last,
               BinaryPredicate _Comp);
```

The sort_heap() *function is not a heap sort algorithm. It is used to sort a range of elements in a specified order, which makes that range no longer a heap.*

SUMMARY

The heap data structure is a very useful ADT container that is based on a binary tree. In this chapter an array-based binary tree was used as the underlying data structure for the heap. We saw along with the heap's implementation a sorting technique called the heap sort and how to implement a priority queue using a heap data structure.

In the next chapter we'll introduce the graph data structure. Trees are a type of graph, and understanding of them will aid in understanding and implementing the various graphs that will be discussed. Graphs are widely used in game development, especially for various path-finding algorithms used by a game's artificial intelligence.

CHAPTER REVIEW QUESTIONS

Answers to the following chapter review questions can be found in Appendix B.

1. What does ADT stand for?
2. A heap:
   a. Is weakly ordered
   b. Uses a priority queue as its underlying data structure
   c. Is a binary search tree
   d. None of the above
3. A priority queue is a:
   a. Type of heap
   b. Abstract data type
   c. Sequence container
   d. Both A and C
   e. None of the above
4. The big-O of an insertion algorithm running on a heap would be:
   a. O(1)
   b. O(log N)
   c. O(N * log N)
   d. O(N)
   e. O(N²)
   f. None of the above

5. The big-O of a searching algorithm running on a heap would be:
    a. O(1)
    b. O(log N)
    c. O(N * log N)
    d. O(N)
    e. O(N²)
    f. None of the above

6. The big-O of a removal algorithm running on a heap would be:
    a. O(1)
    b. O(log N)
    c. O(N * log N)
    d. O(N)
    e. O(N²)
    f. None of the above

7. The big-O of a heap sort would be:
    a. O(1)
    b. O(log N)
    c. O(N * log N)
    d. O(N)
    e. O(N²)
    f. None of the above

8. Another term for percolate is:
    a. Sort
    b. Allocate
    c. Trickle
    d. Bubble
    e. Both C and D
    f. None of the above

9. Which is not a heap condition?
    a. Balanced
    b. Complete
    c. Nodes that are larger than or equal to their children
    d. None of the above

10. A heap is a basic data structure.
    a. True
    b. False

11. The heap sort uses a binary search tree.
    a. True
    b. False

12. Expanding the size of the heap array will invalidate all elements.
    a. True
    b. False
13. A heap is a balanced binary tree.
    a. True
    b. False
14. A binary search tree is weakly ordered compared to a heap data structure.
    a. True
    b. False
15. Heaps are complete like binary search trees.
    a. True
    b. False

PROGRAMMING PROJECTS

Exercise 1: Implement a searching algorithm to test if a key is already inside the container.

Exercise 2: Modify the Heap Sort demo application to perform the sort within the original array instead of making a copy.

Exercise 3: Implement a heap using a tree data structure.

11 | Graphs

In This Chapter

- Introduction to Graphs
- Searching with Graphs
- Topological Sorting
- Weighted Graphs
- Artificial Intelligence

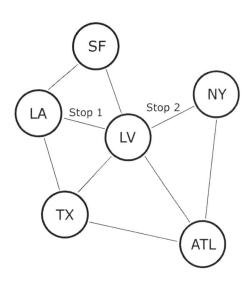

When it comes to data structures, a tree is a type of graph, but although graphs and tree have their similarities, they also have their differences. In a graph the nodes of the data structure represent much more abstract objects used for solving different types of problems. Also, the graph is shaped by the data, and not the algorithms, that operate on it. In Chapter 9 the binary search tree took its shape from its searching algorithm, which made it possible to do a fast search on the data structure. Another example is a heap where the removal algorithm has to return the top element in the structure, in which a binary tree was used. In a graph the nodes are shaped to represent a physical or abstract set of objects, such as the major cities in the United States or the stations in a subway system.

The purpose of this chapter is to examine the data structure known as a graph. Graphs are very powerful data structures and can be used to solve many real-world problems. One such real-world representation is train station stops in a railroad system where each station is connected to one or more other stations. In such a situation a station is not connected directly to every other station in the country but can be connected indirectly by going from one station to another until the end destination is reached. Another real-world situation that comes up often when talking about graphs is a scheduling system for a college campus where some classes have prerequisites that must be completed before they can be taken. In that example all classes that make up a degree program are connected to form the requirements of getting the degree.

Later in this chapter we'll also discuss how graphs are used in game development. One popular and famous use of a graph in game development is for the path-finding algorithm A* (pronounced a-star) in artificial intelligence, using what is known as a weighted graph.

INTRODUCTION TO GRAPHS

There are many similarities between graphs and trees. If you have a strong understanding of one, it will make it easier to learn the other. Graphs and trees use the same type of objects, some of which have different terminology. The things that make a tree and a graph similar include:

- They both have nodes that encapsulate objects.
- They both have edges.
- They both have nodes that can have multiple other nodes related to them.
- They both allow node traversal, which is often used by algorithms.

Although graphs and trees might seem like the same data structure, they are not. By the end of this chapter why they are separate data structures should be clear. A few of the differences between trees and graphs include:

- The relationship of each node is more abstract in a graph than in a tree.
- In graphs nodes are called vertices (plural of vertex).
- Vertices that are connected are called adjacent vertices.
- Graphs have no keys, which binary trees use as a way of structuring the tree.
- The edges of a graph's node can go one way (directed) or both ways (nondirected).
- The edges of a graph are often represented by something known as an adjacency matrix or an adjacency list, whereas the tree uses references to objects or array indexes.
- The nodes of a graph can be unweighted or weighted, which we'll talk about later in this chapter. This can have huge affects on the traversals and algorithms that execute on the graph.
- Different vertices can have different numbers of children without limit, unlike the binary tree, which has a limit of two children per node (e.g., in a graph one vertex can have 10 attached vertices while other vertices can have 0, 1, 4, 15, etc.).
- The relationship between vertices is not a parent-child relationship; the relationship is much more abstract and often takes on a completely different form.

A graph is considered a connected graph if there is a path from all vertices to all other vertices, either directly or indirectly. A path is a sequence of edges that can be taken to get to a destination vertex from a starting vertex. If a vertex cannot directly connect to another, the graph is not considered connected. An example of this is shown in Figure 11.1, where vertex B cannot get to D, but node D can get to B, which is dictated by the directions of the arrows.

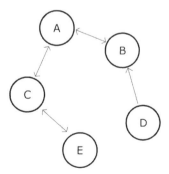

FIGURE 11.1   Connected and nonconnected graphs.

DIRECTED AND NONDIRECTED GRAPHS

There are generally two types of graphs: directed and nondirected. A directed graph is a graph where the edges have a direction. For example, in a singly linked list the edges that connect the nodes go in one direction. This means that to get from node A to node B you can follow node A's edge next pointer, but once at B you can't get back to node A. In a directed graph the idea is similar, where an edge might go from one vertex to another but not in reverse.

A nondirected graph is a graph where the edges do not have a specific direction. In other words, you can travel back and forth from connected vertices. An example of something similar to this is a doubly linked list where the nodes have both next and previous pointers that keep them connected bidirectionally. An illustration of a directed compared to a nondirected graph is shown in Figure 11.2. Using the example of a class scheduling system for a college campus, a directed graph's vertex can be seen in having to take a class called Computer Programming I before being able to take Computer Programming II, but not being able to take the second course before the first.

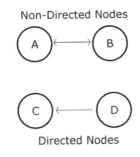

Non-Directed Nodes

Directed Nodes

FIGURE 11.2 Directed and nondirected graphs.

VERTICES OF A GRAPH

The vertices of a graph are its nodes. A vertex in a graph is an object that encapsulates what is being represented abstractly. In a graph various properties can be associated with a vertex, like a weight, which we'll discuss later in this chapter. Our first demo application deals with implementing the depth-first search algorithm, which will be discussed in the next section. The template vertex class from that demo application is shown in Listing 11.1, where the class is used to simply encapsulate any type of object that can be represented by a graph's vertex.

LISTING 11.1 A Vertex Class from the Upcoming Depth First Search Demo

```cpp
template<typename T>
class GraphVertex
{
   public:
      GraphVertex(T node) : m_node(node)
      {

      }


      T GetNode()
      {
         return m_node;
      }


   private:
      T m_node;
};
```

ADJACENCY MATRIX

In Listing 11.1 there are no pointers or indexes to other vertices. In a graph edges from one vertex to others are specified by an adjacency matrix, a two-dimensional array that is the size of $N \times N$, where N is the number of vertices in the graph. An example of an adjacency matrix is shown in Table 11.1, with the vertices called A, B, C, D, E, and F.

TABLE 11.1 An Adjacency Matrix

	A	B	C	D	E	F
A	0	0	1	0	1	0
B	1	0	0	1	1	0
C	0	1	1	1	1	1
D	0	1	0	0	1	1
E	1	0	1	0	0	0
F	0	1	0	1	0	1

By using an array of boolean values, for example, an edge would be defined if the index (row) of a vertex is connected to another (column) by marking true in that matrix entry. In Table 11.1 the vertex A is connected to C and E, and E is connected to A and C, but C is not connected to A and is connected to all other vertices, which would occur in a directed graph where not all edges go in both directions.

The adjacency information can also be represented as an adjacency list. The difference between an adjacency matrix and an adjacency list is that the matrix is a two-dimensional array, while the list is an array of link lists. The array has faster lookups, but the list can save memory by only including elements that are connected. How the graph is used will probably dictate which is more efficient, but that is an application-specific topic.

CREATING A GRAPH

A simple graph data structure can be created by coding a class that holds a list of vertices and an adjacency matrix. The adjacency matrix can be a two-dimensional array of characters where the matrix's data represent true or false states. Using a char instead of other data types can save memory on the array if that is the only thing the elements represent. Using C++ as an example, the vertices can be an std::vector array of GraphVertex objects (see Listing 11.1).

Vertices can be inserted into the graph by adding a new object to the vertex array, which if using the std::vector from the STL would require calling push_back() on the container. The edges can also be added to the adjacency matrix by taking the array index of the first vertex, which will be used for the row, and taking the index for the second vertex, which will be used for the column, and marking that matrix index as true. In a nondirected graph both vertices must be marked, as shown in the addEdge() function in Listing 11.2; adding a directed edge can be seen in the function addDirectedEdge(). Listing 11.2 shows an example graph class that will create and populate a graph object, which is also used in the Depth First Search demo application that we will look at in the following section.

LISTING 11.2   An Example Graph Data Structure

```
template<typename T>
class Graph
{
   public:
      Graph(int numVerts) : m_maxVerts(numVerts), m_adjMatrix(NULL)
      {
         // ALLOCATE NECESSARY MEMORY
      }
```

```
        ~Graph()
        {
            // DELETE ALLOCATED MEMORY
        }


        bool push(T node)
        {
            if((int)m_vertices.size() >= m_maxVerts)
                return false;

            m_vertices.push_back(GraphVertex<T>(node));
            return true;
        }


        void attachEdge(int index1, int index2)
        {
            assert(m_adjMatrix != NULL);

            m_adjMatrix[index1][index2] = 1;
            m_adjMatrix[index2][index1] = 1;
        }


        void attachDirectedEdge(int index1, int index2)
        {
            assert(m_adjMatrix != NULL);

            m_adjMatrix[index1][index2] = 1;
        }


    private:
        vector<GraphVertex<T> > m_vertices;
        int m_maxVerts;

        char **m_adjMatrix;
};
```

SEARCHING WITH GRAPHS

Searching in graphs is done to find which vertices can be reached from a starting vertex by following a path along the edges. Taking the railroad example from earlier in this chapter, a search could be used to find all the stops between city A and city B. Los Angeles does not have a railroad that connects directly (nonstop) to New York City, but it could connect to a station in the next state, which is connected to a station in the state next to that, and so on until one connected to New York is reached. An example of this is shown in Figure 11.3, where each city is a vertex in a graph and the railroad tracks are the edges that connect them.

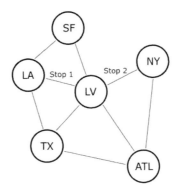

FIGURE 11.3   Finding a path from the vertex Los Angeles to New York.

The two searching algorithms that operate on graphs that will be discussed in this chapter are the depth-first search and the breadth-first search. Both of these functions start at a vertex and visit every vertex between it and a destination vertex. The algorithms find any paths that exist between two vertices. If a path exists, the path data, which is the order of the edges needed to get from start to finish, is built and stored for some meaningful purpose. Using the railroad as an example, a path from one city to another can be found by a travel agency when planning a trip for a client or in a travel directions application where a path from the starting address to a destination address is needed.

DEPTH-FIRST SEARCH

The depth-first search is an algorithm that uses a stack data structure to start at a starting vertex and move until it reaches the destination, assuming it can be reached from that vertex. The steps of the algorithm are:

1. Choose a starting vertex and make it the current vertex.
2. Push the current vertex onto the stack and mark it with a flag that tells us it was checked.
3. If the current vertex is the destination, then the code is done; otherwise, continue.

4. Visit the first adjacent vertex after the current one that was not marked as visited and make it the current vertex.
5. Repeat steps 2 through 4 until the algorithm can't go any further along one path.
6. If the destination vertex was not found, pop the current vertex off the stack and visit the next adjacent vertex that is not marked as visited.
7. Continue steps 2 through 6 until all vertices have been marked visited, which means a path was not found, or until the destination vertex is reached.

The algorithm starts at the starting vertex and recursively checks all vertices that connect to it until the destination is reached or until there are no more vertices to check, which means a path cannot be found. Upon success, the elements in the stack at the end of the algorithm are the path from the start to the destination. See Figure 11.4 for an example with a few simple vertices.

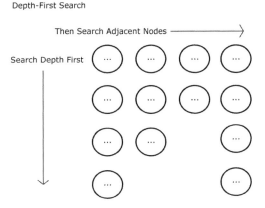

FIGURE 11.4   The depth-first search.

IMPLEMENTING THE DEPTH-FIRST SEARCH

ON THE CD

Implementing the depth-first searching algorithm requires us to take the steps outlined for the algorithm and translate that into code. On accompanying CD-ROM is a demo application called Depth First Search in the Chapter 11 folder. This demo application will create a graph and search for a path between vertices. The graph used in this demo application, as well as those in the upcoming demos, uses character labels as the names of the vertices to make visualization easier.

The Depth First Search demo application is made up of two files: one for the graph (Graph.h) and one for the main source file. In the header file for the graph is the template vertex class, first seen in Listing 11.1, and the template graph class. The graph class is a template so that the data type of the vertices can be specified. The vertex of a graph is abstract and can be used to represent anything. In this demo application it is used to represent letters that can be connected to one another. The graph's vertex and data structure classes are shown in Listing 11.3.

LISTING 11.3 The Graph.h Header File from the Depth First Search Demo

```cpp
template<typename T>
class GraphVertex
{
   public:
      GraphVertex(T node) : m_node(node) { }

      T GetNode() { return m_node; }


   private:
      T m_node;
};


template<typename T>
class Graph
{
   public:
      Graph(int numVerts) : m_maxVerts(numVerts), m_adjMatrix(NULL)
      {
         assert(numVerts > 0);

         m_vertices.reserve(m_maxVerts);


         m_adjMatrix = new char*[m_maxVerts];
         assert(m_adjMatrix != NULL);


         m_vertVisits = new char[m_maxVerts];
         assert(m_vertVisits != NULL);

         memset(m_vertVisits, 0, m_maxVerts);


         for(int i = 0; i < m_maxVerts; i++)
         {
```

```
         m_adjMatrix[i] = new char[m_maxVerts];
         assert(m_adjMatrix[i] != NULL);

         memset(m_adjMatrix[i], O, m_maxVerts);
      }
   }


   ~Graph()
   {
      if(m_adjMatrix != NULL)
      {
         for(int i = O; i < m_maxVerts; i++)
         {
            if(m_adjMatrix[i] != NULL)
            {
               delete[] m_adjMatrix[i];
               m_adjMatrix[i] = NULL;
            }
         }

         delete[] m_adjMatrix;
         m_adjMatrix = NULL;
      }


      if(m_vertVisits != NULL)
      {
         delete[] m_vertVisits;
         m_vertVisits = NULL;
      }
   }


   bool push(T node)
   {
      if((int)m_vertices.size() >= m_maxVerts)
         return false;

      m_vertices.push_back(GraphVertex<T>(node));

      return true;
   }
```

```
void attachEdge(int index1, int index2)
{
   assert(m_adjMatrix != NULL);

   m_adjMatrix[index1][index2] = 1;
   m_adjMatrix[index2][index1] = 1;
}


void attachDirectedEdge(int index1, int index2)
{
   assert(m_adjMatrix != NULL);

   m_adjMatrix[index1][index2] = 1;
}


int getNextUnvisitedVertex(int index)
{
   assert(m_adjMatrix != NULL);
   assert(m_vertVisits != NULL);

   for(int i = 0; i < (int)m_vertices.size(); i++)
   {
      if(m_adjMatrix[index][i] == 1 &&
         m_vertVisits[i] == 0)
      {
         return i;
      }
   }

   return -1;
}


bool DepthFirstSearch(int startIndex, int endIndex)
{
   assert(m_adjMatrix != NULL);
   assert(m_vertVisits != NULL);

   m_vertVisits[startIndex] = 1;
```

```
      // FOR OUTPUT PURPOSES OF THE DEMOS.
      cout << m_vertices[startIndex].GetNode();


      stack<int> searchStack;
      int vert = 0;

      searchStack.push(startIndex);


      while(searchStack.empty() != true)
      {
         vert = getNextUnvisitedVertex(searchStack.top());

         if(vert == -1)
         {
            searchStack.pop();
         }
         else
         {
            m_vertVisits[vert] = 1;

            // FOR OUTPUT PURPOSES OF THE DEMOS.
            cout << m_vertices[vert].GetNode();

            searchStack.push(vert);
         }

         if(vert == endIndex)
         {
            memset(m_vertVisits, 0, m_maxVerts);
            return true;
         }
      }


      memset(m_vertVisits, 0, m_maxVerts);

      return false;
   }


private:
   vector<GraphVertex<T> > m_vertices;
   int m_maxVerts;
```

```
            char **m_adjMatrix;
            char *m_vertVisits;
    };
```

In Listing 11.3 the graph's class is made up of seven functions. The first function is the constructor, which is used to allocate the necessary dynamic memory based on the total number of vertices that will be needed. The second function, the destructor, is used to free that allocated memory upon the object's destruction.

The next three functions are push(), addEdge(), and addDirectedEdge(). The push() function adds a new vertex to the graph until the maximum number of vertices has been reached. The addEdge() function adds a nondirectional edge, which is an edge that goes back and forth between two vertices. The function addDirectedEdge() adds only one directional edge.

The next function is used by the depth-first search algorithm to find the next adjacent vertex not marked as checked from the vertex specified from its parameter called index. The flags used to keep track of which vertices were checked are called m_vertVisits in the graph's class. This array holds true or false values, so it is an array of characters that is the size of the total number of vertices that can be in the graph. Every time a vertex is checked, an entry into this array is set to 1 to indicate that. Marking a vertex as checked will keep the code from becoming an infinite cycle since we have a way of knowing which vertices were already checked and do not need checking again.

The last function is the depth-first searching algorithm itself. This function, called DepthFirstSearch(), takes starting and ending vertices as parameters and pushes the current vertex onto the stack, which is initially the starting vertex, and marks it as checked. It then loops until the stack is empty, which would mean there are no vertices left to check and there is no path from the start to the destination. During the loop the function gets the next adjacent vertex that was not checked. If there is not such a vertex, an element is popped off of the stack. If this happens on the first vertex, the algorithm will stop, and no path off of the staring vertex exists. If an adjacent vertex that was not checked is found, that vertex is marked as checked and pushed onto the stack. The loop then checks to make sure the destination was not reached. This process continues until the current vertex equals the destination or until the stack is empty. If there are no more items on the stack, then no path was found. If the path is found, the function returns true. Throughout the function there are a few cout calls to display output to the console window. These are used to show the search that the algorithm performed.

In the main source file a graph with six vertices is created. To keep things simple the vertices are characters A through F. An edge from A to C and C to A is created, followed by edges between A and D, B and E, and C and F. Once the graph is created, the code performs a depth-first search to see if a path between vertex A and vertex D can be found. During the search the path is displayed to the window. An indication of whether a path was or was not found is displayed to the window to show the results of the algorithm. The main source file's code for the Depth First Search demo application is straightforward and can be seen in Listing 11.4. A screenshot of the demo application is shown in Figure 11.5.

LISTING 11.4   The Main Source File for the Depth First Search Demo

```
#include<iostream>
#include"Graphs.h"

using namespace std;


int main(int args, char **argc)
{
    cout << "Graphs - Depth First Search" << endl;
    cout << "Chapter 11: Graphs" << endl;
    cout << endl;


    Graph<char> demoGraph(6);

    demoGraph.push('A');
    demoGraph.push('B');
    demoGraph.push('C');
    demoGraph.push('D');
    demoGraph.push('E');
    demoGraph.push('F');


    // Attach A to C and C to A.
    demoGraph.attachEdge(0, 2);

    // Attach A to D and D to A.
    demoGraph.attachEdge(0, 3);

    // Attach B to E and E to B.
    demoGraph.attachEdge(1, 4);

    // Attach C to F and F to C.
    demoGraph.attachEdge(2, 5);
```

```
// Perform depth first search for a path from A to D.
cout << "DepthFirstSearch Nodes Visited: ";

int result = demoGraph.DepthFirstSearch(0, 3);
cout << endl << endl;

if(result == 1)
   cout << "Path from A to D found!";
else
   cout << "Path from A to D NOT found!";


cout << endl << endl;

return 1;
}
```

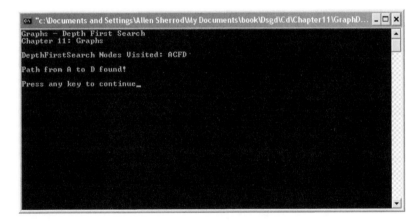

FIGURE 11.5 A screenshot from the Depth First Search demo.

BREADTH-FIRST SEARCH

The depth-first search algorithm started at the starting vertex and eventually made its way down toward the destination, if it existed. This worked by moving away from the starting vertex along the edges of unchecked vertices until one of the algorithm's terminating conditions occurred.

The breadth-first search algorithm acts a little differently. The depth-first search algorithm started at the starting vertex, moved to the first unchecked adjacent vertex, and then moved forward for that vertex's adjacency, and so on. In the breath-first search all adjacent vertices to the current vertex are checked before the algorithm moves forward, and it uses a queue instead of a stack. In the depth-first search the other adjacent vertices were not checked until a chosen path had already been disproved. In the breath-first searching algorithm the steps are:

1. Push the starting vertex into a queue and then start a loop that will execute while the queue is not empty.
2. Once inside the loop, pop a vertex from the queue and make it the current vertex.
3. Place all unchecked vertices adjacent to the current vertex onto the queue and mark them as checked.
4. If there are no more vertices adjacent to the current vertex, check if the current vertex is the destination.
5. If the destination is found, the algorithm is done.
6. If the algorithm did not find the destination, repeat steps 2 through 5.

The breadth-first search is useful if we are looking for the shortest path between two vertices. Use of the vertices in the example in Figure 11.4 for the breath-first search is shown in Figure 11.6.

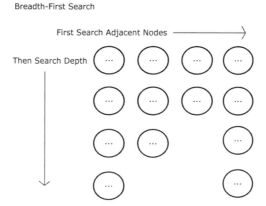

FIGURE 11.6 Breath-first searching algorithm.

IMPLEMENTING BREADTH-FIRST SEARCH

On the accompanying CD-ROM a demo application called Breadth First Search can be found in the Chapter 11 folder. This demo application builds off of the first demo, Depth First Search, and adds a function to the graph class called `BreadthFirstSearch()` for performing the breath-first searching algorithm.

In the Graph.h header file for the Breadth First Search demo application the only new code is the `BreathFirstSearch()` function. This function starts with a starting vertex and searches for a path to the destination vertex. The algorithm pushes the starting vertex onto the queue. It then enters a loop that executes while the queue is not empty. Inside the loop the front of the queue is popped off, and that vertex is made the current vertex. After that a check is made to see if we are at the destination. If not, then all adjacent vertices are added to the queue; otherwise, the destination is found and the function can quit. Once all vertices adjacent to the current vertex have been added to the queue, the loop starts over again and continues the process. The updated graph code is shown in Listing 11.5.

LISTING 11.5 Updated Graph Code to Include Breadth-First Search

```
template<typename T>
class GraphVertex
{
   public:
      GraphVertex(T node) : m_node(node) { }

      T GetNode() { return m_node; }


   private:
      T m_node;
};


template<typename T>
class Graph
{
   public:
      int getNextUnvisitedVertex(int index)
      {
         assert(m_adjMatrix != NULL);
         assert(m_vertVisits != NULL);


         for(int i = 0; i < (int)m_vertices.size(); i++)
         {
            if(m_adjMatrix[index][i] == 1 &&
               m_vertVisits[i] == 0)
            {
               return i;
            }
         }
```

```
      return -1;
}


bool BreadthFirstSearch(int startIndex, int endIndex)
{
   assert(m_adjMatrix != NULL);
   assert(m_vertVisits != NULL);


   m_vertVisits[startIndex] = 1;

   // FOR OUTPUT PURPOSES OF THE DEMOS.
   cout << m_vertices[startIndex].GetNode();


   queue<int> searchQueue;
   int vert1 = 0, vert2 = 0;

   searchQueue.push(startIndex);


   while(searchQueue.empty() != true)
   {
      vert1 = searchQueue.front();
      searchQueue.pop();


      if(vert1 == endIndex)
      {
         memset(m_vertVisits, 0, m_maxVerts);
         return true;
      }


      while((vert2 = getNextUnvisitedVertex(vert1)) != -1)
      {
         m_vertVisits[vert2] = 1;


         // FOR OUTPUT PURPOSES OF THE DEMOS.
         cout << m_vertices[vert2].GetNode();
```

```
                    searchQueue.push(vert2);
            }
        }

        memset(m_vertVisits, 0, m_maxVerts);

        return false;
    }
};
```

The main source file for the Breadth First Search demo application is similar to the Depth First Search demo application, with the addition of a call to the `Breadth-FirstSearch()` function from Listing 11.5. A screenshot for the Breadth First Search demo application is shown in Figure 11.7. If you compare the output from the Depth First Search demo and the Breadth First Search demo you should notice that both algorithms were able to find the path from vertex A to vertex D, but the actual output path taken is slightly different. The main source file for the Breadth First Search demo application is shown in Listing 11.6.

LISTING 11.6 The Main Source File for the Breadth First Search Demo

```cpp
#include<iostream>
#include"Graphs.h"

using namespace std;


int main(int args, char **argc)
{
    cout << "Graphs - Breadth First Search" << endl;
    cout << "Chapter 11: Graphs" << endl;
    cout << endl;


    Graph<char> demoGraph(6);

    demoGraph.push('A');
    demoGraph.push('B');
    demoGraph.push('C');
    demoGraph.push('D');
    demoGraph.push('E');
    demoGraph.push('F');
```

```
// Attach A to C and C to A.
demoGraph.attachEdge(0, 2);

// Attach A to D and D to A.
demoGraph.attachEdge(0, 3);

// Attach B to E and E to B.
demoGraph.attachEdge(1, 4);

// Attach C to F and F to C.
demoGraph.attachEdge(2, 5);


// Perform breadth first search for a path from A to D.
cout << "BreadthFirstSearch Nodes Visited: ";

int result = demoGraph.BreadthFirstSearch(0, 3);
cout << endl << endl;

if(result == 1)
   cout << "Path from A to D found!";
else
   cout << "Path from A to D NOT found!";

cout << endl << endl;

return 1;
}
```

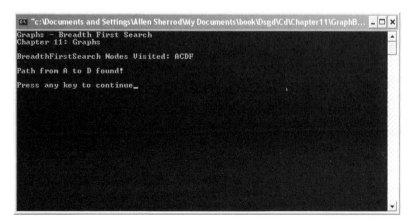

FIGURE 11.7   A screenshot from the Breadth First Search demo.

MINIMAL SPANNING TREE

A minimal spanning tree is an algorithm that can be performed on a graph and will find the minimum number of connected edges needed to visit every vertex in the graph. There are many different paths that will create a valid minimal spanning tree. An example of this is shown in Figure 11.8.

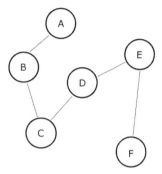

FIGURE 11.8 A minimum spanning tree.

The minimal spanning tree of an unweighted graph represents only the minimal connected edges. This is different from a weighted graph, which we'll discuss later in this chapter.

IMPLEMENTING MINIMAL SPANNING TREE

ON THE CD

On the accompanying CD-ROM is a demo application called Minimal Spanning Tree in the Chapter 11 folder. This demo application will implement and demonstrate the minimal spanning tree algorithm.

After the depth-first and breadth-first searching algorithms, the minimal spanning tree is easy and can be based on the code for either search. The minimal spanning tree algorithm for this demo application is based on the depth-first searching algorithm. In the minimal spanning tree the starting vertex is the first one and the destination is the last vertex. Along the search, the minimal spanning tree is displayed to the console window as a visual output of what it looks like. This is shown in Listing 11.7.

NOTE

The minimal spanning tree in an unweighted graph finds the first minimal spanning tree out of many different possibilities.

LISTING 11.7 The Minimal Spanning Tree Added to the Graph Class

```
template<typename T>
class Graph
```

```
{
    public:
        void DisplayMST()
        {
            assert(m_adjMatrix != NULL);
            assert(m_vertVisits != NULL);


            int startIndex = 0;

            m_vertVisits[startIndex] = 1;

            stack<int> searchStack;
            int vert = 0, currentVert = 0;

            searchStack.push(startIndex);

            while(searchStack.empty() != true)
            {
                currentVert = searchStack.top();
                vert = getNextUnvisitedVertex(currentVert);

                if(vert == -1)
                {
                    searchStack.pop();
                }
                else
                {
                    m_vertVisits[vert] = 1;
                    searchStack.push(vert);

                    // FOR OUTPUT PURPOSES OF THE DEMOS.
                    cout << m_vertices[currentVert].GetNode()
                        << ":" << m_vertices[vert].GetNode()
                        << " ";
                }
            }

            memset(m_vertVisits, 0, m_maxVerts);
        }
};
```

The function DislayMST() in Listing 11.7 starts by making the first vertex the current vertex and pushing it onto the stack. A loop then executes until the stack is empty. Inside the loop the next unchecked adjacent vertex from the current vertex is found. If one was not found, one element would be popped off the stack; otherwise, that vertex, along with the current vertex, is displayed to the console window because it marks one edge in the minimal spanning tree. This process continues until there are no more elements in the stack, which means the entire minimal spanning tree has been displayed.

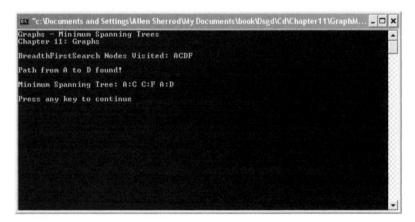

The code in Listing 11.7 assumes the graph is a connected graph.

The main source file for the Minimal Spanning Tree demo application builds off the code in the Breadth First Search demo, with the addition of calling the DisplayMST() function of the Graph class. This function displays the minimal spanning tree based on the edge connections between the nodes. Altering these nodes can generate a different minimal spanning tree. The code for the main source file of the Minimal Spanning Tree demo is shown in Listing 11.8. Figure 11.9 shows a screenshot of the running demo application.

FIGURE 11.9 A screenshot of the Minimal Spanning Tree demo.

LISTING 11.8 The Minimal Spanning Tree Demo's Main Source File

```
#include<iostream>
#include"Graphs.h"

using namespace std;


int main(int args, char **argc)
{
   cout << "Graphs - Minimum Spanning Trees" << endl;
```

```
cout << "Chapter 11: Graphs" << endl;
cout << endl;


// Create the data structure and fill it in.
Graph<char> demoGraph(6);

demoGraph.push('A');
demoGraph.push('B');
demoGraph.push('C');
demoGraph.push('D');
demoGraph.push('E');
demoGraph.push('F');


// Attach A to C and C to A.
demoGraph.attachEdge(0, 2);

// Attach A to D and D to A.
demoGraph.attachEdge(0, 3);

// Attach B to E and E to B.
demoGraph.attachEdge(1, 4);

// Attach C to F and F to C.
demoGraph.attachEdge(2, 5);


// Perform breadth first search for a path from A to D.
cout << "BreadthFirstSearch Nodes Visited: ";

int result = demoGraph.BreadthFirstSearch(0, 3);
cout << endl << endl;

if(result == 1)
   cout << "Path from A to D found!";
else
   cout << "Path from A to D NOT found!";

cout << endl << endl;


// Display the minimum spanning tree.
cout << "Minimum Spanning Tree: ";
demoGraph.DisplayMST();
```

```
        cout << endl << endl;

        return 1;
    }
```

TOPOLOGICAL SORTING

Topological sorting in a graph is an algorithm that can be used with directed graphs where the vertices must be arranged in a specific order dictated by the directed edges. An example of a topological sort can be seen with the college course scheduling where certain courses are prerequisites for other classes. Performing a topological sort on this will give us the order in which the classes must be taken to complete the degree program. If a student is halfway through the degree program, for example, a topological sort can be used to find out which classes remain to be taken and their order. Figure 11.10 shows all the courses needed to get a degree, Figure 11.11 shows what courses the student has already taken, and Figure 11.12 shows the topological order that is needed to complete the degree program.

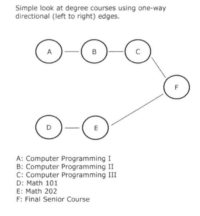

Simple look at degree courses using one-way
directional (left to right) edges.

A: Computer Programming I
B: Computer Programming II
C: Computer Programming III
D: Math 101
E: Math 202
F: Final Senior Course

FIGURE 11.10   Courses in a degree program.

The figures show that the student has three courses that still need to be taken before he or she can graduate. The order of these courses is specified because, as seen in the case of the senior project, some courses can only be taken after others.

Topological sorting works on directed graphs, which are graphs with edges that go in only one direction from one vertex to another. In Figure 11.12 there is no way to take the Senior Project class before Computer Programming II, but Computer Programming II is taken before the Senior Project class (i.e., is a prerequisite to the

Courses Taken vs. Course Remaining

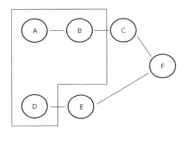

Couses Taken: Couses Taken:
A: Computer Programming I   C: Computer Programming III
B: Computer Programming II   E: Math 202
D: Math 101   F: Final Senior Course

FIGURE 11.11   Courses already taken.

Order of classes to take to graduate (Topological Sort)

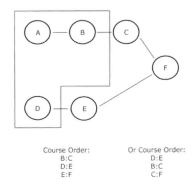

Course Order: Or Course Order:
     B:C   D:E
     D:E   B:C
     E:F   C:F

FIGURE 11.12   Topological sort of courses needed for degree program.

Senior Project class). A directed edge in the graph is specified by the adjacency matrix, where only one entry for a pair of vertices is specified instead of both.

As with the minimal spanning tree, the topological sorting algorithm can have more than one valid outcome. As seen in the college course example there are other combinations that would work. The algorithm finds the first valid answer.

NOTE

For a graph to be a valid candidate for the topological sorting algorithm, it must not have a cycle of connected vertices. For example, if vertex A is connected to B, B is connected to C, and C is connected to A, then there will be a cycle. As we'll discuss in the following section, a topological sort needs at least one vertex to have no vertices it connects to. This doesn't mean that no vertex can connect to, it but it can't connect to any other vertices. To determine if a graph has cycles, just look at the number of edges. If the number of edges is greater than or equal to the number of vertices in the graph, then there is a cycle. If you try this on a piece of paper with three nodes, you'll see that it is not possible to have more than three edges without there being a cycle in a directed graph. A graph without any cycles is called a directed acyclic graph.

A graph without a cycle is a tree, but a graph with a cycle is not a tree. All the types of trees discussed in Chapter 9, had no cycles.

NOTE

IMPLEMENTING A TOPOLOGICAL SORT

ON THE CD

On the accompanying CD-ROM is a demo application called Topological Sort in the Chapter 11 folder. In this section we'll discuss what the topological sort is and how it is implemented.

To implement the topological sort we start with a directed graph. The first step is to find a vertex with no successor. A successor is a vertex that does not connect to another vertex. In other words, if there are two vertices in a graph and vertex A is connected to vertex B, then vertex B is the successor to vertex A since vertex B has no vertices it is connected to (although there are some connected to it).

The next step is to delete the successor vertex from the graph and to add it to a list like a stack. Steps 1 and 2 are repeated until the graph is completely empty, at which time the list stores the topological order. If you are using a stack data structure, the last item in is the first item that needs to be done, followed by the next, and so on until the last item is reached. To handle the deleting of vertices a temporary list of vertices is used so that the original stays intact since this algorithm is to run once to find the information we need but not totally destroy the graph.

Topological sorting works on both connected and nonconnected directed graphs.

NOTE

Determining if a vertex has no successors is easy using the adjacency matrix. The process is to move from row to row in a loop, looking for one that has all 0s in its columns. The row index of a row with all columns equal to 0 is the index for a vertex with no successor. In the Topological Sort demo application this is done in a function called GetVertNoSucessor(), which is called by another function that does the actual topological sort. This function is shown in Listing 11.9. In the GetVert NoSuccessor() function if a vertex cannot be found, a value of –1 is returned.

LISTING 11.9   Finding the Next Vertex Without a Successor

```
template<typename T>
class Graph
{
   private:
      int GetVertNoSuccessor(char **adjMat, int size)
      {
         bool edgeFound = false;

         for(int row = 0; row < size; row++)
         {
            edgeFound = false;

            for(int col = 0; col < size; col++)
            {
               if(adjMat[row][col] != 0)
               {
                  edgeFound = true;
                  break;
               }
            }

            if(edgeFound == false)
               return row;
         }

         return -1;
      }
};
```

If an adjacency list is used instead of an adjacency matrix, then the function used to get the next successor would be as fast as testing if the index of the vertex's link list has any elements. The topological sorting algorithm works as follows:

1. Loop while there are still vertices in the graph.
2. Within the loop get the next vertex that does not have a successor by calling the GetVertNoSucessor() function.
3. If a successor cannot be found, there must be a cycle somewhere within the graph; otherwise, delete the successor from the graph.
4. Add the deleted successor to another list that is used to store the topological order of the vertices.
5. Repeat steps 2 through 4 until complete.

The topological sorting algorithm is implemented in a function called topologicalSort(), which takes a link list as a parameter that will store the topological sorted vertices. This function starts off by making copies of the vertex list and adjacency matrix so that the information can be operated on instead of the original data, which we will want intact once the function is complete. It then loops while there are still vertices inside the temporary list. Within that loop it gets the next vertex without a successor. If such a vertex does not exist, then the loop breaks, the temporary memory is deleted, and the function exits. If a vertex is found, that vertex is added to the output link list and is deleted from the temporary vertex list and matrix before the function moves on to the next iteration of the loop.

The topological sort in the topologicalSort() function is straightforward. The code might look long because the beginning of the function creates the temporary memory that must allocate and copy data and near the end of the function an entry in the temporary lists is deleted. Removing from the vector array can be done by calling the erase() function of the container. To remove from the adjacency matrix the rows underneath the vertex to be deleted and the columns to the right of it are simply moved over. The entries in the temporary adjacency matrix are not deleted but are shifted, which eliminates the need for numerous allocations and de-allocations. Other than creating the temporary memory and removing vertices from those lists, the code for the topological sort is short. The topologicalSort() function is shown in Listing 11.10.

LISTING 11.10 The Updated Graph Class that Adds the Topological Sorting Algorithm

```
template<typename T>
class Graph
{
   public:
      bool topologicalSort(list<T> &output)
      {
         bool hasCycles = false;


         // CREATE COPIES OF DATA

         vector<GraphVertex<T> > tempVerts(m_vertices);

         int tempSize = (int)tempVerts.size();

         char **tempAdjMat = new char*[m_maxVerts];
         assert(tempAdjMat != NULL);
```

```
for(int i = 0; i < m_maxVerts; i++)
{
   tempAdjMat[i] = new char[m_maxVerts];
   assert(tempAdjMat[i] != NULL);

   memcpy(tempAdjMat[i], m_adjMatrix[i],
          m_maxVerts);
}


// PERFORM TOPOLOGICAL SORT

while(tempSize > 0)
{
   int v = GetVertNoSuccessor(tempAdjMat,
                              tempSize);

   if(v == -1)
   {
      hasCycles = true;
      break;
   }


   output.push_front(tempVerts[v].GetNode());


   // DELETE VERTEX FROM THE LIST AND MATRIX
   if(v != (tempSize - 1))
   {
      vector<GraphVertex<T> >::iterator it;
      it = tempVerts.begin() + v;

      tempVerts.erase(it);


      for(int row = v; row < tempSize - 1; row++)
      {
         for(int c = 0; c < tempSize; c++)
         {
            tempAdjMat[row][c] =
               tempAdjMat[row + 1][c];
         }
      }
```

```
            for(int col = v; col < tempSize - 1; col++)
            {
                for(int r = 0; r < tempSize; r++)
                {
                    tempAdjMat[r][col] =
                        tempAdjMat[r][col + 1];
                }
            }
        }

        tempSize-;
    }


    // DELETE TEMP MEMORY
    if(tempAdjMat != NULL)
    {
        for(int i = 0; i < m_maxVerts; i++)
        {
            if(tempAdjMat[i] != NULL)
            {
                delete[] tempAdjMat[i];
                tempAdjMat[i] = NULL;
            }
        }

        delete[] tempAdjMat;
        tempAdjMat = NULL;
    }


    return !hasCycles;
    }
};
```

The main source file for the topological sorting demo application builds off of the Minimal Spanning Tree demo with a few differences. First, the Topological Sort demo creates a directed graph of six vertices with no cycles. The edges from the demo go from A to B, A to C, B to D, C to E, D to E, and E to F.

Once the graph is created, the code performs a breadth-first search to demonstrate that a path from A to D can be found in the directed graph. It then performs a minimal spanning tree algorithm to find the minimal edges that allow the first vertex to visit every node in the graph. The end of the function performs the topological sort and stores the result in a std::list container. This container is then displayed to the console window for output. The entire main source file from the

Toplogical Sort demo application is shown in Listing 11.11. Figure 11.13 shows a screenshot of the running demo application.

LISTING 11.11   The Topological Sort Demo's Main Source File

```cpp
#include<iostream>
#include"Graphs.h"

using namespace std;


int main(int args, char **argc)
{
   cout << "Graphs - Topological Sorting" << endl;
   cout << "Chapter 11: Graphs" << endl;
   cout << endl;


   // Create the data structure and fill it in.
   Graph<char> demoGraph(6);

   demoGraph.push('A'); // 0
   demoGraph.push('B'); // 1
   demoGraph.push('C'); // 2
   demoGraph.push('D'); // 3
   demoGraph.push('E'); // 4
   demoGraph.push('F'); // 5


   // Attach A:B A:C B:D C:E D:E E:F.
   demoGraph.attachDirectedEdge(0, 1);
   demoGraph.attachDirectedEdge(0, 2);
   demoGraph.attachDirectedEdge(1, 3);
   demoGraph.attachDirectedEdge(2, 4);
   demoGraph.attachDirectedEdge(3, 4);
   demoGraph.attachDirectedEdge(4, 5);


   // Perform breadth first search for a path from A to D.
   cout << "BreadthFirstSearch Nodes Visited: ";

   bool result = demoGraph.BreadthFirstSearch(0, 3);
   cout << endl << endl;

   if(result == 1)
      cout << "Path from A to D found!";
```

```
   else
      cout << "Path from A to D NOT found!";

   cout << endl << endl;


   // Display the minimum spanning tree.
   cout << "Minimum Spanning Tree: ";
   demoGraph.DisplayMST();

   cout << endl << endl;


   list<char> tsResult;

   if(demoGraph.topologicalSort(tsResult) == true)
   {
      cout << "Topological Sort: ";
      ostream_iterator<char> output(cout, " ");
      copy(tsResult.begin(), tsResult.end(), output);
   }
   else
   {
      cout << "There are cycles in the graph!";
   }

   cout << endl << endl;

   return 1;
}
```

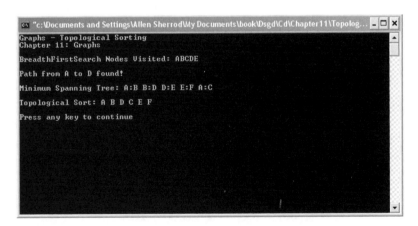

FIGURE 11.13 A screenshot of the Topological Sorting demo.

WEIGHTED GRAPHS

A weighted graph is a graph that adds a weight to each of its vertices. The weight can be anything and it is used to give a much better description of the vertices. For example, using the railroad system from earlier in this chapter, the weight of the vertices can be their distance or longitude and latitude coordinates. If the weight was a distance, the minimal distance from one city to another could be found, which would give us the shortest travel time. Another example from the real world could be the cost of plane travel between cities. Some flights are not nonstop, so not only is a path from one city to another found, but the total monetary cost can also be found. This can be seen in many online airline booking systems where a user can find flights from a staring airport to a destination airport based on the cheapest route.

Another example of using weights in a graph can be seen in artificial intelligence in a video game. If the game world can be broken up into vertices, a path from any starting area to a destination area can be found. In addition, the best route can be found between the two areas, which could include the safest path, the shortest path, and so on that an artificially controlled character or object can take.

Earlier in this chapter we said that the weighted graphs assumed the same weight for all vertices. When the weights of vertices are not the same, the complexity of some algorithms can increase.

Weighted graphs can be directed or nondirected graphs.

NOTE

MINIMAL SPANNING TREES AND WEIGHTED GRAPHS

Finding the minimal spanning tree of a weighted graph requires finding not only the minimal spanning tree but also the cheapest minimal spanning tree that exists for a given set of edges. This can be done by using a priority queue where the priority queue can keep a list of the costs of all edges found by the algorithm. At the end the edges that make up the top elements of the priority queue make up the shortest (or longest, depending on the comparison you are looking for) path from the first vertex to the last vertex in the graph. The algorithm for the minimal spanning tree of a weighted graph can be broken down into the following steps:

1. Mark the first vertex as the current vertex and set its checked flag to true.
2. Loop while the number of checked vertices does not equal the total number of vertices.
3. Loop through and add all unchecked adjacent vertices and their weights to the priority queue.
4. If the priority queue is empty after the last step, then the graph has a cycle.

5. Remove the edge with the lowest weight and add it to a list that makes up the minimal spanning tree.

6. Repeat steps 2 through 5 until the loop in step 2 breaks.

Performing these steps will display the shortest minimal spanning tree of a weighted graph. In the next section we will implement such an algorithm on a weighted graph data structure.

IMPLEMENTING THE MINIMAL SPANNING TREE ON A WEIGHTED GRAPH

ON THE CD
On the accompanying CD-ROM is a demo application called Weighted MST in the Chapter 11 folder. This demo application builds off the previous demo, Minimal Spanning Tree, but uses a weighted graph.

In the Graph.h header file for the Weighted Graph demo application a new class was added to the top. This class is used by the minimal spanning tree algorithm called `EdgeInfo` to store a temporary list of edges that were already checked by the algorithm.

The function for the minimal spanning tree, `DisplayMST()`, starts off by making the first vertex the current vertex and then loops until all vertices have been checked. Within the loop it marks the current vertex as checked and increments the number that holds the total number of checked vertices. Next, the body of the loop loops through each vertex in the graph and looks for an edge between it and the current vertex. Whenever it finds one, it adds the edge to a temporary edge list only if the destination vertex does not already exist somewhere in the temporary edge list. This is done using the find algorithm and the overloaded operator == in the `EdgeInfo` class. If the edge is found, the weights are compared. If the edge we are trying to add has a lower weight than the edge with a matching destination, then we replace that edge; otherwise, we do nothing since the smallest weight is already in the list.

At the end of the inner loop within the `DisplayMST()` function, if there are no vertices in the edge list, the graph must not be a connected graph, which is necessary for the algorithm. If there are elements in the temporary edge list, the edge with the minimum distance is added to the output and is removed from the edge list. Normally a priority queue would be used, but the STL `vector` can make the code easier to look at, so that is used. To find the minimum edge the `vector` array is sorted from greatest to least so that the minimum edge is at the end of the list. Since the elements must be sorted anyhow, sorting by greatest to least will allow for a fast `pop_back()` to be called on the container to remove the minimum edge. The sorting algorithm uses the overloaded operator < to sort the elements by weight from the `EdgeInfo` class.

NOTE
A priority queue based on a heap will lead to better performance than an array.

When the function is complete, you'll have a minimum spanning tree based on the weighted graph. If not, you'll have a message that says the graph is not connected. The code for the `EdgeInfo` class and the new `DisplayMST()` is shown in Listing 11.12.

LISTING 11.12   The Weighted Graph that Includes a New Minimal Spanning Tree

```
class EdgeInfo
{
   public:
      EdgeInfo() : m_v1Index(0), m_v2Index(0), m_weight(0) {}

      bool operator<(const EdgeInfo &e2)
      {
         return (m_weight < e2.m_weight);
      }


      bool operator==(const EdgeInfo &e2)
      {
         return (m_v2Index == e2.m_v2Index);
      }


      int m_v1Index, m_v2Index;
      int m_weight;
};


template<typename T>
class Graph
{
   public:
      void DisplayMST(string &output)
      {
         assert(m_adjMatrix != NULL);
         assert(m_vertVisits != NULL);

         int currentVert = 0, totalChecked = 0;
         int size = (int)m_vertices.size();

         vector<EdgeInfo> vList;
```

```
while(totalChecked < size - 1)
{
   m_vertVisits[currentVert] = 1;
   totalChecked++;


   for(int i = 0; i < size; i++)
   {
      if(i == currentVert || m_vertVisits[i] == 1 ||
         m_adjMatrix[currentVert][i] == 0)
         continue;

      EdgeInfo edge;
      edge.m_v1Index = currentVert;
      edge.m_v2Index = i;
      edge.m_weight = m_adjMatrix[currentVert][i];

      vector<EdgeInfo>::iterator it = find(vList.begin(),
                                           vList.end(),
                                           edge);

      if(it == vList.end())
      {
         vList.push_back(edge);
      }
      else
      {
         if(edge.m_weight <= (*it).m_weight)
         {
            (*it).m_v1Index = edge.m_v1Index;
            (*it).m_v2Index = edge.m_v2Index;
            (*it).m_weight = edge.m_weight;
         }
      }
   }


   if(vList.empty() == true)
   {
      output = "Error: Graph is not connected.";
      return;
   }
```

```
                    // Orders from greatest to least.
                    // Since we have to sort anyhow lets put the
                    // min at the end so pop_back() is fast.
                    sort(vList.rbegin(), vList.rend());

                    int endIndex = (int)vList.size() - 1;
                    int v1 = vList[endIndex].m_v1Index;
                    currentVert = vList[endIndex].m_v2Index;


                    // For demo output.
                    output += m_vertices[v1].GetNode();
                    output += ":";
                    output += m_vertices[currentVert].GetNode();
                    output += " ";


                    // Remove minimum, which was placed at the back.
                    vList.pop_back();
                }

                memset(m_vertVisits, 0, m_maxVerts);
            }
        };
```

The main source file is the same as the Minimal Spanning Tree demo application from earlier in this chapter, with the exception that the weights of the edges are specified. Also, the demo only does a minimal spanning tree. The weights were purposely set so that the minimal spanning tree that is generated is (A, B), (B, C), (C, D), (D, E), so that the visualization is easier. The main source file of the Weighted MST demo application is shown in Listing 11.13. Figure 11.14 shows a screenshot from the running demo application.

LISTING 11.13   Weighted MST Main Source File

```
#include<iostream>
#include"Graphs.h"

using namespace std;


int main(int args, char **argc)
{
```

```
cout << "Graphs - Weighted MST" << endl;
cout << "Chapter 11: Graphs" << endl;
cout << endl;


// Create the data structure and fill it in.
Graph<char> demoGraph(5);
string output;

demoGraph.push('A');
demoGraph.push('B');
demoGraph.push('C');
demoGraph.push('D');
demoGraph.push('E');


// Attach A to each other vertices.
demoGraph.attachEdge(0, 1, 1);
demoGraph.attachEdge(0, 2, 2);
demoGraph.attachEdge(0, 3, 4);
demoGraph.attachEdge(0, 4, 4);

// Attach B to each other vertices.
demoGraph.attachEdge(1, 2, 1);
demoGraph.attachEdge(1, 3, 3);
demoGraph.attachEdge(1, 4, 4);

// Attach C to each other vertices.
demoGraph.attachEdge(2, 3, 1);
demoGraph.attachEdge(2, 4, 4);

// Attach D to each other vertices.
demoGraph.attachEdge(3, 4, 1);

// Vertex E is already attached to all vertices.


// Display the minimum spanning tree.
demoGraph.DisplayMST(output);
cout << "Minimum Spanning Tree: " << output;

cout << endl << endl;

return 1;
}
```

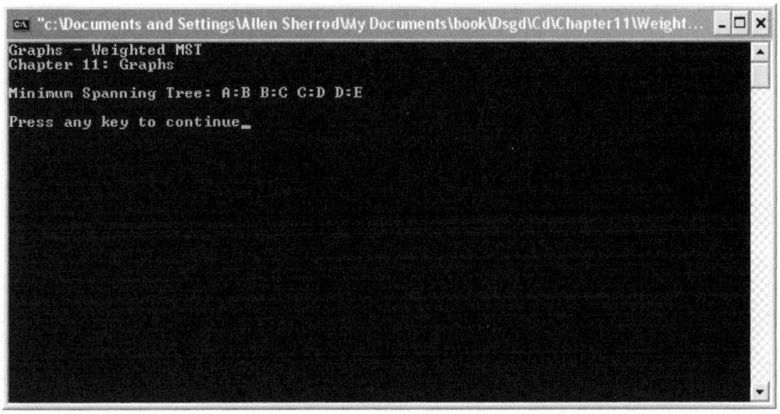

FIGURE 11.14 A screenshot of the Weighted MST demo.

ARTIFICIAL INTELLIGENCE

Artificial intelligence has been used in games practically since the beginning. One of the most important things to do in any game, whether that game is two-dimensional or three-dimensional, is to find a path from one location to another. In some games the illusion of path-finding can be accomplished by moving enemies along predefined paths, but in complex and dynamic scenes the game might need to figure out how to get from one place to another. To complicate matters the path-finding algorithm often must be performed on multiple game objects and perform at interactive rates. In this section we will briefly talk about a very popular path-finding algorithm called the A* algorithm.

A* ALGORITHM

The A* algorithm is performed on a weighted graph. In a game environment the areas of the game world that an artificially controlled character can access are defined by vertices. These vertices are connected to one another by edges that define a path that tells the game how to get from one area (vertex) to another. An example of this is shown in Figure 11.15.

The vertices in a graph data structure that are used in path-finding are known as the search area. This search area does not contain vertices for every microscopic position that an object can possibly be at in a game world because that would be excessive. Instead, the search area is often a simplified representation of where the artificially controlled objects can travel. In Figure 11.15 the vertices of the search area were simplified, which is what most games do to keep the performance of the algorithm acceptable between many game objects. In the A* path-finding algorithm

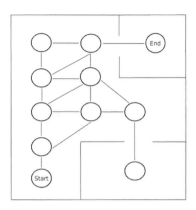

FIGURE 11.15 An overhead view of a game world where vertices define how to get from one area to another.

the number of vertices can affect the performance. These vertices are normally specified using some kind of environment or level editor and by finding a balance between the desired realism and performance.

The weights of the vertices can take on many different meanings, each of which would be application specific. The weights might be the distance from the origin of the game world. They could also be values that reflect the cost of moving to such a location. For example, in a game where the artificially intelligent characters can drive around the game world, the vertices can have varying weights based on the different types of terrains. That way, for example, the roads can have a lower cost than a patch of grass, which can have a lower cost than mud, which can have a lower cost than quicksand.

As mentioned previously, the weights in the A* algorithm are game specific. If the game uses weights to represent the distances of the vertices, then the shortest path from one location to another can be found. If a game uses varying weights to specify the cost of moving to various vertices, as in the example of trying to avoid muddy dirt if a patch of grass or the road is nearby, can also be used to increase the appearance of realism. It is all up to the game-specific requirements.

An understanding of weighted graphs will make the implementation of such a path-finding algorithm much easier. In a game performance is an issue, so modifications would have to be made to the graph data structure to allow it to solve a piece of the path-finding problem instead of calling one function and having it map out the entire route at once. The graphs created in this chapter solved the entire problem when they were asked to do something, but in the A* path-finding algorithm it is more efficient to solve a little bit of the path-finding problem during each frame instead of all at once. With many objects needing to dynamically navigate a game world, this will lead to a huge performance boost. Also, if the destination is dynamic, the end destination can be changed on the fly. For example, in an open world game such as *Saint's Row* (by Volition®) or *Grand Theft Auto*™ (by Rockstar®), the artificially controlled police officers will need to not only chase the player but to also try to stay on the road and avoid as many obstacles as possible. In *Saint's Row* for the Xbox® 360 the police artificial intelligence must be able to locate the players when they spawn. This can be seen if you get in enough trouble during the game and try to flee the scene. In that game, as well as in current and previous *Grand Theft Auto* titles, losing the line-of-sight between you and the police does not make you safe.

Obstacle avoidance brings up another issue associated with artificial intelligence and path finding. Not only does an object need to avoid static geometry in the game world, but they also must avoid dynamic objects. In an open world game this means other cars, pedestrians, and so on. The data structures and algorithms that perform these tasks can work together to create realistic and stunning game play experiences.

SUMMARY

The graph data structure is an impressive set of code that has a lot of uses in general application programming and in game and simulation development. The problems graphs solve are very different from the trees discussed in Chapter 9. In this chapter we discussed nonweighted and weighted graphs, where weighted graphs added a variable to the vertices of a graph that can be used to alter the algorithms seen in this chapter. The shortest path in a weighted graph can also be applied from any vertex to any other vertex using algorithms such as the Dijkstra's algorithm, developed by Edsger Dijkstra in the late 1950s, or Robert Floyd's algorithm, which was developed in the 1960s. These algorithms require modifying the adjacency matrix to show not only the cost of going from one vertex edge to another but the cost of going from all edges.

One very popular algorithm that uses a weighted graph is the A* path-finding algorithm. A* is a very common and popular algorithm that has been used for a long while in video games. Not only can the A* algorithm find a destination every time, assuming it exists, but it can do it at a rate that is beneficial for interactive performance.

In the next chapter we will look at additional C++ STL data structures and algorithms. The STL can make programming easier, and a strong understanding of all aspects of it will make all C++ programmers stronger when it comes to being able to solve problems in code.

Chapter Review Questions

Answers to the following chapter review questions can be found in Appendix B.

1. What is a graph?
2. What is the different between a graph and a tree?
3. What is the difference between a connected graph and a nonconnected graph?
4. What is the difference between a directed edge and a nondirected edge?
5. What is the difference between a weighted and an unweighted graph?
6. The depth-first search algorithm:
   a. Searches for the minimal edges needed to visit each vertex in the graph
   b. Travels all possible paths from a vertex to see if it can find the destination before it moves on to the adjacent vertices
   c. Checks all adjacent vertices before moving down the paths to find the destination
   d. None of the above
7. The breadth-first search algorithm:
   a. Searches for the minimal edges needed to visit each vertex in the graph
   b. Travels all possible paths from a vertex to see if it can find the destination before it moves on to the adjacent vertices
   c. Checks all adjacent vertices before moving down the paths to find the destination
   d. None of the above
8. The minimal spanning tree algorithm:
   a. Searches for the minimal edges needed to visit each vertex in the graph
   b. Travels all possible paths from a vertex to see if it can find the destination before it moves on to the adjacent vertices
   c. Checks all adjacent vertices before moving down the paths to find the destination
   d. None of the above
9. The topological sort algorithm:
   a. Searches for the minimal edges needed to visit each vertex in the graph
   b. Travels all possible paths from a vertex to see if it can find the destination before it moves on to the adjacent vertices
   c. Checks all adjacent vertices before moving down the paths to find the destination
   d. Displays the order of the vertices from a starting vertex to the last vertex
   e. None of the above
10. What difference was there in the minimal spanning algorithm from the weighted graph and the nonweighted one?

11. What is the A*?
    a. A sorting algorithm
    b. A path-finding algorithm
    c. A data structure
    d. None of the above

12. The A* is based on:
    a. A hash table
    b. A stack
    c. A binary tree
    d. A directed graph
    e. A weighted graph
    f. None of the above

13. The minimal spanning tree in an unweighted graph is always the same as in a weighted graph.
    a. True
    b. False

14. A* can only be applied to graphs with cycles.
    a. True
    b. False

15. Performance with the A* is unaffected by the number of vertices.
    a. True
    b. False

16. A topological sorting algorithm can only work on nondirected graphs.
    a. True
    b. False

17. The minimal spanning tree is a list of vertices that specify the order of vertices that can be visited from the start to the end.
    a. True
    b. False

18. A tree is a graph without cycles.
    a. True
    b. False

19. A directed edge is an edge that goes from one vertex to another and vice versa.
    a. True
    b. False

20. The breadth-first search can be used to find the shortest path from a starting vertex to the destination vertex.
    a. True
    b. False

PROGRAMMING PROJECTS

Exercise 1: Modify the Depth First Search demo application to store the output in another container instead of displaying it directly to the console window. Do the same for the Breadth First Search demo.

Exercise 2: Build off of the Depth First Search demo to create a graph that uses an adjacency list instead of an adjacency matrix.

Exercise 3: Add the ability for the graph class to save its data out to a file and to load data in from a file. This will allow the data structure to save its graph or to load one.

12

Additional STL Algorithms

In This Chapter

- Strings
- map and multimap
- set and multiset
- STL Algorithms

```
 "c:\Documents and Settings\Allen Sherrod\My Documents\book\Dsgd\Cd\Chapter12\STL.Mult...
STL Multi-Set Example
Chapter 12: Additional STL

Displaying all items:
     Key/Value: 124.
     Key/Value: 423.
     Key/Value: 634.
     Key/Value: 756.

Found and erased Key 124!

Displaying all items:
     Key/Value: 423.
     Key/Value: 634.
     Key/Value: 756.

Press any key to continue_
```

The C++ STL is a very useful set of template classes that are available to application programmers. So far in this book we've looked at the `vector`, `bit_array`, `list`, `queue`, `priority_queue`, `deque`, and the `stack` STL template classes. We've also looked at a few nonstandard hash containers using STLport including the `hash_set`, `hash_multiset`, `hash_map`, and the `hash_multimap`.

In this chapter we will look at the remaining STL algorithms. We'll also be looking at the `string` container, which isn't a template data structure, as well as the STL `map`, `multimap`, `set`, and `multiset` template classes. This chapter will wrap up the introduction to the C++ STL containers and algorithms, and the chapters that follow will discuss and implement a few data structures and algorithms that are very useful in the field of game and simulation development.

STRINGS

The standard `string` container is useful for creating and manipulating strings in C++. The string class is based on the template class called `basic_string` and is part of the C++ standard. Like other STL containers, the string class has the ability to allocate and manage its own memory and expand as necessary. The string class is also a sequence container, so STL algorithms can be used with it just like with other containers such as the vector. Also, like other STL containers, the `string` container offers methods and operators that make working with strings easier and more convenient.

Using string classes is recommended over using traditional arrays and vectors, because it offers the following benefits:

- They delete themselves.
- They perform allocations and reallocations as necessary.
- They are convenient to work with because they supply various operators and string-related methods.
- You can pass their contents to functions expecting the C-styled arrays so that legacy code can still work.
- For our convenience, the container offers many useful operations that are performed on strings.
- The string is a sequence container, so the STL algorithms will work on it (although normal arrays can also be used with some algorithms).
- The container is standard.

Whenever possible, be sure to use `reserve()` *to avoid unnecessary reallocations.*

NOTE

The `string` class is made up of many different methods and operators. We have seen most of these methods and operators in other containers such as the vector, the list, and so forth. What sets the string apart from the others is that it offers string-related methods as well as the common push_back(), erase(), reserve(), and so forth. Understanding and knowing what functions the string container supplies is important for using the class efficiently. Table 12.1 displays all of the methods and operators of the string class as well as a description of what they do.

TABLE 12.1   Member Functions and Operators of the String Container

Function/Operator	Description
string()	The class's constructor.
append(value_type)	
append(value_type*, count)	
append(str, offset, count)	
append(str)	
append(count, value_type)	
append(inputIteratorBegin, inputIteratorEnd)	Appends characters to the end of the string.
assign(chars)	
assign(value_type, count)	
assign(str, offset, count)	
assign(str)	
assign(count, value_type)	
assign(inputIteratorBegin, inputIteratorEnd)	Assigns new character values to the contents of the string container.
at(offset)	Returns a reference to the character specified by an offset.
begin()	Returns an iterator to the first element in the string.
capacity()	Returns the maximum size the string can hold without reallocations.
clear()	Erases all elements of a string container.
compare(str)	
compare(pos, length, str)	
compare(pos, length, str, offset, count)	
compare(value_type*)	
compare(pos, length, value_type*)	

$\rightarrow$

Function/Operator	Description
`compare(pos, length1, value_type*, length2)`	Compares two strings to see if they are equal or if one is lexicographically less than the other.
`copy(value_type*, count, offset)`	Copies a set of characters from a source to the string.
`c_str()`	Returns an array of the string's contents.
`data()`	Converts the contents of a string container into an array of characters
`empty()`	Tests whether there are characters in the container.
`end()` `size()`	Returns an iterator to the last element in the string.
`length()`	The `size()` and the `length()` functions return the number of characters in the string.
`erase(start, end)`	Deletes a substring from the container.
`replace(start, end, str)` `find(str, index)`	Replaces a substring with another string.
`rfind(str, index)` `find_first_not_of(char, offset)` `find_first_of(value_type*, offset)` `find_first_of(value_type*, offset, count)`	Finds the first occurrence of a substring in the container starting at the index. The `rfind()` function finds the last occurrence.
`find_first_of(str, offset)`	Searches a string for the first character that is not an element of a specified string.
`get_allocator()`	Returns a copy of the container's allocator.
`insert(index, str)`	Inserts a string into the container at a specified position.
`max_size()`	Returns the maximum number of characters the string can contain without being resized.
`push_back(char)`	Adds a character to the end of the string.
`rbegin()`	Returns an iterator to the first element in the reversed string.

$\rightarrow$

Function/Operator	Description
rend()	Returns an iterator to the last element in the reversed string.
reserve(size)	Reserves the minimum size for the string.
substr(index, length)	Returns a substring in the container starting at index for a specified length.
swap(str)	Swaps two strings' contents.
operator=	Operator to make one string equal to another.
operator+	Concatenates strings.
operator+= operator== operator!= operator< operator<= operator>	Concatenates and assigns strings.
operator>=	Boolean comparison operators.
operator[]	Allows the string's contents to be accessed using array subscripts.

Another function that can be used with a string is the getline() method, which reads a stream of data from an input stream. This stream can be an open file, come from the keyboard using std::cin, and so forth. The function takes as parameters the stream object, the string container that is being read to, and a delimiter that specifies when reading should stop. A delimiter in this case is a character that marks when reading should stop and can be anything from a new-line character, a tab character, a letter, a white space, and so forth. The function prototype for the getline() function is:

```
istream& getline (istream& is, string& str, char delim = '\n');
```

NOTE

Use the swap trick to trim excess memory in the container. For a string that could look like string(str.begin(), str.end()).swap(str) *for a string str.*

IMPLEMENTING STL STRINGS

ON THE CD

On the accompanying CD-ROM a demo application called Strings can be found in the Chapter 12 folder. This simple demo application will demonstrate the creation of an STL `string` and perform a few different algorithms on the container. In this section we will look at the demo's main source file in detail.

The demo's main source file starts by creating a string object and using its constructor to pass a set of characters into it. The demo then tests calling the container's `clear()` function to clear the contents of the container, tests the `operator=` to assign a new set of text to the container, and tests the `push_back()` function to add a character to the end of the current string. Once those initial tests are done, the demo uses an output stream iterator along with the `string` iterators to call the `copy()` algorithm to display the contents of the string to the console window in both its forward and reverse order. Last, the demo demonstrates using the `getline()` function to read text from the keyboard and into the container. The `getline()` function will continue to read characters until the Enter key is pressed. Once Enter is pressed, the text that was entered is displayed and the application quits. The Strings demo's main source file is shown in Listing 12.1. Figure 12.1 shows a screenshot of the demo application.

LISTING 12.1   The Strings Demo's Main Source File

```
#include<iostream>
#include<string>
#include<algorithm>

using namespace std;


int main(int args, char **argc)
{
   cout << "Strings Example" << endl;
   cout << "Chapter 12: Additional STL" << endl;
   cout << endl;


   string str("Hello World");

   cout << "                  String contents: " << str << endl;

   str.clear();
   cout << "   String contents after clear: " << str << endl;
```

```
        str = "Goodbye World";
        cout << "      Assigning string contents: " << str << endl;


        str.push_back('!');

        cout << "String contents with iterators: ";

        ostream_iterator<char> output(cout, "");
        copy(str.begin(), str.end(), output);
        cout << endl;


        cout << "              Reverse contents: ";

        copy(str.rbegin(), str.rend(), output);
        cout << endl << endl;


        cout << "Enter in a string and press enter: ";
        getline(cin, str);
        cout << endl;

        cout << "You've entered: " << str << endl << endl;


        return 1;
}
```

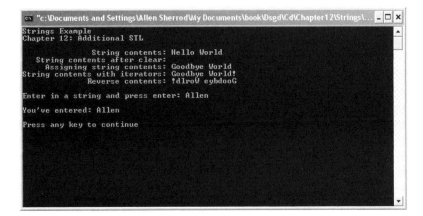

FIGURE 12.1   A screenshot of the Strings demo application.

MAP AND MULTIMAP

In the STL there are also `map` and `multimap` containers. These containers contain a data value and a sorting key pair. The `map` and `multimap` classes are used to retrieve data from a collection using the key value of the pair that is inserted into the container. When declaring one of these containers, the key's data type is a template parameter, the data value's data type is a template parameter, the binary predicate comparison is a template parameter (these were discussed in Chapter 5), and the allocator can be defined, which is optional along with the binary predicate. By default both the `map` and `multimap` classes use the `less<Key>` binary predicate. Using the `map` class as an example, the template declarations would look like the following:

```
template <
    class Key,
    class Type,
    class Traits = less<Key>,
    class Allocator=allocator<pair <const Key, Type> >
    >
    class map
```

Things to remember about the STL `map` and `multimap` are:

- The STL `map` and `multimap` are pair-associative containers.
- Element values are retrieved by using a key.
- They have support for bidirectional iterators.
- They are template classes.
- Each element has a unique key in a `map`, but in a `mutlimap` they do not have to be unique.
- Elements are sorted based on the key.

The `map` and the `multimap` classes share a lot of the same methods but also have a few that are unique to one or the other. The class methods and operators that the STL `map` and `multimap` have in common are listed in Table 12.2. The methods and operators unique to `map` are listed in Table 12.3, and the `multimap` operators are in Table 12.4.

TABLE 12.2   Methods and Operators Shared by `map` and `multimap`

Method/Operator	Description
`begin()`	Returns an iterator to the first element in the container
`clear()`	Clears the container's elements
`count(key)`	Returns the number of elements in the container that matches the key
`empty()`	Boolean test to check if the container is empty
`end()`	Returns an iterator to the last element in the container
`equal_range(key)`	Returns a pair of iterators to the first element that is greater than or equal to the key to the last element that is greater than the key
`erase(it)` `erase(itFirst, itLast)` `erase(key)`	Erases an element from the container based on the iterator position, the range of iterators, or the key value
`find(key)`	Returns an iterator to the element based on the key
`get_allocator()`	Returns the allocator used by the container
`insert(value_type&)` `insert(it, value_type&)` `insert(itFirst, itLast)`	Inserts an element or a range of elements into the container
`key_comp()`	Returns the comparison used for the keys
`lower_bound(key)`	Returns an iterator to the first element that is equal to or greater than the key
`max_size()`	Returns the maximum size of the container without needing a reallocation
`rbegin()`	Returns an iterator to the first reverse element
`rend()`	Returns an iterator to the last reverse element
`size()`	Returns the number of elements in the container
`swap(right)`	Swaps the elements of two containers
`upper_bound(key)`	Returns an iterator to the first element that is less than the key
`value_comp()`	Returns a function object that determines the order of elements in a container by comparing their keys

TABLE 12.3 map Methods and Operators

Method/Operator	Description
map()	
map(comparison)	
map(comparison, allocator)	
map(map&)	
map(itFirst, itLast)	
map(itFirst, itLast, comparison)	
map(itFirst, itLast, comparison, allocator)	Constructors
operator[key]	Inserts an element into the container using key if the key is not found and returns a reference to the data value that exists for that key, which allows for reading and writing (i.e., insertion)

TABLE 12.4 multimap Methods

Method	Description
multimap()	
multimap(comparison)	
multimap(comparison, allocator)	
map(map&)	
map(itFirst, itLast)	
map(itFirst, itLast, comparison)	
map(itFirst, itLast, comparison, allocator)	Constructors

IMPLEMENTING **STL** map AND multimap

ON THE CD

On the accompanying CD-ROM in the Chapter 12 folder is a demo application called STL Map that demonstrates using the map class. In that same folder is another demo application called STL Multi-map that demonstrates how to use a multimap class. These demo applications are very similar but have their differences. The STL Map demo application demonstrates inserting objects into the container using the insert() function and the operator[] overloaded operator. The STL Map demo moves on to demonstrate displaying the contents inside the container using the operator[] and iterators. The STL Map demo finishes by demonstrating how to find a key and its associated data object from the container. The main source file for the STL Map demo application is shown in Listing 12.2. Figure 12.2 shows a screenshot of the running demo application.

LISTING 12.2   The STL Map Demo's Main Source File

```
#include<iostream>
#include<map>
#include<string>
#include<algorithm>

using namespace std;


int main(int args, char **argc)
{
   cout << "STL Maps Example" << endl;
   cout << "Chapter 12: Additional STL" << endl;
   cout << endl;


   // Create and insert into the container.
   map<int, string> mapPair;

   mapPair.insert(map<int, string>::value_type(300, "Test 1"));
   mapPair.insert(map<int, string>::value_type(150, "Test 2"));
   mapPair.insert(map<int, string>::value_type(400, "Test 3"));
   mapPair.insert(map<int, string>::value_type(600, "Test 4"));

   mapPair[100] = "One hundred";

   cout << "Diplaying 400: " << mapPair[400].c_str() <<
           endl << endl;


   // Test displaying contents.
   cout << "Displaying all items:" << endl;

   for(map<int, string>::iterator it = mapPair.begin();
       it != mapPair.end(); it++)
   {
```

```
        cout << "   Key: " << (*it).first << " Value: " <<
            (*it).second << "." << endl;
    }

    cout << endl;


    // Test removing from the container.
    map<int, string>::iterator itPos = mapPair.find(150);

    if(itPos != mapPair.end())
        cout << "Found Key 150!" << endl;


    cout << endl;

    return 1;
}
```

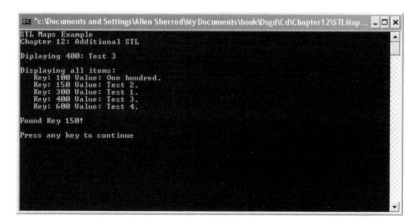

FIGURE 12.2 A Screenshot of the STL Map Demo.

The STL Multi-map demo application starts off by using the insert() function to insert items into the container. Since there is no operator[] for the multimap, it only uses insert(). The demo moves on to show how to display its contents using iterators, how to use the equal_range() function to search for all objects that match a specific key, and how to find an element that matches a key. When the range is displayed, all elements that have that specific key are displayed to the console window. Since multimap objects can have shared keys within the container, during the insertion a few keys are purposely made to share the same key. The main source file for the STL Multi-map demo application is shown in Listing 12.3. Figure 12.3 shows a screenshot of the demo application.

LISTING 12.3   The STL Multi-map Demo's Main Source File

```
#include<iostream>
#include<map>
#include<string>
#include<algorithm>

using namespace std;


int main(int args, char **argc)
{
   cout << "STL Multi-Maps Example" << endl;
   cout << "Chapter 12: Additional STL" << endl;
   cout << endl;


   // Create and insert into the container.
   multimap<int, string> mapPair;

   mapPair.insert(map<int, string>::value_type(300, "Test 1"));
   mapPair.insert(map<int, string>::value_type(150, "Test 2"));
   mapPair.insert(map<int, string>::value_type(100, "Test 3"));
   mapPair.insert(map<int, string>::value_type(275, "Test 4"));
   mapPair.insert(map<int, string>::value_type(150, "Test 5"));


   // Test displaying contents.
   cout << "Displaying all items:" << endl;

   for(multimap<int, string>::iterator it = mapPair.begin();
       it != mapPair.end(); it++)
   {
      cout << "   Key: " << (*it).first << " Value: " <<
              (*it).second << "." << endl;
   }

   cout << endl;
```

```
// Searching for and displaying all values that share a key.
pair<multimap<int, string>::iterator,
     multimap<int, string>::iterator> range;


range = mapPair.equal_range(150);


cout << "Displaying all items in a range:" << endl;


for(it = range.first; it != range.second; it++)
{
   cout << "   Key: " << (*it).first << " Value: " <<
           (*it).second << "." << endl;
}


cout << endl;



// Test removing from the container.
multimap<int, string>::iterator itPos = mapPair.find(150);


if(itPos != mapPair.end())
   cout << "Found Key 100!" << endl;



cout << endl;

return 1;
}
```

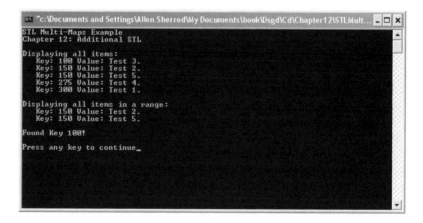

FIGURE 12.3   The STL Multi-map Demo's Screenshot.

SET AND MULTISET

The last STL data structures that will be looked at in this chapter are the set and multiset. The set class is a template class where all elements inserted in the list are to be unique. In a set, as well as a multiset, the elements are sorted by the key, which also serves as the data object. The multiset is the same as the set class, with the exception that the multiset class can have keys that are not unique. Neither set nor multiset can have their elements changed, which mean old keys must be deleted and new keys inserted. Using the set class as an example, the declaration of its template parameters are:

```
template <
    class Key,
    class Traits=less<Key>,
    class Allocator=allocator<Key>
>
class set
```

A few things to keep in mind when working with these containers are:

- set and multiset are simple associative containers in which the key values are their element values.
- The elements are sorted.
- They support bidirectional iterators.
- The set class requires keys that are unique, while the multiset does not.
- Sets, being associative containers, are optimized for insertions, lookups, and removals with a big-O of O(log N).
- Inserting elements do not invalidate iterators, but removing elements do invalidate iterators that point to a place before the element that was removed.

The difference that separates sets from maps is that maps are key-object pair structures, while sets use the object as their keys.

NOTE

The member functions and operators that the set and multiset class offer are the same as the map and multimap classes with the exception that the set does not have an operator[] like the map does.

IMPLEMENTING STL set AND multiset

ON THE CD

On the accompanying CD-ROM in the Chapter 12 folder is a set of demo applications called STL Set and STL Multiset. The STL Set demo creates a set container, populates it with elements, copies the container to another, displays the contents of the copy using iterators, and searches for a value within the container. The main source file for the STL Set demo application is shown in Listing 12.4, and its screenshot is shown in Figure 12.4.

LISTING 12.4 The Main Source File for the STL Set Demo

```
#include<iostream>
#include<set>

using namespace std;


int main(int args, char **argc)
{
    cout << "STL Set Example" << endl;
    cout << "Chapter 12: Additional STL" << endl;
    cout << endl;


    // Create and insert into the container.
    set<int> setContainer;

    setContainer.insert(300);
    setContainer.insert(150);
    setContainer.insert(400);
    setContainer.insert(375);

    set<int> setCopy(setContainer);


    // Test displaying contents.
    cout << "Displaying all items:" << endl;

    for(set<int>::iterator it = setCopy.begin();
        it != setCopy.end(); it++)
      {
         cout << "   Key/Value: " << (*it) << "." << endl;
      }

    cout << endl;


    // Test removing from the container.
    set<int>::iterator itPos = setContainer.find(150);
```

```
    if(itPos != setContainer.end())
        cout << "Found Key 150!" << endl << endl;



    return 1;
}
```

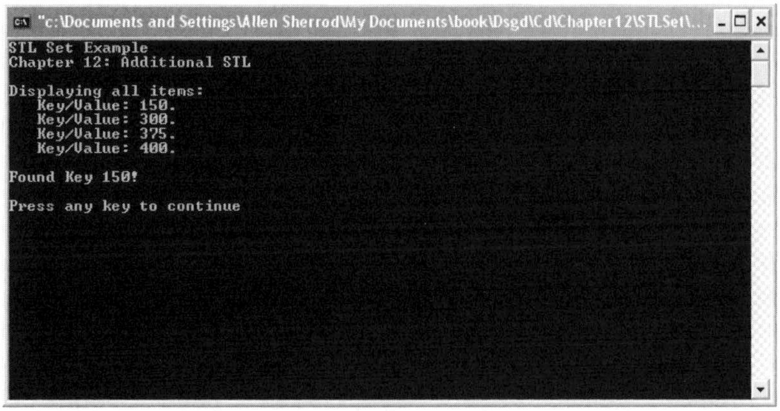

FIGURE 12.4   The STL Set demo's screenshot.

The STL Multiset demo application starts by creating a container and populating it with elements. It then moves on to display the container's contents using iterators, searches for an element based on its key and erases it, and displays the updated container before the application quits to show that the key was actually erased. The biggest difference between the set classes and the map classes is that the set classes use one object for the key and the object while the map classes use two to form a pair (one key and one object). The main source file for the STL Multiset demo is shown in Listing 12.5, and its screenshot is shown in Figure 12.5.

LISTING 12.5   The STL Multiset Demo's Main Source File

```
#include<iostream>
#include<set>

using namespace std;


int main(int args, char **argc)
{
```

```
cout << "STL Multi-Set Example" << endl;
cout << "Chapter 12: Additional STL" << endl;
cout << endl;


// Create and insert into the container.
multiset<int> setContainer;
multiset<int>::iterator it;

setContainer.insert(423);
setContainer.insert(634);
setContainer.insert(124);
setContainer.insert(756);


// Test displaying contents.
cout << "Displaying all items:" << endl;

for(it = setContainer.begin(); it != setContainer.end(); it++)
{
   cout << "   Key/Value: " << (*it) << "." << endl;
}

cout << endl;


// Test removing from the container.
multiset<int>::iterator itPos = setContainer.find(124);

if(itPos != setContainer.end())
{
   setContainer.erase(124);
   cout << "Found and erased Key 124!" << endl << endl;
}


// Test displaying contents.
cout << "Displaying all items:" << endl;

for(it = setContainer.begin(); it != setContainer.end(); it++)
{
   cout << "   Key/Value: " << (*it) << "." << endl;
}
```

```
        cout << endl;


        return 1;
}
```

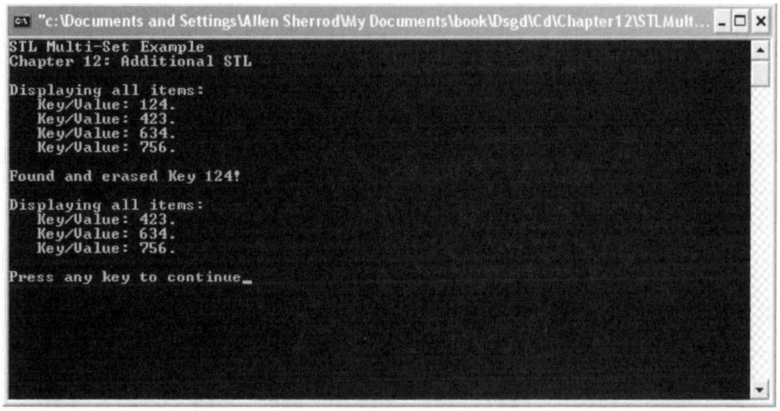

FIGURE 12.5   The STL Multiset demo's screenshot.

STL ALGORITHMS

STL algorithms are sets of algorithms that can be performed efficiently on various STL data structures. When it comes to STL, the algorithms are separated from the containers. Not only does this make it easy for new algorithms to be added to the STL standard, but it means the algorithms do not to have to depend on the individual container's implementation. STL algorithms use the container's iterators. Classes that do not have iterators cannot be used with STL algorithms. Classes that do have iterators, as long as they satisfy the STL requirements, can be used with the STL algorithms.

> *STL algorithms can work not only on STL data structures that have support for iterators, but also with C-style traditional arrays.*

In this section we will discuss various STL algorithms. These algorithms include searching algorithms, copying algorithms, counting algorithms, comparison algorithms, filling algorithms, sorting algorithms, removal algorithms, and so forth.

SEARCHING ALGORITHMS

The first set of STL algorithms that will be discussed deal with searching for values within a container. These algorithms include `adjacent_find()`, `binary_search()`, `lower_bound()`, `upper_bound()`, `search()`, and the `search_n()` functions. The `adjacent_find()` algorithm searches for two adjacent elements that are either equal or satisfy some condition and return an iterator to the result. The function prototype for `adjacent_find()` is as follows:

```
template<class ForwardIterator>
ForwardIterator adjacent_find(ForwardIterator _First,
                              ForwardIterator _Last);



template<class ForwardIterator , class BinaryPredicate>
ForwardIterator adjacent_find(ForwardIterator _First,
                              ForwardIterator _Last,
                              BinaryPredicate _Comp);
```

The `binary_search()` algorithm performs a binary search on an order container to see if a value exists. If the function returns `true`, the value was found; otherwise, it was not found within the container. Binary searches were first discussed in Chapter 2, and STL has an algorithm function for them. The function prototype for the `binary_search()` function is:

```
template<class ForwardIterator, class Type>
bool binary_search(ForwardIterator _First, ForwardIterator _Last,
                   const Type& _Val);



template<class ForwardIterator, class Type, class BinaryPredicate>
bool binary_search(ForwardIterator _First, ForwardIterator _Last,
                   const Type& _Val, BinaryPredicate _Comp);
```

The `lower_bound()` and `upper_bound()` algorithm functions search for an element that is less than or equivalent (`lower_bound()`) to the value that is being searched or that is greater than the value being searched (`upper_bound()`). The return value is an iterator to the element if found or to the element one past the last if not. The function prototypes for the lower and upper bound algorithms are:

```
template<class ForwardIterator, class Type>
ForwardIterator lower_bound(ForwardIterator _First,
                            ForwardIterator _Last,
                            const Type& _Val);
```

```
template<class ForwardIterator, class Type, class BinaryPredicate>
ForwardIterator lower_bound(ForwardIterator _First,
                            ForwardIterator _Last,
                            const Type& _Val,
                            BinaryPredicate _Comp);


template<class ForwardIterator, class Type>
ForwardIterator upper_bound(ForwardIterator _First,
                            ForwardIterator _Last,
                            const Type& _Val);


template<class ForwardIterator, class Type, class BinaryPredicate>
ForwardIterator upper_bound(ForwardIterator _First,
                            ForwardIterator _Last,
                            const Type& _Val,
                            BinaryPredicate _Comp);
```

The search() and search_n() algorithm functions search a container for the first occurrence of a range of values in two sequences. The search_n() function is the same as the search(), with the exception that the search() function takes two pair of beginning and ending iterators, while the search_n() function takes one set of iterators and a count that represents how many elements to search. The function prototypes for the search() and search_n() functions are:

```
template<class ForwardIterator1, class ForwardIterator2>
ForwardIterator1 search(ForwardIterator1 _First1,
                        ForwardIterator1 _Last1,
                        ForwardIterator2 _First2,
                        ForwardIterator2 _Last2);

template<class ForwardIterator1, class ForwardIterator2, class Pr>
ForwardIterator1 search(ForwardIterator1 _First1,
                        ForwardIterator1 _Last1,
                        ForwardIterator2 _First2,
                        ForwardIterator2 _Last2,
                        BinaryPredicate _Comp);


template<class ForwardIterator1, class Diff2, class Type>
ForwardIterator1 search_n(ForwardIterator1 _First1,
                          ForwardIterator1 _Last1,
                          Size2 _Count,
                          const Type& _Val);
```

```
template<class ForwardIterator1, class Size2, class Type,
class BinaryPredicate>
ForwardIterator1 search_n(ForwardIterator1 _First1,
                          ForwardIterator1 _Last1,
                          Size2 _Count,
                          const Type& _Val,
                          BinaryPredicate _Comp);
```

COPYING AND COUNTING ALGORITHMS

The copying algorithms include copy() and copy_backward(). Both algorithm functions copy elements from a source to a destination, while copy_backward() copies the elements from the source in reverse order into the destination. In this book the copying algorithms were first discussed and used in Chapter 2. The copying function prototypes are:

```
template<class InputIterator, class OutputIterator>
OutputIterator copy(InputIterator _First, InputIterator _Last,
                    OutputIterator _DestBeg);
```

```
template<class BidirectionalIterator1, class BidirectionalIterator2>
BidirectionalIterator2 copy_backward(BidirectionalIterator1 _First,
                                     BidirectionalIterator1 _Last,
                                     BidirectionalIterator2 _DestEnd);
```

The counting algorithms return a number of elements in a range that matches the value that is being supplied. In other words, they count how many elements match a value. The counting algorithms consist of count() and count_if(), where count_if() also takes a condition in which the element should be counted or not. The function prototypes for the count() and count_if() are:

```
template<class InputIterator, class Type>
typename iterator_traits<InputIterator>::difference_type count(
    InputIterator _First, InputIterator _Last, const Type& _Val);
```

```
template<class InputIterator, class Predicate>
typename iterator_traits<InputIterator>::difference_type count_if(
    InputIterator _First, InputIterator _Last, Predicate _Pred);
```

COMPARISON ALGORITHMS

The next set of STL algorithms that will be discussed are various comparison operators. These operators include the equal(), equal_range(), min(), max(), min_element(), max_element(), mismatch(), and lexicographical_compare(). The min() and max() algorithms take two parameters and return whichever is either smaller (min()) or larger (max()). The min_element() and max_element() algorithms take iterators that specify a range of values and return either the minimum or maximum value. The prototypes for these four functions are as follows:

```
template<class Type>
const Type& min(const Type& _Left, const Type& _Right);

template<class Type, class Pr>
const Type& min(const Type& _Left, const Type& _Right,
                BinaryPredicate _Comp);


template<class ForwardIterator>
ForwardIterator min_element(ForwardIterator _First,
                            ForwardIterator _Last);

template<class ForwardIterator, class BinaryPredicate>
ForwardIterator min_element(ForwardIterator _First,
                            ForwardIterator _Last,
                            BinaryPredicate _Comp);


template<class Type>
const Type& max(const Type& _Left, const Type& _Right);

template<class Type, class Pr>
const Type& max(const Type& _Left, const Type& _Right,
                BinaryPredicate _Comp);


template<class ForwardIterator>
ForwardIterator max_element(ForwardIterator _First,
                            ForwardIterator _Last);

template<class ForwardIterator, class BinaryPredicate>
ForwardIterator max_element(ForwardIterator _First,
                            ForwardIterator _Last,
                            BinaryPredicate _Comp);
```

The equal() and equal_range() algorithms check to see if elements are equal or have equivalence. Both functions take iterators, but the equal_range() returns a pair within the container, with the first being less than the value and the second being equivalent. Both functions allow for the binary predicate to be specified, which is optional. The function prototypes for the equal() and equal_range() functions are:

```
template<class InputIterator1, class InputIterator2>
bool equal(InputIterator1 _First1, InputIterator1 _Last1,
        InputIterator2 _First2);

template<class InputIterator1, class InputIterator2,
        class BinaryPredicate>
bool equal(InputIterator1 _First1, InputIterator1 _Last1,
        InputIterator2 _First2, BinaryPredicate _Comp);


template<class ForwardIterator, class Type>
pair<ForwardIterator, ForwardIterator> equal_range(
    ForwardIterator _First, ForwardIterator _Last,
    const Type& _Val);

template<class ForwardIterator, class Type, class Pr>
pair<ForwardIterator, ForwardIterator> equal_range(
    ForwardIterator _First, ForwardIterator _Last,
    const Type& _Val,BinaryPredicate _Comp);
```

The next algorithm, mismatch(), tests a range of elements for equality or equivalence. The return value of the mismatch algorithm is a pair of iterators that represent the position in the container where there is a mismatch. If there is no mismatch in the ranges that are being tested, the function will return a pair of iterators that are one past the final element in the container. The function prototype for the mismatch() algorithm is as follows:

```
template<class InputIt1, class InputIt2>
pair<InputIt1, InputIt2> mismatch(InputIt1 _First1,
                                InputIt1 _Last1,
                                InputIt2 _First2);

template<class InputIt1, class InputIt2, class BinaryPredicate>
pair<InputIt1, InputIt2> mismatch(InputIt1 _First1,
                                InputIt1 _Last1,
                                InputIt2 _First2,
                                BinaryPredicate _Comp);
```

The last STL algorithm that we'll look at in this section is called the `lexicographical_compare()` algorithm. This algorithm compares element by element between two containers to determine which one is the lesser of the two. For function parameters it takes the beginning and ending iterators of both containers, and its return type is Boolean. The function prototype for the `lexicographical_compare()` algorithm is as follows:

```
template<class InputIterator1, class InputIterator2>
bool lexicographical_compare(InputIterator1 _First1,
                             InputIterator1 _Last1,
                             InputIterator2 _First2,
                             InputIterator2 _Last2);


template<class InputIterator1, class InputIterator2,
         class BinaryPredicate>
bool lexicographical_compare(InputIterator1 _First1,
                             InputIterator1 _Last1,
                             InputIterator2 _First2,
                             InputIterator2 _Last2,
                             BinaryPredicate _Comp);
```

FILLING ALGORITHMS

The STL includes algorithms for filling a container with elements of a specific value in a range. These algorithms are called `fill()` and `fill_n()`. `fill()` sets the values in a range specified by iterators, and `fill_n()` sets a range specified by a beginning iterator and a count. The function prototypes for the `fill()` and `fill_n()` algorithms are:

```
template<class ForwardIterator, class Type>
void fill(ForwardIterator _First, ForwardIterator _Last,
          const Type& _Val);


template<class OutputIterator, class Size, class Type>
void fill_n(OutputIterator _First, Size _Count,
            const Type& _Val);
```

The filling algorithms can be useful for quickly setting the elements of a newly created container to a specific value, overriding a range of values in an already created container, and so forth. As long as the container has support for iterators it will work with these algorithm functions. An example of their use is:

```
vector<int> array(10);

fill(array.begin(), array.end(), 0);
fill_n(array.begin(), 5, 2);
```

In this code the vector container has its elements set to 0 before setting the first half of the container to the number 2. STL algorithms are fast, so using this can be beneficial when a range of values needs to be set.

GENERATING ALGORITHMS

A generating algorithm uses a generator function to create values in a container within a specified range. The generator function used with a generating algorithm can take no parameters and must return a value. The generating algorithms that are part of the STL include the generate() and generate_n() algorithms. The purpose of these algorithms is to fill a container with a range of values that are generated instead of constant, as seen with the filling algorithms earlier in this chapter. The function prototypes for the generate() and generate_n() algorithms are:

```
template<class ForwardIterator, class Generator>
void generate(ForwardIterator _First, ForwardIterator _Last,
              Generator _Gen);
```

```
template<class OutputIterator, class Size, class Generator>
void generate_n(OutputIterator _First, Size _Count,
                Generator _Gen);
```

In this code the generate() function takes a range specified by a beginning and ending iterator, and the generate_n() function takes a beginning iterator and a count, along with the generator function. A simple example of using the generating functions is:

```
int NextNumber()
{
   static int number = 0;
   return number++;
}

void main()
{
   vector<int> array(10);
```

```
        generate(array.begin(), array.end(), NextNumber);
        generate_n(array.begin(), 5, NextNumber);
}
```

The generator that is used is entirely up to the programmer. In the previous example a function used to return an incremented number every time it is called was used. If the values that need to be inserted into a container must be generated by some means, then the generating algorithms might prove to be of great value.

SORTING ALGORITHMS

The next set of algorithms is the ones that are used for sorting elements within a container. These include the partial_sort(), partial_sort_copy(), prev_permutation(), sort(), sort_heap(), and stable_sort(). The partial_sort() sorts a small set within a container into either descending or user-defined order. The partial_sort_ copy() copied the sorted elements into a destination container. The function prototypes for the partial_sort() and partial_sort_copy() are:

```
template<class RandomAccessIterator>
void partial_sort(RandomAccessIterator _First,
                  RandomAccessIterator _SortEnd,
                  RandomAccessIterator _Last);

template<class RandomAccessIterator, class BinaryPredicate>
void partial_sort(RandomAccessIterator _First,
                  RandomAccessIterator _SortEnd,
                  RandomAccessIterator _Last
                  BinaryPredicate _Comp);


template<class InputIterator, class RandomAccessIterator>
RandomAccessIterator partial_sort_copy(InputIterator _First1,
                                       InputIterator _Last1,
                                       RandomAccessIterator _First2,
                                       RandomAccessIterator _Last2);

template<class InputIterator, class RandomAccessIterator, class
      BinaryPredicate>
RandomAccessIterator partial_sort_copy(InputIterator _First1,
                                       InputIterator _Last1,
                                       RandomAccessIterator _First2,
                                       RandomAccessIterator _Last2,
                                       BinaryPredicate _Comp);
```

The prev_permutation() algorithm reorders a container's contents into the lexicographical next-greater permutation if it exists. The function takes as parameters the beginning and ending iterators of the container that is using the algorithm. The function prototypes for the prev_permutation() algorithm are:

```
template<class BidirectionalIterator>
bool prev_permutation(BidirectionalIterator _First,
                      BidirectionalIterator _Last);


template<class BidirectionalIterator, class BinaryPredicate>
bool prev_permutation(BidirectionalIterator _First,
                      BidirectionalIterator _Last,
                      BinaryPredicate _Comp);
```

The last three algorithms that will be looked at in this section are the sort(), sort_heap(), and stable_sort() algorithms. The sort() algorithm arranges the elements of a container based on a condition or in nondescending order (default). The sort_heap() algorithm converts a heap into a sorted range. If the elements do not meet the requirements of a heap, the sort_heap() algorithms will not be a stable sort. The stable_sort() algorithm sorts elements into nondescending order or a user-defined order and preserves the relative ordering of equivalence of the elements. The function prototypes of the sort(), sort_heap(), and stable_sort() algorithms are:

```
template<class RandomAccessIterator>
void sort(RandomAccessIterator _First,
          RandomAccessIterator _Last);

template<class RandomAccessIterator, class Pr>
void sort(RandomAccessIterator _First,
          RandomAccessIterator _Last,
          BinaryPredicate _Comp);


template<class RandomAccessIterator>
void sort_heap(RandomAccessIterator _First,
               RandomAccessIterator _Last);

template<class RandomAccessIterator, class Pr>
void sort_heap(RandomAccessIterator _First,
               RandomAccessIterator _Last,
               BinaryPredicate _Comp);
```

```
template<class BidirectionalIterator>
void stable_sort(BidirectionalIterator _First,
                 BidirectionalIterator _Last);


template<class BidirectionalIterator, class BinaryPredicate>
void stable_sort(BidirectionalIterator _First,
                 BidirectionalIterator _Last,
                 BinaryPredicate _Comp);
```

REMOVING ALGORITHMS

The removing algorithms allow programmers to remove elements from an STL container. The remove() algorithm takes a range of iterators and a value that is to be removed from the container. The remove_if() algorithm takes a value to be removed and a range of iterators and will only remove the value if a specified condition is met. The remove_copy() algorithm copies a source container to the destination, with the exception of the value that is to be removed. remove_copy_if() does the same as remove_if()but only removes a value if a certain condition is met. The function prototypes for the remove(), remove_if(), remove_copy(), and remove_copy_if() algorithms are:

```
template<class ForwardIterator, class Type>
ForwardIterator remove(ForwardIterator _First,
                       ForwardIterator _Last, const Type& _Val);


template<class ForwardIterator, class Predicate>
ForwardIterator remove_if(ForwardIterator _First,
                          ForwardIterator _Last, Predicate _Pred);


template<class InputIterator, class OutputIterator, class Type>
OutputIterator remove_copy(InputIterator _First,
                           InputIterator _Last,
                           OutputIterator _Result,
                           const Type& _Val);


template<class InputIterator, class OutputIterator,
         class Predicate>
OutputIterator remove_copy_if(InputIterator _First,
                              InputIterator _Last,
                              OutputIterator _Result,
                              Predicate _Pred);
```

REPLACING ALGORITHMS

The STL algorithms that are used to replace elements in a container are called `replace()`, `replace_if()`, `replace_copy()`, and `replace_copy_if()`. These functions are similar to the removing functions except that they replace one value with another instead of removing it. The parameters for these algorithms are also similar to the removing functions, but there is one additional parameter when dealing with replacing, and that is for the value that will replace the old one. The function prototypes for the replacing algorithms are:

```
template<class ForwardIterator, class Type>
ForwardIterator replace(ForwardIterator _First,
                        ForwardIterator _Last,
                        const Type& _OldVal,
                        const Type& _NewVal);


template<class ForwardIterator, class Predicate>
ForwardIterator replace_if(ForwardIterator _First,
                           ForwardIterator _Last,
                           Predicate _Pred,
                           const Type& _Val);


template<class InputIterator, class OutputIterator, class Type>
OutputIterator replace_copy(InputIterator _First,
                            InputIterator _Last,
                            OutputIterator _Result,
                            const Type& _OldVal,
                            const Type& _NewVal);


template<class InputIterator, class OutputIterator,
         class Predicate>
OutputIterator replace_copy_if(InputIterator _First,
                               InputIterator _Last,
                               OutputIterator _Result,
                               Predicate _Pred,
                               const Type& _Val);
```

REVERSING AND ROTATING ALGORITHMS

The next set of STL algorithms that we will look at deal with reversing elements and rotating them. The reversing algorithms include `reverse()` and `reverse_copy()`, and both algorithms reverse the order of a container's elements. reverse_copy()copies the reverse contents from one container to another (destination). The function prototypes for the reverse() and reverse_copy() are:

```
template<class BidirectionalIterator>
void reverse(BidirectionalIterator _First,
             BidirectionalIterator _Last);
```

```
template<class BidirectionalIterator, class OutputIterator>
OutputIterator reverse_copy(BidirectionalIterator _First,
                            BidirectionalIterator _Last,
                            OutputIterator _Result);
```

The rotating algorithms in the STL are swapping algorithms. The rotate() and rotate_copy() algorithms swap the elements in two adjacent containers. rotate_copy()copies the results to another container as well as performing the rotation algorithm. The function prototypes for the rotate() and rotate_copy() algorithms are:

```
template<class ForwardIterator>
void rotate(ForwardIterator _First, ForwardIterator _Middle,
            ForwardIterator _Last);
```

```
template<class ForwardIterator, class OutputIterator>
OutputIterator rotate_copy(ForwardIterator _First,
                           ForwardIterator _Middle,
                           ForwardIterator _Last,
                           OutputIterator _Result);
```

SUMMARY

In this chapter we discussed a few STL data structures and several STL algorithms that C++ programmers can use. These data structures included the set, multiset, map, and multimap template classes as well as the STL string container. Whenever possible in an application, unless there are special circumstances, STL algorithms should always be preferred to custom implementations or even to doing things the long way (e.g., using a loop instead of using for_each()).

In the next chapter we will look at game- and simulation-related data structures and algorithms. We will discuss and implement many different techniques that go a long way to making modern video games and other such applications possible.

CHAPTER REVIEW QUESTIONS

Answers to the following chapter review questions can be found in Appendix B.

1. What kind of a container is the STL string?
   a. Associate container
   b. Template associate container
   c. Sequence container
   d. Template sequence container
   e. None of the above
2. What class is the STL string based on?
   a. vector<char>
   b. basic_string
   c. list<char>
   d. None of the above
3. What are set STL containers?
4. What are multiset STL containers?
5. What is the difference between set and multiset?
6. What are map containers?
7. What are multimap containers?
8. What is the difference between a map and a multimap?
9. Generally, what is the main difference between a set and a map?
10. The STL string is a template class.
    a. True
    b. False
11. The STL string can be used with legacy code that requires C-like arrays.
    a. True
    b. False
12. The string class is used with STL algorithms.
    a. True
    b. False
13. STL algorithms can be used with C-styled arrays.
    a. True
    b. False
14. STL algorithms depend on the container's implementation.
    a. True
    b. False
15. Because of the nature of STL algorithms, it is hard to add new algorithms to the standard.
    a. True
    b. False

PROGRAMMING PROJECTS

Exercise 1: Write an application that allows the user to enter text, from the keyboard, into a link list of strings where each string is added to the link list. Save the link list to a text file.

Exercise 2: Write an application for game player characters (which include character name, character race, character level, and player ID) and insert it into a map. Use the employee ID as the hash key and use the STL `map` along with a custom hash function so that only the player ID (integer) is hashed.

Exercise 3: Build off of Exercise 2 and use a `multimap` to allow the same players to have more than one character.

13 Scene Management

Game developers are faced with a challenge when it comes to creating complex and realistic scenes in modern games. The expectations of gamers are rising every generation, and the cost of keeping up with this trend is also rising. Not only is this increase in cost monetary, but it also comes in the form of increased hardware requirements. Since the beginning of video games there have been techniques to help manage the data used in an application.

In this chapter we will discuss scene management. Scene management is very important in trying to achieve real-time performance in interactive applications such as video games because developers must be able to manage all the data that can be part of an environment. The topic of scene management is huge, so this chapter will take a general look at it and implement some of the different topics that will be discussed.

INTRODUCTION TO SCENE MANAGEMENT

Scene management is a general term used to describe the management of a game's data as the game is being played. Many kinds of resources can be placed into a game world, and this data is becoming larger in size and more complex in its commercial quality. The resources that can be found in the average game include but are not limited to:

- Scripts
- Static objects
- Dynamic objects
- Animations
- Environments
- Particles
- Sounds
- Textures
- Graphical user interface elements
- Fonts
- Cinematic videos

Each of the resources in a video game needs to be managed by the application. On top of that the hardware can also play a part in how the data is managed. For example, on video game consoles resources often need to be read off a CD-ROM or DVD-ROM disk, which takes time. Video game consoles also have limited amounts of memory, which can have a huge impact on the amount of data that can be read and stored. This falls under the scope of resources management, and various techniques can be used to allow for gameplay experiences that are more complex than what the hardware can handle. An example of this can be seen in the *Grand Theft Auto* series, where the massive open-world environments are dynamically managed and loaded as the player explores the game world. Without complex resource management data structures and algorithms, the game world would be much too large and complex for consoles such as Sony's PlayStation® 2 to render using a brute force approach.

The purpose of this chapter is to look at general scene management, particularly that used to speed up the rendering efficiency of complex environments. Some of the topics discussed in this chapter are the management of environment geometry to allow for fast processing of what needs to be rendered, the general management of game objects, and state management. The topics that will be discussed in this chapter deal with organizing and processing complex scenes so that they can be rendered as quickly as possible on the hardware.

One major difference between resource management and scene management is that resource management aims are managing the data of the resources in terms of loading, unloading, and so on, while scene management generally organizes the data of a scene so that it can be efficiently processed once loaded.

STATE MANAGEMENT

In games there are often a lot of rendering state changes in a scene. These state changes can include changing textures, shaders, material information, and so forth. If a new object needs to be rendered, its states must be applied so that the rendering system can display the geometry as intended.

The problem with changing states is that some of them can be expensive. Changing textures and changing shaders are among the most expensive state changes that occur. The cost of changing states can add up and have an impact on a game's performance. The more objects that are in the scene, the worse is the potential for the state changes to have a negative impact on performance.

The idea behind state management is to try to minimize the state changes as much as possible to improve performance. One way to do this can be seen with textures. If five objects use texture A, and five objects use texture B, it makes sense to render all the objects that use texture A first and then render all the objects that use texture B. It also makes sense to not reapply the texture data for every object, by only sending the data once and using it for all objects that share it. An example of this is shown in Figure 13.1, where the number of state changes goes from 10 to 2 when objects are grouped based on their material.

We'll revisit the topic of state management later when we discuss scene graphs. In modern games state management is a topic that should be taken seriously because poor state management can have an impact on performance. This falls under

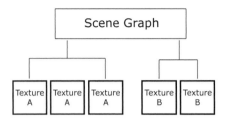

FIGURE 13.1   Grouping by states.

the topic of general scene management because the objects in the scene that need to be rendered are managed in a way that allows them to be displayed in a manner that can be beneficial to performance. If you are developing your own game, you might want to keep state management in mind.

State management deals not only with shaders and textures but with any state that can be changed. This includes alpha blending, culling, and so forth. Normally the most expensive state changes that add up quickly are shaders and textures in OpenGL and Direct3D.

TEXTURE ATLASES

Another way to reduce state changes, as far as textures are concerned, is to group textures together into larger ones so that objects that don't share the same decal can still use the same larger texture data. A texture atlas is a large texture made up of multiple smaller textures. By grouping those textures, the need to apply different textures before the rendering of an object or objects can be reduced. The downside is that the larger textures can be very large, which increases the size of the data that is being sent to the hardware when a texture is applied for rendering. Also, since graphics hardware supports a maximum resolution for textures, the smaller textures in the atlas have a limited resolution because more than one of them must fit in the larger texture. An example of a texture atlas is shown in Figure 13.2, where four textures are placed in one atlas.

The objects using any of those subtextures access the same larger texture, which means they can be grouped together in a state management system. There is slight added complexity when working with texture coordinates of a geometric model and textures in an atlas that must also be taken into account since adjustments to those coordinates must be made.

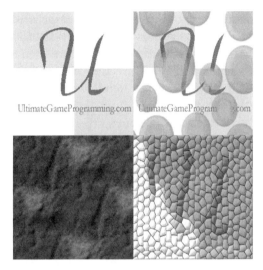

FIGURE 13.2 A texture atlas.

GAME MATH

Mathematics is used throughout many aspects of a video game, and having an understanding of the different kinds of math is important to being able to create the kinds of applications that gamers expect. In this section we will briefly discuss a few math objects that will be used later in this chapter. These math objects include vectors, bounding volumes, planes, frustums, and cameras.

This section is not an introduction to or review of game math, and it assumes that you already have a fair amount of knowledge on the subject. Instead, this section is a quick summary of the math code that will be used in a few of the demo applications in this chapter. Appendix A, Additional Resources, lists a number of resources that can be used to brush up on various game mathematics.

The math code used for the demos in this chapter is straightforward and does not take into consideration possible optimizations or implement every possible operation a math object can perform. The code is kept clear to make it easier to understand the topic at hand, which isn't how to create a powerful and robust math engine.

VECTORS

Vectors are used heavily in three-dimensional games and are the foundation for many calculations that take place. A vector is a direction, and when talking about two-dimensional vectors, those are directions specified in terms of an x- and y-axis, while three-dimensional vectors have an x-, y-, and z-axis.

A vertex is a point in a virtual space. Most often the term *vector* is used to describe either a vertex point or a direction vector. A vector with a magnitude of 1 is known as a unit-length normal, often just called a normal. The demos later in this chapter will use vectors to great length.

A class was created to represent a three-dimensional vector and includes overloaded operators for basic arithmetic (e.g., +, –, *, /, etc.) as well as operations such as normalizing a vector (creating a normal), finding the magnitude of a vector, and calculating the cross product of a vector as well as the dot product. These are few common operations that are found when working with vectors and will all be used in the demos later in this chapter. The three-dimensional vector class is shown in Listing 13.1.

Don't mistake the vertex of a point in a geometric primitive for that of a vertex in a graph, which is what a graph's node is called.

LISTING 13.1   The Three-Dimensional Vector Class

```
class Vector3D
{
   public:
      Vector3D() : x(0), y(0), z(0) { }
      Vector3D(float X, float Y, float Z) : x(X), y(Y), z(Z) { }
      Vector3D(const Vector3D &v) { x = v.x; y = v.y; z = v.z; }


      void operator=(const Vector3D &v)
      {
         x = v.x; y = v.y; z = v.z;
      }


      Vector3D operator+(const Vector3D &v2)
      {
         return Vector3D(x + v2.x, y + v2.y, z + v2.z);
      }


      Vector3D operator-(const Vector3D &v2)
      {
         return Vector3D(x - v2.x, y - v2.y, z - v2.z);
      }
```

```
Vector3D operator/(const Vector3D &v2)
{
   return Vector3D(x / v2.x, y / v2.y, z / v2.z);
}


Vector3D operator*(const Vector3D &v2)
{
   return Vector3D(x * v2.x, y * v2.y, z * v2.z);
}


Vector3D operator+(float f)
{
   return Vector3D(x + f, y + f, z + f);
}


Vector3D operator-(float f)
{
   return Vector3D(x - f, y - f, z - f);
}


Vector3D operator/(float f)
{
   return Vector3D(x / f, y / f, z / f);
}


Vector3D operator*(float f)
{
   return Vector3D(x * f, y * f, z * f);
}


float Dot3(const Vector3D &v)
{
   return x * x + y * y + z * z;
}


float Magnitude()
{
```

```
            return (float)sqrt(x * x + y * y + z * z);
        }


        void Normalize()
        {
            float len = Magnitude();

            if(len <= 0.00001) len = 1;
            len = 1 / len;

            x *= len; y *= len; z *= len;
        }


        Vector3D CrossProduct(const Vector3D &v)
        {
            return Vector3D(y * v.z - z * v.y,
                            z * v.x - x * v.z,
                            x * v.y - y * v.x);
        }


        float x, y, z;
    };
```

PLANES

A plane is an infinitely flat surface that extends in two axes. Planes are used for many things such as collision detection. In this chapter the binary space partitioning data structure and various algorithms use planes to perform their duties. A plane object is made up of a normal, which is normally expressed as A, B, and C, and it is made up of a distance. This distance specifies how far the plane is from the point of origin, which has an x, y, and z location of (0, 0, 0).

The plane class in this chapter will have a function used to calculate a plane from a triangle; test if a box, sphere, or point intersects a plane; and test which side of a plane a point is on. A vertex point can be either on the front side of the plane, on back side, or on the plane. Geometric primitives such as triangles, can also span both sides of a plane, with a piece being on the front side and the rest crossing over to the back side. The side of the plane is determined by the plane's normal. The plane class used in this chapter is shown in Listing 13.2.

LISTING 13.2   The Plane Class

```cpp
class Plane
{
   public:
      Plane() : a(0), b(0), c(0), d(0) { }
      Plane(float A, float B, float C, float D) :
         a(A), b(B), c(C), d(D) { }


      void Create(Vector3D &t1, Vector3D &t2, Vector3D &t3)
      {
         Vector3D e1, e2, n;

         e1 = t2 - t1;
         e2 = t3 - t1;

         n = e1.CrossProduct(e2);
         n.Normalize();

         a = n.x; b = n.y; c = n.z;
         d = - (a * t1.x + b * t1.y + c * t1.z);
      }


      bool Intersect(const Vector3D &bbMin, const Vector3D &bbMax)
      {
         Vector3D min, max;
         Vector3D normal(a, b, c);

         if(normal.x >= 0.0f)
         {
            min.x = bbMin.x; max.x = bbMax.x;
         }
         else
         {
            min.x = bbMax.x; max.x = bbMin.x;
         }

         if(normal.y >= 0.0f)
         {
            min.y = bbMin.y; max.y = bbMax.y;
         }
         else
```

```
   {
      min.y = bbMax.y; max.y = bbMin.y;
   }

   if(normal.z >= 0.0f)
   {
      min.z = bbMin.z; max.z = bbMax.z;
   }
   else
   {
      min.z = bbMax.z; max.z = bbMin.z;
   }

   if((normal.Dot3(min) + d) > 0.0f)
      return false;

   if((normal.Dot3(max) + d) >= 0.0f)
      return true;

   return false;
}


bool Intersect(const Vector3D &position, float radius)
{
   float dp = fabs(GetDistance(position));

    if(dp <= radius)
       return true;

   return false;
}


PLANE_STATUS ClassifyPoint(float x, float y,
                           float z, float *dist)
{
   float distance = a * x + b * y + c * z + d;

   if(dist != 0)
      *dist = distance;

   if(distance > 0.001)
      return PLANE_FRONT;
```

```
    if(distance < -0.001)
        return PLANE_BACK;

    return PLANE_ON_PLANE;
}


float Plane::GetDistance(float x, float y, float z)
{
    return a * x + b * y + c * z + d;
}


float a, b, c, d;
};
```

BOUNDING VOLUMES

Bounding volumes are shapes used to surround a geometric object. There are many different types of bounding volumes, but the most popular are the axis-aligned bounding box and bounding sphere. Bounding volumes are used to enclose (tightly surround) a geometric object so that they can be used as very simplified and general representations of those objects. For example, if a bounding box is surrounding a three-dimensional character model, early tests can be done on the bounding box instead of the more complex three-dimensional character model. An example of one test is visibility determination, which can be used to quickly determine if the geometric model is visible to the viewer. Since the bounding volume tightly surrounds the object, it can act as a simple stand-in for many tests that would otherwise be expensive to do on a polygonal object with hundreds if not thousands of polygons.

In this chapter we will create an axis-aligned bounding box class since that is used by the octree demo later on. To create a bounding box, or any bounding volume, we have to loop through the geometric object and determine its extents so that the simplified bounding shape can be calculated around the object. For a box the minimum and maximum x, y, and z axes must be determined, which can be used to specify the corners of the bounding box. For a bounding sphere the same operation can be used, but the center of the object must be calculated, which is the maximum and minimum axes added together and divided by two, as well as the sphere's radius, which is the square root of the maximum axis's distance from the sphere's center. A screenshot of a bounding volume surrounding an object is shown in Figure 13.3. The bounding box class is shown in Listing 13.3.

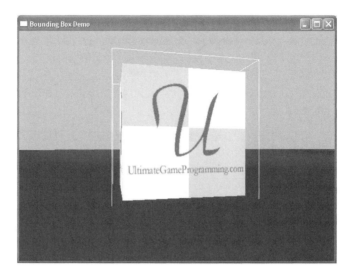

FIGURE 13.3 Bounding volumes.

LISTING 13.3 Bounding Box Class

```cpp
class BoundingBox
{
   public:
      BoundingBox()
      {

      }


      BoundingBox(const BoundingBox &aabb)
      {
         m_min = aabb.m_min;
         m_max = aabb.m_max;
         m_center = aabb.m_center;
      }


      void Calculate(Vector3D *v, int numPoints)
      {
         if(v == NULL)
            return;
```

```
for(int i = 0; i < numPoints; i++)
{
    if(v[i].x < m_min.x) m_min.x = v[i].x;
    if(v[i].x > m_max.x) m_max.x = v[i].x;

    if(v[i].y < m_min.y) m_min.y = v[i].y;
    if(v[i].y > m_max.y) m_max.y = v[i].y;

    if(v[i].z < m_min.z) m_min.z = v[i].z;
    if(v[i].z > m_max.z) m_max.z = v[i].z;
}

m_center.x = (m_min.x + m_max.x) * 0.5f;
m_center.y = (m_min.y + m_max.y) * 0.5f;
m_center.z = (m_min.z + m_max.z) * 0.5f;
}


Vector3D m_min, m_max, m_center;
};
```

Algorithms on bounding spheres are faster to process on the CPU than a bounding box. The downside is that the spheres waste more virtual space than the boxes, as shown in Figure 13.3.

FRUSTUM CULLING

Frustum culling is the process of determining what objects are visible within a view frustum so that those objects are the only ones sent to the rendering system. To create a view frustum six planes are needed. These planes represent the left, right, top, bottom, far, and near planes that, when working together, completely enclose a volume around the virtual camera.

A frustum is calculated by creating six planes based on the camera's information. This information includes the near and far distances, which are basically how far and how close the camera can see, the aspect ratio, the field of view, and the camera's state, such as its position, looking direction, and so forth. Once a frustum has been created, geometric objects can be tested against it for visibility determination. If an object is on the front side of all planes that make up the frustum, it is visible. If an object is behind at least one of these planes, the object is not visible. An example of this is shown in Figure 13.4.

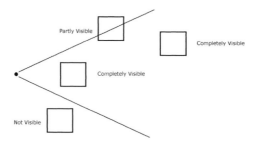

FIGURE 13.4   A frustum where some objects are outside, some inside, and others spanning.

When testing against a frustum, it is common to test the bounding volume of an object instead of the object itself. This can lead to a very fast visibility test, which is important in trying to keep the frame rate of an application acceptable. By testing the object itself, all polygons of the model would have to be tested, which would cause a major slowdown in the performance with a few high polygonal models compared to using the bounding volume. Testing simple bounding volumes drastically reduces this workload. The frustum class is shown in Listing 13.4 and can be used to test if a point, box, or sphere is visible.

LISTING 13.4   A View Frustum Class

```
class Frustum
{
   public:
      Frustum()
      {

      }


      void CalculateFrustum(float angle, float ratio,
                            float near, float far,
                            Vector3D &camPos, Vector3D &lookAt,
                            Vector3D &up)
      {
         Vector3D xVec, yVec, zVec, vecN, vecF;
         Vector3D nearTopLeft, nearTopRight,
                  nearBottomLeft, nearBottomRight;
         Vector3D farTopLeft, farTopRight,
                  farBottomLeft, farBottomRight;
```

```
float radians = (float)tan((DEG_TO_RAD(angle)) * 0.5);
float nearH = near  * radians;
float nearW = nearH * ratio;
float farH  = far   * radians;
float farW  = farH  * ratio;

zVec = camPos - lookAt;
zVec.Normalize();

xVec = up.CrossProduct(zVec);
xVec.Normalize();

yVec = zVec.CrossProduct(xVec);

vecN = camPos - zVec * near;
vecF = camPos - zVec * far;

nearTopLeft     = vecN + yVec * nearH - xVec * nearW;
nearTopRight    = vecN + yVec * nearH + xVec * nearW;
nearBottomLeft  = vecN - yVec * nearH - xVec * nearW;
nearBottomRight = vecN - yVec * nearH + xVec * nearW;

farTopLeft      = vecF + yVec * farH - xVec * farW;
farTopRight     = vecF + yVec * farH + xVec * farW;
farBottomLeft   = vecF - yVec * farH - xVec * farW;
farBottomRight  = vecF - yVec * farH + xVec * farW;

m_frustum.clear();
Plane plane;

plane.CreatePlaneFromTri(nearTopRight, nearTopLeft,
                         farTopLeft);
AddPlane(plane);

plane.CreatePlaneFromTri(nearBottomLeft, nearBottomRight,
                         farBottomRight);
AddPlane(plane);

plane.CreatePlaneFromTri(nearTopLeft, nearBottomLeft,
                         farBottomLeft);
AddPlane(plane);

plane.CreatePlaneFromTri(nearBottomRight, nearTopRight,
                         farBottomRight);
AddPlane(plane);
```

```
                       plane.CreatePlaneFromTri(nearTopLeft, nearTopRight,
                                          nearBottomRight);
                       AddPlane(plane);

                       plane.CreatePlaneFromTri(farTopRight, farTopLeft,
                                          farBottomLeft);
                       AddPlane(plane);
                   }


                   void AddPlane(Plane &pl)
                   {
                      m_frustum.push_back(pl);
                   }


                   bool isPointVisible(float x, float y, float z)
                   {
                      for(int i = 0; i < (int)m_frustum.size(); i++)
                      {
                         if(m_frustum[i].GetDistance(x, y, z) < 0)
                            return false;
                      }

                      return true;
                   }


                   bool isSphereVisible(float x, float y, float z, float radius)
                   {
                      float distance = 0;

                      for(int i = 0; i < (int)m_frustum.size(); i++)
                      {
                         distance = m_frustum[i].GetDistance(x, y, z);

                         if(distance < -radius)
                            return false;
                      }

                      return true;
                   }
```

```
      bool isBoxVisible(Vector3D min, Vector3D max)
      {
          if(isPointVisible(min.x, min.y, min.z)) return true;
          if(isPointVisible(max.x, min.y, min.z)) return true;
          if(isPointVisible(min.x, max.y, min.z)) return true;
          if(isPointVisible(max.x, max.y, min.z)) return true;
          if(isPointVisible(min.x, min.y, max.z)) return true;
          if(isPointVisible(max.x, min.y, max.z)) return true;
          if(isPointVisible(min.x, max.y, max.z)) return true;
          if(isPointVisible(max.x, max.y, max.z)) return true;

          return false;
      }


      int GetTotalPlanes()
      {
          return (int)m_frustum.size();
      }
  };


  private:
      vector<Plane> m_frustum;
};
```

VIEWS AND CAMERAS

The upcoming demo applications can benefit from allowing the user to roam around the virtual environment. Since a full-blown, complex camera system is not needed, a simple one is made available in this chapter. This simple camera class will keep track of the camera's position and a view direction. The camera is always moved along its viewing direction. If the direction is rotated, which it is in the function RotateView(), then the direction the camera is moving can be altered. The members of the camera class can be fed directly to OpenGL, which we'll see later in this chapter. The simple camera class is shown in Listing 13.5.

LISTING 13.5   A Simple Camera Class

```
class Camera
{
   public:
      Camera(Vector3D &pos, Vector3D &lookAt)
      {
```

```
            m_pos = pos;
            m_lookAt = lookAt;
        }


        void MoveCamera(Vector3D &direction, float speed)
        {
            m_pos += direction * speed;
            m_lookAt += direction * speed;
        }


        void RotateView(float angle);


        void SetPosition(Vector3D &pos) { m_pos = pos; }
        void SetLookDirection(Vector3D &at) { m_lookAt = at; }

        Vector3D GetPosition() { return m_pos; }
        Vector3D GetLookDirection() { return m_lookAt; }


    private:
        Vector3D m_pos, m_lookAt;
    };
```

ADDITIONAL GAME MATH

In this chapter only the math objects used in this chapter's demos were created, and the functionality needed by these demos was also all that was coded. Creating a full-blown math engine is no easy task, and there are many optimizations that can be made to speed up the math code. Other types of math objects include:

- Rays
- Matrices
- Quaternion rotations
- Additional bounding volumes
- Occlusion fields

Appendix A, Additional Resources, lists resources that could be helpful to anyone looking to expand their game math and physics knowledge.

SCENE GRAPHS

A scene graph is a data structure that is used to specify the relationships between objects in a virtual environment. The relationships between objects form a hierarchy in which nodes are connected to one another by edges and can be objects' spatial relationships, materials, physical relationships (e.g., a character picking up a weapon or a character riding in a vehicle), and so forth. An example of a scene graph is shown in Figure 13.5.

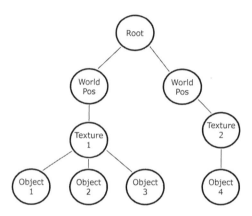

FIGURE 13.5   A scene graph.

A scene graph is a very general data structure. In video games this data structure is often highly application specific and is generally not made up of a concrete set of rules or definitions. Because scene graphs are so general, there is no right or wrong way to create them. In Figure 13.5 the illustration defines a scene graph that specifies spatial and material relationships. During the creation of a scene graph, the implementation depends highly on the game specifics. If a game has static objects in specific areas like in Figure 13.5, then grouping objects by location might be a feature of that game's scene graph. If objects can be grouped by material, all objects that share the same texture, shader, and so forth can be conveniently grouped in a subtree. Another situation in which scene graphs can be used is to define physical relationships, such as when a character model hops in a vehicle and drives it around the environment, which causes a relationship between the two objects to allow one model's movements and orientations to affect the other. Implementing a scene graph requires taking the basic ideas and principles of a scene graph and building on them for the needs of a specific game.

NODES OF A SCENE GRAPH

In a scene graph the data structure can be implemented using a graph or a tree. In some cases scene graphs can be implemented using basic data structures such as an array or a link list as well. In a scene graph built from a tree or graph a node can have multiple children but only one parent. Depending on the game specifics, the parent node affects the children and so forth down the hierarchy. In Figure 13.5 a transformation node was used to position all objects in a subgroup to one general location. Each of these objects had their own transformations that were added and applied further to that main transformation.

In this chapter the scene graph will be simple and will implement transformation nodes and sphere nodes. The transformation nodes will be used to apply transformation information to the OpenGL API, while the sphere nodes will be used to draw a sphere shape. The nodes will use inheritance, and both types (transformation and sphere) will derive from one node.

A game's scene graph can have additional types of nodes that are specific to the game. Nodes can be used to group objects by material, physical relationship, which was discussed in the example of a character model getting into a vehicle, and whatever else the game needs to group by.

IMPLEMENTING A SCENE GRAPH

The implementation for this chapter's scene graph is straightforward and simple. The scene graph will be implemented using a general tree data structure similar to the first tree discussed in Chapter 9. The scene graph will have a class for the nodes which will act as a base class from which the other two classes, one for transformations and one for the spheres, will be derived. In the base class for the nodes, the nodes will store their child pointers and their sibling pointers. The sibling pointers form a doubly linked list and are used to chain the nodes together. The base class for the nodes is shown in Listing 13.6. The entire scene graph is processed by calling the Process() function on the root node, which will recursively handle all nodes in the graph. This is used in this demo to display and apply the information in each node so that we can see it on the screen.

LISTING 13.6 The node Class

```
class Node
{
   public:
      Node()
      {
         m_next = NULL;
         m_prev = NULL;
```

```
      m_child = NULL;
}


virtual ~Node()
{
   m_prev = NULL;

   if(m_child != NULL)
   {
      delete m_child;
      m_child = NULL;
   }


   if(m_next != NULL)
   {
      delete m_next;
      m_next = NULL;
   }
}


void AddChild(Node *node)
{
   if(m_child == NULL)
   {
      m_child = node;
   }
   else
   {
      m_child->AddSibling(node);
   }
}


void AddSibling(Node *node)
{
   Node *ptr = m_next;

   if(m_next == NULL)
   {
      m_next = node;
      node->m_prev = this;
```

```
            }
            else
            {
               while(ptr->m_next != NULL)
               {
                  ptr = ptr->m_next;
               }

               ptr->m_next = node;
               node->m_prev = ptr;
            }
         }


         virtual void Process()
         {
            if(m_child != NULL)
               m_child->Process();

            if(m_next != NULL)
               m_next->Process();
         }


      protected:
         Node *m_next;
         Node *m_prev;
         Node *m_child;
   };
```

The first node that will be looked at is the transformation node called `TransformationNode`. This class takes a three-dimensional position, using the `Vector3D` class from earlier in this chapter, and is used to apply the translation. Other attributes such as the orientation can be added to this class, but that can be left as an exercise at the end of the chapter. Since the code for this scene graph is supposed to be simple and straightforward, the necessary OpenGL calls are made directly in the `Process()` function. Transformations of any kind are only applied to child nodes, so sibling nodes will have to be processed without that information applied in order to get the correct results. The `TransformationNode` is shown in Listing 13.7.

LISTING 13.7   The Node for Transformations

```cpp
class TransformationNode : public Node
{
    public:
        TransformationNode(Vector3D &pos) : m_pos(pos)
        {

        }


        ~TransformationNode()
        {

        }


        void Process()
        {
            glPushMatrix();

            glTranslatef(m_pos.x, m_pos.y, m_pos.z);

            if(m_child != NULL)
                m_child->Process();

            glPopMatrix();

            if(m_next != NULL)
                m_next->Process();
        }


    protected:
        Vector3D m_pos;
};
```

The last node is for the sphere meshes. Again, since this demo is straightforward, this class will allow us to specify the dimensions and color of a sphere and display it to the screen using the OpenGL class. The radius of the sphere specifies its size, the slices specify the number of subdivisions along the longitude, and the stacks specify the number of subdivisions along the latitude. The SphereNode class is shown in Listing 13.8.

LISTING 13.8 The Node for the Spheres

```
class SphereNode : public Node
{
   public:
      SphereNode(double rd, int slices, int stacks,
                 float r, float g, float b) :
                 m_radius(rd), m_slices(slices), m_stacks(stacks),
                 m_red(r), m_green(g), m_blue(b)
      {

      }


      ~SphereNode()
      {

      }


      void Process()
      {
         glColor3f(m_red, m_green, m_blue);
         glutSolidSphere(m_radius, m_slices, m_stacks);

         if(m_child != NULL)
            m_child->Process();

         if(m_next != NULL)
            m_next->Process();
      }


   protected:
      double m_radius;
      int m_slices, m_stacks;
      float m_red, m_green, m_blue;
};
```

The last class is the class for the scene graph. This class will need to add nodes (which is done using a function called AddNode()) to delete the hierarchy (which is done using Release()) and to recursively process the scene graph (which is done with a function called Process()). Each of these functions operates on the root node of the scene graph. To build the scene graph we must first create all of the subtrees for the scene, which we'll see in the main application of the Scene Graph demo later on, and add those subtrees to the scene graph. Another method would be to allow the scene graph to add nodes to subtrees internally, but that would require having to identify nodes (possibly by name, integer id, etc.) and having to look up those nodes in the scene graph to find where a new node should be attached. This is not necessary for this demo but can be useful. The scene graph class is shown in Listing 13.9.

LISTING 13.9   The Scene Graph

```cpp
#include"node.h"


class SceneGraph
{
   public:
      SceneGraph()
      {
         m_root = NULL;
      }

      ~SceneGraph()
      {
         Release();
      }


      void Release()
      {
         if(m_root != NULL)
         {
            delete m_root;
            m_root = NULL;
         }
      }


      void AddNode(Node *node)
      {
         if(m_root == NULL)
            m_root = new Node;

         m_root->AddChild(node);
      }
```

```
            void Process()
            {
               if(m_root != NULL)
                  m_root->Process();
            }


         private:
            Node *m_root;
      };
```

ON THE CD   On the accompanying CD-ROM is a demo application called Scene Graph that demonstrates the code discussed in this chapter. The demo application creates two groups of spheres, each with its own local position and color, and renders them to the screen. Each group adds as its child the positions of each of the spheres, which in turns add each of their children (the sphere positions are parents to the sphere meshes), to the sphere objects themselves. Each of these subtrees (groups) is added as children to the scene graph's root node. The processing of the scene graph takes place in the RenderScene() function by calling the scene graph's Process() function. The scene graph is deleted by calling the Release() function in ShutdownApp(), and it is built in the InitializeApp() function. The entire main source file for the Scene Graph demo application is shown in Listing 13.10. Figure 13.6 shows a screenshot of the running application.

LISTING 13.10   The Main Source File

```
#include<gl/glut.h>
#include<stdio.h>
#include"SceneGraph.h"
#include"TransformationNode.h"
#include"SphereNode.h"


void RenderScene();
void KeyDown(unsigned char key, int x, int y);
void Resize(int width, int height);
bool InitializeApp();
void ShutdownApp();


// Scene graph.
SceneGraph g_sceneGraph;
```

```
int main(int arg, char **argc)
{
   glutInitWindowSize(800, 600);
   glutInitWindowPosition(100, 100);
   glutInitDisplayMode(GLUT_RGB | GLUT_DOUBLE | GLUT_DEPTH);
   glutInit(&arg, argc);

   glutCreateWindow("Scene Graph");

   glutDisplayFunc(RenderScene);
   glutReshapeFunc(Resize);
   glutKeyboardFunc(KeyDown);

   if(InitializeApp() == true)
      glutMainLoop();
   else
      printf("Error in InitializeApp()!\n\n");

   ShutdownApp();

   return 1;
}


void Resize(int width, int height)
{
   glViewport(0, 0, width, height);
   glMatrixMode(GL_PROJECTION);

   gluPerspective(45, width/height, 0.1, 200.0);
   glMatrixMode(GL_MODELVIEW);
}


void KeyDown(unsigned char key, int x, int y)
{
   switch(key)
   {
      case 27:
         exit(0);
         break;
   }
}
```

```
bool InitializeApp()
{
  glClearColor(0.0f, 0.0f, 0.0f, 1.0f);
  glShadeModel(GL_SMOOTH);
  glEnable(GL_DEPTH_TEST);
  glEnable(GL_LIGHTING);

  float diffuseLight[] = {0.8f, 0.8f, 0.8f, 1.0f};
  float specularLight[] = {1.0f, 1.0f, 1.0f, 1.0f};
  float LightPosition[] = {1.0f, 0.0f, 8.0f, 1.0f};

  glLightfv(GL_LIGHT0, GL_DIFFUSE, diffuseLight);
  glLightfv(GL_LIGHT0, GL_SPECULAR, specularLight);
  glLightfv(GL_LIGHT0, GL_POSITION, LightPosition);
  glEnable(GL_LIGHT0);

  glEnable(GL_COLOR_MATERIAL);
  glColorMaterial(GL_FRONT, GL_AMBIENT_AND_DIFFUSE);
  glMaterialfv(GL_FRONT, GL_SPECULAR, specularLight);
  glMateriali(GL_FRONT, GL_SHININESS, 128);


  TransformationNode *group1 = NULL,  *group2 = NULL,
                     *spherePos1 = NULL, *spherePos2 = NULL,
                     *spherePos3 = NULL, *spherePos4 = NULL,
                     *spherePos5 = NULL, *spherePos6 = NULL;

  SphereNode *sphere1 = NULL, *sphere2 = NULL, *sphere3 = NULL,
             *sphere4 = NULL, *sphere5 = NULL, *sphere6 = NULL;


  group1 = new TransformationNode(Vector3D(5, 0, 0));

  spherePos1 = new TransformationNode(Vector3D(-1, 0, 0));
  spherePos2 = new TransformationNode(Vector3D(1, 0, 0));
  spherePos3 = new TransformationNode(Vector3D(0, 0, -1));

  sphere1 = new SphereNode(1, 20, 20, 1, 0, 0);
  sphere2 = new SphereNode(1, 20, 20, 0, 1, 0);
  sphere3 = new SphereNode(1, 20, 20, 0, 0, 1);

  spherePos1->AddChild(sphere1);
  spherePos2->AddChild(sphere2);
  spherePos3->AddChild(sphere3);
```

```
    group1->AddChild(spherePos1);
    group1->AddChild(spherePos2);
    group1->AddChild(spherePos3);


    group2 = new TransformationNode(Vector3D(-5, 0, 0));

    spherePos4 = new TransformationNode(Vector3D(-1, 0, 0));
    spherePos5 = new TransformationNode(Vector3D(1, 0, 0));
    spherePos6 = new TransformationNode(Vector3D(0, 0, -1));

    sphere4 = new SphereNode(1, 20, 20, 1, 1, 0);
    sphere5 = new SphereNode(1, 20, 20, 0, 1, 1);
    sphere6 = new SphereNode(1, 20, 20, 1, 0, 1);

    spherePos4->AddChild(sphere4);
    spherePos5->AddChild(sphere5);
    spherePos6->AddChild(sphere6);

    group2->AddChild(spherePos4);
    group2->AddChild(spherePos5);
    group2->AddChild(spherePos6);


    g_sceneGraph.AddNode(group1);
    g_sceneGraph.AddNode(group2);

    return true;
}


void ShutdownApp()
{
    g_sceneGraph.Release();
}


void RenderScene()
{
    glClear(GL_COLOR_BUFFER_BIT | GL_DEPTH_BUFFER_BIT);
    glLoadIdentity();

    gluLookAt(0, 5, -20, 0, 0, 0, 0, 1, 0);
```

```
        g_sceneGraph.Process();


        glutSwapBuffers();
        glutPostRedisplay();
    }
```

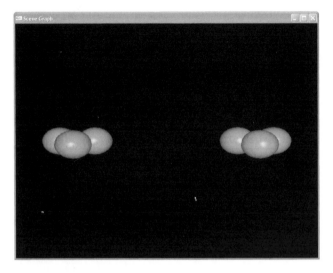

FIGURE 13.6 A screenshot of the Scene Graph demo.

BINARY SPACE PARTITIONING TREES

The binary space partitioning (BSP) data structure has been used for a long time in the game industry for processing three-dimensional virtual scenes. With a BSP tree a tool is used to take the polygons of a level and create a hierarchy out of them. This hierarchy can quickly be processed by the application at run time to increase overall performance. In a BSP tree it is possible to traverse through the data structure's contents in front-to-back or back-to-front order. The BSP tree can be used for rendering, collision detection, or large-scale culling of the scene's geometry through the use of other structures such as potential visibility sets, which we'll discuss later in this chapter.

In a BSP tree the child nodes are often called the front and back nodes instead of left and right. The BSP recursively partitions a scene into two sections. First, a plane is chosen as the splitter plane. This plane is tested against all polygons, and the ones on the front are placed in the front node for further processing, the ones on the back of the plane are placed in the back node, and all polygons that span both sides of the plane are broken into two pieces so that one can be placed on the front and the other on the back. Figure 13.7 shows a simple environment split into halves using a plane. The idea behind the BSP tree is that a plane is chosen, the scene is partitioned into halves, and this recursively happens until some condition is met. This condition can be that a certain number of polygons (minimum) has been reached in one node or a certain depth level has been reached.

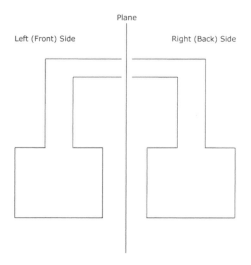

FIGURE 13.7 A simple scene divided using a plane.

Many games use the BSP tree. Among the most popular are the early *Doom* and *Quake*™ games from Id Software. Modern games that use BSP trees include *Half-Life 2*, *Quake 4*, *Doom 3*, and many others. Although games today use BSP trees that are slightly different than in the past, they are still a part of game development. When it comes to rendering, BSP trees are often used with other structures such as potential visibility sets. In the early days this was first done with the first *Quake*, where the performance of the traditional BSP tree suffered in some areas of game levels.

Before there were Z-buffers in the graphics hardware there was a need to be able to correctly render polygons in the right order (from back to front). If polygons were not rendered is a specific order, polygons that are supposed to appear behind others might be rendered on top. The BSP tree was a way to partition the scene so this order can be quickly determined and the polygons of a level rendered correctly.

In today's games we have fast Z-buffers in the graphics hardware, so using BSP trees to render the faces in the correct order is not necessary. However, when combined with frustum culling and potential visibility sets, new BSP trees can be created and rendered that benefit speed. BSP trees can also be used for very fast collision detection, which is important in three-dimensional games.

The planes used to split the nodes of a BSP tree are often axis-aligned, arbitrary, or coplanar with the polygons. Axis-aligned means that the planes align to an axis (x, y, or z), arbitrary planes are used to divide the scene into near two equal or equal parts, and planes that are coplanar with the polygons are planes that are created out of chosen polygons from the scene. An example of each type is shown in Figure 13.8.

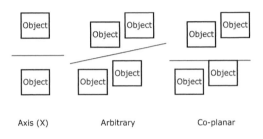

FIGURE 13.8   Splitting plane types.

BSP TREE NODES

The nodes of a BSP tree can have a list of polygons and two child nodes. Leaf nodes have no children and have a list of polygons. The BSP tree is a binary search tree for polygons. By understanding the binary search tree in Chapter 9, you already have some of the knowledge necessary to understand BSP trees. The creation of a BSP tree is a generally simple process (in theory) and is made up of the following steps:

1. Take a list of polygons and send it to the node (root node if this is the first node).
2. Calculate a plane that will be used as the splitter plane.
3. Loop through all polygons and determine which side the polygons lie on. If any span the plane, split them into two new planes.
4. Repeat steps 1 through 3 for the left (front) and right (back) nodes recursively until a certain number of polygons are in a node, until a certain depth is reached, or until some other condition (whatever condition you see fit to stop the recursion) is met.
5. The pseudo-code for the creation of a BSP tree can look like the following:

```
// Get a list of polygons (possibly load from a file).
// Build BSP tree recursivly by returning the root node.

listOfPolygons = new PolygonList(...);
bspTree = CreateBSPNode(listOfPolygons);
```

```
CreateBSPNode(listOfPolygons)
{
   node = new BSPNode();

   // If threshold is met then stop recursion.

   if(listOfPolygon.count <= MIN_NODE_POLY_COUNT)
      {
         node.polygonList = listOfPolygons;
         return node;
      }

   // Else continue.

   splitPlane = GetBestSplitter(listOfPolygons);

   for each(element i in listOfPolygons)
   {
      if(splitPlane.Classify(listOfPolygons[i]) == FRONT)
      {
         subPolyList1.push(listOfPolygons[i]);
      }
      else if(splitPlane.Classify(listOfPolygons[i]) == BACK)
      {
         subPolyList2.push(listOfPolygons[i]);
      }
      else
      {
         // Return two split polygons in p1, p2.
         splitPlane.ClipPolygon(listOfPolygons[i], &p1, &p2);

         subPolyList1.push(p1);
         subPolyList2.push(p2);
      }
   }

   node.frontNode = CreateBSPNode(subPolyList1);
   node.backNode  = CreateBSPNode(subPolyList2);

   return node;
}
```

The first thing to note is that BSP trees by themselves are better for indoor scenes than outdoor scenes. This is because the splitting planes on the terrain of an outdoor scene will not be as efficient as an indoor one. One of the challenges of making a BSP tree is to pick a good splitter plane. If the tree is severely unbalanced, performance traversing the tree can suffer. On the accompanying CD-ROM is a demo application called BSP Tree that creates a BSP tree out of a simple list of polygons. This BSP tree is rendered to the screen in back-to-front order. The splitting plane is chosen using a scoring algorithm that performs these steps:

ON THE CD

1. Loop through all polygons and create a plane for each one.
2. For each plane add up the number of polygons that are on the front side and on the back side.
3. Whichever plane has the lowest absolute difference (abs[front total – back total]) is the best polygon to use for the splitting plane (also known as the score).

Such a simple algorithm should create a fairly balanced tree since it chooses planes that have equal or close to equal numbers of polygons on each side. To implement such an algorithm a loop can be used to create and score each polygon while keeping track of the current best. Once the algorithm is done, the one marked as the current best is the one to use. Pseudo-code for finding the best splitter using this algorithm can look like the following:

```
GetBestSplitter(listOfPolygons)
{
    plane = Plane();
    minPlane = Plane();
    minCount = 9999999999, currentCount = 0;

    for each(element i in listOfPolygons)
    {
        // Create plane out of this polygon.

        plane.Create(listOfPolygons[i]);

        // Determine how many polys are on the front and back.

        for each(element j in listOfPolygons)
        {
            frontCount = 0, backCount = 0;

            // Wouldn't test current (plane) polygon.
```

```
        if(i != j)
        {
            if(plane.Classify(listOfPolygons[j]) == FRONT)
            {
                frontCount++;
            }
            else if(plane.Classify(listOfPolygons[j]) == BACK)
            {
                backCount++;
            }
            else
            {
                // The split polygon would create one on each.

                frontCount++;
                backCount++;
            }
        }
    }

    // Score the current polygon.

    currentCount = abs(frontCount - backCount);

    // If current polygon proves to be the smallest so far...

    if(currentCount < minCount)
    {
        minPlane = plane;
        minCount = currentCount;
    }
}

return minPlane;
}
```

Building a BSP tree is often a preprocessing step because of the time it will take to create the data structure. Adding potential visibility sets can drastically increase this build time. This is not a problem, since a level is loaded during runtime, but it does require the geometry of the environment itself be static. The objects do not need to be static and would not be part of the BSP tree anyway. A screenshot from the BSP TREE demo is shown in Figure 13.9.

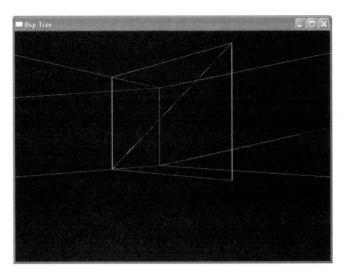

FIGURE 13.9 A screenshot from the BSP Tree demo.

QUAD-TREES AND OCTREES

Bounding volume hierarchies are used for fast culling of a scene's geometry. In a bounding volume hierarchy a bounding volume is created to enclose the entire scene. The main bounding volume is then recursively divided into smaller sections. When a bounding volume is divided, all polygons that fall within that volume are added to that node. This recursion continues until a certain depth level is reached or until a minimum number of polygons have been reached. In this section we will talk about two popular bounding volume hierarchies known as the quad-tree and the octree.

QUAD-TREES

A quad-tree starts with one large axis-aligned bounding box around the environment. It then recursively splits this box into four equal subboxes. These four subboxes are the four child nodes, just like the front and back were child nodes of a BSP tree node. All polygons are then placed into the node within which it falls. This process continues for the child nodes downward until some condition is met to stop the recursion, which is often until a minimum number of polygons are reached. A quad-tree is shown in Figure 13.10.

Building a bounding volume hierarchy like the quad-tree is easier than building a BSP tree. In a quad-tree there are four nodes that each represent an equal area of the parent. The polygons are separated based on if they fall within one of these

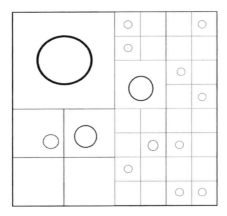

FIGURE 13.10   A quad tree.

boxes, and the process continues until the recursion-ending condition is met. Using frustum culling on such a data structure would require starting at the root node and testing if it is visible. If so, each of the child nodes are tested to see if they are visible. The children of every child node that is visible are tested until the entire tree has been processed. If some nodes are not visible, they and their children are rejected. Thus, if a view is facing away from a section of the level, those nodes would have been quickly rejected because some of the nodes higher up in the hierarchy closest to the root would have been rejected, and thus those children that eventually did hold geometry would have also been rejected automatically. The process of building a quad-tree is shown in Figure 13.11, and using a quad-tree with frustum culling is shown in Figure 13.12.

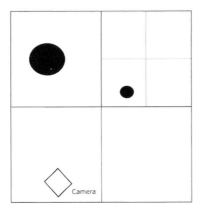

FIGURE 13.11   Building a quad tree out of a few objects.

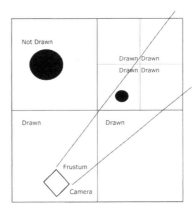

FIGURE 13.12   Culling objects in a quad tree.

The pseudo-code for creating a quad-tree can look like the following:

```
// Get list of polygons (maybe from a file).

listOfPolygons = new PolygonList(...);

// Create quad tree by returning root node.

quadTree = CreateQuadNode(listOfPolygons);


CreateQuadNode(listOfPolygons)
{
   node = new QuadNode();

   aabb = CalculateBoundingBox(listOfPolygons);
   node.aabb = aabb;


   // Stop recursion once list becomes small.

   if(listOfPolygons.count <= MIN_NODE_POLY_COUNT)
   {
      node.polygons = listOfPolygons;
      return node;
   }


   // Else continue.

   // Divide large bounding box into four areas (quad).
   // In other words SPLIT ALONG X and Y axis.

   frontLeftBox  = CalculateSubBox(aabb, FRONT_LEFT);
   backLeftBox   = CalculateSubBox(aabb, BACK_LEFT);
   frontRightBox = CalculateSubBox(aabb, FRONT_RIGHT);
   backRightBox  = CalculateSubBox(aabb, BACK_RIGHT);


   // Divide main polygon list into sublists.

   frontLeftList  = new PolygonList();
   backLeftList   = new PolygonList();
   frontRightList = new PolygonList();
   backRightList  = new PolygonList();
```

```
for each(element i in listOfPolygons)
{
   if(frontLeftBox.IsPolyIn(listOfPolygons[i]) == true)
   {
      frontLeftList.push(listOfPolygons[i]);
   }
   else if(backLeftBox.IsPolyIn(listOfPolygons[i]) == true)
   {
      backLeftList.push(listOfPolygons[i]);
   }
   else if(frontRightBox.IsPolyIn(listOfPolygons[i]) == true)
   {
      frontRightList.push(listOfPolygons[i]);
   }
   else if(backRightBox.IsPolyIn(listOfPolygons[i]) == true)
   {
      backRightList.push(listOfPolygons[i]);
   }
}

node.frontLeftNode  = CreateQuadNode(frontLeftList);
node.backLeftNode   = CreateQuadNode(backLeftList);
node.frontRightNode = CreateQuadNode(frontRightList);
node.backRightNode  = CreateQuadNode(backRightList);

return node;
}
```

Note that the pseudo-code for creating a quad-tree does not take into account polygons that span multiple boxes. In this case you would have to split the polygons similarly to what was discussed for the BSP tree. The pseudo-code adds the polygon to whatever box it touches.

The pseudo-code for culling with a quad-tree can look like the following:

```
// Create quad-tree out of polygon list and a frustum.

listOfPolygons = new PolygonList(...);
quadTree = CreateQuadNode(listOfPolygons);
frustum = Frustum(camera)


// Render by calling this recursively on root node.
```

```
        RenderQuadTree(frustum, quadTree);


        // Recursive rendering function.

        RenderQuadTree(frustum, node)
        {
           if(node == NULL)
              return;


           // Cull (return) if camera cannot see this node.

           if(frustum.isVisible(node.aabb) == FALSE)
              return;


           // Either rendering a leaf node or must traverse.

           if(node.polygons != NULL)
           {
              for each(element i in node.polygons)
              {
                 // Render poly using API like OpenGL, Direct3D, etc.
              }
           }
           else
           {
              RenderQuadTree(frustum, node.frontLeftNode);
              RenderQuadTree(frustum, node.backLeftNode);
              RenderQuadTree(frustum, node.frontRightNode);
              RenderQuadTree(frustum, node.backRightNode);
           }
        }
```

Quad-trees can also be used to create terrains with nodes that have varying levels of detail. As nodes are determined to be farther and farther away from the viewer (camera), low-detail versions of that node's geometry can be used to decrease the rendering load on the graphics hardware. As geometry moves further away from the camera, the detail that it holds is not as visible. Using lower levels of detail as geometry is farther away can lead to renders that show no real noticeable difference. We'll discuss level of detail more later on this chapter.

Octrees

Octrees are essentially the same as quad-trees, but a node is split into eight boxes instead of four. Octrees can be useful for environments where a large number of polygons can appear above a camera's frustum and can be culled out of the rendering process. In a quad-tree the polygons of a node are rendered if the node is visible or partially visible. It would be more expensive to cull individual polygons than groups of them, and because of this, if there are large numbers of polygons that can appear above a camera, they will be rendered even if not visible in a quad-tree. By using an octree, these polygons can be possibly culled out. This situation is shown in Figure 13.13.

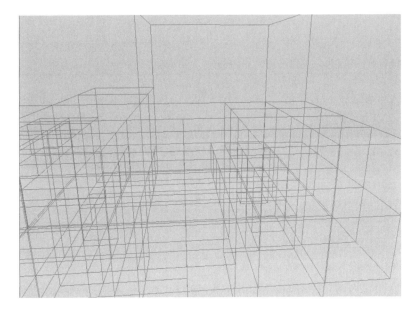

FIGURE 13.13 An octree.

Implementing an Octree

On the accompanying CD-ROM a demo application called Octree is in the Chapter 13 folder. The Octree demo will take a simple wire-frame terrain and build an octree out of it. It will also use frustum culling on the octree's nodes to render only what geometry is visible. The octree is implemented using the information for the quad-tree, with the exception of eight child nodes instead of four. A screenshot of the demo application is shown in Figure 13.14.

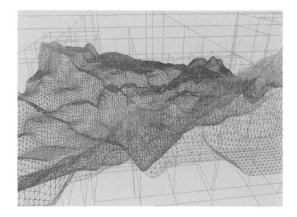

FIGURE 13.14 A screenshot from the Octree demo.

ADDITIONAL MANAGEMENT TOPICS

The management of a scene can be very complex, with all the pieces of data that are brought together to make a virtual experience. In this chapter the main focus has been on introducing space partitioning, but other topics are also important for game developers. These topics include the following:

- Texture compression
- Level of detail
- Occlusion culling
- Potential visibility sets
- Portal rendering

In this section we will briefly discuss a few of these topics that can be used to increase the rendering performance of a scene.

TEXTURE COMPRESSION

Textures are becoming larger in resolution and larger in numbers. With more textures and with more textures that are made up of high resolutions, more memory is needed to store them. There are many kinds of textures outside of color maps (also known as decal textures). The other kinds of textures that can be applied to a surface include:

- Specular maps (gloss maps)
- Alpha maps
- Height and displacement maps

- Bump and normal maps
- Detail maps
- Ambient occlusion maps
- Light maps
- Environment maps (i.e., cube maps, sphere maps, etc.)
- High-dynamic-range light probes

Compression is a technique used to reduce the size of data in memory. Compressing textures used by a game reduces the total amount of memory used. This can allow for more textures and/or higher-resolution images. In the next chapter, Data Compression, we'll briefly discuss and implement texture compression as well as other topics.

LEVEL OF DETAIL

Many geometric objects and sections of the game world are often visible at one time in a complex game. Earlier in this chapter we discussed a few ways to quickly determine what polygons are visible so the rendering system can draw only that information. This allows applications to spend less time on what is not visible and more time on what is.

What about the objects that are visible to the viewer? If you take a high polygonal object and render it close to the viewer, the full detail of the character will be visible. As the object moves farther away from the viewer, the detail becomes less visible because the object is not as close but that amount of data is still being rendered. Level of detail is used to create different versions of a virtual object, where each level is made up of less detail than the previous one. A screenshot of this is shown in Figure 13.15.

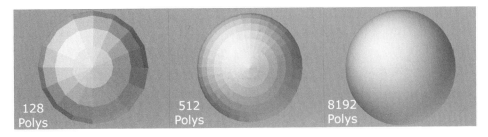

FIGURE 13.15   Level of detail on a sphere.

The idea is that when an object is farther from the viewer, less information can be used to render that object without a noticeable difference. Since the object is farther away, it would be hard for a user to realize that the objects are different meshes.

Drawing lower and lower polygonal versions of an object as it gets farther away from the viewer gives the graphics hardware less work, which increases performance. If this is done on all objects and sections of the environment (e.g., using level of detail on octree nodes), a complex scene can be rendered quickly that would have otherwise have had the potential for low performance.

Occlusion Culling

In frustum culling, discussed earlier in the chapter, everything outside of the frustum is culled, or, in other words, not rendered. For geometry that falls within the frustum, another technique, called occlusion culling, is used to cull geometry further.

Within a frustum some visible objects can block others. For example, a wall might block the view of objects behind it. If objects are not visible because other objects block them, they should not be rendered if this can be quickly determined. That is what occlusion culling is. It is a technique used to eliminate nonvisible geometry that passes the frustum culling test.

Occlusion culling has advantages and disadvantages. On the one hand, a test can be used to determine if objects completely block the view of other objects. On the other hand, if too many tests are being performed, in some cases the test can result in the same or worse performance than not doing anything and simply rendering the object. As with many things in video games, a balance must be found to achieve the best results. An illustration of occlusion culling is shown in Figure 13.16.

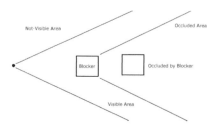

FIGURE 13.16   Occlusion culling.

Potential Visibility Sets

Earlier in this chapter we looked at various data structures there are used to partition a virtual world into manageable blocks of bounding volumes. Quad-trees and octrees are used to quickly determine what parts of a scene are visible and to draw only those. In a BSP tree things are a little different, and rendering and the tree's algorithms normally allow for front-to-back rendering. In the early days of three-dimensional games this was fine, but, as seen with *Quake 1*, it was determined that the BSP tree can result in bad performance depending on the design of a level.

Using potential visibility sets was the answer John Carmack of id Software used to solve the rendering performance issues in *Quake*, and they have been used ever since in many games such as *Doom 3*, *Quake 4*, and *Half-Life 2*. Potential visibility sets are straightforward. Using the BSP tree as an example, although any tree would work, every node stores a list of other nodes that it can possibly see. *Potential* in the name potential visibility set means there is at least one position where the player can be within that node that can see another node. By having each node store what other nodes it can see, the BSP tree can be used to render only what is visible. In the demo application seen earlier in this chapter the BSP tree was used to render the entire scene. Since most of the scene was not visible, this was a waste of processing cycles. If potential visibility sets were used, the algorithm would change to determine what node the player was in, render that node, and then render all nodes in the potential visibility set for the node the player is in. Since octrees and quad-trees are designed to quickly reject large portions of a scene, they might not benefit too much from potential visibility sets in some situations.

Originally BSP trees were designed to be able to render the polygons of an environment in the proper order. Since BSP trees are used mostly for indoor areas, there is also a lot of occluded geometry. By creating a potential visibility sets list during the build of a level in a level editor, the in-game engine can quickly use that precomputed data to know what nodes to draw and what nodes to reject. The process of building a potential visibility set out of the quad-tree in Figure 13.7 is shown in Figure 13.17, where each node knows which other nodes it can potentially see. Use of potential visibility sets is shown in Figure 13.18, where the current node the viewer is in is rendered, followed by all of the potentially visible nodes.

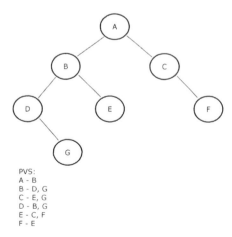

FIGURE 13.17   A BSP tree where each node knows which other nodes it can see.

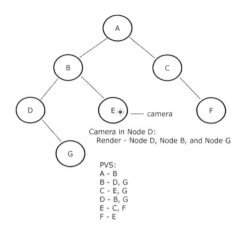

FIGURE 13.18 Using potential visibility sets.

Using a bit array is one way to save memory space when using potential visibility sets if the potential visibility set data represent true or false boolean values for whether or not the other nodes can be seen from that node.

PORTAL RENDERING

Another rendering technique used from the early days of games to the present is the portal rendering technique. In portal rendering the game world is separated into sectors. Using a house as an example, a sector can be a room such as a bedroom or kitchen. Each sector is connected by a portal that is often a plane used to specify which portals are connected. For example, a bedroom door can be a portal that is used to connect the bedroom sector with the hallway sector. An example is shown in Figure 13.19.

A number of tricks can be used for portal rendering. The system can be set up so that the geometries of two connecting sectors are not physically next to one another. This creates a wormhole-like situation where you can cross into a portal and end up in a part of the game world that is nowhere near the area you just left. In the Xbox® 360 game *Prey* this was used to create some very unique gameplay elements where portals existed throughout the game world and the players could not only move through them but could also look through them, sometimes even being able to look at themselves, almost as if they were looking into another universe.

The possibilities are remarkable with portal rendering. If a player can start in a completely closed room where there is a box in the middle of the area, a portal can be attached to one of the faces on the box so that the player can walk through and

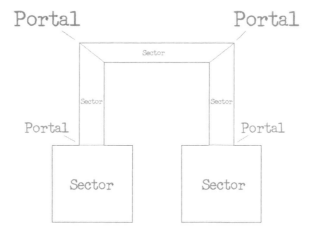

FIGURE 13.19   A scene divided by portals and sectors.

end up in a completely new area. Maybe a player can hit a switch to open the portal, or the portal can already be there waiting. Either way, the trick can be used for some very weird things, such as a portal that acts like a window on one side but looks into a completely different area or a solid surface from the other side or, as in Value's upcoming game *Portal*, in which sectors can have a portal that connects the sector to itself, creating a loop.

SUMMARY

The purpose of this chapter was to introduce the topic of using data structures and algorithms to perform scene management. This chapter covered a lot of information dealing with the general management of a virtual scene in a video game. As seen so far, the subject of scene management can be very complex. So much data makes up a game world that efficiently processing it all calls for data structures and algorithms that manage and feed the information to the systems that require it. Some of these data structures were mentioned in this chapter, but there are many others:

- CLOD for terrains
- ROAM
- *k*d-trees
- Sphere trees
- Loose trees

In the next chapter we'll discuss topics such as data encryption and compression. Compression can be used to compress textures to increase the performance of a rendered scene, so this topic is very important for game developers.

CHAPTER REVIEW QUESTIONS

Answers to the following chapter review questions can be found in Appendix B.

1. What is state management?
2. What is a texture atlas?
3. What is the difference between managing resources and managing states?
4. A vector with a magnitude of 1 is:
   a. The cross product of two vectors
   b. The dot product of a vector
   c. A unit-length vector
   d. None of the above
5. What is frustum culling?
6. What is a scene graph?
7. The scene graph discussed in this chapter is a type of:
   a. Graph
   b. Weighted graph
   c. Multiway tree
   d. Binary tree
   e. None of the above
8. What is occlusion culling and how can it be used to increase rendering times?
9. What is the difference between an octree and a quad-tree?
10. What bounding volume do quad-trees and octrees use?
    a. Spheres
    b. Ellipsoids
    c. Axis-aligned boxes
    d. None of the above
11. What kind of trees are quad-trees and octrees?
    a. Multiway
    b. Binary
    c. Graph
    d. None of the above
12. What is a binary space partitioning tree?

13. In a BSP tree the left and right nodes of the binary tree are also known as the:
    a. Sibling/child
    b. Splitting planes
    c. Front/back
    d. None of the above
14. What are potential visibility sets and how do they aid in the rendering of a scene?
15. Bounding boxes are generally faster than bounding spheres.
    a. True
    b. False
16. A scene graph is a binary tree.
    a. True
    b. False
17. A quad-tree splits on the y-axis, while an octree splits on the x and y axes.
    a. True
    b. False
18. Binary space partitioning trees are obsolete in today's games.
    a. True
    b. False
19. BSP trees are not better suited to open spaces such as the outdoors.
    a. True
    b. False
20. Octrees are not better suited to open spaces such as the outdoors.
    a. True
    b. False

PROGRAMMING PROJECTS

Exercise 1: Implement a bounding sphere and modify the Scene Graph demo application to use the spheres instead of the bounding boxes.

Exercise 2: Do Exercise 1 and add the ability to specify the orientation of the transformation. Also change the spheres to teapots using the `glutSolidTeapot()` function in the GLUT library.

Exercise 3: Build off of Exercise 2 and allow nodes to have identifiers, such as names, and allow the scene graph to attach nodes to specific other nodes in the hierarchy.

Exercise 4: Modify the Octree demo application to use a quad-tree. This can be done by performing splits along the x and y axes but not the z-axis.

14

Data Compression

In This Chapter

- Introduction to Data Compression
- Introduction to Texture Compression
- Introduction to Data Encryption

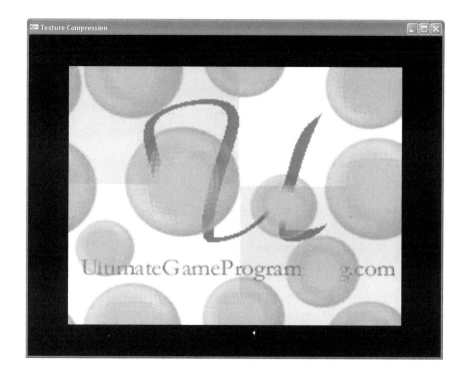

The transfer of data is very important for machines connected to one another and for data stored on different mediums. The Internet is one type of connection where millions of individuals are able to share all types of information on virtually any subject. Since the early days of computers there has always been a need to (a) protect sensitive data and (b) increase the transfer speed of information from a source to a destination. Today these goals are just as important, if not more important, than ever before.

Data can be protected using something known as encryption. Encryption essentially takes data that is in its original form and converts it into another form that makes it hard to read and process. This conversion is done using an algorithm, and there are many different types of these algorithms. Encrypted data is considered more secure than unencrypted data. Some types of encryption can be cracked more easily than others, and the goal of encryption is to make that process as difficult as possible.

The transfer speed of data can increased by increasing the transfer rate of a device such as a modem or by taking the information that needs to be transmitted and reducing its size in memory. The second option is known as compression, which attempts to take data and reduce its size while keeping the data acceptably intact. Two major kinds of compression will be discussed later in this chapter: lossless and lossy compression. All compression algorithms fall in one of these two categories.

This chapter will discuss data encryption and compression in general computer programming and in game development. The purpose of this chapter is to introduce both topics as well as discuss their implications in game and simulation development. Although each of these topics can fill their own books, this chapter will give some insight into each one.

INTRODUCTION TO DATA COMPRESSION

Many different types of files have information in them that has some kind of redundancy and/or can be represented using less information than the original data. For example, in a database it might be acceptable to represent a person's birth month using a number between 1 and 12 instead of a string for the month's text. Another example is an image file that might have large numbers of consecutive pixels that use the same color value throughout the picture. Compression is all about taking advantage of short cuts that a piece of data can allow so that the information is the same or is close to the same.

There are many ways to compress information in a file. In this chapter we will discuss a few methods that are well known in computer science. The main two types of compression are lossless compression and lossy compression.

LOSSLESS VERSUS LOSSY COMPRESSION

Lossless compression refers to a compression algorithm that can take information and compress it without sacrificing the original data's quality. With a lossless compression scheme it is possible to compress data and then decompress that data back into its original form and in its original condition and quality. The kind of file being compressed determines whether lossless compression is desired or is essential.

Lossy compression is the opposite of lossless compression. Lossy compression is a compression algorithm that takes information and compress it as small as possible by sacrificing the quality or accuracy of the data for file size. Many algorithms use lossy compression. One famous file type that uses lossy compression is the JPEG image file format. In a JPEG the original quality of the image is lost so that the image can be small. If you try to save a JPEG to a lossless file format or try to compare a JPEG to the original, depending on the color variations between the pixels in the original file, you'll see a clear difference in the image quality in most cases. Usually this loss of quality is more than acceptable. In the case of transmitting JPEG images across the Internet, most files are small enough in resolution that a loss in quality can't even be recognized by everyday Web surfers, especially if the compression ratio is not very high to begin with. Once data has been compressed using a lossy compression algorithm, if there is a drop in quality then there is little to nothing that can be done to restore that data to the original form unless you keep a copy of the original. Also, recompressing data that has been compressed using a lossy algorithm will cause a further reduction in quality. In some cases this is okay, but in others it is important not to compress already compressed data but to instead keep a copy of the original and perform compressions only on that.

The choice to use either lossless compression or lossy compression comes down to what is being compressed. Lossy compression is often used on images because the loss in quality can go unnoticed in some cases, but when data quality and accuracy are essential, lossless compression is often the preferred solution.

RUN-LENGTH ENCODING

Traditional run-length encoding is a very well-known and popular lossless compression algorithm. In run-length encoding a run is a number that defines how many times a piece of information repeats itself consecutively. For example, take this string:

```
AAAAAbbCCCCCCd
```

In this string the letter "A" is repeated five times, "b" is repeated twice, "C" is repeated six times, and "d" only appears once. If run-length encoding was performed on this string, the compressed result could look like the following encoded data:

```
5A2b6C1d
```

In run-length encoding the run tells the algorithm how many times the data that follows it is repeated. If the runs are large enough, this can lead to a significant reduction in data size by replacing the original data with a shorter form that can be translated back later. The compressed data in a run-length encoded piece of information are abbreviated to shorten their representation. Generally every piece of data is in the form of a (n, val) pair, where n is a number and val is the value that was encoded. A visual representation of run-length encoding is shown in Figure 14.1.

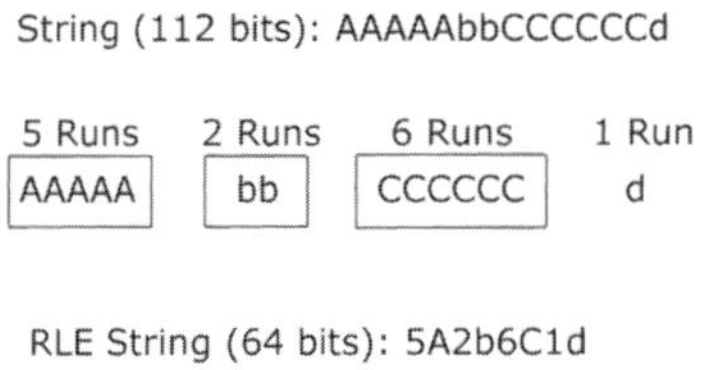

String (112 bits): AAAAAbbCCCCCCd

5 Runs	2 Runs	6 Runs	1 Run
AAAAA	bb	CCCCC	d

RLE String (64 bits): 5A2b6C1d

FIGURE 14.1   Run-length encoding.

A situation to consider when using run-length encoding is the number of runs for each piece of information. If many runs are not greater than 1, then the data used to represent the encoded value will be twice as long as the original value itself. For example, take the following piece of information:

```
ABCCDEEEFFGH
```

The encoded form of the string would look like the following:

```
1A1B2C1D3E2F1G1H
```

The run-length encoded version of this example string leads to four more characters in the string than in the original version. One way around this is to use a marker character in the pair so that the encoded data consist of a (m, n, val), where m is a marker character, n is the run number, and val is the encoded data. If the marker character is a unique character, meaning it does not show up in the original data, then when the algorithm reads a byte from the data, it can perform this general test:

```
read from the data: m

if(m == marker)
{
```

```
    read the run number: n
    read the encoded value: val

    do something with it:
}
else
{
    // The value in m is not a marker but is the data.

    do something with it:
}
```

Looking for a marker first can allow the algorithm to know if the data is encoded or not. Because encoded data are composed of three values (*m*, *n*, *val*), it makes sense to encode runs that are four or larger. Since it takes at least three values to represent an encoded piece of data, if the original set of data has three or fewer runs, it might as well not be encoded. If it is, the encoded version will be bigger than the original set of data and would defeat the purpose of encoding it.

If the marker used by the algorithm must exist in the data being encoded, one solution to allowing this is to place the marker twice. When the algorithm first reads the marker it will then read the next value. If the next value is another marker, the algorithm will know there is no run here and will work with the character used as the marker. This is similar to escape characters in C, C++, and other languages (e.g, "\n"). An example can look like the following:

Original: AAAAABBBBBB~C

Encoded: ~5A~6B~~C

In games a common use for run-length encoding is for texture images. Although run-length encoding-compressed data cannot be used directly on the graphics hardware like some texture compression algorithms that will be discussed later, it can be used to save disk space with images that can make good use of the technique. In the case of compressing an image with run-length encoding, the value of each encoded piece of data is an image pixel. Because of the nature of images, this brings up another point. What if the following RGB color values were found: Five pixels of (255, 128, 74), five pixels of (255, 125, 70), and so on. If there is a run of five pixels that use (255, 128, 74) and a run of five pixels that use (255, 125, 70), then, since the two colors are very close without any major noticeable difference, they can both be represented as (255, 128, 74), which would give us 10 (255, 128, 74).

Adjusting close-by pixels to match one another to improve the run-length encoding efficiency in this manner will turn the algorithm from lossless to lossy because the original data's quality or accuracy has been altered. If this was done and the image was decompressed and saved, the areas where there was once a slight change in color would now be one solid color. Recompressing the compressed data might even cause pixels that were originally not close to one another but were close after the first compression to be further optimized into a longer run of the same value. This is one reason it is not always desirable to recompress compressed information when using a lossy algorithm and to instead just compress the original data again.

If the data being encoded have little or no redundancy, the run-length encoding algorithm can prove ineffective. Using the character marker technique will allow the data to keep its original size or a size close to the original in a situation like that.

NOTE

IMPLEMENTING RUN-LENGTH ENCODING

ON THE CD

This section includes a simple implementation of run-length encoding being performed on strings. On the accompanying CD-ROM a demo application called run length Encoding is in the Chapter 14 folder. In this demo application there are three functions, Encode(), Decode(), and main(), in the application's main source file.

The Encode() function takes a source string and a destination string as parameters. The source string is the original information, while the destination string is where the encoded information will be saved. The Encode() function starts by looping through the entire source data byte by byte. For each byte it keeps track of how many runs are in the sequence. If the total runs are four or more, the character marker, run total, and value are saved to the destination. If there are fewer than four runs, the value is simply copied to the destination. A loop is used to save the values that have fewer than four runs for run values of 1, 2, or 3. The function is straightforward and is shown in Listing 14.1. To save bytes on the value stored for the run, a character is used instead of an integer. In this demo a run longer than 255 is highly unlikely. Even so, a short (two-bytes) would probably be enough for most applications if a char was not. In general it is not important to group runs in blocks of 255, but this could be application specific.

Adding the ability of the marker to exist in the original data will be an exercise for the end of the chapter.

NOTE

LISTING 14.1   Encoding Data Using Run-Length Encoding

```
void Encode(string &src, string &dst)
{
   int index = 0;
   char runTotal = 0, currentChar = 0;
```

```
    while(index < (int)src.length())
    {
       runTotal = 0;
       currentChar = src[index];


       while(currentChar == src[index] && runTotal < 255)
       {
          runTotal++;
          index++;
       }


       if(runTotal > 3)
       {
          dst += '~';
          dst += runTotal;
          dst += currentChar;
       }
       else
       {
          for(int i = 0; i < runTotal; i++)
          {
             dst += currentChar;
          }
       }
    }
  }
```

The decoding algorithm for run-length encoding is simpler than the encoding algorithm in Listing 14.1. The Decode() function takes a source and a destination string as parameters. Inside the function a loop is used to loop through each byte of the source. If the current character matches the character marker, the next byte is the number of runs followed by the value itself. If the current byte is not a character marker, the byte is simply copied to the destination. The Decode() function for the decoding algorithm is shown in Listing 14.2.

LISTING 14.2   Decoding data using Run-Length Encoding

```
    void Decode(string &src, string &dst)
    {
       int index = 0, runTotal = 0;
       char currentChar = 0;
```

```
        while(index < (int)src.length())
        {
           if(src[index++] == '~')
           {
              runTotal = (int)src[index++];
              currentChar = src[index++];


              for(int i = 0; i < runTotal; i++)
              {
                 dst += currentChar;
              }
           }
           else
           {
              dst += src[index - 1];
           }
        }
     }
```

The `main()` function of the demo application is straightforward. The main source file takes a simple string of characters, displays it to the console window along with its size, encodes it using run-length encoding, displays the encoded data to the console window along with its compressed size, decodes the encoded data, and displays the decoded data to the console window to prove everything worked as planned. The `main()` function from the Run Length Encoding demo application is shown in Listing 14.3. Figure 14.2 shows a screenshot of the application.

LISTING 14.3 The `main()` Function of the Run Length Encoding Demo

```
int main(int args, char **argc)
{
   cout << "Run Length Encoding" << endl;
   cout << "Chapter 14: Data Compression and Encryption" << endl;
   cout << endl;


   string str = "AAAAaaBBBBBBCCCCCCddddddEEEEEeeeeFFFFGGGG";
   string encodedStr, decodedStr;

   cout << "Original Data Size: " << str.length() << endl;
   cout << "Original Data:" << endl;
   cout << str << endl << endl;
```

```
Encode(str, encodedStr);

cout << "Compressed Size: " << encodedStr.length() << endl;
cout << "Compressed Data:" << endl;
cout << encodedStr << endl << endl;


Decode(encodedStr, decodedStr);

cout << "Decompressed Size: " << decodedStr.length() << endl;
cout << "Decompressed Data:" << endl;
cout << decodedStr << endl << endl;


    return 1;
}
```

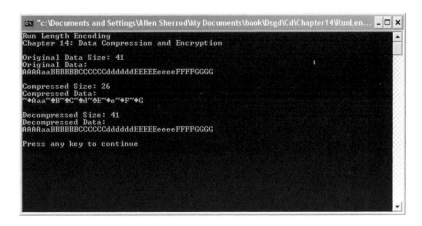

FIGURE 14.2   A screenshot of the Run Length Encoding demo.

HUFFMAN CODING

The Huffman coding algorithm is a lossless data compression algorithm created by David A. Huffman in the 1950s. The Huffman coding algorithm uses various data structures such as the binary tree and priority queue to compress data efficiently. The Huffman code uses binary digits to traverse a binary tree. For example, if 0 means to go left and 1 means to go right, a binary tree of letters in the alphabet could look like Figure 14.3

In Figure 14.3 only 3 bits are used to represent the letter "A" instead of the normal 8 bits that a byte normally uses. Doing this with all bytes in a source of data

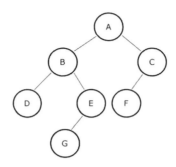

FIGURE 14.3   A binary tree with letters.

can allow the data to be compressed very tightly while remaining lossless in its compression scheme.

The Huffman algorithm is generally quite simple to implement for those with knowledge of priority queues and binary trees. In this section, to make the visualization easier, we will use the letters of the alphabet as an example of data that are being compressed. For example, take the following string:

```
Susie sells sea shells at the sea shore
```

The first step of the algorithm is to figure the frequency of every letter in the string. For the letter "S" this frequency is the number of times it shows up in the data, which is eight times. Every letter in the message has a frequency that is determined by the algorithm.

The next step is to create a node for each letter in the message and to store each of these nodes in a priority queue. A node in a Huffman tree has pointers to the left and right child nodes and a frequency number. The priority queue will sort the nodes by frequency from least to greatest.

The third step is to use a loop to remove the top two nodes from the priority queue. Since the priority queue stores its elements from least to greatest, these two nodes are the nodes with the smallest frequencies. The two removed nodes are made child nodes of a new node, and the new node has a frequency that equals the first node's plus the second node's frequency. This new node is then inserted into the priority queue, which is shown in Figure 14.4.

Performing this until there is only one large node left in the priority queue will create the Huffman tree. The Huffman tree is a binary tree of all the pieces of information that make up the data. If the value 0 means to go left and 1 means to go right, then every letter in the example string can be mapped to a few binary digits. The higher the frequency (i.e., the most times a letter is used in the data), the lower the number of bits that are used to store it. An example of this Huffman tree is shown in Figure 14.5.

String:
Susie
Character Frequency:
s - 2
u - 1
i - 1
e - 1
A 010
...
E 1111
I 110
S 10
...

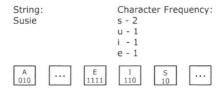

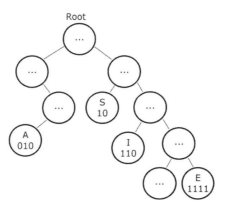

FIGURE 14.4 Removing two nodes, combining them, and placing them back on the queue.

Root
S 10
A 010
I 110
E 1111

FIGURE 14.5 A binary tree for "Susie sells sea shells at the sea shore."

The next step to the Huffman coding algorithm is to create a Huffman table. This table is an array that holds the bits necessary to traverse through the binary tree to find a letter. An example of this is shown in Figure 14.6.

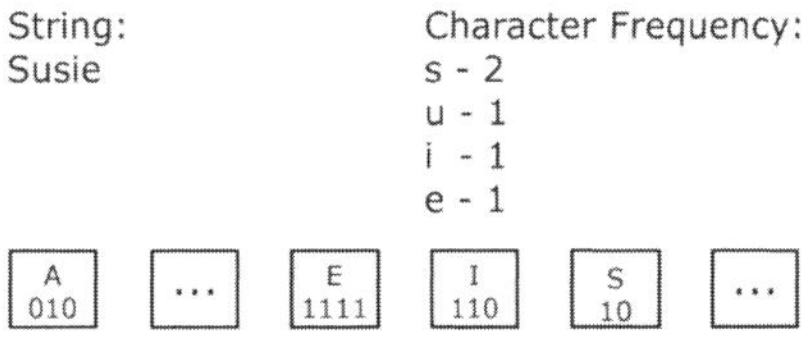

String:
Susie
Character Frequency:
s - 2
u - 1
i - 1
e - 1
A 010
...
E 1111
I 110
S 10
...

FIGURE 14.6 A Huffman table.

Encoding data using the Huffman coding algorithm would require a loop to go through the original data and replace each (using strings as an example) letter with the binary digits necessary to look it up in the binary tree. This encoded data along with the Huffman table can be saved and decoded later. To decode the information the Huffman tree can be generated out of the Huffman table, and the binary digits of the encoded message can be processed and decompressed. An example of this is shown in Figure 14.7.

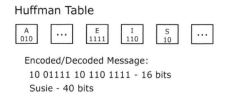

Encoded/Decoded Message:
10 01111 10 110 1111 - 16 bits
Susie - 40 bits

FIGURE 14.7 Compressing and decompressing using the Huffman code.

The Huffman coding algorithm for encoding can be summarized as the following:

1. Get the frequency for every piece of data.
2. Create a node for each of these pieces and place them into a priority queue based on their frequencies from least to greatest.
3. Remove two nodes at a time from the priority queue. Make those nodes child nodes of a new node, where the new node's frequency is equal to the frequencies of its children added together, and place the new node into the priority queue. Continue until there is only one node left, which is the Huffman tree.
4. Go through all the leaf nodes of the Huffman tree to determine what path is necessary to get to each piece of data. Store this path data of 0s and 1s in an array known as a Huffman table.
5. Encode the data using the Huffman table.

The Huffman coding algorithm for decoding can be summarized as the following:

1. When decoding the data, use the Huffman table to generate the Huffman tree.
2. When processing the data to be decoded, use each bit as a direction for traversing the Huffman tree.
3. When a leaf node is reached, that piece of data at the node is the decoded value.
4. Continue until all compressed data have been processed.

To decode data the algorithm you will need is either the Huffman table, so that the Huffman tree can be generated, or the Huffman tree itself. The Huffman table can easily be saved to a file with the compressed data or transferred across a connection much more easily and efficiently than a tree that uses pointers to nodes. The tree itself is used for decoding a message and for creating the Huffman table. The Huffman table, along with being used for generating the tree if needed, serves as a look-up table for encoding the original data. For example, the piece of information being encoded is looked up in the Huffman table and that series of bits is what is saved to the compressed file. Because the Huffman table stores the traversing information for the binary tree, the binary tree can be generated using this table if needed. The same can be said for the Huffman tree being used to generate the Huffman table. The Huffman tree can also be generated using the priority queue and frequencies, which are necessary for the first step of the algorithm. Pseudo-code for the encoding algorithm can look like the following:

```
// Determine frequencies.

for each(element i in array of data)
{
   if(element i does not have frequency)
   {
      frequency = GetFreqency(i, data);

      node = CreateNode(freqencyList);
      AddNode(node, priorityQueue);
   }
}


// Build huffman tree.

while(priorityQueue.count > 1)
{
   node1 = RemoveTopNode(priorityQueue);
   node2 = RemoveTopNode(priorityQueue);

   newSubNode = CreateNode(node1, node2);

   AddNode(newSubNode, priorityQueue);
}


// Last node left in queue is huffman tree.
// Create huffman table from it.

huffmanTree = RemoveTopNode(priorityQueue);
huffmanTable = CreateHuffmanTable(huffmanTree);
```

```
// Compress data using huffman table.

for each(element i in array of data)
{
    // Look up this element's compressed representation.
    compressedData[i] = huffmanTable[data[i]];
}
```

Assuming you have the Huffman table and tree, the decoding pseudo-code can look like the following:

```
// Decoding.

index = 0;

for each(bit i in array of compressedData)
{
    // 0 means move left, 1 means move right.
    huffmanTree.MoveToNextTreeBranch(compressedData[i]);

    if(huffmanTree.AtLeafNode())
    {
        data[index++] = huffmanTree.GetCurrentNodeValue();
    }
}
```

You can think of the Huffman table as a tool used to encode a message and the Huffman tree as a tool used to decode the message. The Huffman tree is also used to generate the Huffman table and vice versa.

INTRODUCTION TO TEXTURE COMPRESSION

The amount of data used to represent virtual worlds in a video game is growing with every generation. A lot of this increase in data comes from increased numbers of textures and an increase in their resolutions. Texture data takes up a lot of space. Of course, there are other resources that take up a lot of space such as video, audio, geometry, and so on, but textures have become a major focus for compression.

Compressing textures have quite a few benefits in game development. The first benefit is that the textures take up less space on the storage device. With the number of textures a game uses increasing, the extra space can come in handy. Using a compression algorithm that gives a 4:1 compression ratio on a 32-bit 1024 × 1024 texture would give you the following comparison:

Original data size: 4 bytes per pixel $\times (1024 \times 1024) = 4{,}194{,}304$ bytes or 4.2 MB

Compressed size: Original size/4 = 1 MB (give or take a few kilobytes)

If the compression ratio was 6:1, like one of the techniques that will be discussed shortly, the compressed size for a 32-bit 1024×1024 texture would be 700 kilobytes. Such a savings is huge for a large texture.

The great thing about texture compression is that the benefits do not end there. Modern graphics hardware is designed to internally work with data that was compressed with certain algorithms. This means that not only does the compressed data take up less storage space on a disk, but it also takes up less bandwidth and memory inside the game. The faster a texture can be moved through the pipeline, the better the performance. When it comes to rendering, one of the most expensive operations is switching textures. This cost can be minimized by using state-management techniques, which were first discussed in Chapter 13. Because graphics hardware is able to load and work with compressed data, there are many opportunities to use high-definition content in video games. Using the best compression method for the type of texture you are dealing with can go a long way toward create stunning, high-definition and high-resolution virtual scenes.

In this section we will look at some popular compression methods used in the game industry for compressing color maps and normal maps. Each method has its strengths and weaknesses, which will be examined in the following subsections. The first types of image compression algorithms that will be discussed for textures are S3 texture compression algorithm formats (the OpenGL version of DirectX DXTC), which include DXT1 through DXT5. Before moving on let's briefly discuss normal maps.

Bump mapping is an extension to per-pixel lighting. In per-pixel lighting the lighting algorithms are performed on each fragment of a rendered object. In traditional per-pixel lighting this leads to smooth lighting contributions across an entire surface. With per-vertex lighting, the lighting quality mostly depended on the number of vertices in the mesh, while in per-pixel lighting it mostly depends on the screen resolution of the rendered scene.

Bump mapping extends per-pixel lighting by varying the normals at the fragment level to create patterns that have different lighting contributions. These patterns can give the illusion of detail on an object. Bump maps are images that store the normal X, Y, Z in the color components R, G, B. Texture mapping can apply a bump map onto a surface that allows the pixel shader to access that information. The main difference between bump mapping and per-pixel lighting is the normal it uses for the lighting. For bump mapping this is a normal it fetches from the bump map, while for per-pixel lighting it is the normal at the surface normal. Bump maps are height maps that specify a pattern.

Normal mapping is essentially bump mapping, but instead of using a height map with a pattern, which is normally created by an artist, normal maps use height maps that are calculated from a low-polygon mesh and a high-polygon mesh. Calculating the difference between a low- and high-polygon model, the resulting normal map can be used to perform bump mapping on the low-polygon model so that it looks like the high-polygon version. This technique is used in many of today's games to give models and environments the appearance of detail and complexity while keeping the polygon count low enough for real-time rendering.

DXTC COMPRESSION

The DXTC image compression methods are texture compression formats that are good for getting a compression ratio of 6:1 on color images using DXT1 and a 4:1 compression ratio using the other DXT formats. The DXTC compression formats use a lossy type of compression, so the quality of color maps can be less than the original, and they are not the best choice for compressing normal map images. The reason they are not good to use with normal maps lies with the normal values themselves. To provide accurate lighting across a surface, the normals will need to be relatively intact. A screenshot of a normal map using lossy compression is shown in Figure 14.8. Later we'll see another compression format that is efficient for compressing normal maps. By using a lossy compression like the DXTC formats on normal maps you will be giving up lighting accuracy and quality, and this can hurt the look of a scene.

FIGURE 14.8 Compressing a normal map image.

The DXTC formats are great for decal images, but the format version used depends on the quality given from the compression. The DXT1 gives the lowest overall quality but also gives the most compression. Each version above the DXT1 has better quality than the one that came before it but at the cost of compression size. The DXT5 often gives the best quality but does not get the most compression. A comparison of a texture image compressed with DXT1 and DXT5 is shown in Figure 14.9. A comparison of these formats on a normal map is shown in Figure 14.10.

FIGURE 14.9   DXT1 compared to DXT5 on decals.

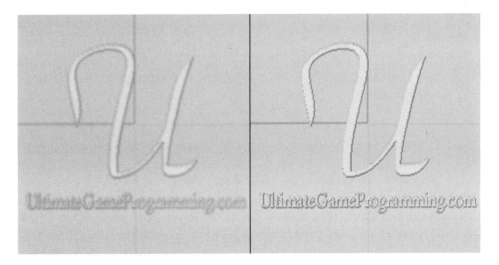

FIGURE 14.10   DXT1 compared to DXT5 on normal maps.

Normal Maps and DXTC Formats

Normal maps are not good candidates for DXTC compression because the DXTC formats assume that the image data are smooth across its pixels. In a normal map there are often sharp changes that are used to give detail and variations for the lighting algorithms. Because normal maps are often not smooth, the normals can be compressed and altered to a point where the detail is lost and the lighting does not look as intended. Using only 16 bits for each color component is not enough precision for normals in a normal map. Also, specular lighting and normal maps compressed with a DXTC format can further amplify the rendering artifacts that exist on the rendered surface.

There are a few tricks to getting normal maps to compress with DXTC formats while retaining an acceptable level of quality. These options are not as useful as the 3Dc compression format, which will be examined later, but they can work if DXTC must be used. The tricks that can be used to increase the quality of a normal map using a DXTC format include:

- Renormalizing normals as they are fetched from a texture.
- Placing the x-axis of a normal in the alpha channel of a DXT5 compression since the alpha channel is compressed separately.
- Taking the previous trick, fetching the y-axis from the normal, and generating the z-axis instead of using the one from the normal map.

Generating the z-axis is a clever and easy means of working with compressed normals. By generating the z-axis, the normal can always be unit-length without needing to renormalize the vector. A unit normal is a vector whose length (magnitude) equals 1, like so:

$$1 = \text{square\_root}(X * X + Y * Y + Z * Z).$$

If we know the x-axis and the y-axis, the z-axis can be calculated using the simple formula

$$Z = \text{square\_root}(1 - (X * X - Y * Y)).$$

Generating the z-axis and using DXT5 with the x-axis stored in the alpha channel can give you the best results when compressing normal maps using the DXTC formats. A screenshot is shown in Figure 14.11.

The DXT1 format gives the most compression at a ratio of 8:1 but does not use an alpha channel. The DXT1 format uses 16-bit color values at 5-6-5 (red 5, green 5, blue 5). The algorithm for the DXT1 format splits the image up into 4 x 4 pixel blocks. Each block stores only two unique colors and uses a 16-bit palette. The pixels in each block reference an entry in the block's palette, allowing the colors to be

FIGURE 14.11   DXT5 and normal maps using various tricks.

represented using less data. Because the format uses 4 × 4 blocks, gradient information often becomes clearly blocky, with many unwanted visual artifacts. These artifacts can be seen on the three-dimensional object that is textured with a DXT1 compressed image in Figure 14.12.

FIGURE 14.12   Artifacts caused by DXT1 compression.

Extensions to the DXT1 format allow it to use a 1-bit alpha channel.

The DXT1 format can give a compression ratio of 8:1. The extension to the DXT1 that allows for an alpha channel can give a compression ratio of 6:1.

The DXT2 format is similar to the DXT1 format, with the exception that the DXT2 format uses a 4-bit alpha that is multiplied before the compression so that more transparent pixels appear darker than opaque ones. The DXT3 format is similar to the DXT2 format, with the exception that the DXT2 format premuliplies the data by the alpha channel and the DXT3 does not. The DXT4 and DXT5 compression formats are similar to the DXT3 format, but the DXT4 alpha channel is premultiplied as it is with the DXT2 format, and the DXT5 format interpolates the alpha channel when compressing the original image data.

CREATING DXTC TEXTURES

Many tools can save textures that use DXTC-compressed formats. One tool, which was used for this book, is the NVIDIA DDS Photoshop® plug-in tool for Adobe® Photoshop CS2. A screenshot of the tool running in Photoshop is shown in Figure 14.13. This tool allows a normal map to be generated and saved.

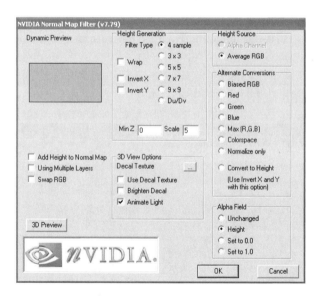

FIGURE 14.13 The NVIDIA DDS and Normal Map plug-ins.

Other tools include the texture tool that comes with the DirectX® SDK as well as numerous freeware and software applications that can be found on the Internet or as plug-ins to existing popular tools such as Photoshop.

3Dc COMPRESSION

The 3Dc texture compression, created by ATI, is a lossy compression format used for normal map images. The 3Dc texture compression offers a compression ratio of

4:1. With the 3Dc format a texture is broken up into 4 x 4 blocks of pixels of 16 values each. Each of these values has two components that are compressed separately. When compressing normal maps, this is good because the z-axis can be calculated and the x and y axes can be compressed and stored. A comparison of the 3Dc and DXT5 formats and an uncompressed normal map is shown in Figure 14.14.

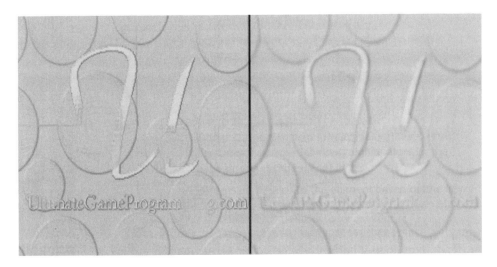

FIGURE 14.14   Comparison of 3Dc and DXT5.

Because the 3Dc works on two components, it can be used on normal maps but not on color maps. This is because there is no way to generate a blue component, whereas in the normal map a z-axis can be computed.

3Dc is the compression format of choice for normal map images, while DXT5 can be a good general choice for color maps (depending on the texture and the visual requirements). A free tool to create 3Dc texture images can be found on ATI's Web site and is called the ATI Compressonator.

A8L8 FORMAT

The format that will be discussed next is not a compression format as much as it is a format used for normal maps. A normal map can calculate the z-axis (or any axis for that matter, as long as two are already known). With the A8L8 format the texture data are represented just as they are for a normal texture, but minus the blue component (z-axis). The Direct3D and OpenGL graphics API allows for two component texture images to be created and used. Because of this, a file that uses only two components in this manner can be used directly in the API, and the missing component can be calculated in a pixel shader. Note that because the data in an A8L8 texture are not lossy compressed, the quality of the data remains unaffected.

IMPLEMENTING TEXTURE COMPRESSION

In this section an implementation of DXTC texture compression will be discussed. This implementation will use OpenGL as the rendering API and will also use the DDS (Direct-Draw Surface) image format. The DDS file format is a DirectX file format used for storing image information. Although the file format was first used in DirectX, it can be easily loaded and used outside of the Windows graphics API. When loading a DXTC-compressed image in OpenGL, the compressed contents can be loaded directly into the rending API so that the compressed information is used internally.

To load compressed textures in Direct3D, the 3D graphics API of DirectX, no special steps need to be taken. They can be loaded just like noncompressed textures when using the D3DX library because the file format is supported.

On the accompanying CD-ROM is a demo application called GL Texture Compression in the Chapter 14 folder that demonstrates using DXTC-compressed textures in OpenGL. The demo application uses GLUT so that there is no operating-specific code inside it, and it uses GLEE for the OpenGL extensions that will be used. If you are unfamiliar with OpenGL, GLUT, and GLEE, see Appendix C, OpenGL, for a quick review.

The GL Texture Compression demo's source code is split up into three files. The first file is the main source file, which has the application code. The other two files are a header and source file used for loading DDS images into memory. The information that will be read out of a DDS image is the image's width, height, compression type, number of color components (e.g., RGB, RGBA, etc.), number of mipmaps, and the compressed image data itself. A simple structure that will hold most of this information is called ImageInfoDDS in the demo's code. A function called to fill in this structure and return the compressed image data in the demo is called LoadDDS(). The LoadDDS() function returns the loaded image data upon success or NULL if it has failed. The function also takes as parameters the file that is to be loaded and the address to an ImageInfoDDS structure that will be filled in by this function. The entire DDSLoader.h header file from the GL Texture Compression demo application is shown in Listing 14.4.

LISTING 14.4 The DDSLoader.h Header File

```
enum DDS_COMPRESSION {DDS_NULL = 0, DDS_DXT1, DDS_DXT3, DDS_DXT5};


struct ImageInfoDDS
{
   ImageInfoDDS() : m_width(0), m_height(0), m_type(DDS_NULL),
                    m_components(0), m_numMipMaps(0)
   {

   }


   int m_width;
   int m_height;
   DDS_COMPRESSION m_type;
   int m_components;
   int m_numMipMaps;
};


unsigned char *LoadDDS(char *file, ImageInfoDDS &info);
```

The next file is the DDSLoader.cpp source file. DDS images store multibyte values. Saving a multibyte value such as an integer when using a little-endian processor (e.g., Pentium® processors) will store the information in a different byte order than that of a big-endian processor (e.g., PowerPC® processors). Because of this, there are portability issues when writing files that are going to be accessed in a cross-platform manner. This is related to endianess and affects not only data being saved to a disk but also data being transmitted across a network from a machine that uses one byte-order to a machine that uses a different byte-order. For example, a Windows XP desktop running a Pentium 4 processor has a different byte-order than a Mac PowerBook®. This is illustrated in Figure 14.15.

value = 0xAABB

Little Endian	Big Endian
43707	*48042*

FIGURE 14.15 Byte ordering.

Byte ordering can be in little-endian order, big-endian order, or middle-endian order.

This book is meant to be used by different platforms regardless of byte ordering. Luckily, handling the byte ordering of a value is straightforward. A simple test can be done to check the order of a multibyte variable by comparing it with what it would be if the application was running on a little-endian machine compared to a big-endian machine. This simple if/else statement is executed in a function called GetEndian(), which returns one of the enumeration values shown in Listing 14.4, which is located at the top of the DDSLoader.cpp source file. The DDS files are written in little-endian order. If the machine running the demo's code uses big-endian order, as the bytes are read from the file they are swapped around so that the machine can obtain the intended value. This swapping is done in a function called SwapBytes() that follows the GetEndian() function in the DDSLoader.cpp source file . The SwapBytes() function is another simple function that casts a variable to a character pointer and loops through the bytes, switching their order. The code used to handle the byte ordering is shown in Listing 14.5 along with a few macros that are used to determine what type of compression the DDS image uses. The MAKE4CC macro creates an unsigned long variable that can be tested with one read from the DDS image to see which one of the DXTC format types it uses.

There is no way to automatically determine a file's byte order. When creating a file format that stores multibyte values, it is important to pick a byte order and make it part of the file's structure standard. Anyone reading that file should know what byte order it uses so that it can be read correctly. Many popular file formats have their byte order in their documentation.

LISTING 14.5   First Section of the DDSLoader.cpp Source File

```
#include<stdio.h>
#include<string.h>
#include<assert.h>
#include"DDSLoader.h"


#ifndef MAKE4CC
    #define MAKE4CC(ch0, ch1, ch2, ch3)                    \
            ((unsigned long)(unsigned char)(ch0) |         \
            ((unsigned long)(unsigned char)(ch1) << 8) |   \
            ((unsigned long)(unsigned char)(ch2) << 16) |  \
            ((unsigned long)(unsigned char)(ch3) << 24 ))
    #endif
```

```
#define DS_FOURCC_DXT1   (MAKE4CC('D','X','T','1'))
#define DS_FOURCC_DXT2   (MAKE4CC('D','X','T','2'))
#define DS_FOURCC_DXT3   (MAKE4CC('D','X','T','3'))
#define DS_FOURCC_DXT4   (MAKE4CC('D','X','T','4'))
#define DS_FOURCC_DXT5   (MAKE4CC('D','X','T','5'))


enum ENDIAN { ENDIAN_UNKNOWN = 0, ENDIAN_LITTLE, ENDIAN_BIG };


ENDIAN GetEndian()
{
   unsigned long data = 0x12345678;
   unsigned char *ptr = (unsigned char*)&data;


   if(*ptr == 0x12 && *(ptr+1) == 0x34 &&
      *(ptr+2) == 0x56 && *(ptr+3) == 0x78)
   {
      return ENDIAN_BIG;
   }
   else if(*ptr == 0x78 && *(ptr + 1) == 0x56 &&
           *(ptr + 2) == 0x34 && *(ptr + 3) == 0x12)
   {
      return ENDIAN_LITTLE;
   }


   return ENDIAN_UNKNOWN;
}


void SwapBytes(char *data, int size)
{
   assert((size & 1) == 0);

   char *ptr = data;
   char temp = 0;


   for(int i = 0, j = size - 1; i < size / 2; i++, j--)
   {
      temp = ptr[i];
      ptr[i] = ptr[j];
```

```
                ptr[j] = temp;
        }
    }
}
```

The next part of the DDSLoader.cpp source file is the LoadDDS() function, which is designed to load DDS images that use DXTC compression formats 1, 3, and 5. The steps to reading the file are as follows:

1. Read the file ID (first four bytes) and see if the character data is "DDS."
2. Move the file pointer to the image resolution and read the height and width.
3. Read the size of the data followed by the number of mipmaps.
4. Read the compression type.
5. Read the compressed image data.

The LoadDDS() function starts by determining the byte order of the machine running the application code. If the byte order is not little, the following code will swap the bytes of any multibyte variable it reads. After the endian order has been determined, the function opens the file, reads the first four bytes, and tests to see if it equals "DDS," which is the file ID for a DDS file.

The next step in the function is to read the width and height resolutions, which are the dimensions of the image. Then the function will read the size of the data, the number of mipmaps, and the type of compression the image uses. This type is tested against the macros in Listing 14.5. The last bit of information read from the DDS image file is the compressed image data itself. These image data are returned to the caller and use dynamic memory allocation. When calling this function, it is important to delete the allocated memory. The entire code for the LoadDDS() function is shown in Listing 14.16.

LISTING 14.6 The LoadDDS() Function

```
unsigned char *LoadDDS(char *file, ImageInfoDDS &info)
{
    const int ddsHeightOffset = 12;
    const int ddsWidthOffset = 16;
    const int ddsLinearSizeOffset = 20;
    const int ddsMipMapNumOffset = 28;
    const int ddsFourCCOffset = 84;
    const int ddsImageDataOffset = 128;


    ENDIAN e = GetEndian();
    bool byteSwap = false;
```

```
if(e == ENDIAN_BIG)
   byteSwap = true;


FILE *fp = fopen(file, "rb");

if(fp == NULL)
   return NULL;


char imageID[4];
fread(imageID, 1, 4, fp);

if(strncmp(imageID, "DDS ", 4) != 0)
{
   fclose(fp);
   return false;
}


unsigned int dwHeight = 0, dwWidth = 0,
             dwLinearSize, dwMipMaps = 0,
             dwFourCC = 0;

fseek(fp, ddsHeightOffset, SEEK_SET);
fread(&dwHeight, sizeof(unsigned int), 1, fp);

if(byteSwap == true)
   SwapBytes((char*)&dwHeight, sizeof(unsigned int));

fseek(fp, ddsWidthOffset, SEEK_SET);
fread(&dwWidth, sizeof(unsigned int), 1, fp);

if(byteSwap == true)
   SwapBytes((char*)&dwWidth, sizeof(unsigned int));

fseek(fp, ddsLinearSizeOffset, SEEK_SET);
fread(&dwLinearSize, sizeof(unsigned int), 1, fp);

if(byteSwap == true)
   SwapBytes((char*)&dwLinearSize, sizeof(unsigned int));

fseek(fp, ddsMipMapNumOffset, SEEK_SET);
fread(&dwMipMaps, sizeof(unsigned int), 1, fp);

if(byteSwap == true)
   SwapBytes((char*)&dwMipMaps, sizeof(unsigned int));
```

```
fseek(fp, ddsFourCCOffset, SEEK_SET);
fread(&dwFourCC, sizeof(unsigned int), 1, fp);

if(byteSwap == true)
   SwapBytes((char*)&dwFourCC, sizeof(unsigned int));

if(dwLinearSize == 0)
   dwLinearSize = dwHeight * dwWidth;

if(dwLinearSize <= 0)
{
   fclose(fp);
   return NULL;
}

info.m_numMipMaps = dwMipMaps;
info.m_width = dwWidth;
info.m_height = dwHeight;


int mipFactor = 0;

switch(dwFourCC)
{
   case DS_FOURCC_DXT1:
      mipFactor = 2;
      info.m_components = 3;
      info.m_type = DDS_DXT1;
      break;

   case DS_FOURCC_DXT3:
      mipFactor = 4;
      info.m_components = 4;
      info.m_type = DDS_DXT3;
      break;

   case DS_FOURCC_DXT5:
      mipFactor = 4;
      info.m_components = 4;
      info.m_type = DDS_DXT5;
      break;

   default:
      fclose(fp);
      return NULL;
```

```
            break;
    }


    int totalSize = 0;

    // Take into account multiple mip maps.
    if(dwMipMaps > 1)
        totalSize = dwLinearSize * mipFactor;
    else
        totalSize = dwLinearSize;

    unsigned char *image = NULL;

    image = new unsigned char[totalSize * sizeof(unsigned char)];

    if(image != NULL)
    {
        fseek(fp, ddsImageDataOffset, SEEK_SET);
        fread(image, 1, totalSize, fp);
    }

    fclose(fp);

    return image;
}
```

The last file in the demo application is the main source file main.cpp. The demo application uses the GLUT utility for OpenGL. Appendix C, OpenGL, has more information on both and this chapter assumes at least some knowledge of the OpenGL rendering API. Listing 14.7 lists the beginning section of the GL Texture Compression demo application starting with the main() function. The texture object is a global called g_texture.

LISTING 14.7   The Headers, Function Prototypes, and main() Function

```
#include<gl/glee.h>
#include<gl/glut.h>
#include<stdio.h>
#include"DDSLoader.h"


void RenderScene();
void KeyDown(unsigned char key, int x, int y);
void Resize(int width, int height);
```

```
bool InitializeApp();
void ShutdownApp();


// DDS Texture.
GLuint g_texture;


int main(int arg, char **argc)
{
   glutInitWindowSize(640, 480);
   glutInitWindowPosition(100, 100);
   glutInitDisplayMode(GLUT_RGB | GLUT_DOUBLE | GLUT_DEPTH);
   glutInit(&arg, argc);


   glutCreateWindow("Texture Compression");


   glutDisplayFunc(RenderScene);
   glutReshapeFunc(Resize);
   glutKeyboardFunc(KeyDown);


   if(InitializeApp() == true)
      glutMainLoop();
   else
      printf("Error in InitializeApp()!\n\n");


   ShutdownApp();

   return 1;
}
```

The next three functions in the main source file are Resize(), KeyDown(), and ShutdownApp(). The Resize() function is used to set up perspective projection and is called whenever the window is resized. The KeyDown() function is called whenever a key is pressed. This function only tests to see if the escape key is pressed, which has the code of 27. The ShutdownApp() function is used to delete the OpenGL texture object by calling glDeleteTextures(). In OpenGL textures are automatically deleted, so this is not really necessary for the end of the application, but it is a good habit. The Resize(), KeyDown(), and Shutdown() functions are shown listed in Listing 14.8.

LISTING 14.8   The Function Used to Resize the Window, Detect Input, and Shut Down the Application

```
void Resize(int width, int height)
{
   glViewport(0, 0, width, height);
   glMatrixMode(GL_PROJECTION);

   gluPerspective(45, width/height, 0.1, 200.0);
   glMatrixMode(GL_MODELVIEW);
}


void KeyDown(unsigned char key, int x, int y)
{
   switch(key)
   {
      case 27:
         exit(0);
         break;
   }
}


void ShutdownApp()
{
   glDeleteTextures(1, &g_texture);
}
```

The next function is `InitializeApp()`. This function starts off by setting up the OpenGL rendering states. It then loads the DDS texture image by calling `LoadDDS()`. As long as the returned memory is not `NULL`, the texture was loaded. The next step is to set the data up in OpenGL. When sending compressed texture data to OpenGL, we use the function `glCompressTexImage2DARB()`, which is part of the `ARB_texture_comperssion` extension. When loading compressed texture data, each mipmap of the image is loaded, which is done by the for-loop. Once this is done, the memory that was allocated for the compressed texture data is freed and the function returns. The `InitializeApp()` function is shown in Listing 14.9.

LISTING 14.9   The Initialization Function

```
bool InitializeApp()
{
   glClearColor(0.0f, 0.0f, 0.0f, 1.0f);
```

```
glShadeModel(GL_SMOOTH);
glEnable(GL_DEPTH_TEST);
glEnable(GL_TEXTURE_2D);


// Load DDS image.
ImageInfoDDS info;
unsigned char *image = LoadDDS("../image.dds", info);

if(image == NULL)
   return false;


glGenTextures(1, &g_texture);
glBindTexture(GL_TEXTURE_2D, g_texture);


int w = info.m_width;
int h = info.m_height;
int mipFactor = 0;

if(info.m_type == DDS_DXT1)
   mipFactor = 8;
else
   mipFactor = 16;

int mipSize;
int mipOffset = 0;

int type = 0;

switch(info.m_type)
{
   case DDS_DXT1:
      type = GL_COMPRESSED_RGBA_S3TC_DXT1_EXT;
      break;

   case DDS_DXT3:
      type = GL_COMPRESSED_RGBA_S3TC_DXT3_EXT;
      break;

   case DDS_DXT5:
      type = GL_COMPRESSED_RGBA_S3TC_DXT5_EXT;
      break;
}
```

```
for(int i = 0; i < info.m_numMipMaps; i++)
{
   mipSize = ((w + 3) / 4) * ((h + 3) / 4) * mipFactor;

   glTexParameteri(GL_TEXTURE_2D, GL_TEXTURE_MIN_FILTER,
                   GL_LINEAR);
  glTexParameteri(GL_TEXTURE_2D, GL_TEXTURE_MAG_FILTER,
                  GL_LINEAR);


   glCompressedTexImage2DARB(GL_TEXTURE_2D, i, type, w, h,
                             0, mipSize, image + mipOffset);

   // Half the image size for the next mip-map level...
   w >>= 1;
   h >>= 1;

   // Move the offset to the next mip map.
   mipOffset += mipSize;
}

delete[] image;

return true;
}
```

The last function in the GL Texture Compression demo application is the rendering function, a straightforward function that renders a textured square to the screen. Using texture objects that represent compressed textures is no different than using noncompressed ones. The rendering function from the GL Texture Compression demo application is shown in Listing 14.10. Figure 14.16 shows a screenshot of the running application.

LISTING 14.10   The Rendering Function of the GL Texture Compression Demo

```
void RenderScene()
{
   glClear(GL_COLOR_BUFFER_BIT | GL_DEPTH_BUFFER_BIT);
   glLoadIdentity();

   glTranslatef(0.0f, 0.0f, -3.0f);

   glBindTexture(GL_TEXTURE_2D, g_texture);
```

```
glBegin(GL_QUADS);

    glTexCoord2f(0, 0);  glVertex3f(-1, -1, 0);
    glTexCoord2f(1, 0);  glVertex3f( 1, -1, 0);
    glTexCoord2f(1, 1);  glVertex3f( 1,  1, 0);
    glTexCoord2f(0, 1);  glVertex3f(-1,  1, 0);

glEnd();

glutSwapBuffers();
glutPostRedisplay();
}
```

FIGURE 14.16   A screenshot of the Texture Compression demo.

INTRODUCTION TO DATA ENCRYPTION

Another topic that is important to software development is encryption. Information has become an important part of the age we live in. Information on everything and anything can be shared by billions through media like the Internet, and the need to protect this information is very important. Not only is this needed to protect sensitive data such as credit card numbers, but in video games data sometimes needs protecting from malicious users who intend to cheat or disrupt a network.

Cryptography is the process of scrambling data into a form that is unreadable without some special way to translate the information. In cryptography a cipher is used to perform encryption and decryption. A cipher is an algorithm that is performed on the data. These algorithms often depend on a key that the algorithm uses to transform the data. This key is like a password, and without it the encrypted message can not be decrypted, or at least it would be very difficult. The different kinds of ciphers include stream ciphers and block ciphers. The different kinds of keys include asymmetric and symmetric keys. A symmetric key is a key that is used for both the encryption and the decryption, while an asymmetric key is used in conjunction with other keys to encrypt or decrypt.

The data that are encrypted are known as ciphertext.

Cryptography is a huge and complex field of study that grows more complex as time moves on. For those interested in encryption, various resources in Appendix A, Additional Resources, might prove helpful.

SUMMARY

The compression and encryption of data can be very useful for many different types of applications. Compression can be used to reduce the size of a file on a storage device. In video games compression can also be used on texture images, which can allow for an increased number of textures and an increase in texture resolution and can benefit a game's performance. Knowing what compression algorithm to use for the different types of texture data is important for retaining a certain level of quality in the rendered scenes.

Encryption is necessary in the information age in which we live. The purpose of encryption is to make it as hard as possible for individuals to gain access to information that they do not have permission to access. Although encryption is a complex topic that can span an entire book on its own, it is a subject that is definitely worth researching if an application must work with or transmit sensitive information.

CHAPTER REVIEW QUESTIONS

Answers to the following chapter review questions can be found in Appendix B.

1. What is the purpose of compression?
2. What is the purpose of encryption?
3. What is lossy compression?

4. What is lossless compression?
5. The JPEG image format uses what kind of compression?
   a. Lossless
   b. Lossy
   c. DXTC
   d. None of the above
6. What is run-length encoding?
7. What kind of compression do the DXTC formats use?
8. What kind of compression does the 3Dc format use?
9. Which of the following is a type of DXTC format?
   a. DXT1
   b. 3Dc
   c. DXT6
   d. DXT3
   e. Both A and D
   f. None of the above
10. Why is 3Dc preferable to DXTC formats even though they both are lossy compression formats?
11. What is encryption?
12. What is cryptography?
13. What is a symmetric key used for in encryption?
    a. Encryption
    b. Opening a password protected file
    c. Decryption
    d. Both A and C
    e. None of the above
14. What is another name for an encryption-decryption algorithm?
    a. Cryptography
    b. Cryptanalysis
    c. Cipher
    d. None of the above
15. What is another name for encrypted data?
    a. Encryption
    b. Ciphertext
    c. Key
    d. None of the above

PROGRAMMING PROJECTS

Exercise 1: Modify the Run Length Encoding demo application to allow the character used as the marker to exist in the original data.

Exercise 2: Modify the Run Length Encoding demo application to be a template class that allows a programmer to specify the character marker and the data type of each value being encoded. This should allow someone to encode an array of integers, pixels, and so forth.

Exercise 3: Implement the Huffman compression algorithm as described in this chapter.

15 Conclusions

In This Chapter

- Quick Review
- The Next Step

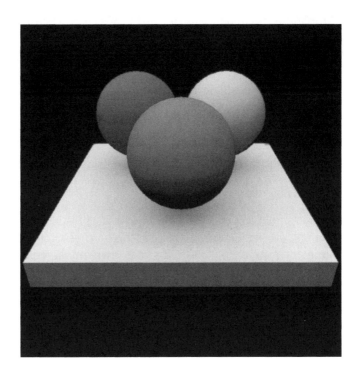

Many data structures and algorithms exist in computer science and game development. The foundation of all application programming lies in the use of these structures and the efficiency of the algorithms that operate on them. All meaningful applications have some kind of data structure and algorithm within their code, and a general understanding of them and of specific topics can go a long way toward creating professional applications. Data structures and their algorithms come up often in programming, and this is a topic that every serious programmer should tackle to some degree. Also, common data structures and algorithms can solve complex programming problems.

The purpose of this book was to introduce the topic of data structures and algorithms to readers as well as to serve as a reference for the many topics discussed within this book. In this chapter we will take a brief look at what was covered in this book and what steps those looking to expand their knowledge should take.

QUICK REVIEW

Throughout this book we looked at various data structures and algorithms that are used in general computer programming and in game and simulation development. These data structures include arrays, link lists, queues, hash tables, stacks, trees, graphs, scene graphs, space partitioning trees, and various standard and nonstandard data structures. The algorithms discussed include various sorting and searching methods, insertions and removals, recursion, space partitioning, compression, encryption, and culling. Although this book covered a lot of information, much remains to learn about data structures, algorithms, and optimizations and their uses in application development, especially game and simulation development.

STANDARD DATA STRUCTURES

The data structures and algorithms discussed in this book include the data structures and algorithms from the C++ STL. Using a standard set of code frees programmers from having to develop their own implementations. This not only saves developers time but also saves them from having to test, debug, and correct bugs that might result from a custom implementation. Among the several advantages and disadvantages to using a standard library for both data structures and algorithms include:

- They provide proven and tested code.
- They are portable.
- They allow programmers to use a standard set of code instead of having to develop and test their own implementations.

- They are maintained by professionals.
- They are coded with performance in mind.
- They are documented in great detail.
- They save development time.
- They do not offer all data structures and algorithms that commonly arise in application development (e.g., hash tables).
- Some optimizations might not be beneficial or acceptable in all types of applications (e.g., some `string` implementations use reference counting, which can cause problems when passing strings around).

NONSTANDARD DATA STRUCTURES

The standard library is a very useful tool for developers, but it does not offer every type of data structure and algorithm that has common use in application development. Many nonstandard data structures, algorithms, and extensions to the standard library can prove just as useful. This code, although useful and written in C++, is not always going to be as portable as standard implementations. A few things to note about the advantages and disadvantages of nonstandard data structures and algorithms include:

- They have efficient code.
- They are tested and maintained by professionals.
- Some libraries, such as the ones provided by Boost, are peer reviewed.
- They give programmers the ability to use containers and algorithms that are not available through the C++ standard library.
- Programmers can avoid having to develop and test their own implementations.
- They offer many data structures and algorithms outside of the standard.
- They are not standardized.
- Different providers can have slightly different implementations with some class containers.

Many resources offer STL-related code, documentation, and nonstandard libraries. Three highly recommended websites include the SGI STL site (*http://www.sgi.com/tech/stl*), the STLport site (*http://www.stlport.org*), and the Boost site (*http://www.boost.org*). Each of these websites offers nonstandard libraries that are filled with free data structures, function objects, adapters, and algorithms. The SGI STL websites also offers comprehensive STL-related documentation, which is always a valuable resource for developers. In this book we looked at implementing nonstandard hash containers using STLport in Chapter 7, Hash Tables.

DATA STRUCTURES FOR SCENE MANAGEMENT

In Chapter 13, Scene Management, we discussed many game- and simulation-related uses for data structures. Data structures have always played a vital role in video games. When 3D games started to become popular, the complexity and creative use of data structures and algorithms allowed some advanced and legendary games to be created. The scenes in the average three-dimensional video game are far too complex to process without using advanced data structures and algorithms to feed scene data to the hardware. As hardware becomes more advanced, so does the scene complexity in cutting-edge video games.

Many data structures and algorithms can be used for managing scene data. Some of those discussed in this book are scene graphs, quad-trees, binary space partitioning trees, octrees, kd-trees, potential visibility sets, portals, and sections. Other data structures and algorithms that are used for processing scene information include:

- Resource managers
- Sphere trees
- ROAM algorithm for terrains
- CLOD (continuous level of detail)
- Skeleton hierarchy for animations
- Global illumination algorithms for lights and shadows

DATA STRUCTURES FOR GAME PHYSICS

Game physics is becoming more and more popular and offers game developers the ability to simulate interactions between virtual objects and their environments in a more realistic manner. Many games on the market make heavy use of physics, and the feature is starting to become a standard for many three-dimensional games that thrive on realism. In game physics the three main types of objects are the following:

- Point masses
- Rigid bodies
- Soft bodies

Point masses are the simplest of the three major types and normally consist of particles. Particles and particle systems can add many effects to a three-dimensional scene including sparks, smoke, fire, snow, rain, dust, smoke trails, and debris. Particles in games are normally rendered as small textured squares that face the camera and are alpha-blended. The data structure in the case of a point mass stores physical properties such as velocity, position, and size and are normally kept in an array. The particle system is usually an object that applies various algorithms on the point mass objects such as applying forces such gravity and so forth. In a full-blown physics system the physics system itself applies the physics while the particle system and its particles supply properties that control the simulation.

Rigid bodies are used to represent the translation and rotation of objects in a virtual world. Rigid bodies are more complex to implement than point masses since point masses take into account only the translation and not the angular velocity. Rigid bodies can be used for character models, crates, boxes, weapons, destructible environments, and so forth. They are often represented similarly to point masses but with many more properties. These properties include orientation, bounding volumes, inertia, and tensors.

Soft bodies are becoming more popular. Soft bodies are bodies that can have their shapes changed, while rigid bodies remain unchanged. A soft body could be a piece of cloth or a cape in a game. In the *Splinter Cell*™ series from Ubisoft™ cloth is used in many game levels as curtains that the players can hide behind and move through realistically. Soft bodies are represented by point masses and springs. Springs are used to connect and deform the point masses, which affects the vertices attached to those masses, to create the soft body effect. Although point masses by themselves do not have an orientation, soft bodies do, because the springs that connect point masses create a three-dimensional grid. Moving one point mass affects the ones attached to it and changes the physical appearance of the mesh.

DATA STRUCTURES FOR ARTIFICIAL INTELLIGENCE

Artificial intelligence is an important area of study because it brings the games to life. When it comes to artificial intelligence, it doesn't take much to make a virtual character appear intelligent when there is no user interaction, but if you add interaction from the player and from other characters, the artificial intelligence in a game can make or break the experience.

In Chapter 11, Graphs, we discussed how a weighted graph can be used for path finding. Many popular and well-known algorithms for path finding use graphs. One such algorithm, which is among the most popular, is the A* algorithm. The speed at which these algorithms execute is very important in games because the many areas of a game are already demanding on their own (e.g., the physics system, the rendering system, etc.).

DATA STRUCTURE GAME SCRIPTING

Scripting in games is not new to the industry, and it has many different uses in video games. These uses include:

- Altering game properties without recompiling and redistributing any executables
- Defining game objects and items like those used in a massively multiplayer online roleplaying game.

- Driving artificial intelligence
- Allowing gamers to modify or extend their games
- Defining entire environments

Game scripting that uses compiled binaries requires a compiler and a virtual machine. The compiler is used to parse a text file containing the code and transform it into a form that is faster and easier for applications to read, which isn't necessarily simple but sounds more complicated than it generally is. A virtual machine is a data structure that resides in an application and is responsible for reading and executing a compiled script. Java is a famous language that uses a virtual machine. By creating a virtual machine for every supported platform, the same code can be executed on all of them, thus achieving platform independence. Breaking a source file down into a simpler form will allow the virtual machine to quickly open the data and work on it without the slow string parsing and so on that would otherwise be needed.

THE IMPORTANCE OF OPTIMIZATIONS

In video games speed is everything, and it is commonplace to sacrifice realism for the sake of speed. Real-time applications that are media intensive often require quite a bit of speed to keep the experience interactive. All data structures and algorithms can benefit from optimizations under these general conditions:

- The code being optimized is a serious source of a bottleneck (i.e., is among the biggest causes of slow performance); optimizing code that is a minor source first can waste time and resources.
- Optimizations can be based on the hardware's architecture.
- Optimizations should be done in the later cycles of development rather than at the start to avoid spending unnecessary time on code that does not need optimization.
- Some optimizations might require sacrificing memory for speed, speed for memory, or realism for both, and the choice should be appropriate for the application in question.
- If an application has bad performance, several things can be done to make major improvements without having to rewrite or reengineer code modules.

THE NEXT STEP

This book mentioned many advanced data structures and algorithms that can prove beneficial to implement in an application. After reading this book, readers should have the knowledge necessary to tackle more advanced topics as well as optimizations. Game development is a huge field, so the learning does not stop here at the end of this book.

Game engines also make heavy use of data structures and algorithms in their frameworks. The uses an engine can have include:

- Automatic and manual memory management
- Resource management
- Scheduling services
- Journaling services
- Scene management utilities
- Physics systems
- Networking systems
- Scripting systems
- Sound processing
- Data streaming utilities

ADDITIONAL RESOURCES

Appendix A, Additional Resources, lists several resources that might prove useful for learning more advanced data structures and algorithms and applying them to games and game engines. These resources include books and Internet resources, one of which is *www.UltimateGameProgramming.com*, where there is a large and detailed list of resources that span all areas of game development as well as data structures and algorithms.

SUMMARY

This book served as an introduction to a very important, complex, and large field of study. Video games thrive off of data structures, algorithms, and the speed at which they can perform their duties. Developing solid data structures and algorithms that can be reused and flexible for many types of projects can prove very beneficial in the long run. As seen with the C++ STL, having solid, reusable, and proven code can make application development a faster process. Although standard and nonstandard libraries make the need to develop custom implementations less important for some data structures and algorithms, there are still many cases when code must be created to solve a problem. As seen throughout this book, many data structures are application specific.

Appendix

A | Additional Resources

In This Appendix:

- Recommended books
- Recommended websites

This appendix lists recommended books and websites that you can explore for more advanced information dealing with various subjects. Additional resources that might be of some use beyond those listed here can be found at *www.UltimateGameProgramming.com*.

RECOMMENDED BOOKS

Ultimate Game Engine Design and Architecture (Charles River Media) is my second book published by Charles River Media. This book deals with designing and building a platform-independent game engine and is targeted at more advanced audiences. The information gained from this book can be combined with the engine book to take you to the next level.

Ultimate Game Programming with DirectX (Charles River Media) is my first book that dealt with learning DirectX using C++ for beginner hobbyist and student programmers. At the end of this book a very simple first-person shooter game was put together. The majority of the book's content focused on learning DirectX and the tools that make up Microsoft's suite.

Memory Management: Algorithms and Implementation in C++ (Wordare Publishing) discusses the ins and outs of writing a memory management system in C++. This book includes information on performance, garbage collection, and so forth. This book can be useful for anyone wanted to go deeper into the subject or implement their own system.

The *Game Programming Gems* (Charles River Media) series is a long-running series of books written by game developers for game developers. These books are targeted to an advanced audience and are not suited for beginners, but they are valuable for anyone looking to get into game development and can be a great asset. This series can be a valuable resource for many years to come.

AI for Game Developers (O'Reilly Media) is an artificial intelligence book aimed at the game development community. This inexpensive and lightweight book is a great resource for anyone who wants to get into artificial intelligence programming in video games.

Physics for Game Developers (O'Reilly Media) is another lightweight book aimed at game developers. This book deals with physics, mathematics, and programming and is a great resource for getting into the topic. Physics is not an easy subject, and a book aimed at game developers is very useful.

Game Scripting Mastery (Course Technology) deals with scripting in video games. The author takes readers from the basics to advanced topics dealing with creating a scripting language from scratch. The book shows how to implement an assembler, virtual machine, high-level compiler, and custom high and low programming languages.

Head First Design Patterns (O'Reilly Media) is one of my favorite books on design patterns. The book is easy to read and fun. Design patterns are very important in professional software development and are something that everyone can find some value in.

RECOMMENDED WEBSITES

http://www.UltimateGameProgramming.com: This is a general game programming site that focuses on areas such as graphics with OpenGL, Direct3D, ray tracing, input, sound, and much more. There is a community at the website that anyone can access for game development help, news, and other such information.

http://www.sgi.com/tech/stl: The SGI STL website has documentation on the C++ STL as well as downloads of all STL containers, function objects, algorithms, and so forth.

http://www.stlport.org: The STLport has C++ containers, algorithms, and other objects that expand upon SGI's STL implementations including many non-standard objects.

http://www.boost.org: The Boost website has peer-reviewed C++ data structures and algorithms available for download.

http://www.OpenGL.org: OpenGL is the rendering system used in this book for the graphics aspects of the some of the later demos. The OpenGL website has a lot of information on the API and can be a valuable resource for anyone using it for graphics. The website also has a community that can be used to gain additional information on the various aspects of OpenGL.

http://www.opengl.org/resources/libraries/glut/glut_downloads.php: The GLUT (OpenGL Utility Toolkit) is a useful tool for creating cross-platform OpenGL windows.

http://elf-stone.com/glee.php: The GLee (GL Easy Extension Library) is a cross-platform extension loading library that can be used for OpenGL applications. This library makes loading and using extensions effortless, which is a plus for Windows and Linux users.

http://MSDN.Microsoft.com: The Microsoft Developer Network (MSDN) is a great place to visit if you need documentation on a well-known API, language. Not only can you get DirectX documentation here, but you can also get OpenGL, C/C++, Visual Basic, and many others.

Chapter Review Question Answers

CHAPTER 1

1. c. Memory
2. An algorithm is code that is executed on a data structure to produce some meaningful result.
3. e. Both B and C
4. b. Standard Template Library
5. c. List, vector, queue
6. a. True
7. a. True
8. b. False
9. a. True
10. b. False

CHAPTER 2

1. c. Standard STL sequence container
2. c. When no pointers are pointing to a memory location and can't release the resource
3. a. O(N)
4. c. O(log N)
5. To specify the size of the container's total number of elements.
6. An iterator is used to point to an element in a container. They can also be used to move throughout the container's other elements. There are input, container, and output iterators.
7. a. True
8. b. False
9. a. True, but it is simulated using bit operators.
10. b. False

CHAPTER 3

1. Recursion is a self-referencing function that is often executed in a controlled manner.
2. With tail recursion that is a type of recursive definition that calls itself at the end of the function where no statements follow it and no recursive statements come before it. Nontail recursion is a method that defines statements after the recursive call and/or if there is more than one recursive call in the same body.
3. A triangular number is a number defined by taking the nth term and adding it to the previous result. They are called triangular numbers based on their visual representation, which often looks triangular.
4. c. 28
5. Factorials multiply terms, while triangular numbers use addition.
6. a. 5040
7. b. False
8. a. True
9. a. True
10. b. False

CHAPTER 4

1. c. $O(N^2)$
2. b. $O(N^2)$
3. a. $O(N)$
4. a. $O(N^2)$
5. d. $O(N * \log N)$
6. b. Quicksort
7. d. Intro-sort
8. e. Merge-sort
9. To set how the container does its comparisons for its internal sorting.
10. The selection-sort, mainly because not as many swaps are being performed.
11. a. True
12. a. True
13. b. False
14. a. True
15. a. True

CHAPTER 5

1. (1) Fast deletions, (2) fast growth, (3) fast to sort
2. Link lists where elements can be inserted and removed from both ends of the container.
3. Link lists with nodes that can traverse in both directions.
4. b. Doubly linked-list
5. To access other elements in the container.
6. Because the algorithm functions that exist outside of the class do not know the container implementation details, unlike the class's algorithm member functions.
7. b. False
8. b. False
9. b. False
10. a. True

CHAPTER 6

1. c. Restricted-access adapters
2. b. First-in, last-out
3. a. First-in, first-out
4. b. Only one item
5. To sort elements based on their priority.
6. One uses first-in, first-out, while the other uses first-in, last-out.
7. Because link lists can grow and shrink more efficiently.
8. b. False
9. b. False
10. b. False

CHAPTER 7

1. The ratio of the number of objects in the hash table and the table's maximum size.
2. In open addressing when a collision occurs, a new array position is sought out. The three types are linear and quadric probing and double hashing.
3. Separate chaining stores more than one object at a hashed index by using an array of containers for the hash table.
4. Upon collision, linear probing will look for a new index position linearly (one at a time) until it finds a valid index.

5. Upon collision, quadric probing will look for a new index position using a varying step size until it finds a valid index.

6. Upon collision, double hashing will rehash the key using a different hash function.

7. a. Primary clustering

8. b. Secondary clustering

9. It will ensure that all elements are eventually checked when working with open addressing.

10. Robin-hood hashing is a variation of double hashing and is where a key is displaced by an already existing key if the probe count is larger than the key at a position. In perfect hashing a hash table with no collisions can be created if all the keys are known ahead of time and the array size is already known.

11. b. False

12. b. False

13. b. False

14. a. True

15. a. True

CHAPTER 8

1. Donald Shell

2. c. Insertion sort

3. b. Gap sequence

4. The insertion sort requires many more copies and comparisons than the Shellsort.

5. e. O(N * (log N)²)

6. a. 364

7. It is an algorithm that splits a container into two halves based on a condition.

8. c. O(N²)

9. The pivot value is the value used to specify how the two sections should be partitioned. Usually the first section is less than the pivot value, while the second section is greater than or equal to it.

10. The pivot index is the index in the partitioned array that marks where the first section ends and the second section begins.

11. d. Quicksort

12. c. O(N * log N)

13. The median-of-three is when the median of the values in three indexes is used as the pivot value.

14. b. False
15. b. False
16. The radix-sort is a sorting algorithm that uses containers and simple operators to perform the sorting without any comparisons taking place.
17. c. O(N * log N)
18. The bit radix uses two containers because a binary bit is either a 0 or a 1.
19. b. False
20. b. False

CHAPTER 9

1. A tree is a data structure that is made up of a root node that has a series of connected nodes attached to it.
2. A root node is the first node that starts a tree and has no parent.
3. c. Leaf node
4. a. Sibling node
5. An edge is a connection between two nodes. An example of this in C++ is using pointers.
6. b. 2
7. a. 1
8. c. 20
9. a. In-order, pre-order, post-order
10. d. In-order successor
11. *kd*-trees have keys that have multiple dimensions. The algorithms (for example, insertion) depend on the keys and their dimensions.
12. b. Depth level, key dimension, and key value
13. b. Trees are multiway trees. Examples of b-trees are the 2-3 and 2-3-4 trees.
14. The 2-3 tree has up to three nodes, and a 2-3-4 tree has up to four.
15. AVL trees are self-balancing binary trees.
16. b. False
17. b. False
18. a. True
19. a. True
20. b. False

CHAPTER 10

1. ADT stands for abstract data type.
2. a. Weakly ordered

3. b. Abstract data type
4. b. O(log N)
5. d. O(N)
6. b. O(log N)
7. c. O(N * log N)
8. e. Both C and D
9. a. Balanced
10. b. False
11. b. False
12. b. False
13. b. False
14. b. False
15. b. False (binary trees are not required to be complete)

CHAPTER 11

1. A graph is a data structure made up of nodes, called vertices, which are connected by edges.
2. A tree is a regular graph with no cycles.
3. A connected graph is one in which all vertices can reach all other vertices either directly or indirectly. In a nonconnected graph there is one or more vertices that can't be reached by other vertices.
4. A directed edge goes in one direction, while a nondirected edge goes in both directions.
5. In weighted graphs the edges have a property called a weight, which affects the algorithms performed on the data structure.
6. b. Travels all possible paths from a vertex to see if it can find the destination before it moves on to the adjacent vertices
7. c. Checks all adjacent vertices before moving down the paths to find the destination
8. a. Searches for the minimal edges needed to visit each vertex in the graph
9. d. Displays the order of the vertices from a starting vertex to the last vertex
10. The MST of a weighted graph takes into consideration the weights of the vertices.
11. b. A path-finding algorithm
12. e. Weighted graph
13. b. False
14. b. False
15. b. False
16. b. False

17. a. True
18. a. True
19. b. False
20. a. True

CHAPTER 12

1. c. Sequence container
2. b. `basic_string`
3. The `set` container contains a data value that is also used as a unique sorting key in its elements.
4. The `multiset` container contains a data value that is also used as a sorting key (does not need to be unique) in its elements.
5. The `set` requires unique keys, and the `mutliset` does not require unique keys.
6. The `map` container contains a data value and a unique sorting key pair in its elements.
7. The `multimap` container contains a data value and a sorting key (does not need to be unique) pair in its elements.
8. A `map` uses unique keys, while a `multimap` can use keys multiple times.
9. A `set` uses a key as the object, while the `map` uses a key-object pair.
10. b. False
11. a. True
12. a. True
13. a. True
14. b. False
15. b. False

CHAPTER 13

1. Managing the rendering states in a game or simulation in an effort to increase performance.
2. A texture atlas is a texture with smaller subtextures within it.
3. Managing states deals with managing the changes in rendering states, while resource management manages the physical data that is loaded and saved to and from storage.
4. c. A unit-length vector
5. Culling (rejecting) geometric objects that are outside of the camera's view.
6. A graph that represents the relationship between objects in a virtual environment.

7. a. Graph
8. It is used to cull out (reject) geometry that is occluded by other pieces of geometry.
9. An octree splits along the x, y, and z axes, while the quad-tree splits against the x and y axes.
10. c. Axis-aligned boxes
11. a. Multiway
12. It is a binary tree that is used to partition a geometric entity into sections.
13. c. Front/back
14. They are a node's list of other nodes that are potentially visible from it.
15. b. False
16. b. False
17. b. False (the octree splits on all three axes and the quad-tree on two)
18. b. False
19. a. True
20. a. True

CHAPTER 14

1. To reduce the size of data so that it is smaller than its original.
2. To add a layer of protection to data to keep unauthorized individuals from accessing its contents.
3. Lossy compression is compression that sacrifices quality for data size.
4. Lossless compression is compression that suffers from no quality loss from the original.
5. b. Lossy
6. Run-length encoding is encoding the runs in a data sequence in an effort to save space on redundant information.
7. DXTC formats use lossy compression.
8. 3Dc uses lossy compression.
9. d. Both A and D
10. 3Dc is designed for compressing normal maps. The quality loss from DXTC formats can make using them with normal maps visually unacceptable.
11. Encryption is converting data from one from to another form that is often much harder to read and to process without special knowledge.
12. A field of study dealing with encryption and decryption.
13. d. Both A and C
14. c. Cipher
15. b. Ciphertext

Appendix

C OpenGL

In This Appendix:

- Latest version of OpenGL
- GLUT
- GLEE

In this appendix we will discuss OpenGL and some of the tools used throughout this book. Two of the tools are the OpenGL Utility Toolkit (GLUT) and the OpenGL Easy Extension (GLEE). In this book it is assumed that you already have some previous experience with and knowledge of the OpenGL graphics API.

LATEST VERSION OF OPENGL

The latest version of OpenGL can be obtained by installing the latest drivers for your video graphics hardware. These drivers can be downloaded from the manufacturer's Web site for the operating system and platform you are using.

New functionality of OpenGL is exposed through extensions. Extensions in Windows and Linux must be loaded during runtime, which is platform specific. In the following section we will discuss a way to easily load and work with extensions in a portable manner.

OPENGL EASY EXTENSION

GLEE is used to make loading extensions easy across multiple platforms. New features of OpenGL are exposed through extensions. To use these features the hardware must support the extensions that you want to use. In addition, when dealing with Windows and Linux operating systems, the application must obtain function pointers to the OpenGL extension functions it wants to use. Although OpenGL is cross platform, the way to load functions from dynamic libraries is platform specific.

The good thing about GLEE is that it hides the querying of extension functions. Trying to use one of the OpenGL extension functions in an application that is using GLEE will cause that function to be automatically queried and obtained. GLEE has no setup and no special requirements other than including the GLEE header and source file.

GLEE definitely makes working with OpenGL extensions much easier and much more convenient. GLEE can be downloaded from the Web site *http:// elf-stone.com/glee.php*. Although Mac users do not have to obtain function pointers to OpenGL extension functions like Linux and Windows users, the code can still compile on that platform to allow your code to be compatible.

Other extension libraries like this are available across the Internet that you can use for free. GLEE is one that is very popular and simple to use.

GLUT

The OpenGL samples in Chapters 13 and 14 use the OpenGL Utility Toolkit for cross-platform window creation in the code. In this section we will briefly discuss the GLUT functions used in those samples in more detail, starting with `glutInit()`. The `glutInit()` function initializes the GLUT library and takes as parameters the main function's `argc` parameter and `argv` parameter. The function can be passed with NULL values. The function prototype for the `glutInit()` is:

```
void glutInit(int *argcp, char **argv);
```

The next functions we'll look at are the `glutInitWindowSize()` and `glutInit WindowPosition()` functions. The `glutInitWindowSize()` function takes as parameters the desired width and height of the window's resolution and sets it. The `glutInitWindowPosition()` takes an x and y location for where the window will appear on the screen. The function prototypes for both functions are as follows:

```
void glutInitWindowSize(int width, int height);
void glutInitWindowPosition(int x, int y);
```

The next function is the `glutInitDisplayMode()`. This function takes a flag for the display mode and will set it. The flags for the function can be one or more of the following values:

- GLUT_RGBA
- GLUT_RGB
- GLUT_INDEX

- GLUT_SINGLE
- GLUT_DOUBLE
- GLUT_ACCUM
- GLUT_ALPHA
- GLUT_DEPTH
- GLUT_STENCIL
- GLUT_MULTISAMPLE
- GLUT_STEREO
- GLUT_LUMINANCE

The function prototype for the `glutInitDisplayMode()` GLUT function is as follows:

```
void glutInitDisplayMode(unsigned int mode);
```

The next function is the `glutCreateWindow()`, which is used to create the actual window. The only parameter it takes is the desired name of the window, which is sent into a character pointer. The return value of the `glutCreateWindow()` function is a unique identifier for the newly created window, which starts at 1 for the first window. The function prototype is:

```
int glutCreateWindow(char *name);
```

The next three functions are `glutDisplayFunc()`, `glutReshapeFunc()`, and `glutKeyboardFunc()`, which are callback functions. As a parameter, each of these functions takes a function prototype to a function that will be called upon when some condition occurs. The `glutDisplayFunc()` function is used to set the function that will be called each time the scene needs to be rendered. The `glutReshape-Func()` function is called when the window is being resized, and it takes a function prototype to a function that specifies two integer parameters. `glutKeyboardFunc()` is the callback function that is called when a key-press occurs. It takes a function prototype that takes an unsigned char and two integers, which is used for the mouse x and y position. The function prototypes for these three functions are:

```
void glutDisplayFunc(void (*func)(void));

void glutReshapeFunc(void (*func)(int width, int height));

void glutKeyboardFunc(void (*func)(unsigned char key, int x,
int y));
```

The last function that is called to complete setting up GLUT is `glutMainLoop()`, which is used to enter the application loop of the program. Once in the main loop, the code will render the scene by calling the display callback function and all other callback functions that were set when appropriate. The function prototype for `glutMainLoop()` is:

```
void glutMainLoop(void);
```

Additional GLUT-related functions in this book include using GLUT to render spheres. This is done using the function `glutSolidSphere()`, which also has a wire-frame version called `glutWireSphere()`. In addition, one of the exercises asked to render a teapot to the window using GLUT, which is done using the `glutSolidTeapot()` function. The sphere functions take as parameters the radius, detail level along the longitude (slices), and detail level along the latitude (stacks). The teapot function takes the size of the teapot mesh in units. The function proto-types for these functions are:

```
void glutSolidSphere(GLdouble radius, GLint slices, GLint stacks);
void glutWireSphere(GLdouble radius, GLint slices, GLint stacks);

void glutSolidTeapot(GLdouble size);
void glutWireTeapot(GLdouble size);
```

Documentation on the GLUT library can be found at `http://www.opengl.org/documentation/specs/glut/spec3/spec3.html`. GLUT itself can be downloaded, if necessary, from OpenGL's Web site, *http://www.opengl.org/resources/libraries/glut/glut_downloads.php*, for various operating systems.

NonStandard Containers and Algorithms

In This Appendix:

- SGI STL
- STLport
- Boost

This appendix offers a more detailed discussion of the STL-related websites that can prove useful to C++ developers. Each of the resources in this chapter was briefly discussed in this book.

SGI STL

The SGI STL website (*http://www.sgi.com/tech/stl/*) has a lot of information on the C++ STL. This information can prove valuable to all professional programmers and is definitely worth exploring. The information on the SGI STL website includes:

- An introduction to STL
- Detailed documentation on all of the STL data structures, algorithms, function objects, iterators, memory management, and utilities
- A list of STL website resources
- An experimental I/O library
- A download of the entire STL in its current and previous versions
- Release information on changes in the STL

This website is definitely recommended as a documentation reference and will give you all the information you'll need that is related to the STL. The STL code at this website is implemented in header files, so there is no need to compile or link source objects. Also, all compilers with good template class support should work with the STL if you need to download them for your tool of choice.

STLPORT

STLport Consulting (*http://www.stlport.org/*) is a company that was started in 1997 by a small group of developers. The STLport is free and offers many data structures, algorithms, and other objects for download. The STLport builds off of the STL and adds a lot of code that is not part of the C++ standard. Unlike STL, the STLport does require compiling of source files.

When you download the STLport, it must be set up for your compiler. The download has makefile files for each of the supported compilers that can be executed to set up the STLport for your tool of choice. The STLport website also has the following:

- Community
- Forums
- Online documentation
- STLport download, which includes the latest version, past versions, and beta snapshots
- A list of STL-related resources

BOOST

The Boost website (*www.Boost.org*) provides free-of-charge peer-reviewed portable C++ libraries for C++ application programmers. Some of the libraries available on Boost are included in the C++ Standards Committee's Library Technical Report, which means they are being considered as a future part of the C++ Standard Library. The Boost website is similar to the others in that it includes:

- Downloads for the Boost libraries
- Documentation for the Boost libraries
- Community and developer groups
- Newsgroups and mailing lists

The Boost website encourages participation in contributing to the development of Boost and to discussions and formal reviews of libraries. The Boost libraries are huge and have many types of data structures and algorithms. For example, Boost has containers for graphs, hash tables, and much more.

Appendix

E : About the CD-ROM

The companion CD-ROM for *Data Structures and Algorithms for Game Developers* contains all of the projects files for your use as you work through the book.

FOLDERS

The files on this disc are organized into folders as follows:

Figures: All of the figures from the book, organized in folders by chapter.

Chapter 1: Contains all of the source code samples from Chapter 1.

Chapter 2: Contains all of the source code samples from Chapter 2.

Chapter 3: Contains all of the source code samples from Chapter 3.

Chapter 4: Contains all of the source code samples from Chapter 4.

Chapter 5: Contains all of the source code samples from Chapter 5.

Chapter 6: Contains all of the source code samples from Chapter 6.

Chapter 7: Contains all of the source code samples from Chapter 7.

Chapter 8: Contains all of the source code samples from Chapter 8.

Chapter 9: Contains all of the source code samples from Chapter 9.

Chapter 10: Contains all of the source code samples from Chapter 10.

Chapter 11: Contains all of the source code samples from Chapter 11.

Chapter 12: Contains all of the source code samples from Chapter 12.

Chapter 13: Contains all of the source code samples from Chapter 13.

Chapter 14: Contains all of the source code samples from Chapter 14.

GENERAL SYSTEM REQUIREMENTS

The system requirements for this CD-ROM are:

- Windows 2000/XP Operating System or better
- Mac OS X
- Linux
- Pentium 2 GHz
- 256 MB RAM
- 300 MB Hard-Drive Space
- CD-ROM Drive
- OpenGL Compatible 3D Graphics Accelerator

Index